Flyover History: Remembering Our Ignored Past

Volume I

Seventh Edition

Peter Myers | Robert Hines | Rex Field

CENGAGE
Learning™

Australia • Brazil • Japan • Korea • Mexico • Singapore • Spain • United Kingdom • United States

Flyover History:
Remembering Our Ignored Past: Volume I,
Seventh Edition

Peter Myers | Robert Hines | Rex Field

Executive Editors:
 Maureen Staudt
 Michael Stranz

Senior Project Development Manager:
 Linda DeStefano

Marketing Specialist:
 Sara Mercurio

Senior Production / Manufacturing Manager:
 Donna M. Brown

PreMedia Supervisor:
 Joel Brennecke

Rights & Permissions Specialist:
 Kalina Hintz
 Todd Osborne

Cover Image:
 Getty Images*

* Unless otherwise noted, all cover images used by Custom Solutions, a part of Cengage Learning, have been supplied courtesy of Getty Images with the exception of the Earthview cover image, which has been supplied by the National Aeronautics and Space Administration (NASA).

For product information and technology assistance, contact us at
Cengage Learning Customer & Sales Support, 1-800-354-9706
For permission to use material from this text or product,
submit all requests online at **cengage.com/permissions**
Further permissions questions can be emailed to
permissionrequest@cengage.com

Library of Congress Control Number: 2007930689

ISBN-13: 978-1-4266-2967-9

ISBN-10: 1-4266-2967-2

Cengage Learning
5191 Natorp Boulevard
Mason, Ohio 45040
USA

Cengage Learning is a leading provider of customized learning solutions with office locations around the globe, including Singapore, the United Kingdom, Australia, Mexico, Brazil, and Japan. Locate your local office at:
international.cengage.com/region

Cengage Learning products are represented in Canada by Nelson Education, Ltd.

For your lifelong learning solutions, visit **www.cengage.com/custom**

Visit our corporate website at **www.cengage.com**

CONTENTS

I

EARLY NORTH AMERICA   1

II

EXPLORATION AND COLONIZATION   23

III
ROADS TO REVOLUTION   61

IV
EARLY AMERICA   97

V
TECHNOLOGY OF THE NINETEENTH CENTURY   117

VIII
SLAVERY   219

IX
THE CIVIL WAR AND IT'S AFTERMATH   271

PREFACE

FLYOVER HISTORY:

REMEMBERING OUR IGNORED PAST

An open letter to you:

*Taking an American history course is probably nothing new for you. You have had many social studies classes throughout your education. It's required by law that you do so. Texas mandates that all high school students complete a full year of United States history. And the state legislature requires that you do so in college. So the question is—what can you possibly learn in a college survey history course that you have not learned already? That's **the reason** why we have created this book.*

Flyover History: Remembering Our Ignored Past is not a textbook. We did not intend it to be. It is a collection of readings to whet your appetite to learn about the American experience from different perspectives. Our history is full of characters, who have made things interesting, and often complicated for those who interpret the past. Flyover History is a compilation of articles that emphasize "everyday people" and their roles in the making of America.

As editors of Flyover History: Remembering Our Ignored Past, we have attempted to fill in many of the missing pieces in American history. Flyover refers to how certain topics in American history received little—or no—coverage in your previous education; those areas, which were almost literally "flown over." Consider what you know about: how people lived and died in the nineteenth century, or the obstacles that all minorities faced in achieving civil rights, or the role women played in controlling their own lives. These are only a few of the topics that you will learn about in Flyover History.

We appreciate all of our Palo Alto College colleagues, who have shared their thoughts and comments with us. Special thanks to Javier Aguirre, for his firsthand account in Boy Scouts of America. Irene Scharf wrote the introduction and questions for Against All Odds. Many students offered us their suggestions to make this anthology the best one yet. Crystal Vyvlecka wrote the introduction for A Village Disappeared, while Maria Gloria Flores's interview of Judy Babbit is incorporated in Conquering Polio. We are thankful to our proofreader Tori Beckman-Wilson, who checked the manuscript for errors. Finally, we would not have been able to complete this task without the love and support from those on the homefront—our families.

Have an enlightening semester.

Peter J. Myers
Rex Lewis Field
Robert R. Hines

October 2007

I

EARLY NORTH AMERICA

1   One of the most taxing tasks placed upon the shoulders of students of history involves interpretation, for even the most documented events require considerable care and investigation. Consider how much more difficult a problem we face when investigating periods void of the written record. Such is the case with most Native American history. Considerable work has been accomplished in the study of native cultures, yet we must rely quite heavily upon speculation as we try to tie together **millennia** of archeological and environmental evidence. So many of the questions that could have been answered in a short note here or government document there must wait for further evidence or remain mysteries.

2   We are able to piece together some of the facets of the great migrations of the earliest arrivals in the Americas. Naturally, the place names and landmarks that we are accustomed to did not define those early settlers' world. From the ethnic evidence, we can assume that they arrived from Asia, perhaps over a land bridge linking Siberia with present-day Alaska. For well over 10,000 years, perhaps far longer, the movement of people followed a more or less north to south direction. By the time of the arrival of the first Europeans millions of Native Americans, representing a collage of cultures, peopled the Americas from the northern most reaches to the southern extremes of the continent. Their cultures, shaped by environment and geography, were varied and distinct, though the ethnic group that we call "Native American" dominated all areas.

3   The ethnic uniformity and isolation of these early settlers, separated from the old world for many millennia, was significant when considering the disastrous consequences of contact with Europeans. When the European invasion finally began, it represented a bacteriological and viral disaster of the first order. Native Americans, ill-equipped to fight the plagues that had been incubated in the Old World, died in veritable droves and suffered dislocations and demoralization from which they could not recover.

4   During the years immediately following the arrival of Columbus, Spaniards sought to consolidate their hold on the Caribbean, and then invade the mainland in present-day Mexico. Their success at defeating the Aztecs, inheritors of the great culture of Mesoamerica, can be directly attributed to the pathogens they propagated by their mere presence.

5   Mesoamerica, that area encompassing the Mexican plateau southward to Costa Rica, was an area of the most advanced civilizations of the New World. By around 2000 B.C. some Native American societies had domesticated many animals and crops. However, the greatest progress was brought about by the

---

millennia: a span of one thousand years.

successful cultivation of a storable grain, corn. Indeed, the Old World already experienced an "agricultural revolution," but at much earlier times, with the development of wheat in ancient Mesopotamia. The historical consequences were the same, however, in that cereal grain crops presented opportunities to societies that could not be enjoyed under any other circumstances. Just as the Biblical Pharaoh could monopolize grain stores and force nomads like the Hebrews into slavery, so early civilizations like the Olmecs and their successors could dominate large empires through control of the food supply and monopolization of the means to produce. The basis of that civilization rested upon a kind of cultural template established by an ancient people, the Olmec, who dominated much of central Mexico at their height, and affected its history long after their demise. Though scholars still debate the earliest dates of the Olmec, we know that they experienced a rapid decline by 100 B.C. (It should be noted that as students of history we can not rely upon precise dating of any ancient people. One cannot turn the pages of a book to discover what happened on July 4, 1776 B.C. Dating is an imprecise science under the best circumstances, so dealing with Native Americans necessarily means that dates should be looked upon with, at best, skepticism.)

6   The Olmec created urban centers, the core of a loose empire based on connecting the rural corn growing communities. They institutionalized religion, developed calendars, and laid the groundwork for the "writing" that was carried through other cultures over the centuries. A pantheon of gods and rituals pervaded all aspects of Olmec existence. The great cultures to follow, including the Maya, Toltec, and even Aztec were borrowers from this earlier age.

7   Indeed, the Maya arrived at their cultural apex long after the Olmec were gone, but well before the arrival of the first Europeans. Scholars tend to refer to a "classical Period," a truly western concept, to describe and date the Maya. Their greatest cultural undertakings, initiated on a huge scale, were underway by 300 A.D. and in decline by 900 A.D. Scholars, such as Linda Schele of the University of Texas, have deciphered much of the Maya writing and revealed a great deal about their lives and world. They lived with a sense of limbo, an existence both spiritual and secular, a state of being that defies descriptions in western or Eurocentric terms. They sought to please their many gods with incredible architectural creations and blood rituals. Their temple cities, built on grids aligned to the cosmos, litter a geographic region of Yucatan, Guatemala, and Honduras. Great pyramids in places like "Edzna" and "Tikal" testify to great communal societies, organized and directed to particular ends. Like all Native American groups, the Maya force upon us the need to be open-minded and sensitive to their beliefs and ways of life. Preconceptions of any people are detrimental to critical analysis, and such is especially the case with Native Americans.

8   The decline of the Maya around 900 A.D. left a vacuum that would be filled successively by different powerful tribes, including the Toltec and Aztec. Warlike and nomadic, the first Aztecs settled into the area around present-day Mexico City, establishing their capital of Tenochtitlan. From around 1300s to the arrival of Hernando Cortes in 1519 they dominated most of Mesoamerica. As with those who preceded them, they built an empire based upon military power and tribute. Gods like Quetzalcoatl and Huitzilopochtli not only gave them a religious focus, but shaped their violent world view.

9   Into this ancient land the Spaniards arrived, fresh from the "reconquista" in Spain, expressing both abhorrence of what they saw as barbarism, while at the same time humiliating, torturing and subjugating whole societies of the Americas. They left behind paradoxical place-names like "Vera Cruz" (true cross) and "Matamoros" (kill Moors). Thus, they initiated one of the great cultural collisions of human history.

1

AMERICA'S FIRST IMMIGRANTS

BY EVAN HADINGHAM

*You were probably taught that the hemisphere's first people
came from Siberia across a long-gone land bridge. Now a sea
route looks increasingly likely, from Asia or even Europe*

Archeology seeks out and provides the material evidence by which students of history can come to understand the lives of people who did not otherwise record their experience in writing, or in the case of some literate cultures, composed a written record in characters whose meanings were long lost. Ongoing excavations at far-flung sites from Siberia and Gault, TX to New Mexico and Chile have yielded numerous clues, and likewise forced a reevaluation of interpretations of the prehistoric presence of people in the Americas. If anything, the modern techniques and refinements in archeology have at once devalued the simple answers proffered by work conducted by an earlier generation of scholars, while causing considerable consternation and puzzlement at the plethora of diverse finds now extant.

Archeologists read the evidence from educated perspectives, reinforced by evolving scientific methods, and the accumulated experiences of many hardworking people devoting their lives to the discipline. They have mastered the ability to recognize important objects that might otherwise incite little interest from untrained eyes and have come to appreciate the vital need to study all discoveries in what they deem proper contexts. Indeed, one can observe quite a variety reflecting up from unearthed stones, bones and artifacts as they are associated with one site or another. Greater numbers of discoveries translate into more broadly accepted consensus, and taken in total hint at answers that could never be teased from them separately.

The story of the human experience and American life would always seem to ultimately include, or even depend upon the histories of many other places. The storied infusion of innumerable cultures brought by waves of immigrants has become almost cliché in modern analyses. Yet, archeologists have done nothing to alter this perspective of American history, and certainly prove that the nature of the migratory movements of ancients arriving in this land are a solid realization that there really never was a single, disassociated American history. In the immensity of that diversity we can see the one and only recurring theme, an irony that will gain even more credence as new finds push back the centuries to when the "first" arrivals trekked from their particular homes of origin and came here.

- *What are "Clovis" points and how do they help archeologists identify sites?*
- *How does the Clovis site at Gault, TX contradict traditional interpretations?*
- *What kinds of historical information can be gained from genetic testing of living people?*
- *In what way do archeologists use the word "convergence"?*
- *What was "Solutrean" culture?*

1 About four miles from the tiny cattle town of Florence, Texas, a narrow dirt road winds across parched limestone, through juniper, prickly pear and stunted oaks, and drops down to a creek. A lush parkland of shade trees offers welcome relief from the 100-degree heat of summer. Running beside the creek for almost half a mile is a swath of chipped, gray stone flakes and soil blackened by cooking fires—thousands of years of cooking fires. This blackened earth, covering 40 acres and almost six feet thick in places, marks a settlement dating back as far as the last ice age 13,000 years ago, when mammoths, giant sloths and sabertoothed cats roamed the North American wilderness.

2 Since archaeologists began working here systematically seven years ago, they have amassed an astonishing collection of early prehistoric artifacts—nearly half a million so far. Among these are large, stone spearheads skillfully flaked on both sides to give an elegant, leaf-shaped appearance. These projectiles, found by archaeologists throughout North America and as far south as Costa Rica, are known as Clovis points, and their makers, who lived roughly 12,500 to 13,500 years ago, are known as Clovis people, after the town in New Mexico near where the first such point was identified some seven decades ago.

3 A visit to the Gault site—named after the family who owned the land when the site was first investigated in 1929—along the cottonwood- and walnut-shaded creek in central Texas raises two monumental questions. The first, of course, is, Who were these people? The emerging answer is that they were not simple-minded big-game hunters as they have often been depicted. Rather, they led a less nomadic and more sophisticated life than previously believed.

4 The second question—Where did they come from?—lies at the center of one of archaeology's most contentious debates. The standard view holds that Clovis people were the first to enter the Americas, migrating from Siberia 13,500 years ago by a now-submerged land bridge across the Bering Strait. This view has been challenged recently by a wide range of discoveries, including an astonishingly well-preserved site in South America predating the supposed migration by at least 1,000 years.

5 Researchers delving into the origins question have sought to make sense of archaeological finds far and wide, from Canada, California and Chile; from Siberia; and even, most controversially, from France and Spain. The possibility that the first people in the Americas came from Europe is the boldest proposal among a host of new ideas. According to University of Texas at Austin archaeologist Michael Collins, the chief excavator of the Gault site, "you couldn't have a more exciting time to be involved in the whole issue of the peopling of the Americas. You can't write a paper on it and get it published before it's out of date. Surprising new finds keep rocking the boat and launching fresh waves of debate."

6 For prehistoric people, one of the chief attractions of the Gault site was a knobby outcrop of a creamy white rock called chert, which conceals a fine, gray, glasslike interior. If struck expertly with a stone or antler tool, the rock fractures in predictable ways, yielding a Clovis point. In the end, each spearhead has distinctive grooves, or "flutes," at the base of each face and was fastened to a wooden shaft with sinew and resin.

7 Ancient pollen and soil clues tell archaeologists that the climate in Clovis-era Texas was cooler, drier and more tolerable than today's summertime cauldron. Vast herds of mammoths, bison, horses and antelope ranged on the grasslands southeast of Gault, and deer and turkeys inhabited the plateau to the west. Along the creek, based on bones found at the site, Clovis hunters also preyed on frogs, birds, turtles and other small animals.

8 This abundance of food, coupled with the exceptional quality of the chert, drew people to Gault in large numbers. Unlike the majority of Clovis sites, which are mostly the remains of temporary camps, Gault appears to have been inhabited over long periods and thus contradicts the standard view that Clovis people were always highly mobile, nomadic hunters. Michael Collins says that of the vast quantity of artifacts found at the site, many are tool fragments, left behind by people who'd stuck around long enough to not only break their tools but also to salvage and rework them. The researchers also unearthed a seven by seven foot square of gravel—perhaps the floor of a house—and a possible well, both signs of more than a fleeting presence.

9 Another clue was concealed on a 13,000-year-old Clovis blade about the size of a dinner knife. Under a magnifying lens, the blade's edge is glossy, rounded and smooth. Marilyn Shoberg, a stone tool analyst on the Gault team who has experimented with replicas, says the blade's polish probably came from cutting grass. This grass could have been used for basketry, bedding, or thatching to make roofs for huts.

10 Among the most unusual and tantalizing finds at the Gault site are a hundred or so fragments of limestone covered with lightly scratched patterns. Some resemble nets or basketry, while a few could be simple outlines of plants or animals. Although only a dozen can be securely dated to Clovis times, these enigmatic rocks are among the very few surviving artworks from ice age America.

11 "What this site tells us is that Clovis folks were not specialized mammoth hunters constantly wandering over the landscape," says Collins. "They exploited a variety of animals, they had tools for gathering plants and working wood, stone and hide, and they stayed through the useful life of those tools. All these things are contrary to what you'd expect if they were highly nomadic, dedicated big-game hunters." Yet this unexpected complexity sheds only

a feeble glimmer on the more contentious issue of where the Clovis people came from and how they got here.

12   In the old scenario, still popular in classrooms and picture books, fur-clad hunters in the waning moments of the last ice age, when so much seawater was locked up in the polar ice caps that the sea level was as much as 300 feet lower than today, ventured across a land bridge from Siberia to Alaska. Then, pursuing big game, the hunters trekked south through present-day Canada. They passed down a narrow, 1,000-mile-long treeless corridor bounded by the towering walls of retreating ice sheets until they reached the Great Plains, which teemed with prey. The human population exploded, and the hunters soon drove into extinction some 35 genera of big animals (see sidebar, p. 94). All of these were supposedly dispatched by the Clovis point, a Stone Age weapon of mass destruction.

13   For more than half a century, this plausible, "big-game" theory carried with it an appealing, heroic image. As James Adovasio of Mercyhurst College puts it in his book *The First Americans,* it was as if the ice sheets had parted "like the Red Sea for some Clovis Moses to lead his intrepid band of spear-toting, mammoth-slaying wayfarers to the south." But recent discoveries are indicating that almost everything about the theory could be wrong. For one thing, the latest studies show that the ice-free corridor didn't exist until around 12,000 years ago— too late to have served as the route for the very first people to come to America.

14   Perhaps the strongest ammunition against the old scenario comes from Monte Verde, an archaeological site on a remote terrace, which is today some 40 miles from the Pacific in southern Chile. Here, about 14,500 years ago, a hunting and gathering band lived year-round beside a creek in a long, oval hide tent, partitioned with logs. Archaeologist Tom Dillehay of Vanderbilt University began probing Monte Verde in 1977, unearthing the surface of the ancient encampment, complete with wood, plants and even remains of food, all preserved under a layer of waterlogged peat. Dillehay recovered three human footprints, two chunks of uneaten mastodon meat and possibly even traces of herbal medicine (indicated by nonfood plants still used by healers in the Andes). The dating of these extraordinary finds, at least 1,000 years before the earliest Clovis sites in North America, aroused skepticism for two decades until, in 1997, a group of leading archaeologists inspected the site and vindicated Dillehay's meticulous work.

15   No such triumph has emerged for any of the dozen or so sites in North America claimed to predate Clovis. But among the most intriguing is a rock overhang in Pennsylvania called Meadowcroft, where a 30-year campaign of excavation suggests that hunters may have reached the Northeast 3,000 or 4,000 years before the Clovis era.

16   Meanwhile, genetics studies are pointing even more strongly to an early entry into the continent. By analyzing the mitochondrial DNA of living Native Americans, Douglas Wallace, a geneticist at the University of California at Irvine, and his colleagues have identified five distinct lineages that stretch back like family trees. Mitochondria are the cells' energy factories. Their DNA changes very little from one generation to the next, altered only by tiny variations that creep in at a steady and predictable rate. By counting the number of these variations in related lineages, Wallace's team can estimate their ages. When the team applied this technique to the DNA of Native Americans, they reached the stunning conclusion that there were at least four separate waves of prehistoric migration into the Americas, the earliest well over 20,000 years ago.

17   If the first Americans did arrive well before the oldest known Clovis settlements, how did they get here? The most radical theory for the peopling of the New World argues that Stone Age mariners journeyed from Europe around the southern fringes of the great ice sheets in the North Atlantic. Many archaeologists greet this idea with head-shaking scorn, but the proposition is getting harder to dismiss outright.

18   Dennis Stanford, a Clovis expert at the Smithsonian Institution's Department of Anthropology who delights in prodding his colleagues with unconventional thinking, was a longtime supporter of the land bridge scenario. Then, with the end of the cold war came the chance to visit archaeological sites and museums in Siberia—museums that should have been filled with tools that were predecessors of the Clovis point. "The result was a big disappointment," says Stanford. "What we found was nothing like we expected, and I was surprised that the technologies were so different." Instead of a single leaf-shaped Clovis spearhead, ice age Siberian hunters made projectiles that were bristling with rows of tiny razor-like blades embedded in wooden shafts. To Stanford, that meant no Siberian hunters armed with Clovis technology had walked to the Americas.

19   Meanwhile, Bruce Bradley, a prehistoric stone tool specialist at Britain's University of Exeter, had noticed a strong resemblance between Clovis points and weapons from ice age Europe. But the idea that the two cultures might be directly connected was heretical. "It certainly wasn't part of the scientific process at that point," Bradley says. "There was no possibility, forget it, don't even think about it." Bradley eventually pursued it to the storerooms of the Musée National de Préhistoire in Les Eyzies-de-Tayac in southwest France, where he pored through boxes of local prehistoric stone tools and waste flakes. "I was absolutely flabbergasted," he recalls. "If somebody

had brought out a box of this stuff in the United States and set it down in front of me, I'd have said, 'Man, where did you get all that great Clovis stuff?'" But the material was the work of a culture called the Solutrean that thrived in southwest France and northern Spain during the coldest spell of the ice age, from around 24,000 to 19,000 years ago.

20   Thousands of years before their successors created the masterworks of Lascaux and Altamira, Solutrean-age artists began painting vivid murals in the depths of caves such as Cougnac and Cosquer. They made delicate, eyed sewing needles out of bone, enabling them to stitch tightfitting skin garments to repel the cold. They devised the *atlatl*, or spear thrower, a hooked bone or wood handle that extends the reach of the hunter's arm to multiply throwing power. But their most distinctive creation was a stone spearhead shaped like a laurel leaf.

21   Apart from the absence of a fluted base, the Solutrean laurel leaf strongly resembles the Clovis point and was made using the same, highly skillful flaking technique. Both Clovis and Solutrean stone crafters practiced controlled overshot flaking, which involved trimming one edge by striking a flake off the opposite side, a virtuoso feat of handiwork rarely seen in other prehistoric cultures. To Bradley, "there had to be some sort of historic connection" between the Solutrean and Clovis peoples.

22   Critics of the theory point to a yawning gap between the two peoples: roughly 5,000 years divide the end of Solutrean culture and the emergence of Clovis. But Stanford and Bradley say that recent claims of pre-Clovis sites in the southeastern United States may bridge the time gap. In the mid-1990s at Cactus Hill, the remains of an ancient sand dune overlooking the Nottoway River on Virginia's coastal plain, project director Joseph McAvoy dug down a few inches beneath a Clovis layer and uncovered simple stone blades and projectile points associated with a hearth, radiocarbon dated to some 17,000 to 19,000 years ago. This startlingly early date has drawn skeptical fire, but the site's age was recently confirmed by an independent dating technique. Stanford and Bradley suggest that the early people at Cactus Hill were Clovis forerunners who had not yet developed the full-blown Clovis style. They are convinced that many more sites like Cactus Hill will turn up on the East Coast. But the burning question is, Did these ice age Virginians invent the Clovis point all by themselves, or were they descendants of Solutreans who brought the point with them from Europe?

23   Many archaeologists ridicule the notion that people made an arduous, 3,000-mile journey during the bleakest period of the ice age, when the Atlantic would have been much colder and stormier than today. Stanford believes that traditional Inuit technology suggests otherwise; he has witnessed traditional seagoing skills among Inupiat communities in Barrow, Alaska. Inupiat hunters still build large skin-covered canoes, or *umiaks*, which enable them to catch seals, walrus and other sea mammals that abound along the frozen edges of the pack ice. When twilight arrives or storms threaten, the hunters pull their boats up on the ice and camp beneath them. Ronald Brower of the Inupiat Heritage Center in Barrow says, "There's nothing that would have prevented . . . people from crossing the Atlantic into the Americas 19,000 years ago. It would be a perfectly normal situation from my perspective."

24   A different critique of the out-of-Europe theory dismisses the resemblance between Solutrean and Clovis points. Many archaeologists suggest that similarities between Clovis and Solutrean artifacts are coincidental, the result of what they call convergence. "These were people faced with similar problems," says Solutrean expert Lawrence Straus of the University of New Mexico. "And the problems involved hunting large- and medium-sized game with a similar, limited range of raw materials—stone, bone, ivory, antler, wood and sinew. They're going to come up with similar solutions."

25   More tellingly, in Straus' view, is that he can find little evidence of seafaring technology in the Solutrean sites he has dug in northern Spain. Although rising sea levels have drowned sites on the ice age coastline, Straus has investigated surviving inland cave sites no more than a couple of hours' walk from the beach. "There's no evidence of deep-sea fishing," says Straus, "no evidence of marine mammal hunting, and consequently no evidence, even indirect, for their possession of seaworthy boats."

26   And David Meltzer, an archaeologist at Southern Methodist University and a critic of the European-origins idea, is struck more by the differences between the Solutrean and Clovis cultures than their similarities—particularly the near-absence of art and personal ornaments from Clovis. Still, he says, the controversy is good for the field. "In the process of either killing or curing" the theory, "we will have learned a whole lot more about the archaeological record, and we'll all come out smarter than we went in."

27   Besides crossing the land bridge from Asia and traveling to ice age America from Europe by boat, a third possible entryway is a sea route down the west coast. Using maritime skills later perfected by the Inuit, prehistoric south Asians might have spread gradually around the northern rim of the Pacific in small skin-covered boats. They skirt the southern edge of the Bering land bridge and paddle down the coast of Alaska, dodging calving glaciers and icebergs as they pursue seals and other marine mammals. They keep going all the way to the beaches of Central and South America. They arrive at Monte Verde, inland from the Chilean coast, some 14,500 years ago. Each new generation claims fresh hunting grounds a

few miles beyond the last, and in a matter of centuries these first immigrants have populated the entire west coast of the Americas. Soon the hunters start moving inland and, in the north, their descendants become the Clovis people.

28 Many archaeologists now accept the west coast theory as a likely solution to the origin of the earliest Americans. On Prince of Wales Island in southeastern Alaska, inside the aptly named On Your Knees Cave, University of South Dakota paleontologist Timothy Heaton and University of Colorado at Boulder archaeologist E. James Dixon recovered an accumulation of animal bones from the last ice age. When mile-high ice sheets still straddled the interior of the continent 17,000 years ago, ringed seals, foxes and seabirds made their home on the island. "Humans could easily have survived there," Heaton says.

29 The ultimate evidence for the western sea route would be the discovery of pre-Clovis human remains on the coast. No such luck. Dixon and Heaton have found human jaw fragments and other remains in the On Your Knees Cave, but those date to about 11,000 years ago—too recent to establish the theory. And what may be the oldest-known human remains in North America—leg bones found on Santa Rosa Island, off the California coast—are from 13,000 years ago, the heart of the Clovis era. Still, those remains hint that by then people were plying the waters along the Pacific Coast.

30 If the trail of the very earliest Americans remains elusive, so, too, does the origin of the Clovis point. "Although the technology needed to produce a Clovis point was found among other cultures during the ice age," says Ken Tankersley of Northern Kentucky University, "the actual point itself is unique to the Americas, suggesting that it was invented here in the New World." If so, the spearhead would be the first great American invention—the Stone Age equivalent of the Swiss Army Knife, a trademark tool that would be widely imitated. The demand for the weapon and the high-quality stone it required probably encouraged Clovis people to begin long distance trading and social exchanges. The spearhead may also have delivered a new level of hunting proficiency and this, in turn, would have fueled a population spurt, giving Clovis people their lasting presence in the archaeological record.

31 Sheltering from the broiling heat under the cottonwoods at Gault, Michael Collins told me of his conviction that the Clovis people who flocked to the shady creek were not pioneers but had profited from a long line of forebears. "Clovis represents the end product of centuries, if not millennia, of learning how to live in North American environments," he said. "The Clovis culture is too widespread, is found in too many environments, and has too much evidence for diverse activities to be the leavings of people just coming into the country." Collins reminded me that his team has investigated less than 10 percent of the enormous site. And archaeologists have barely scratched the surface of a handful of other Gault-size, Clovis-era sites—Williamsburg, in Virginia, for instance, or Shoop, in Pennsylvania. "One thing you can be sure," he said, beaming, "there'll be great new discoveries just around the corner."

HUNTED TO EXTINCTION?

32 At the end of the last ice age, 35 genera of big animals, or 'megafauna,' went extinct in the Americas, including mammoths, mastodons, giant ground sloths, giant beavers, horses, short-faced bears and saber-toothed cats. Archaeologists have argued for decades that the arrival of hunters wielding Clovis spear points at around the same time was no coincidence. Clovis hunters pursued big game, their signature stone points are found with the bones of mammoths and mastodons at 14 kill sites in North America. Experiments carried out with replica spears thrust into the corpses of circus elephants indicate that the Clovis point could have penetrated a mammoth's hide. And computer simulations suggest that large, slowbreeding animals could have easily been wiped out by hunting as the human population expanded.

33 But humans might not be entirely to blame. The rapidly cycling climate at the end of the ice age may have changed the distribution of plants that the big herbivores grazed on, leading to a population crash among meat-eating predators too. New research on DNA fragments recovered from ice age bison bones suggests that some species were suffering a slow decline in diversity—probably caused by dwindling populations—long before any Clovis hunters showed up. Indigenous horses are now thought to have died out in Alaska about 500 years before the Clovis era. For mammoths and other beasts who did meet their demise during the Clovis times, many experts believe that a combination of factors—climate change plus pressure from human hunters—drove them into oblivion.

34 Amid all the debate, one point is clear: the Clovis hunter wasn't as macho as people once thought. Bones at the Gault site in central Texas reveal that the hunters there were feeding on less daunting prey—frogs, birds, turtles and antelope—as well as mammoth, mastodon and bison. As the late, renowned archaeologist Richard (Scotty) MacNeish is said to have remarked, 'Each Clovis generation probably killed one mammoth, then spent the rest of their lives talking about it.'

2

CORN, THE NEW WORLD'S SECRET WEAPON AND THE BUILDER OF ITS CIVILIZATIONS

BY ALAN LINN

Corn is a uniquely American crop, unknown to Europeans prior to the age of exploration, yet widely disseminated throughout the Americas and grown by countless native peoples. The great civilizations of Meso-America were literally built and sustained by corn. Though corn's historical results and ongoing importance are readily documented, its origins remain a mystery.

Corn has proven to be an exceedingly adaptable crop, grown in many climates, ranging throughout countries all over the globe. The most important genetic materials, however, remain locked in the few, original corn species raised by Native Americans during many centuries prior to its appropriation by alien people.

- *How did corn change the lives of ancient people in the Americas?*
- *Why was corn so important to Europeans once they arrived on American shores?*
- *What happened to corn over the centuries?*

---

1 Indian cultures and settlers whose lives it saved revered it, and research into its origin is vital to today's beneficiaries

2 On Corn Hill in Truro, Massachusetts, there is a plain bronze plaque dedicated to a plant. The inscription is in the words of William Bradford, governor of Plymouth Colony, written in 1621:

> *And sure it was God's good providence*
> *that we found this corn, for else we*
> *know not how we should have done.*

3 In point of fact, Governor Bradford and the Pilgrims cannot claim credit for "finding" the corn, even under divine supervision. Captain John Smith was more accurate when in 1607 he wrote gratefully (he was starving), "It pleased God . . . to move the Indians to bring us corn," but even he denied the

Indians any credit for their hospitable act. They were instruments of God's innate friendliness toward colonists.

4 Far grander monuments lie some 1,500 miles southwest of the one on Cape Cod, deep within the tangled jungles of Mexico's Yucatan peninsula. Here you can stand atop pyramids hundreds of feet above the jungle floor and gaze across courtyards, ball parks, temples and sacrificial altars, built more than a millennium before the Pilgrims huddled at Plymouth. Almost every place the eye rests it can discern a carved facsimile of an ear of corn or some other symbol concerned with its cultivation.

5 If an observer could stand on a much higher pyramid, one tall enough to make the Americas appear like a map, he could not help but notice similar monuments to corn spread throughout Mesoamerica, Peru and Bolivia, adobe cities in the sides of cliffs in

the Southwestern United States and earthen mounds heaped up along the Mississippi River and its tributaries. The names of the builders would ring euphoniously in his ears—Olmec, Maya, Inca, Toltec, Aztec, Zapotec, cliff dwellers, Mound Builders—and each of them depended on corn.

6   The Americas are covered with other monuments to corn. Cathedral-like grain elevators in the corn belt, glass-and-steel spires in modern cities, roads and highways and trains and factories and universities—all owe their debt to corn. It is the core of American civilization, the most efficient device for trapping the energy of the sun and turning it to our uses. It is the top crop, earning $7.1 billion a year, more than double that of wheat. Corn is indeed, as historians have remarked, "the grain that built a hemisphere."

7   In its own way, and perhaps more beautifully, corn is a monument to Man. Look at it the next time you have corn on the cob or are surprised by one of those tiny ears of corn in your hors d'oeuvres at a cocktail party. The ear is the ultimate in efficient food packaging, a highly specialized flower cluster with hundreds of naked, energy-crammed seeds, compactly arranged on a rigid cob enclosed in husks. Remarkable!

8   "An ear of corn has no counterpart anywhere else in the plant kingdom," says Dr. Paul C. Mangelsdorf, a retired Harvard professor of botany, who has spent nearly all his adult lifetime studying the plant. "There is nothing like it either in nature or among cultivated plants." But the ear is a paradox, for it cannot live without Man. But for him, its seeds would fall on the ground and sprout together in a tangled mass. This is a case of what Darwin called parallel evolution: Corn and Man have become interdependent.

9   It seems almost a shame that this perfect plant has placed its future in the hands of so capricious a creature as Man. On the other hand, men have greatly benefited the plant. When corn first met our primitive ancestors its cobs were about the size of a stubby pencil, contained some 50 tiny kernels and were supported by a short spindly stalk. Some modern hybrids have ears nearly as long as a man's forearm, bearing more than 1,000 large kernels. Plant breeders, mostly since World War I, have made corn higher in protein (field corn), higher in sugar (sweet corn), disease resistant, insect resistant, mold resistant, drought resistant and wind resistant. Plants have been bred to bear ears at a uniform height for easier mechanical harvesting. Farmers have learned to plant them with a density per acre that allows each one to absorb the maximum possible sunlight.

10   In most cases, improvements in modern corn have come from using ancient types as breeding stock. All of today's major types of corn—dent, flint, flour, pop and sweet corn—were in existence by the time Columbus discovered America. When some of these ancient races were inbred (bred to close "relatives"), the vigor of successive generations decreased. But when separate inbred lines were crossbred, the result was an explosive burst of hybrid vigor—one of the most important breakthroughs in all agriculture. Between 1929 and 1969 average corn yields in the United States shot up from 26 bushels to 80 bushels per acre.

11   The results have been a bounty. Captain Smith's corn farmers could barely feed themselves, even with Indian tutoring. Henry A. Wallace, a corn breeder and farm editor before becoming Secretary of Agriculture and Vice President under Franklin D. Roosevelt, introduced hybrid corn seed commercially in 1926. Before then, one farmer fed about nine people. Today a corn-belt farmer can grow enough corn to produce enough livestock products to feed about 400 people (it takes 10 pounds of corn to raise a pound of steak). Of course, mechanization, fertilizers and pesticides aid this production, but corn now has the capacity to repay all these inputs.

12   One Ohio farmer found he could significantly increase corn yields by putting aluminum foil between the rows to throw sunlight on the *bottom* of the leaves and by keeping the corn growing all night with high powered lights! It is generally true that the more we learn about corn's origins, the more we can improve the modern crop.

13   After three centuries of speculation about which came first, the corn or the Indians who planted it, several tiny charred vegetable scraps were found in Mexico's Tehuacán Valley, about 150 miles south of Mexico City. Their discovery can be compared to that of the Dead Sea Scrolls and the ruins of Troy, for these humble pieces have caused the rewriting of the book about our transition from savagery to civilization.

14   The scraps were found in a large cavelike cliff shelter near Coxcatlán by Dr. Richard S. MacNeish, director of the Robert S. Peabody Foundation for Archaeology in Andover, Massachusetts. He had sought them for a decade and through some 35 other excavations. A workman digging through the rubble of ancient human occupation six feet below the floor of the modern cave found the black remains, about the size of a cigarette butt. MacNeish, who has the face of a philosopher and the physique of a boxer, leaped into the trench and, swinging the pick for an hour, unearthed two more similar remnants. He hurried his crew back to the local *cantina* for a congratulatory beer and then wired home, "We've hit corn!"

15   A short time ago, MacNeish recalled that day in Mexico: "A most exciting moment. There they were, small black cobs, the source of energy, comparable to our discovery of the energy within the atom, which enabled primitive man of the New World to carve his empires in the jungle."

16   The cobs were identified by Mangelsdorf at Harvard as "the earliest corn yet found . . . very close to wild." Carbon dating showed them to be about 5,600 years old. The point in time and space where the paths of Man and corn had crossed seemed about to be revealed.

17   In the dozen years since his finding the first corn in Tehuacán, and in many new excavation sites, MacNeish has found about 26,000 more intact cobs, 50,000 plant and animal remains, 10,000 artifacts such as projectile points and 500,000 potsherds. Today, in the orderly clutter of his workrooms, he is piecing together a mosaic of a people's way of life from the beginnings of human occupation. (Four volumes of a planned six–volume report on Tehuacán by MacNeish and the team of scientists who cooperated on the project have been published by the University of Texas Press.)

18   Some 12,000 years ago, Man arrived in the Valley of Tehuacán, a 20-by-70-mile basin ringed by the Sierra Madre Oriental and the Mixteca Hills. In the beginning there were probably no more than three family groups of four to eight people each (most campsites had only two fireplaces). They were primarily hunters, changing camps seasonally in search of jackrabbits, rats, birds, turtles and other small animals and some plant foods such as pods, seeds and cactus leaves. Their meager tools were simple flaked-stone implements, leaf-shaped projectile points and scrapers for working hides and wood.

19   Occasionally the nomads managed to snare or ambush one of the now-extinct horses or antelopes. This life is often portrayed by museum muralists as the "Great Mammoth Hunt," depicting the giant animal going down in a hail of spears. Actually, as MacNeish says, quoting a colleague, "They probably found one mammoth in a lifetime and never got over talking about it."

20   About 6700 B.C. the Tehuacanos began a shift from hunting to gathering wild plants. The Pleistocene era, the last Ice Age, was drying up, and game animals were moving on or becoming extinct. When plants were abundant during the wet season, the families could gather in temporary settlements. They were eating a few plants such as squash and avocados, but they had no corn and probably often starved. MacNeish speculates that about this time the idea occurred to these nomads: "If you drop a seed in the ground a plant comes up."

21   About 5000 B.C. the concept of agriculture was put to use. The inhabitants were still basically plant gatherers, but they domesticated more and more plants, including the water-bottle gourd, squash, beans, peppers, amaranth—and, for the first time, corn. Their stone implements, now polished, included the forerunner of the classic New World roller and stone device for grinding corn—the *mano* and the *metate*—which can still be seen in almost every rural Mexican village. However, the great Mexican food staple, the tortilla, had not yet been invented. The Tehuacanos probably ate corn as a gruel, like corn-meal mush today.

22   Their more efficient use of plants gave these people surplus energy; they could afford to meet seasonally in larger numbers at some favorite collecting spot, and stay together longer. As their dependence on agriculture increased, the importance of rainfall and weather became more crucial to them. The shaman and religious functions in all likelihood gained more significance, not only in rituals of birth and death but in those of planting and harvesting. Their subsistence agriculture, says MacNeish, "can be regarded as the foundation for the beginning of civilization."

23   The inhabitants of the Tehuacán Valley were growing about 30 percent of their food by 3400 B.C. They had many plants, some of which had been domesticated earlier than corn, but only corn furnished them with a storable energy reservoir that would last through the dry season and eliminate the need to move on. For the first time, Americans settled down and lived in hamlets the year round.

24   By about 1500 B.C. the hamlets formed a solid corn nurtured base for a civilization stretching 4,000 miles from central Mexico to southern Peru. But the only evidence of art or religion from this period is clay figurines, and there is nothing to indicate a political organization above the village level.

25   Alongside the cultivated patches of Indian corn grew closely related highland grasses: teosinte (an Anglicization of the Aztec name *téozinté*) and *Trip-sacum*, which had not been changed by the centuries of Man's selection and cultivation. These plants grow small ear-like seed heads and tassels which produce millions of grains of pollen. With every spring breeze, clouds of pollen mixed and fertilized them. The result was the same explosive burst of hybrid energy which revolutionized modern agriculture. Accidental hybridization gave the people of Tehuacán Valley "supercorn."

26   "It was this corn," Dr. Mangelsdorf has written, "more than any other, which initiated the rapid expansion of agriculture that was accompanied by the development of, first, large villages and, later, secular cities, the practice of irrigation, and the establishment of a complex religion."

27   Mexican farmers still revere two races of Mexican corn resulting from this hybridization, Nal-Tel and Chapalote, and grow it next to their modern corn for good luck.

28   Scientists think it may have been during this period that Mesoamerica became divided into two cultural units. One was the highland culture, such as in Tehuacán, based on irrigation agriculture and culminating in the rise of secular cities. The other was the lowland culture, beginning with the Olmecs of Veracruz, known to most people today by the huge,

thick-lipped stone heads that have been discovered half-buried in the jungle. The first of these, six-and-a-half-feet tall and weighing ten tons, was brought to the world's attention by Dr. Matthew W. Stirling of the Smithsonian Institution in 1938. The lowlanders practiced slash-and-burn agriculture and built the classical ceremonial cities with immense stone pyramids, ruled by a hierarchy of priests.

29   Despite their differences, highlanders and lowlanders relied on the same crop. As MacNeish says, "It was highland corn that made the lowland culture jump."

30   The Tehuacanos were not the first or only people in the Western Hemisphere to bring wild corn under cultivation. MacNeish believes the New World's invention of agriculture was fragmented and that some other areas, probably nearer Mexico City, were slightly earlier. However, the origins of civilization in Tehuacán are the first to be traced. The valley has yielded an almost unbroken detailed record of nearly 12,000 years of prehistory—the longest span for any New World area and the most complete record for either the New or Old World.

31   The actual origin of corn is still unclear. The Aztecs believed their hero-god, Quetzalcoatl ("who created mankind from his own blood"), once turned himself into an ant in order to steal a grain of corn from the ants' treasury inside a great mountain and give it, the gift of agriculture, to Man. Many modern theories seem just about as likely. Did it originate (1) from teosinte, (2) from primitive "pod" corn, or (3) along with the closely related teosinte and *Tripsacum,* from a common ancestor, now extinct?

32   The teosinte theory was favored until Mangelsdorf's experiments indicated teosinte was the daughter, not the mother, of corn. Mangelsdorf favors the pod corn theory. He believes the pods of chaff (the tissues between the kernels which stick in your teeth when you eat corn-on-the-cob) extended over the kernels; the husks opened at maturity, allowing the kernels to seed themselves without the help of man. Some ancient corn resembles this form. Yet recent experiments by Professor George W. Beadle of the University of Chicago are giving new impetus to the teosinte theory.

33   The search for corn's beginnings has a practical aspect, for it is still the most important grain of the Americas and if geneticists can identify corn's predecessors, they would have important new gene pools with which to improve modern hybrids. One example is a new variety called "prolific" corn. Under good conditions it produces some 20 percent more than other varieties by growing two or three ears on a plant (some modern hybrids have only one large ear). Under stress conditions, such as drought, this corn still manages to produce one ear, where other varieties can grow none at all. This corn was bred in part from an "archaic" South American popcorn.

34   A more dramatic example of our need for new genes came with the corn blight of 1970, which reduced the nation's corn production by some 700 million bushels (worth about $1.33 per bushel). The devastation resulted from too narrow a gene pool for breeding our corn crop. The corn was so similar that when a damaging disease came along, virtually every field in the country was susceptible. Here was a case of carrying all our corn, generically speaking, in one basket.

35   Discovery of corn's true family tree could produce a "son-of-supercorn." Even though the benefits would not change our lives as much as "supercorn" affected the Tehuacanos and other primitive cultures, it could not help but feed more of our hungry.

36   It behooves us in the late 20th century to heed the Zuñi Indian proverb:

"Love and cherish your corn as you love and cherish your women."

3

SECRETS OF THE MAYA: DECIPHERING TIKAL

BY DAVID ROBERTS

*After decades of intense research, the ancient ruins of Mexico
and Central America are yielding new insights into the
pre-Columbia culture*

David Roberts attempts to bring the Maya into focus by developing his discussion around the long abandoned city of Tikal, located in Guatemala. The ruins are an example of extraordinary architecture seen throughout a large, geographic territory that was once the domain of the Maya stretching from the Yucatan to Honduras. Early scholars who studied these amazing people interpreted the evidence far differently from today's investigators. The images and hieroglyphs originally seemed to hint at a people devoted to mysteries and contemplation rather than war and strife. Only recently have those ideas been tested and disproved. Likewise, what were once thought to be sparsely populated cities reserved for selective elite have been reintroduced into the record as vibrant, crowded places where many people lived.

Cracking the Maya writing system provided an opportunity to not only gain a fuller, more authentic appraisal of their society, but showed the degree to which they revered time and documented their society's existence by its exquisite precision. Trustworthy notations of years that can be compared to modern calendars allow for verifiable credibility in their accounts and give us insights into the importance that they imparted to their leaders and their deeds. Their devotion affords us the opportunity to know something about when their society began, and the sad time at which their civilization faded away.

We can also evaluate the Maya presence in Mexico in consideration of other cultures that thrived elsewhere but which apparently interacted and traded with them. Each new piece of material discovered and brought under the gaze of interested parties lends more complexity to those trade and other relationships.

- Why did deciphering the Mayan writing system make such a difference to scholars?
- What role did the colonizing Spaniards play in the long process of understanding the Maya?
- How did the Maya employ time and by what means did they calibrate a calendar?
- How could early discoverers of the Maya ruins, such as that at Tikal, have been so mistaken in describing the people who had once lived in them?
- What is the one mystery of the Maya yet to be answered?

---

1   Tikal's great plaza, at the heart of what was one of the most powerful city-states in the Americas, is surrounded by monumental structures: the stepped terraces of the North Acropolis, festooned with grotesque giant masks carved out of plaster and masonry; a steep pyramid called Temple I, whose roof comb towers 145 feet above the ground, and its mate across the plaza, Temple II, soaring 125 feet above the grass; and a complex of mysterious buildings called the Central Acropolis. At the peak of its glory, around a.d. 750, Tikal was home to at least 60,000 Maya and held sway over several other city-states scattered through the rain forest from the Yucatán Peninsula to western Honduras.

2   Though magnificent, the ruins of Tikal visible today represent but a fraction of the original city-state. During its heyday, archaeologists say, "downtown" Tikal was about six square miles, though research indicates that the city-state's population may have sprawled over at least 47 square miles. Yet most of Tikal—the heart of Guatemala's Tikal National Park, about an hour's drive northeast of the modern city of Flores—has not even been excavated. And until recently, the same could be said about the nature of the Maya themselves.

3   For much of the 20th century, Maya experts followed the lead of Carnegie Institution of Washington archaeologist J. Eric Thompson, who argued that the Maya were peaceful philosophers and extraordinary observers of celestial events content to ponder the nature of time and the cosmos. Thompson, who died in 1975, theorized that Tikal and other sites were virtually unpopulated "ceremonial centers" where priests studied planets and stars and the mysteries of the calendar. It was a beautiful vision—but nearly all wrong. "For all of Eric Thompson's important findings in many areas of Maya studies," writes anthropologist Michael Coe in his 1992 book *Breaking the Maya Code*, "he singlehandedly held back the decipherment [of Mayan hieroglyphs] for four decades" and, consequently, the study of the Maya.

4   When, in the 1960s, the hieroglyphs—the most sophisticated writing system created in the New World—were at last beginning to be deciphered, a new picture of these people emerged. Mayan art and writing, it turned out, contained stories of battles, sacrificial offerings and torture. Far from being peaceful, the Maya were warriors, their kings vainglorious despots. Maya cities were not merely ceremonial; instead, they were a patchwork of feudal fiefdoms bent on conquest and living in constant fear of attack. "Blood was the mortar of ancient Maya ritual life," wrote groundbreaking epigrapher Linda Schele and art historian Mary Miller in their 1986 book *The Blood of Kings*.

5   It is one of the ironies of this view that evidence for it has long been in plain sight. At the base of Tikal's North Acropolis stands a row of tall carved stones, or stelae. Each stela depicts a sumptuously bedecked king, and the monoliths are covered in hieroglyphs that, once deciphered, illuminated our view of Maya life.

6   During the Spanish conquest of Mesoamerica in the 16th century, the Catholic Church's Friar Diego de Landa supervised the burning of hundreds of Maya codices—fig-bark books rich in mythological and astronomical information. Only four Maya codices are known to have survived. And one key to the glyphs from that time was saved: a manuscript that Landa wrote in 1566 about his contact with the Maya. It recorded what he mistakenly thought was the Mayan alphabet. Although parts of his manuscript were first published in 1864, nearly a century would pass before epigraphers understood that Mayan hieroglyphs are actually a combination of symbols using both logographs (words) and syllabic signs (units of sound). However, it was not until the 1970s that the full meaning of many hieroglyphs was understood. Today at least 85 percent of known Mayan texts have been read and translated.

7   The descendants of the ancient Maya, who long ago lost the ability to read their ancestors' writings, have been in the midst of a cultural revival. Having weathered the Catholic Church's suppression of their culture during the 16th and 17th centuries and later endured a string of brutal dictators, including the notorious Efrain Ríos Montt—responsible for the murder of more than 100,000 Maya in the early 1980s—some Maya have begun openly to celebrate their heritage with pilgrimages to Tikal and other sites.

8   Abandoned by its original inhabitants more than a thousand years ago, the city remained unknown to outsiders for almost a millennium. In 1525, Spanish conquistador Hernando Cortés passed within a few dozen miles of the place without learning of it. Likewise, in 1841, the American diplomat, journalist and explorer John Lloyd Stephens and the British illustrator Frederick Catherwood reported with great fanfare their "discovery" of ruins in the Maya region, but they missed Tikal. Guatemalan archives mention that local people lived in Tikal in the 18th century, but the first official expedition to the ruin wasn't until 1848. Even "Tikal" is a relatively recent name, derived from the Mayan word *ti ak'al*, or "at the water hole."

9   A leader in the field of Mayan epigraphy is David Stuart, who was awarded a MacArthur Fellowship in 1984 at age 18—the youngest recipient of the so-called genius award—for his several publications and papers about deciphering Mayan hieroglyphs. He defined some previously unknown glyphs and refined the spelling rules of the Mayan writing system. Now 38, Stuart is the curator of Mayan hieroglyphs at Harvard University's Peabody Museum of Archaeology and Ethnology. He has a special fondness for Tikal. "It's the atmosphere of the place,"

Stuart says. "Tikal is simply one of the most overpowering archaeological sites in the world."

10   Though Tikal may have been settled by at least 600 b.c., most of the city's edifices were built during what is called the Classic period of Maya history, from a.d. 250 to 900. It was a time when the Maya created great artwork and amazing architecture across the region. Recent finds may yet force scholars to redefine the beginning of this period. This spring, archaeologists working at the nearby city of Cival uncovered evidence that distinctively Mayan art and writing may have developed as early as 300 b.c., and a wall painting dating to about a.d. 100, the oldest known intact Maya mural to date, was discovered in an 80-foot-high pyramid at the ruins of San Bartolo, a ceremonial site in Guatemala. Still, Tikal stands out. "The buildings at Tikal are particularly well built, and they have stood up quite well against the onslaught of the jungle," says Stan Loten, an architectural archaeologist and retired professor who conducted surface surveys of Tikal's standing structures from 1964 to 1970.

11   Beginning in the 1880s, well before other glyphs yielded up their meanings, researchers began decoding the Maya calendar from glyphs on stelae at sites all over the Maya world. Most stelae include the date of their creation, written in a five-number sequence known to scholars as the Long Count, or the number of days since the beginning of this current era. This system is built on a base of 20 rather than 10 and is made up of glyphs and combinations of a single dot for "one," a bar for "five," and a glyph that translated to *mih*, or "zero." Once scholars figured out this system, they were able to correlate it with the Gregorian calendar, revealing an astonishing sense of time: the Long Count starts in 3114 b.c. The earliest dated monument yet discovered in Tikal and all of the Maya lowlands, Stela 29, has a Long Count date of 8.12.14.13.15, which translates to a.d. 292.

12   Understanding this calendar was an important step in understanding the history of the Maya. Of all the dated stelae found at Tikal, not one is from between a.d. 562 and 692. This period of monumental silence is known as the Hiatus. For decades, scholars were at a loss to explain what happened during those years. But after the discovery of the Long Count, one of the next breakthroughs in deciphering the Mayan writing system was recognizing what experts call the emblem glyph—a unique hieroglyph that represents a specific city-state. Tikal's emblem glyph is read as *mutal*, which is based on the word *mut*, meaning "bound" or "tied." The glyph resembles how a ruler's tied-back hair might look from behind, and appears on stelae in ancient Maya city-states as far away as Copán, about 180 miles to the southeast. But why?

13   As experts translated more glyphs, they learned that Tikal had lost a war with Caracol, a Maya city in present-day Belize. The evidence is a boast of the victory, in a.d. 562, inscribed on an altar found in Caracol. That crushing defeat must have hung over Tikal like a pall. Before the glyphs were read, no archaeologist would have dreamed that Caracol, though a substantial city-state, could have laid low the mighty Tikal. Other stelae at Caracol suggest that the key to its triumph was an alliance with Calakmul, another Maya powerhouse in present-day Mexico. For more than 100 years, then, Tikal may have been a conquered city-state, languishing in thrall to foreign rulers.

14   Somehow, Tikal recovered. In 672, the city launched a war against Dos Pilas, about 70 miles to the southwest. An upstart Maya city less than 50 years old at the time, Dos Pilas had the nerve to use Tikal's emblem glyph, calling itself in effect "New Tikal." In the war, Tikal was triumphant. Glyph-covered stone stairways at Dos Pilas record the city's defeat.

15   So explicit are Mayan glyphs that archaeologists have by now compiled a chronology of 33 rulers of Tikal (including at least one queen) spanning 800 years. Scholars formerly named these rulers after the glyphs that signified them, such as Double Bird, Jaguar Paw and Curl Snout. As epigraphers learned to sound out the glyphs, they assigned phonetic names. The architect of the first phase of Tikal's revival was Nuun Ujol Chaak, a warrior king also known as Shield Skull.

16   Nuun Ujol Chaak's era was hardly peaceful. As a young king, he fled Tikal when Calakmul declared war in a.d. 657. But he returned to lead Tikal's defeat of Dos Pilas in 672. Then, only five years later, Nuun Ujol Chaak lost again to Dos Pilas, which was most likely collaborating with Calakmul, probably the greatest Maya power at the end of the seventh century. Victory over Tikal's rivals was finally achieved by his son, Jasaw Chan K'awiil I, on August 5, 695. A drawing on a building in the Central Acropolis shows Jasaw carried in triumph into the city on a litter, leading his captive—perhaps the defeated lord of Calakmul—by a tether.

17   Temple IV, erected about a.d. 741, is a dizzying pyramid that stands 212 feet above the ground, the tallest Maya structure ever built. Only the upper levels of Temple IV have been restored, but thanks to a pair of wooden staircases that surmount the rubble, visitors can climb nearly to the top of this structure for the finest view at Tikal. A seemingly limitless green expanse of rain forest billows into the distance like waves on a chlorophyll ocean. There is no sign of any other human settlement.

18   Yet hidden in the jungle below is another of Tikal's mysteries. The Lost World is a complex of pyramids and buildings southwest of the Great Plaza. It was excavated and restored between 1979

and 1985 by Guatemalan archaeologists working on the Tikal National Project. The area, according to Guatemalan epigrapher Federico Fahsen, served as an observatory from about 500 b.c. to a.d. 250. During the early Classic period, it vied with the North Acropolis as the ceremonial epicenter of Tikal and served as a royal burial ground.

19   Around the Lost World, architectural and artistic features suggest Tikal had links to Teotihuacán, a city in the highlands of Mexico whose culture flourished between a.d. 150 and 650, entirely separate from the Maya. Because Teotihuacán lies 630 miles from Tikal, many scholars originally doubted that the two empires were even aware of the other's existence. Yet ceramic designs found at Tikal and other Maya sites seem to mirror the iconography of the Teotihuacán culture—especially its grim-visaged storm god, Tlaloc.

20   Only six years ago, David Stuart untangled a series of fourth-century glyphic texts from Tikal's Stela 31 that helped connect the two empires. Remarkably, he was able to read the glyph that confirmed scholarly speculation pinpointing the day when a lord from Teotihuacán named Siyah K'ak', or Fire is Born, arrived at Tikal: a.d. January 31, 378. It is probably no coincidence that the 14th king of Tikal, Chak Tok

Ich'aak I, long known as Jaguar Paw, died the same day. The impact that other civilizations have had on the Maya is just beginning to be understood, researchers say.

21   Perhaps the greatest Maya mystery of all is the cause of the civilization's abrupt decline. The last dated stela erected at Tikal was put up in a.d. 869; the last anywhere in the Maya world, in 909. The causes of what University of Pennsylvania archaeologist Robert Sharer calls "one of the most profound cultural failures in human history" have been debated for a century. The stelae are no help—the collapse seems to have ended most of the carving. Most likely, researchers speculate, a severe drought devastated a society that was already suffering from overpopulation and famine.

22   Tikal still keeps some secrets. Scanning a map of the ruins laid out on his desk, Stuart points to an area of nameless, unexcavated mounds just south of the Lost World. "I've always been curious about this group," Stuart says. "You can spend five or six years digging a site and not greatly change our understanding of Classic Maya civilization. What changes it is the fortuitous discovery of a new inscription." His finger rests on the area. "Who knows what you might find there?"

4

AMERICA BEFORE COLUMBUS

BY LEWIS LORD AND SARAH BURKE

At the moment of Columbus' first encounters with Native Americans, misunderstandings spawned tragedies ranging from wrongly identifying the people of this land and their numbers to outright exploitation and extermination of their civilizations. Historians of past generations have tended to downplay the value of Native Americans in history, ignoring some of the greatest architectural feats and social achievements seen anywhere in the world.

The authors of this article discuss one of the most traumatic historical events, the "Columbian Exchange," which affected the world's populations, especially native people. Europeans, Africans, and Asians benefitted by the great food stores of America, while the Native people of the Western Hemisphere suffered from the deadly diseases passed on by the newcomers from those regions.

- *What kind of place was America before Columbus came?*
- *Why do we know so little about native people, and what sort of speculation do the authors provide for explaining their behavior prior to and after first encounters with Europeans?*

---

1 Most vacationers on Interstate 70 speed right by ancient Cahokia and its 15-acre ceremonial mound, the one that's two acres bigger than the Great Pyramid of Egypt. Only a curious few pull off to learn how a feather-crowned dictator known as the Great Sun used to kneel atop the earthen temple every morning and howl when the real sun came up. At its peak, the town across the Mississippi from present-day St. Louis boasted a trade network that stretched from the Gulf of Mexico to the Dakotas and probably had as many residents as did London at that time. But modern textbooks barely take notice. Cahokia's problem is that American history, in the minds of many, started just 500 years ago, back when Columbus discovered the New World. By 1492, Cahokia was an Illinois Babylon, a city that had thrived and vanished.

2 Like many 20th-century metropolises, 13th-century Cahokia could not handle growth, even though its developers were sharp enough to grasp geometry and astronomy. Besides building more than 100 neatly proportioned mounds, they constructed a circle of tall poles—archaeologists call it "Woodhenge"—that aligned with the sun at equinox and solstice. Despite this evidence of advanced thinking, however, no Cahokian appears to have anticipated the consequences of ecological change and environmental degradation. Cornfields that fed 20,000 to 40,000 urbanites gradually lost their fertility. Forests were stripped of trees not only to fuel thousands of daily household fires but also to form a 2½-mile stockade wall. As hard times set in, Cahokians moved or perished. Centuries later, the French arrived and found only grown-over mounds. The Europeans who peopled America in Columbus's wake believed the land had never been settled, much less civilized. "North America was inhabited only by wandering tribes who had no thought of profiting by the natural riches of the soil," wrote Alex de Tocqueville in 1835. It was, the French observer concluded, "an empty continent, a desert land awaiting its inhabitants." Tocqueville's "empty continent"

phrase endures today in Fourth of July speeches that hail the building of the nation, but in fact the New World was anything but empty in Columbus's day. Give or take several million, the Western Hemisphere in 1492 had as many people as Europe. It was the teeming and majestic civilizations of Mexico's Aztecs and Peru's Incas that awed the Spanish conquistadors initially—some gawked like country bumpkins at Montezuma's capital, with its several hundred thousand people—but ancient societies had also been rising and falling for centuries above the Rio Grande. More than 1,000 tribes—with upward of two million people–still inhabited the northern forests, prairies and mesas when whites arrived.

3   Newcomers from Europe, though accustomed to people being burned or beheaded, were shocked at what went on in America. Columbus claimed he had to take hundreds of Carib Indians to Spain for their own good and that of their Arawak neighbors, whom they were eating. (He had a harder time explaining why he also enslaved the gentle Arawaks.) While cannibalism and human sacrifice were rare among Indians north of Mexico, people in some tribes killed unwanted infants, had multiple wives and, in the case of the Hurons, wiped their hands on dogs that ambled by. Other traits seemed alien as well: an awed reverence of nature, a desire to share and, for many, societies free of oppression and class stratification. In addition, most took a daily bath, a practice the Europeans abhorred. America was not new, but it was different.

4   As whites moved westward across what is now the United States, they encountered a familiar question among tribesmen in their path: "Why do you call us Indians?" The answer, of course, was that Columbus was mistaken. He thought he was in the distant Indies, somewhere between Japan and India, and labeled his hosts *los Indios*. The Indians had no word for their race. They called their own tribes "people" or "real people," and other tribes names like "friend," "enemy" or "poisonous snake."

5   The diversity that Americans relish today actually existed long before Columbus arrived. Most of the hundreds of languages the Indians spoke were as different from one another as Farsi is from French. Some Indians loved war. Others hated it. After every reluctant fight, Arizona's Pimas subjected their warriors to a 16-day cure for insanity. Some tribes banned women from their councils. Others were ruled by female chiefs, like Georgia's "Lady of Cofltachequi," who greeted Hernando De Soto with pearls from the Savannah River. (He ungraciously kidnapped her.) Puppies were a gourmet's delight in some huts. Elsewhere, Indians would rather die than eat dog meat. Premarital sex was unthinkable among the Cheyenne. But Mississippi's Natchez tribe encouraged teenagers to have flings while they could. Once a Natchez girl wed, an extramarital affair could cost her hair or even an ear.

6   Every American Indian, from the Abenakis of Maine to the Zunis of New Mexico, descended from immigrant stock. Asian-Americans were the first Americans, and they came over 12,000 to 20,000 years ago, probably crossing a glacial land bridge between Siberia and Alaska. For some time, they hunted the **mastodon** and the long-horned bison, perhaps speeding their extinction. As long ago as 5,000 years, people in Mexico may have cultivated maize, better known as corn, and early residents of Arizona were growing it in A.D. 1. Many people in what is now the United States existed the next 10 or 15 centuries as nomads, moving about in search of game, fish and wild plants for food, but some accomplished much more.

7   Pioneers who found thousands of abandoned mounds in the Ohio and Mississippi valleys refused to believe they had been built by Indians. "The natural indolence of the Indian and his averseness to any kind of manual labor are well known," wrote author William Pidgeon in 1858. Other 19th-century writers speculated that the mound builders were stray Vikings, Phoenicians or a lost tribe of Israel— obviously an intelligent people who were annihilated by Indian savages. Settlers liked that theory, because it seemed to justify the treatment they inflicted on the Indians on the frontier. Not until the 1890s did educated people agree that the mounds in fact were built by the Indians' ancestors.

8   The genius of the mound builders has become even more evident in recent years. Just west of the Mississippi in northeast Louisiana lies Poverty Point, a 3,500-year-old collection of concentric semicircles of earth, the biggest nearly three quarters of a mile long. Visitors can stand atop a mound just west of Poverty Point's rings during the spring and fall equinox and see the sun rise over what was the town's central plaza—a view like that at England's Stonehenge during similar conjunctions of earth and sun. On Moundbuilders Golf Course in Newark, Ohio, stands an earthen ring that is 15 centuries old. Its diameter is the same, 1,050 feet, as those of two more circles within 50 miles of Newark. Other precisely measured mounds in central Ohio include three 1,200-foot circles and five 27-acre squares. "Such nice equivalences of shapes and sizes are not the work of savages," says Roger Kennedy, director of the Smithsonian's Museum of American History, who is writing a book entitled "Medieval America."

---

mastodon: Any of the several extinct mammals of the genus

"I doubt that the Harvard freshman class would be capable of similar intellectual achivement."

9   Every explorer and early settler seemed to notice the aroma of America. Robert Beverley was awed by "the pleasantest Smell" of Virginia's giant magnolias. De Soto's men admired Georgia's "very savoury, palatable and fragrant" strawberries. Henry Hudson paused in New York's harbor to enjoy the "very sweet smells" of grass and flowers on the New Jersey shore. But the visitors also smelled smoke. Many soon concluded that Indian women did all the work, while the men idled away their time hunting, fishing and setting the woods on fire.

10   The native men, it turned out, were practicing a form of forest management that put food in their wigwams and longhouses. With torches and stone hatchets, the Nootkas and Haidas of the Pacific Northwest toppled giant redwoods and turned them into whaling canoes. In the eastern forests, Indians slashed and burned to clear the way for cornfields fertilized by the ashes and to create meadows for grazing deer and elk. Every autumn, Indians burned huge chunks of woodland to clear away underbrush. The sprouts that poked each spring through the charred ground boosted populations of game animals, which the Indians could easily spot in the open forests. The trees that survived flourished, too. Sycamores in Ohio grew seven feet in diameter, and the white pines of New England towered 200 to 250 feet. Governor's Island, now in the shadow of Manhattan's skyscrapers, had so many big hickory and walnut trees that the Dutch settlers called it Nut Island.

11   Colonists enjoyed describing the country they settled as a "howling wilderness"—a phrase from the Book of Jeremiah—and in many places it was. Bamboo canebrakes, 20 to 30 feet high and impenetrable, stretched in parts of the Southeast for 100 miles or more, and tangles of brier and grapevines crowded the cottonwoods of the river bottoms. The forests were so boundless, the settlers like to say, that a squirrel could travel from Maine to the Mississippi and never touch the ground. But wherever Indians hunted, the forest floor was usually clear, reminding one observer of "our parks in England."

12   Early English settlers, accustomed to woods with only a few doves, were startled by the spectacle in America's skies. The colonists especially admired the green-and-gold Carolina parakeet, "a fowle most swift of wing [and] very beautiful." Passenger pigeons passed in flocks "for three or foure houres . . . so thicke they have shaddowed the skie from us." Out west, Meriwether Lewis and William Clark would see huge flocks of pelicans and sandhill cranes along the Missouri and dense clouds of geese over the Columbia River.

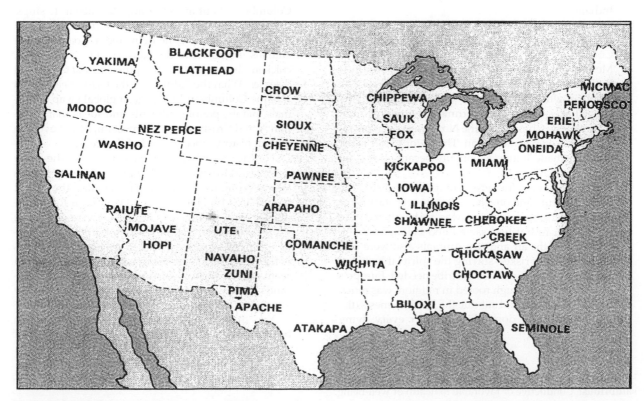

Major Indian Tribes in America Prior to European Colonization

13   Animals were bigger then. Pennsylvania trout, nearly two feet long, were easy targets for Algonquian arrows. Virginia sturgeon stretched six to nine feet, and Mississippi catfish topped 120 pounds. Off Cape Cod, a few Indians could catch 30 lobsters in a half hour, some weighing 20 pounds, and many Massachusetts oysters had to be sliced into thirds to be swallowed.

14   Bison roamed not only the Great Plains but also the meadows and open forests of Ohio, Pennsylvania and Virginia. The western bison were infinitely more numerous, thundering along in herds 25 miles long, but the woods buffalo was bigger and blacker with shorter hair and no hump. A few still remained in George Washington's time; he considered crossing them with domestic cattle.

15   The white man's Bible taught that it is better to give than to receive, and the Indians couldn't agree more. Long after the Arawaks showered Columbus with birds, cloth and "trifles too tedious to describe," natives were offering Europeans virtually anything they had, from fish and turkeys to persimmon bread and the companionship of a chief's daughter. Colonists interpreted the Indians' generosity as evidence they were childlike. That they had no desire to accumulate wealth was seen as a symptom of laziness. The Indians, concluded one New Englander, must develop a love of property. "Wherever this can be established, Indians may be civilized; wherever it cannot, they will still remain Indians."

16   The Indians felt quite civilized with what they did own, often things a Puritan wouldn't appreciate. Colorado's Pueblos kept parrots that came from Mexico. The Cayuse of Eastern Oregon swapped buffalo robes for the shells of coastal Indians. The Ottawas, whose name meant "to trade," traveled the Great Lakes exchanging cornmeal, herbs, furs and tobacco. The Chinooks of the Northwest even developed their own trade jargon. Their word *hootchenoo*, for homemade liquor, eventually became the slang word "hootch."

17   Above all else, Indians were religious. They saw order in nature and obeyed elaborate sets of rules for fear of disturbing it. Land was to be shared, not owned, because it was sacred and belonged to everyone, like the air and sea. Animals also were precious. A hunter risked stirring the spirits if he killed two deer when one was all his tribe needed. Europe's view of nature, though rooted in religion, was much different. Man should subdue the Earth, Genesis dictated, "and have dominion . . . over every living thing."

18   Rituals surrounded each important Indian event. To prove their courage, the Arikara of North Dakota danced barefoot on hot coals and, with bare hands, retrieved and devoured hunks of meat from pots of boiling water. Timucuan leaders started council meetings in Florida with a round of emetics brewed from holly leaves. The Hurons of the Great Lakes carried smoldering coals in their mouths to invoke a spirit to cure the sick. But often the rituals were painless. From New York to New Mexico, tradition allowed a woman to end her marriage by putting her husband's belongings outside their door—a sign for him to live with his mother.

19   Three centuries before the U.S. Constitution took shape, the Iroquois League ran a Congress-like council, exercised the veto, protected freedom of speech and let women choose officeholders. The New Yorkers ran a classless society, as did many tribes across America. But ancient caste systems also endured. The Great Sun of the Natchez, a mound dweller like Cahokia's Great Sun, used his feet to push his leftovers to his noble subordinates. The nobles were not about to complain; below them was a class known as "Stinkards." Besides, the chief's feet were clean. He was carried everywhere, a French guest reported, and his toes never touched the ground.

20   Columbus's second voyage—the one in which Europeans came to stay—began the process that changed nearly everything. Instead of 90 sailors on the *Niña*, the *Pinta* and the *Santa Maria* as in 1492, Columbus set out in 1493 with 1,200 men in 17 ships. In addition to starting the world's most significant movement of people, he delivered a Noah's Ark of animals unknown to the New World—sheep, pigs, chickens, horses and cows— plus a host of Old World diseases. What the Admiral of the Ocean Sea created was the Columbian Exchange, a global swap of animals, plants, people, ailments and ideas that historian Alfred Crosby calls "the most important event in human history since the end of the Ice Age."

21   For the Old World as well as the New, the event was both **salubrious** and **calamitous**. Twenty years after Columbus colonized Hispaniola—the island now shared by Haiti and the Dominican Republic—diseases and taskmasters reduced its Arawaks from a quarter million down to 14,000. Within two centuries, Old World diseases killed probably two thirds of the New World's natives, and America did indeed seem empty. Africans also were dying by the thousands. They were brought to the New World to grow sugar, another import from the Old World.

22   Yet, thanks to Columbus, Africa's population boomed. Corn, an American staple for thousands of

---

salubrious: Conductive or favorable to health or well-being.
Calamitous: Disastrous.

CHAPTER 4: AMERICA BEFORE COLUMBUS

years, augmented African diets, boosting the continent's birth rates and life spans. The same thing happened in Europe with the potato, also from America. The Columbian Exchange thickened Italy's sauces with tomatoes, seeded Kentucky with European bluegrass and covered the gullies of Georgia with Chinese kudzu. China, in return, became the globe's No. 1 consumer of the American-born sweet potato. "The Columbus story is not an Old World, New World story," explains Smithsonian historian Herman Viola, who heads the Museum of Natural History's Columbus Quincentenary programs. "It is two old worlds that linked up, making one new world."

23   It is also a story of winning and losing, with many of the losers gone before the winners ever showed up. When whites first penetrated the fertile Ohio Valley, they found many mounds but few Indians. The Southeast also seemed vacant when the French came to stay around 1700. As they moved into lands that abounded in natural food resources, the settlers kept wondering where the Indians had gone. Some scholars believe they were wiped out or chased away by epidemics of European diseases that moved north along Indian trade routes in the century after Columbus. Two years before DeSoto visited Cofitachequi's female chief in the 1540s, pestilence swept her province, decimating her town and emptying others nearby. In one village, the Spaniards found nothing but large houses full of bodies. It was the same medical disaster the conquistadors at that time were discovering in Mexico and Peru and the Pilgrims would notice much later in Massachusetts. Four years before the Mayflower landed, disease killed tens of thousands of Indians on the New England coast, including the inhabitants of a village where Plymouth would stand. John Winthrop, admiring the abandoned cornfields, saw the epidemic as divine providence. "God," he said, "hath hereby cleared out title to this place."

24   Indians in the forests shuddered every time they found honeybees in a hollow tree. The "English flies" moved 100 miles ahead of the frontier—a sign that the white man was on his way. The smart tribes moved west, pushing whatever band was in their way. The Chippewas pushed the Sioux out of the woods of Minnesota into the Dakotas. The Sioux pushed the Cheyenne into Nebraska. The Cheyenne pushed the Kiowas into Oklahoma. Yet not every Indian fled. The Comanches, with horses descended

from Columbus's stock, thwarted Spain's colonial designs on Texas with frequent raids on Spanish outposts. Apaches did the same thing in Arizona and New Mexico. Parts of Pennsylvania and New York today might be part of Quebec had the Iroquois rolled over for the French.

25   Many, who didn't move, perished. A generation after their gifts of corn saved England's toehold settlement at Jamestown, the Powhatan Indians were systematically wiped out, their crops and villages torched by settlers who wanted more land to grow tobacco. Florida's Timucuas—of whom it was said "it would be good if among Christians there was as little greed to torment men's minds and hearts"—vanished in the early 19th century, victims of epidemics and conflicts with the Spanish, English and Creeks. Natchez's Great Sun wound up with his feet on the ground, enslaved in the West Indies by the French, who eradicated his tribe. California's Chumash shrank from 70,000 to 15,000 toiling for the friars. Soon after the Gold Rush, the tribe, like most in California, ceased to exist. The four-century clash of cultures made two of every three tribes as extinct as the Carolina parakeet.

26   The land they left is different now. The white pines that towered over New England became masts for the Royal Navy's sailing ships. The redwoods that stretched from the Rockies to the Pacific, like the cypresses that crowded the Mississippi Valley, exist in pockets smaller than the Indians' shrunken reservations. The hours-long thunder of bison hooves no longer shakes Kansas or Nebraska, where only a few stretches of grassland remain like the prairie John Muir described a century ago—"one sheet of plant gold, hazy and vanishing in the distance." The prairie now feeds the nation with Old World food like wheat and pork.

27   Yet at least one ancient American community endures. Shunning electricity, 3,000 Pueblo Indians live today in Acoma atop a mesa in the high New Mexico desert. The town's adobe apartments have been inhabited since the 12th century, through droughts, Apache raids and a brutal occupation in which the enslaving Spaniards chopped off one foot of each adult male. Acomans are reluctant to promote the fact that their settlement is nearly twice as old as St. Augustine, Fla., the Spanish-settled city that is generally considered the nation's oldest community. The people of Acoma figure they have had enough visitors.

II

EXPLORATION AND COLONIZATION

1   European exploration cannot be understood in the isolated context of the voyages begun by Columbus under the aegis of his Spanish sponsors. Europeans, like all peoples, were products of their past. We must grasp the great, wrenching events of Medieval and Renaissance Europe to fully appreciate the great quests that resulted in the events of 1492.

2   Europe had suffered severe decline following the disintegration of the Roman Empire. The "Dark Ages," a period lasting from roughly the sixth century until around the 15th, represented a birthing of unique European institutions. Feudalism and its codes of chivalry created a society of religious devotees who nonetheless glorified martial pursuits.

3   The Renaissance dawned with European society still fractured by war and confusion, but perched for the leap into the era of nation-states. Great strides in science and technology extended the horizons of first the Italian states, and finally most of the rest of Europe. Populations grew, despite setbacks caused by plague; and prosperity helped ignite commercial ventures that were themselves the basis of state support for exploration.

4   At the forefront of this activity was tiny Portugal, hinged on the western Iberian Peninsula, and facing a single, reliable right of way to trade, the sea. In the early 15th century Prince Henry the Navigator, a monarch well aware of the value of modernization, insured Portugal's place in history as a state devoted to great exploration, as well as exploitation. He set the stage for the phenomenal European obsession with conquest and colonization.

5   In 1440 Johann Gutenburg invented the printing press, a device that revolutionized the dissemination of information. Hence, any interested party could gain access to accounts, maps, and other materials associated with the great discoveries. This one innovation came about at a time of many converging forces in European history, and was certainly a catalyst to ignite the imaginations of dreamers like Christopher Columbus.

6   Columbus, the son of a Genoan weaver, was a tenacious self-promoter who succeeded in convincing the Spanish crown to sponsor his scheme to cross the Atlantic. Fresh from victories against the Moors, Ferdinand and Isabella were inclined to support Columbus' pursuit for new avenues of wealth. His successful crossing was by no means a certainty of great wealth, and certainly the greatest part of Spain's majestic colonial campaigns were still to be initiated. The Aztecs and Incas, along with their gold, were yet to be plundered. However, Columbus set events into motion, the inertia of which is still being felt in our own age.

7   The Spaniards carried with them a culture fashioned out of centuries of conflict. They professed a devout religious conviction born out of their experiences as a Catholic bastion in the face of

Moorish occupation. The Muslim armies that occupied the Iberian Peninsula in 732 A.D. help to sculpt that brand of Spanish duality, faith and violence, that culminated in Hernan Cortes victory over the Aztecs in 1521. Cortes was a true Spanish Conquistador, he felt no qualms about naming his landfall in Mexico "Vera Cruz" (True Cross) and then ruthlessly crushing the indigenous populations. Spaniards were aghast at the sight of Aztecs carving the hearts out of captives, yet they were the fervent sword of the inquisition, burning people at the stake and garotting criminals and heretics in scenes of incredible barbarity.

8 Spain's claim to the "New World" was contested by other Europeans, even before the full extent of the geography was understood. The Portuguese, French, Dutch, English, and others took their turns at either exploring new lands or colonizing at the expense of the overextended Spanish. Of course, in all cases the indigenous populations were seen as no more than slave labor at best or expendable populations at worst.

5

THE SAILORS OF PALOS

BY PETER F. COPELAND

The voyage undertaken by Christopher Columbus is universally remembered in the context of the famous Genoese weaver's son and his Spanish patrons. The three ships, the long ocean voyage, the encounter with alien people, and the ultimate return to Spain are memorialized as an odyssey led by Columbus, but void of consideration of the many men who sailed under him. Historian Peter Copeland steers the reader's attention away from the glory of Spain and Columbus's singular extravaganza, and instead attempts to bring common seaman into the discussion. He tries to peek into the hulls and spaces of three divine ships, as well as consider the sailor's archetypical comrades elsewhere in the world.

Simply clad, irreverent, cynical, and superstitious, the sailors of Columbus's time were in some ways just like those who stayed rooted to shore; however, in others very distinct ways, they were exposed to a larger world of seaports and strange lands. Sailors might use salty language and remain walled off from respectable society while ashore, but at sea those same chafed souls recited daily prayers and followed a routine of invocations heavenward. Libido and credo were somehow melded into a single person.

Life at sea was no watery copy of existence on land, but the sailors manning Europe's ships acted according to norms well-established for common folk. The unique life experienced by men of humble origin did not compel them to stop eating "from their lap" in the fashion of peasants. A sailor stood to earn wages for his efforts, a truly remarkable enticement for men from a class who could never hope to see real money. These common folk, the labor, and talent that made Columbus's voyage possible, had so much to tell, but historians did a poor job of listening.

- *How much persuasion might a person like Columbus have had to use to gain ships and crews for such as voyage as he envisioned?*
- *What sorts of challenges must the historian confront when truly attempting to appraise the life and role of sailors manning ships like those that Columbus prized from royal patrons?*

---

1   When Christopher Columbus's two surviving ships arrived back in Europe from the New World in March 1493, the Admiral of the Ocean Sea returned to lasting but troubled fame. But the mariners who had accompanied him across unknown seas and through storm and shipwreck remained virtually forgotten to history.

2   It was early March 1493, and the great voyage was nearly over. En route back to Spain from the far-off Indies, the storm-beater *Niña*, flagship of Christopher Columbus, had put into Lisbon. Her consort, the original flagship *Santa María*—or what was left of her—lay shattered on a reef off the island of Hispaniola.

3   The *Niña* sailors were at work, repairing and re-newing their weathered ship, and anticipating a speedy return to Spain and their home port of Palos. They had little time to speculate on the fate of the *Pinta*, the sister caravel last seen one stormy night a month before in mid ocean.(**) There was much to be done. A new set of sails must be laid out, cut, and sewn. Running rigging must be renewed; standing rigging needed repair. Already shoreside carpenters were measuring and sawing aloft and on deck, while caulkers worked at sealing the leaky hull, other sail-ors turned-to to clean and wash down the hold. Soon they would load sacks and barrels of stones from the banks of the River Tagus, to be packed as ballast in the now lightly laden vessel.

4   Within a few days, news of Columbus's epochal seven-month voyage and discovery of a sea route across the Western ocean to the Indies and far Cathay would begin to reverberate across Portugal and Spain, and indeed be trumpeted throughout Europe. Greeted as a hero by all who heard of his enterprise, the admiral already basked in his celebrity It was, at least for the moment, everything for which the determined explorer could hope.

5   Columbus returned to Europe in 1493 to lasting but troubled fame for achievements that still cast an imposing shadow today, 500 years later. But what of the nearly 90 officers and sailors who accompanied him across unknown seas, enduring storm and shipwreck? Unlike Columbus, his mariners have passed the succeeding centuries in virtual obscurity. Who were these sailors and what were their lives like—both in port and during their odyssey of discovery?

6   Most of the men and boys who signed on for the Voyage of Discovery during the summer of 1492 came from Palos and the other seaside towns and villages of Andalusia in southern Spain. A few, however, were Basques and Gallicians from the northern part of the country, and five—a Portuguese, a Venetian, a Calabrian, and two Genoese-were foreigners.

7   The crewmen ranged in age and experience from seasoned veterans of the sea accustomed to the rigors of shipboard life to youths no older than 12 years of age. They included skilled specialists such as boatswains, carpenters, caulkers, coopers, gunners, pilots, stewards, and surgeons, as well as untrained boys.

8   Legend suggests that Columbus's sailors were criminals and convicts, dragooned for a desperate enterprise, but in fact only one man among them was a convicted murderer. He and two cohorts were pardoned on condition of volunteering to serve. The vast majority of the sailors joined the expedition—after initial hesitation—for the adventure of the voyage and the hope of gaining riches in the far-off Indies.

9   Strange and picturesque to the shore-folk he encountered, the seaman of Columbus's time lived apart in his own world of ships and seaports. He had been to distant lands and seen fascinating sights. He wore odd clothes and spoke a language that sounded peculiar and sometimes even incomprehensible.

10   To landsmen unfamiliar with the fifteenth-century sailor's world, the bustling seaports he frequented must have seemed exciting and exotic places. In many harbors the waterfront itself was called the "lowere city" and sometimes was sepa-rated by a tall wooden palisade from the rest of the town—the "upper city"—where dwelt the merchants and well-to-do tradesmen.

11   This lower city—with its population of fisherfolk, chandlers, peddlers, ship-wrights, rogues, slat-terns, and drunks—was a place of noise and smells and mud. Packs of half-wild dogs roamed through the narrow, filthy alleys that led down to the ships. The air was filled with the raw stench of hides, fish, and sewage and the sounds of wine vendors, soap sellers, and other street peddlers crying their wares. Here, too, one might hear the chanted prayers of a blackrobed priest—his pious petitions for the mariners laboring on the seas occasionally inter-rupted by songs and shouts emanating from nearby taverns.

12   The waterfront itself was crowded with mer-chants, beggars, sailors, and itinerant laborers look-ing for odd jobs. Ships at the quayside loaded and discharged such cargoes as fish, salt, oil, grain, wine, and hides. Windlasses cracked and groaned as gangs of chanteysinging sailors, clad only in wide-bottomed underdrawers, strained at the capstan bars.

13   Some of the vessels anchored in the harbor or tied alongside the wharves might have hailed from such far-off places as Denmark and Egypt. Most were lateen-rigged caravels built in western Andalusia—familiar sights along the shores of Spain, Portugal, and throughout the Mediterranean.

14   A large three-masted deep-sea ship loading horses through a side-port opening also might be seen on the waterfront, tied up alongside tiny coastal trading vessels manned by crews of two men each, or near a fishing boat newly arrived from Iceland and deeply laden with a cargo of dried codfish. Here also might be a ship-of-war, with banners fluttering from her fore and aft castles, taking aboard chests of arms and casks of salt-meat and wine.

15   Columbus's flagship *Santa María* was a Gallician-built nao—a round-bellied, three-masted, square-rigged former merchantman of the type commonly seen in the Mediterranean. Heavy and unwieldy, she measured about 85 feet long, had a beam of 30 feet, and displaced more than one hundred tons. Colum-bus called her "a dull sailor, and unfit for discovery." During the voyage of discovery the *Santa María* shipped a crew of 40 men and boys.

16 The *Niña* and *Pinta* both were caravels, small, lightly-built, broad-bowed vessels that had begun life as lateen-rigged ships with no square sails—a typical Mediterranean rig. Both ultimately were re-rigged as caravela redondas, with square sails on the fore and mainmasts, and lateen sails on their mizzens. The *Niña* had a fourth mast aft of the mizzen, called a bonaventura mast, upon which was shipped a smaller lateen sail; it is possible that the *Pinta* did also. The *Niña* was about 67 feet long, with a beam of 21 feet; tradition tells us that the *Pinta* was somewhat larger. The *Niña* carried a crew of 24 men and boys, and the *Pinta* shipped 26 crewmen.

17 A typical merchant ship of the era was described as a "grim and dark city, full of bad odors, filth, and uncomfortable living conditions." At sea the vessel's masts and hull creaked and groaned continually as, with her short keel and round bilges, she pitched and rolled heavily even in a moderate sea. Built with timber from the high Pyrenees, Columbus's ships were fastened with wooden pegs and handwrought iron spikes, and they leaked like weathered wash tubs.

18 The captain of a Spanish ship of the fifteenth century was commander of the vessel and crew, but not necessarily a seaman. He might be a military officer of the crown, a member of a noble family, or, like Columbus, the holder of a Royal Commission that in Columbus's case declared him "Captain General" of the fleet as well as captain of the *Santa María.*

19 Second to the captain in line of command stood the master—the man who actually supervised the operation of the ship. He was an experienced seaman in overall charge of each day's sailing, getting the vessel underway, stowing cargo, and anchoring. Sometimes the master also was the ship's captain; occasionally he was its owner as well.

20 Below the master was the first mate or pilot (*piloto* in Spanish), the navigation officer responsible to the master for the operation of the ship and the work of the seamen. He was, ideally, an experienced ship handler, wise in the ways of the weather, the tides, and the sea. The pilot brought aboard with him such navigational materials as charts, compass, sandglasses, astrolabe or quadrant, and sounding leads. Both master and pilot received a rate of pay about twice that of the sailors.

21 The *Santa María*, as flagship of Columbus's expedition, carried several additional officials to fulfill special assignments. There was an interpreter to converse with the Asians the explorer expected to meet; a secretary of the fleet to record the discovery of new lands that might be found and claimed; and two royal agents to note expenses and take charge of the Crown's portion of any treasure recovered. There were also a comptroller of the fleet and a silversmith.

22 Also serving aboard the *Santa María* was the *alguazil de la armada*, or marshal of the fleet. Each of the two other vessels had a marshal of the ship. These men were responsible for maintaining discipline and administering punishment as required.

23 A surgeon aboard each vessel served the medical needs of the crew, and a steward was responsible for the food stores, firewood, water, and wine. The steward saw to trimming and maintaining lamps and tending the fires over which hot meals were prepared.

24 Equal in rank with the steward was the boatswain, who led the seamen in their daily tasks and who reported to the mate. The boatswain carried out the orders of the master and mate in the stowing of cargo; he continually inspected masts, spars, rigging, and sails for wear and repair; and he had charge of all the ship's cable and lines. He also was responsible for keeping the deck clean and shipshape; for maintaining the good condition of the ship's boat; and for making sure that the galley fire was put out each night.

25 Next below the steward and boatswain were the ship's petty officers, or *oficiales*—sailors who practiced special trades such as carpentry, caulking, or cooperage. The caulker, responsible for keeping the deck and hull watertight, had a store of rope yarn, oakum, tallow, oil, pitch, scupper nails, and lead sheets for stopping leaks. He also was in charge of the ship's pumps. The cooper had the important job of making up, caulking, and repairing the ship's casks and barrels, buckets, tubs, hogsheads, and other such wooden containers—all vital for the storage of water, wine, and oil.

26 Next in this shipboard hierarchy were the experienced seamen or *marineros*, and finally, at the bottom, the apprentices and boys or *grumetes*. There were 26 watch-standing sailors aboard the *Santa María*, 14 aboard the *Niña*, and 15 aboard the *Pinta*.

27 Columbus was captain of the *Santa María* as well as admiral of the fleet. The ship's owner, Juan de la Cosa, sailed as master, with Peralonso Nino as his mate. Juan Sanchez was surgeon, and Pedro de Terreros was Columbus's personal steward. Diego de Arana was marshal of the fleet, and Rodrigo de Escobedo was secretary or *escrivano* of the armada. Luis de Torres, a converted Jew, was the official interpreter. He spoke Hebrew, Aramaic, and some Arabic.

28 Thirty-year-old Vicente Yanez Pinzon was captain of the *Niña*, and Juan Nino was master. Sancho Ruiz de Gama served as pilot; Bartolome Garcia was the boatswain; and Alonso de Moguer was surgeon.

29 Martin Alonzo Pinzon—brother of Vicente—was captain of the *Pinta*, and his other brother Francisco Martin Pinzon sailed as master. Cristobal Garcia Sarmiento was pilot, and Juan Quintero was boatswain. Garcia Fernandez was steward, and a man named Diego was surgeon.

30   Most of the ordinary seamen and apprentices whose names appeared on the rosters of Columbus's ships were listed only by their first name and place of origin. Among those assigned to the *Santa María,* for example, was a boy known to us only as Juan, who was listed as a servant. Juan could have been a ship's boy, an apprentice seaman, or the personal servant of one of the officials aboard the ship. Probably coming from a village in Andalusia, he may have been recommended by a brother or cousin among the members of the crew. His parents could have been peasants who worked the stony coastal land, or possibly fisherfolk. In any case, the social standing of Juan's family would have been very near the bottom of medieval society.

31   The average seafarer of Columbus's time was illiterate, as were the great majority of people ashore. His life expectancy was short due to his exposure to the perils of the sea, warfare, and waterfront life. Accustomed to coping with primitive conditions, he was tough and cynical, with not much respect for the law but a realistic fear of the strong arm of authority.

32   Sailors are mentioned briefly here and there in the reminiscences of travelers of the medieval world—ship's passengers, pilgrims, merchants, and clerics. They also appear in some of the works of authors and playwrights of the day In his *Canterbury Tales,* fourteenth-century writer Geoffrey Chaucer described a "shipman" who was traveling to the shrine to make a votive offering, perhaps in obedience to a vow made in time of peril on the sea. The sailor's rough and homely attire, his awkwardness on horseback, his weather-beaten complexion, and his seafaring speech made him a subject of jest to his fellow pilgrims. He nevertheless was a jovial and welcome companion for the travelers and "certainly he was a good felawe."

33   Medieval seamen also appeared in a morality play given by the Guild of Shipwrights for the pageant of Corpus Christi in London in the year 1415. Portrayed as being distinctly different from shore folk, the sailors were distinguished by the "quaint expressions of their profession," their rough and boisterous humor, and their contempt for the soft and sheltered life of their shore-side cousins.

34   Superstitious, as so many seafarers through the ages have been, the typical sailor of Columbus's time deeply believed in omens and portents of doom. He accepted the existence of gigantic sea monsters that lived far out in the depths of the unknown ocean. He looked with a child's eyes upon odd things seen in far places and had a great faith in the miraculous. Anything that frightened him or seemed unexplainable, he believed to be of supernatural origin. If a strange bird alighted upon his ship, he took it as an unfavorable omen; and he feared the presence on board of a priest or woman as a sure way to raise up the devil. One medieval ocean traveler recalled that "during the night hours when the wind was high, the sailors would think they could hear sirens singing, wailing and jeering, like insolent men in their cups."

35   Columbus's sailors were as superstitious as any. They had been skeptical and uneasy about this voyage of exploration to the far Indies. There were old-timers among them who had sailed down the African coast to Guinea and out into the Western ocean to the Canary Islands and the Azores. They knew that the Portuguese had sailed far reaches of the Atlantic in quest of the mythical islands of Brazil, Antilla of the Seven Cities, and the fabled isles of St. Brendan, but without success.

36   The same circumstances that made the sailor prone to superstition tended to make him more religious than his kinfolk ashore. His religious convictions conformed to a deeply devout though violent and authoritarian period. The cruelty and amorality of his time did not shake his belief in the existence of an avenging deity or in the strict authority of the Holy Church.

37   Although lacking in formal education, the able-bodied sailor of the fifteenth century was proficient at the peculiar skills of his trade through years of apprenticeship. He had to be able to steer at the tiller, splice line, caulk seams, make and mend sails, take accurate soundings, and be adept at small-boat handling. He was required, among his other duties, to work at loading and discharging the ship's cargo and to make and take in sail in all weather. He had to be familiar with the process of weighing and letting go the anchors and of securing them when brought aboard. He also had to be fairly skilled at rough carpentry and to be practiced in the use of weapons and in gunnery, for he would be called upon to defend his ship in time of need. Hardy and strong, he was as agile as a monkey; when going aloft he often climbed hand-over-hand up the lines of the standing rigging.

38   The sailors of Columbus proved as talented as any in the skills of the marinero. Before the expedition departed from the Canary Islands on its outbound voyage, Columbus decided to convert the *Niña* from a lateen to a square rig. With no shipyards or skilled artisans available, Captain Pinzon chose a gang from among the ship's own crew to do the job, which included cutting and sewing new sails for the fore and main yards. The work began on August 26, and the *Niña* was ready to sail just three days later. It is a tribute to Columbus's sailors that the only complaint voiced by the admiral about poor workmanship concerned the shipwrights of Palos, whose faulty caulking caused the *Niña* and *Pinta* to leak badly.

39   The clothing of Columbus's sailors was simple and their possessions few. Typical garb consisted of wide-bottomed knee-length breeches; a loose-fitting

hooded blouse of coarse linen or old sail cloth; and, perhaps, a sleeveless vest-like overgarment slit at the sides and tied with laces. Although the sailor sometimes wore stockings and shoes, in milder climes he usually went barefoot. Most seamen wore red woolen stocking caps of the type made in Toledo. Columbus gave several of these caps as gifts to the natives he encountered in the New World.

40 The Spanish seaman's foul-weather garment has been described as a brown cloth robe or overcoat called papahigo or "storm sail" in sailors' slang, that resembled the habit of the Franciscan friars. This, the sea gown worn by mariners all over western Europe, was the distinctive garment that identified them as seafarers. Chaucer's shipman of the Canterbury Tales, for example, wore "a gown of falding (a coarse cloth) to the knee." This, plus the pilgrim's habit of wearing his sailors' knife hung from a thong slung over his shoulder, marked him as a seaman in the eyes of his fellow travelers.

41 The sailor tightened his sea gown at the waist with a belt or perhaps a bit of ships' hempen line; when working on deck he often knotted the front or tucked it through his waist belt to keep it out of the way.

42 Ships' officers wore cloaks, jackets, or doublets of cloth or dressed leather that laced down the front; hose and a variety of styles of hats or caps, all in brighter colors than the rough simple clothing of the sailors. At his belt, the ship's officer wore a dagger rather than a sailor's sheath knife. At sea the officers sometimes reverted, in part at least, to more common sailors' garb. Columbus is reported habitually to have worn a brown sea gown, which was mistaken by some observers as being the hooded brown habit of a Franciscan monk. It is interesting that a man so vain of his rank and titles would choose to wear a garment so rough and uncouth in medieval eyes.

43 Sleeping and sanitary accommodations aboard Columbus's ships were primitive. The captain and sailing master probably had small cabins, each barely large enough to contain a narrow wooden bunk. other officers slept on mattresses under the quarter-deck, forward of the helmsman. When not in use, the mattresses were rolled up in grass sacks and lashed along the bulwarks.

44 The ordinary sailors generally had to sleep in the open on the cambered deck, where hatch covers offered the only flat surfaces and coils of line served as pillows—or if more fortunate, to huddle under the shelter of the forecastle. on many vessels of that time the sailors were forbidden to sleep in the protection of the ship's hold, even during stormy weather, as it would take too long to roust them out in an emergency. In the *Santa María,* with her large crew, this rule may not have been enforced.

45 To relieve a call of nature the sailor had to swing up over the bulwarks and hang in the rigging over the ship's lee side, "making reverence to the sun," as the saying was, and hope that he would not be swept away by a visiting wave. The lower rigging had to be washed down each day as a consequence of this necessity.

46 When the ship was becalmed, the men might bathe themselves on deck, scooping up sea water in buckets; the more adventurous might, in calm weather, even go over the side if there were no sharks about. Most sailors wore whiskers or a full beard, because the average man of that day shaved only once a week if he shaved at all.

47 The staples of the Spanish sailor's diet were hard biscuit; bacon; salt meat and fish; chick peas and beans; garlic and olive oil; rice and raisins. No cook was carried to prepare the sailors' meals; this duty probably fell to one of the ships' boys. The officers ate aft, their food prepared by the captain's servant.

48 Hot meals, when they were available, always were soups or stews prepared with salt meat or fish, broken ship's biscuit, rice, and whatever spices were available, with rare additions of onions or potatoes. one such stew, called lobscouse, was eaten by seafaring men until the end of the age of sail. On Fridays, if the weather held, the sailors' hot meal was bean soup seasoned with garlic and peppers.

49 Columbus described his idea of the stores to be carried on a voyage of discovery thus: good biscuit seasoned and not old, flour salted at the time of milling, wine, salt meat, oil, vinegar, cheese, chick peas, lentils, beans, salt fish, honey, rice, almonds, and raisins. The salted flour could be mixed with water or wine, made into cakes of unleavened bread, and baked in the ashes at the bottom of the open iron firebox in which the hot meals were prepared. This primitive stove, called a fogon, was brought up from below in fair weather and set on deck near the lee rail. The fire was kindled upon a bed of earth or sand that covered the bottom of the firebox. Supplies of firewood were stowed in every available corner of the ship.

50 When conditions permitted, a hot meal was prepared before noon so that the watch below could eat before turning to and the watch on deck could dine after being relieved. Gathering around the smoking firebox, the hungry sailors extended their bowls for stew or soup and then found a place on the crowded, cluttered deck or on the hatch. Sprawling or kneeling or sitting as conditions allowed, and with a knife their only utensil, they ate "from their lap" in the fashion of the poor folk in the Middle Ages. As one observer noted, they "pull out their knives of different shapes made to kill hogs or skin lambs or for cutting bags, and then grab in their hands the poor bones and peel them clean of their sinews and meat as if all their lives they had practiced anatomy in Guadelupe or Valencia. In a prayer, they leave them clean as ivory."

51   It did not take many days at sea for the food supplies to become wormy and rancid in the damp shipboard environment. And the casks of fresh water soon became foul and stinking—though when laced with wine the brackish liquid became at least barely palatable. Sometimes sailors carried their ration below decks to eat in the dark—to avoid seeing the maggots that infested it.

52   To supplement their diets, the sailors caught fish as often as possible. On Columbus's outward voyage, when supplies were still relatively plentiful and fresh, such catches were a luxury. During the return, however, they became a dire necessity. The admiral recorded in his Diario on January 25—more than three weeks before reaching the Azores—that the crew of the *Niña* had "killed a porpoise and a tremendous shark . . . [they] had quite some need of it because they were carrying nothing to eat except bread and wine and yams from the Indies."

53   Mariners marked the passage of time at sea with the turning of a sandglass, which was done by an apprentice seaman. As the sand ran out at the end of each half-hour, the helmsman rang a bell to remind the apprentice to turn the glass. This was the origin of the ship's-bell time used to this day.

54   With each turning of the glass during the night watch, the grumete called out to the lookout in the masthead "Ah! de proa! Alerta, buena guardia!" to which the lookout called back "Buena guardia!' to prove he was awake—a procedure still followed aboard some merchant ships in recent times.

55   Ceremony and formality accompanied the passage of each watch at sea. Just before sundown and before the first night watch, the crew was called to evening prayers. An apprentice carried the binnacle lamp aft along the deck, singing "Amen and God give us a good night and a good sailing. May the ship make a good passage, captain and master and good company." Then the apprentices led the sailors in prayer, chanting the Pater Noster, the Ave Maria, and the Credo, after which all hands sang the Salve Regina. For the sailors these chanted rituals of the church were comforting and expected, their only link to their distant homeland.

56   The night watches also had their moments of formal spoken reverence, as described by Felix Fabri, a traveler of 1480: "When the wind is quite fair and not too strong all is still save only he who watches the compass and he who holds the handle on the tiller, for these, by way of returning thanks for a voyage and good luck, continually greet the breeze, praise God, the Blessed Virgin and the Saints, on answering the other, and they are never silent so long as the wind is fair. Anyone on board who hears this chant of theirs would fall asleep."

57   At daybreak the youngest boy of the watch sang or chanted a prayer that invoked a blessing of the True Cross, the Holy Trinity, and the true God, keeper of the immortal soul, concluding:

Blessed be the light of day
And he who sends the night away.

Then the boy recited the Pater Noster and the Ave Maria and added a plea to God for a good voyage and the hope that he would grant good days to the officers of the after guard and to the sailors forward.

58   The sailors and apprentices were divided into two watches, each group alternating at watch-standing duties of four hours each. If he was not already on watch, the sailor's day began at seven in the morning when the deck boy sang out "Al quarto!" (on deck) and the men of the morning watch crawled out from whatever sheltering spot they had found to sleep away their few hours of rest. No one needed time to dress, for all hands slept in their clothes. one sailor went aft to relieve the helmsman, who steered from his position under the quarterdeck in an enclosed, gloomy little space cut off from the rest of the ship. He handled the heavy tiller below decks, without any view of the sea or the sails; his orders were shouted down to him through a small hatch by the mate standing on the quarterdeck above. Before him, secured to the mizzenmast, was the binnacle, a box containing the compass and its lantern.

59   In maintaining his assigned compass course the helmsman was aided by the feel of the ship under his feet and the orders of the mate from above. Steering was a rough job. When a heavy sea slammed against the rudder, the swinging tiller might knock the helmsman off his feet. To minimize this, a relieving tackle, which could be adjusted to allow for the set of the sea, was rigged to the tiller. Not every sailor was a skilled helmsman. Columbus noted in his journal that his sailors sometimes steered badly, carelessly allowing the *Santa María* to run as much as several points off the ordered course.

60   The first duty of the men of the morning watch was to man the wooden pumps that stood just forward of midships on the main deck, to remove the water that had accumulated in the bilges during the night. The bilge water came up "foaming like hell and stinking like the devil." Seamen believed, however, that if the bilges stank they would enjoy a lucky voyage; the stale water sloshing about in the bottom of the hold ensured that the beams and planks would remain swollen tight and that the crew would not be laboring forever at the pumps.

61   The men then scrubbed the deck with buckets of sea water and stiff-bristled brooms. In hot, dry climates this scrubbing and sloshing of water over the decks was repeated several times a day to keep the planking from drying out and shrinking in the hot sun. With their buckets, the men then washed down the lower rigging, deadeyes, and main shrouds

where they had been soiled by men relieving themselves over the side during the night.

62 Those on the morning watch were responsible for taking up the slack in the running gear so that all the lines were taut. The sailors also regularly tarred all of the standing rigging, stays, and shrouds. The deck boys were put to making up spun yarn and chafing gear out of old lines and making oakum from old rope yarns for the caulker's use.

63 When sail was to be taken in, the main yard was quickly lowered to the deck and the sailors gathered the canvas and secured it to the yard with lashings, after which all hands manned the topping lifts and hauled the yard and its furled sail back up to the masthead. In good weather there was no need to raise and lower the heavy yard because sailors could climb the rigging and straddle the yard while gathering up the sail.

64 When rain was expected and the wind permitted, the sailors manned the mainsail clew lines and raised a corner of the sail to form a belly in the canvas with which to catch some of the precious rainwater, which then would be drained into buckets and casks.

65 During a storm at sea, life was a nightmarish struggle, with the sailors fighting to take in sails and all hands laboring constantly at the crude hand pumps or (when as often happened, the pumps broke down) forming bucket brigades to bail the ship out by hand. Steering with the heavy wooden tiller in bad weather was a brutal wrestling match that left the helmsman exhausted and covered with bumps and bruises.

66 In storm and howling winds many among the crew were both sick and terrified, and the sailors were not reluctant to pray to God and call upon the saints for mercy. During Columbus's homeward voyage, when the *Niña* fought to survive a February storm off the Azores, the admiral himself "ordered that lots should be drawn for a pilgrimage to Santa Maria de Guadalupe and to take a five-pound wax candle [and] for another pilgrim to go to spend a night at vigil in Santa Clara de Moguer and to have a Mass said. . . . After this the admiral and all the men made a vow that, as soon as they reached the first land, all would go in their shirtsleeves in procession to pray in a church dedicated to Our Lady".

67 During such miserable times there were no hot meals and little sleep. At the end of his watch the sailor, soaked to the skin, rolled himself in his rough gown and napped, perhaps curled up in a sodden coil of mooring line among the rats and roaches under the forecastle, until the boatswain's whistle rousted him out for another emergency. After the storm passed, the mariners often discovered to their further dismay that the sea stores had suffered storm damage or that wine or water casks had been stove in, requiring that both food and drink thereafter be severely rationed.

68 During most of his time at sea, the sailor had precious little leisure time that was not spent in trying to sleep or tending to necessary personal chores. When in port or at anchor, however, or in gentler hemispheres where emergencies were infrequent, the seamen found time for entertainment. Storytelling was a universal pastime among mariners and included tall tales of adventures past and hardships endured, of feats of gluttony and drinking bouts ashore, and of romances in different ports. The board game of checkers (*damas* in Spanish) was widely played, and men off watch squandered many a hard-earned coin gambling with dice under the forecastle head.

69 Singing was another popular recreation for sailors far from home. We are told that after sighting the islands of the New World, the crew of the *Pinta* sang and danced around the mainmast to the accompaniment of pipes and a tambourine. Shipmates also passed their free hours at sea fishing with hand line and harpoon; gathering flying fish that landed on deck; and spotting and identifying types of birds that approached the ships.

70 Yet another leisure-hour activity was described by a seafaring pilgrim in 1401: "Among all the occupations of seafarers there is one which, though loathsome, is yet very common, daily and necessary. I mean the hunting and catching of lice and vermin. Unless a man spends several hours in this work when he is on pilgrimage, he will have but unquiet slumbers."

71 Although there always have been men who loved the sea in spite of all of its hardships and dangers, there was one feature of the fifteenth-century sailor's calling that probably attracted him more than anything else—the lure of money. The peasant farmer seldom saw hard cash in his life. What his family could not grow, weave, or craft itself must be obtained through barter. To a youth growing up in such a world the idea of regular wages was most attractive. The sailor was paid in cash for his time and labor.

72 A sailor's monthly wage of 800 maravedis—enough to buy two fat pigs—was about the same as that earned by the manservant to a nobleman. A ship's master earned more than double that amount—the price of a cow. For those who sailed with Columbus, the enterprise held both the distant promise of a fortune to be discovered in the Indies and also a stipulated monthly salary to be earned in hard money paid from the Royal treasury.

73 Despite all they had experienced and endured, the crews of the *Niña* and *Pinta* who returned to Palos in March 1493 were in remarkably good shape. None had been lost due to disease or accidents at sea. (***) Before setting out in August 1492 they had received four months' pay in advance. Now, as they prepared to drop anchor, the seamen could look forward to collecting the balance owed them and to telling all who would listen of the strange sights they had seen. Although history would focus its gaze on

the man who commanded the expedition, the seamen whose labors brought the two surviving ships back to their home port could bask, at least for a time, in his reflected glory.

74   (*) On Christmas Eve 1492, as the flagship sailed along the coast of Hispaniola, Columbus, who had been on deck for several days, went below for a few hours of sleep. The night being fine and the sea calm, the officer of the watch also went below, and the watch on deck settled down to sleep—with the helmsman (disobeying the admiral's standing orders) leaving the tiller in the hands of one of the ship's boys. During the night, with the youth at the helm, the *Santa María* went aground on a coral bank, wedging in so firmly that all efforts to kedge her off proved fruitless. Her seams eventually opened and she had to be abandoned.

75   (**) The two ships and their crews were unexpectedly reunited on March 15, when both entered the harbor of Palos on the same tide.

76   (***) Sadly, more than a third of Columbus's sailors did not survive to enjoy their hard-won rewards. When the *Santa María* ran aground and was wrecked off Hispaniola, the admiral, having insufficient room aboard the remaining ships for all of his crewmen, built a fort—named La Villa de Navidad in honor of the Christmas feast day—and left thirty-nine men behind. When his second expedition returned to Villa de Navidad in November 1493, Columbus found the fort in ashes and the men dead at the hands of local Taino tribesmen—the Navidad garrison having allowed greed and lust to destroy the good relations that Columbus had established with the natives.

6

THE GREAT DISEASE MIGRATION

BY GEOFFREY COWLEY & MARY TALBOT

*It wasn't swords or guns that devastated the Native Americans.
It was germs the Europeans carried.*

Disease is everywhere: HIV, SARS, Ebola, and countless other flu's bacteria, viruses and contagions. We have been conditioned to isolate, inoculate, and most of all fear those who have these diseases. Most Americans know of the historical component involved: that smallpox has been wiped off the face of the earth (at least for now); that plague killed millions in the middle ages; that diseases our children are routinely inoculated against in this country are big killers in poor, underserved countries around the world; and that disease enabled Europeans to take the western hemisphere from its native inhabitants.

Recently, Bill Gates, the founder and C.E.O. of Microsoft, Corporation, committed $22 billion of his own rather sizeable fortune to fight diseases like HIV and malaria around the world. He challenged governments to ante up and kick in, to do their part in dealing with these world-wide problems. To date, only one nation, Uganda, in central Africa, has answered the challenge. Besides the obvious generosity and commitment of Gates, the world-wide lack of resolve illustrates one exceedingly glaring fact: too often, we do not want to deal with problems faced by others. But it would seem obvious, would it not, that if governments do not deal with these problems now, they most certainly will be dealing with them later.

Five hundred years ago, the Aztec government in Tenochtitlan was incapable of dealing with the problem of smallpox, measles and other diseases decimating its population, since they had no idea what was happening. Likewise, their Spanish enemies, witnessing the piles of corpses around them, could not possibly have fathomed what had transpired. But without a doubt, within a few decades of the arrival of the Spanish, most of the roughly 30 million people in Mexico before the Spanish arrival were dead.

- *Why were people in the "Old World" immune from the diseases that were killing Native Americans?*
- *What enabled Pizarro to conquer the Incas so easily?*
- *What effect did the epidemics have upon marriage customs, local cultures, and the slave trade?*
- *Who started syphilis?*
- *What can we learn from this chapter in history?*

1   Only weeks before the great conquistador Hernan Cortes seized control of Tenochtitlan (Mexico City) in 1521, his forces were on the verge of defeat. The Aztecs had repeatedly repelled the invaders and were preparing a final offensive. But the attack never came, and the beleaguered Spaniards got an unlikely chance to regroup. On Aug. 21 they stormed the city, only to find that some greater force had already pillaged it. "I solemnly swear that all the houses and stockades in the lake were full of heads and corpses," Cortes's chronicler Bernal Diaz wrote of the scene. "It was the same in the streets and courts. . . . We could not walk without treading on the bodies and heads of dead Indians. I have read about the destruction of Jerusalem, but I do not think the mortality was greater there than here in Mexico. . . . Indeed, the stench was so bad that no one could endure it . . . and even Cortes was ill from the odors which assailed his nostrils."

2   The same scent followed the Spaniards throughout the Americas. Many experts now believe that the New World was home to 40 million to 50 million people before Columbus arrived and that most of them died within decades. In Mexico alone, the native population fell from roughly 30 million in 1519 to three million in 1568. There was similar devastation throughout the Caribbean islands, Central America and Peru. The eminent Yale historian David Brion Davis says this was "the greatest genocide in the history of man." Yet it's increasingly clear that most of the carnage had nothing to do with European barbarism. The worst of the suffering was caused not by swords or guns but by germs.

3   Contrary to popular belief, viruses, bacteria and other invisible parasites aren't designed to cause harm; they fare best in the struggle to survive and reproduce when they don't destroy their hosts. But when a new germ invades a previously unexposed population, it often causes devastating epidemics, killing all but the most resistant individuals. Gradually, as natural selection weeds out the most susceptible hosts and the deadliest strains of the parasite, a sort of mutual tolerance emerges. The survivors repopulate, and a killer plague becomes a routine childhood illness. As University of Chicago historian William McNeill observes in his book *Plagues and Peoples*, "The more diseased a community, the less destructive its epidemics become."

4   By the time Columbus set sail, the people of the Old World held the distinction of being thoroughly diseased. By domesticating pigs, horses, sheep and cattle, they had infected themselves with a wide array of pathogens. And through centuries of war, exploration and city-building, they had kept those agents in constant circulation. Virtually any European who crossed the Atlantic during the 16th century had battled such illnesses as smallpox and measles during childhood and emerged fully immune.

5   By contrast, the people of the Americas had spent thousands of years in biological isolation. Their own distant ancestors had migrated from the Old World, crossing the Bering Strait from Siberia into Alaska. But they traveled in bands of several hundred at most. The microbes that cause measles, smallpox and other "crowd type" diseases require pools of several million people to sustain themselves. By the time Columbus arrived, groups like the Aztecs and Maya of Central America and Peru's Incas had built cities large enough to sustain major epidemics. Archeological evidence suggests they suffered from syphilis, tuberculosis, a few intestinal parasites and some types of influenza (probably those carried by waterfowl). Yet they remained untouched by diseases that had raged for centuries in the Old World. When the newcomers arrived carrying mumps, measles, whooping cough, smallpox, cholera, gonorrhea and yellow fever, the Indians were immunologically defenseless.

6   The disaster began almost as soon as Columbus arrived, fueled mainly by smallpox and measles. Smallpox—the disease that so ravaged Tenochtitlan on the eve of Cortes's final siege—was a particularly efficient killer. Alfred Crosby, author of *The Columbian Exchange*, likens its effect on American history to "that of the Black Death on the history of the Old World." Smallpox made its American debut in 1519, when it struck the Caribbean island of Santo Domingo, killing up to half of the indigenous population. From there outbreaks spread across the Antilles islands, onto the Mexican mainland, through the Isthmus of Panama and into South America. The Spaniards were moving in the same direction, but their diseases often outpaced them. "Such is the communicability of smallpox and the other eruptive fevers," Crosby notes, "that any Indian who received news of the Spaniards could also have easily received the infection."

7   By the time the conquistadors reached Peru in the 1520s, smallpox was already decimating the local Incan civilization and undermining its political structure. The empire's beloved ruler, Huayna Capaj, had died. So had most of his family, including the son he had designated as his heir. The ensuing succession struggle had split the empire into two factions that were easily conquered by Francisco Pizarro and his troops. "Had the land not been divided," one Spanish soldier recalled, "we would not have been able to enter or win."

8   Smallpox was just one of many afflictions parading through defenseless communities, leaving people too weak and demoralized to harvest food or tend their young. Some native populations died out altogether; others continued to wither for 100 to 150 years after surviving particularly harsh epidemics. The experience wrought irrevocable changes in the way people lived.

9   Persuaded that their ancestral gods had abandoned them, some Indians became more susceptible to the Christianity of their conquerors. Others united to form intertribal healing societies and Pan-Indian sects. Marriage patterns changed, too. In North America most pre-Columbian Indians lived in communities of several hundred relatives. Tradition required that they marry outside their own clans and observe other restrictions. As populations died off and appropriate marriage partners became scarce, such customs became unsustainable. People had two choices, says University of Washington anthropologist Tsianina Lomawaima. They could "break the rules or become extinct." Occasionally, whole new tribes arose as the survivors of dying groups banded together. The epidemics even fueled the African slave trade. "The fact that Africans shared immunities with Europeans meant that they made better slaves," says anthropologist Charles Merbs of Arizona State University. "That, in part, determined their fate."

10   The great germ migration was largely a one-way affair; syphilis is the only disease suspected of traveling from the Americas to the Old World aboard Spanish ships (see box). But that does not diminish the epochal consequences of the exchange. Columbus's voyage forever changed the world's epidemiological landscape. "Biologically," says Crosby, "this was the most spectacular thing that has ever happened to humans."

11   That isn't to say it was unique. Changes in human activity are still creating rich new opportunities for disease-causing organisms. The story of AIDS—an affliction that has emerged on a large scale only during the past decade and that now threatens the stability and survival of entire nations—is a case in point. No one knows exactly where or how the AIDS virus (HIV) was born. Many experts suspect it originated in central Africa, decades or even centuries ago, when a related virus crossed from monkeys into people and adapted itself to human cells.

12   Like venereal syphilis, AIDS presumably haunted isolated communities for hundreds of years before going global. And just as sailing ships brought syphilis out of isolation during the 16th century, jet planes and worldwide social changes have unleashed AIDS in the 20th. War, commercial trucking and the growth of cities helped propel HIV through equatorial Africa during the 1960s. And when the virus reached the developed world during the 1970s, everything from changing sexual mores to the rise of new medical technologies (such as blood transfusion) helped it take root and thrive.

13   AIDS won't be the last pandemic to afflict humankind. As the Columbian Exchange makes clear, social changes that spawn one epidemic tend to spawn others as well. Researchers have documented outbreaks of more than a dozen previously unknown diseases since the 1960s. Like smallpox or syphilis or AIDS, most seem to result from old bugs exploiting new opportunities. "What's happening today is just what we've been doing for thousands of years," Crosby says. "Bit by bit by bit, we're getting more homogenized. In the Middle Ages the population got big enough to send out a boat and bring back the Black Death. Columbus brought together two worlds that were a huge distance apart. People were living side by side, then elbow to elbow. Soon we'll be living cheek to jowl. Everybody's diseases will be everybody else's diseases."

Who Started Syphilis?

Experts have long suspected Columbus and his sailors of infecting the Old World with syphilis. It's a reasonable suspicion. The **disease**, unknown east of the Atlantic until 1493 suddenly raced through Europe and Asia in the decades following Columbus's crossing. Yet skeptics dismiss the seeming connection as a coincidence. Treponemas, the bacteria responsible for syphilis also cause three milder, nonvenereal **diseases** (yaws, pinta and bejel). Since those conditions were already common in the Old World, the skeptics reason, venereal syphilis must have been present, too, just unrecognized. Today many experts favor a third explanation midway between the other two. According to this theory, 15th century Europe was no stranger to the syphilis bacterium (Treponema pallidum), but local strains had never mastered the art of venereal transmission. What Columbus brought home was an American strain of T. pallidum that made syphilis a sexually transmitted **disease**.

7

MISSION SAN FRANCISCO DE LA ESPADA OF SAN ANTONIO

BY REX LEWIS FIELD

"Founded in 1690 as San Francisco de los Tejas near present-day Weches, this was the first mission in Texas. In 1731, the mission was transferred to the San Antonio River area and renamed Mission San Francisco de la Espada. A friary was built at Espada in 1745. The church was completed in 1756."—National Historical Park's description (courtesy of the National Park Service)

This is what the visitor reads when first entering the Mission San Francisco de la Espada in San Antonio. However, there is definitely more to Mission Espada than what meets the eye. The following selection (published here for the first time) was written by Rex Lewis Field, co-editor of Flyover History: Remembering Our Ignored Past. *Every semester he tours Mission Espada with dozens of Palo Alto College students and presents them with an enlightening discussion similar to the one you are about to read.*

- *What role did Mission San Francisco de la Espada of San Antonio play in Spain's colonial empire?*
- *How did Native Americans react to the arrival of Europeans in their midst?*
- *How has Mission Espada changed over the centuries?*
- *Who were the "Mestizaje"?*

1　The "camposanto," or cemetery, at Mission San Francisco de la Espada bears no markers and has no clear boundaries. Extending out from the east wall of the mission church, the grassy plot is identified by a sign placed there by the National Park Service, the modern-day trustees of the San Antonio Missions. Yet, shorn of its long-decayed wooden crosses and picked clean of weeds by the current resident friars, the sanctity and history of the spot strikes the senses in ways that can only be explained by what makes us and the people interred there human. Many who rest under the tourist-pressed grass were born centuries ago into the native world of shamans and many gods, but buried under the symbolic cross of alien invaders. A strange ambivalence must have inhabited those souls, as it still does among those who wander the site today. Beyond the grounds of the mission, barely yards away from this spot, the descendants of mission deceased go about their day tending homes, yards and fields in full view of their ancestor's ghosts.

2　Mission Espada is part of a series of National Park Service sites in San Antonio, Texas, one of four small missions that represent a huge place in Texas history. Though "rating" the missions is obviously a subjective exercise, the Espada mission is undoubtedly one of the most authentic, rustic, and true-to-life examples of an outpost of Spanish Colonial efforts. Founded in 1731 at its present site, it was neither the first nor last of the missions created in

37

Spain's vast empire, but it defines the concept and exemplifies the origins of Spain's incursion northward into Texas. Success or failure of the scheme can be debated, but millions of people in Texas speak Spanish, worship in Catholic churches, while continuing to expand a unique gene pool of both Indian and European origins that historians refer to as "Mestizaje," a process that began when the first Spaniards entered the native world in 1492.

3   The cultural identifiers at all San Antonio missions are mixed, even confused. Entry into Espada involves walking under an arch held aloft by stone and saltillo tiles, elements bequeathed from ancient Roman engineers. In colonial times, Espada was a major producer of fired tiles and boasted true "hornos," or kilns. The walls are broken and interrupted, but were once high and protective. After the "secularization" of the mission lands, the stones were "liberated" from the derelict structures and used in other places nearby by locals. The outlines of Espada are, nonetheless, quite obvious. The thick mission walls performed dual purposes, serving as storage as well as residences for native people at the mission. Grain was kept in one large chamber, and provided the basic staples of wheat and corn, ready supplies of which had provided potential for sedentary societies in both European and Native societies for a millennia.

4   Espada is now surrounded by trees and invasive vegetation brought in the wake of Spanish settlement. The land was originally attractive to cattle ranchers because of the vast grassland stretching out in all directions from the San Antonio River. The Spaniards drove sheep, goats and cattle up from Mexico and took advantage of the grassy range, but likewise triggered significant environmental change, destroying the sod and native grasses with overgrazing, and helping to propagate woody plants and alien scrub brush and grasses. In a sense, a similar, opposite ecological process was underway in faraway Spain and Europe. Corn, tomatoes, potatoes, and melons shared by the New World were altering the landscape of the Old, while the Old World reciprocated with weeds, grackles, and aggressive, exotic diseases.

5   A workshop was located at Espada that provided both the center of crafting and repair of needed items, as well as a learning place for Natives at the mission. No cities existed close to Espada, or any other mission in "El Norte." Procurement of manufactured goods, materials, or anything commonly produced in this pre-industrial age society had to be engineered on the grounds. Though trade and commerce would eventually thread its way up and down the "Camino Real," or King's Road, the time it took to move goods by ox-cart or mule over rugged terrain was difficult to a distant outpost like San Antonio. For modern consumer-citizens, it is hard to imagine as there was no "quick" trip to the store, or anywhere else for that matter.

6   The grand plan for a large church to act as a communal place of worship at the center of Espada's grounds was nullified by the soft soil and unstable walls of the structure designated for that purpose. The Esapda chapel remained the church at the mission by default, and as such has gained a photogenic reputation as the most unique relic on the site. All members of the mission community were communicants. The Spaniards looked upon religion as part of the national identity and duty sanctioned by law. The Church provided the great avenue to spiritual peace and eventual glory. Women, the home-bound wards of men, vassals drafted to lives of work and childbearing, joined in religious life with the men. Theirs was a life of kneading, knitting, weaning, and kneeling.

7   The defense of Espada required training and trust in the inhabitants. In 1731, when Mission San Francisco de la Espada was inaugurated, Apaches who refused to assimilate in the fashion of the local Coahuiltecans represented the greatest early threat. By the mid-eighteenth century the Comanche, mounted on horses, stormed into south Texas. The most obvious remnants of those dangers are represented by gun ports in the mission walls, points at which one could fire through toward an approaching enemy. "Neophytes," new believers, were indoctrinated in both muzzle and missal. In this sense, the mission was compelled to defend itself as a far-flung outpost in Spain's grand empire and establish a secure bastion of believers.

8   The Chapel at Espada is a typical example of Spain's influence on culture, as well as its role as a conduit of other cultures. The façade of the chapel is the product of centuries of Islamic Moorish occupation of Spain, though the thrust of the upper most peak of the structure is the cross. Entry into the chapel is via a "Moorish keyhole," and the Christ figure is first viewed from under the Muslim door carvings that were originally installed by Native and Mestizo workers. Upon entry the faithful were feasted with images to inspire and pews in which to sit, hence no one would confuse this hall with a Muslim venue. Though kneeling and honoring the proper feast, good Catholics weren't bowing to Allah's East.

9   The "convento," a residence for the Father and Brothers of the order, was typical to all missions. The Franciscans lived in these cubicles and lived out their lives in single-minded pursuit of religious conversion and maintenance of the faith. The Franciscans were willing co-conspirators in alliance with the secular powers of Spain, to bring Spanish rule to Texas and subjugate the inhabitants to church and crown. Changing native people and fastening them to an absentee Royalty was a theme throughout Spanish history, and would be taken up in some

form by virtually all European colonial powers. The church might be the cocoon into which unchecked, pagan souls were squeezed for spiritual metamorphosis, but the emerging butterflies were the colors of Spain's imperial ensign.

10   Mission Espada, like the rest of the Spanish missions, was secularized by independent Mexico in 1823. The inhabitants were given "labores," or parcels of mission lands and released from the bond that tethered them to the old system. By that date the descendents of the native and settler inhabitants of the previous century had firmly anchored their lives in Hispanic culture. Ultimately, the "mestizaje" and proselytizing that had been pursued as a strategic policy to bring all under Spanish skies, resulted in development of a society that would, ironically, revolt against that paternity and struggle toward a separate future.

8

RETHINKING JAMESTOWN

BY JEFFERY L. SHELER

*America's first permanent colonists have long been considered
lazy and incompetent. But new evidence suggests that it was a
prolonged drought—not indolence—that almost did them in*

Mention the term *Revisionist* History *to a group of people and someone is bound to
express his contempt for it.* Why don't historians leave history as it is? The way I was
taught about the past was good enough for my generation. What has changed in the
past that historians feel the need to revise it?

Rethinking Jamestown *is a prime example on why history should be revised,
when new evidence is discovered about the past. Since 1994 when the Association
of the Preservation of Virginia Antiquities (APVA) launched a ten year archeological
dig to uncover Jamestown's past, the story of England's first permanent colony in
North America has changed to reflect a far, more complex history. And new evidence
leads to revised thoughts about the past. The late nineteenth century English writer
Oscar Wilde said "The one duty we owe history is to re-write it."*

- *What obstacles did the Jamestown settlers encounter? How did they attempt to
  overcome those problems?*
- *What role have archeologists played in revising the history of Jamestown? What
  have they discovered to change that history?*
- *What longheld assumptions are being reconsidered due to the APVA?*
- *Why did the relationship of the Jamestown settlers and the Native Americans
  change?*
- *What does Bill Kelso mean by saying that John Smith comes out the star in his own
  movie?*
- *Do you agree with Bill Kelso's assessment that the roots of American society began
  at Jamestown?*

---

1 To the English voyagers who waded ashore at the
mouth of the Chesapeake Bay on a balmy April day
in 1607, the lush Virginia landscape must have
seemed like a garden paradise after four and a half
months at sea. One ebullient adventurer later wrote
that he was "almost ravished" by the sight of the
freshwater streams and "faire meddowes and goodly
tall trees" they encountered when they first landed
at Cape Henry. After skirmishing with a band of
Natives and planting a cross, the men of the Virginia
Company expedition returned to their ships—the
Susan Constant, Godspeed and *Discovery*—and the 104
passengers and crew continued up the Powhatan
River (soon to be renamed the James in honor of
their King, James I) in search of a more secure site.

2 They thought they had found it on a marshy peninsula some 50 miles upstream—a spot they believed
could be defended against Indians attacking from
the mainland and that was far enough from the coast
to ensure ample warning of approaching Spanish

warships. They set about building a fortress and clearing land for the commercial outpost they had been sent to establish and which they called "James Cittie." They were eager to get down to the business of extracting gold, timber and other commodities to ship back to London.

3   But Jamestown proved to be neither paradise nor gold mine. In the heat of that first summer at the mosquito-infested settlement, 46 of the colonists died of fever, starvation or Indian arrows. By year's end, only 38 remained. Were it not for the timely arrival of British supply ships in January 1608, and again the following October, Jamestown, like Roanoke a few years before, almost certainly would have vanished.

4   It is little wonder that history has not smiled on the colonists of Jamestown. Though recognized as the first permanent English settlement in North America and the setting for the charming (if apocryphal) tale of Pocahontas and Capt. John Smith, Jamestown has been largely ignored in colonial lore in favor of Massachusetts' Plymouth Colony. And what has survived is not flattering, especially when compared with the image of industrious and devout Pilgrims seeking religious freedom in a new land. In contrast, the Jamestown settlers are largely remembered as a motley assortment of inept and indolent English gentlemen who came looking for easy money and instead found self-inflicted catastrophe. "Without a trace of foresight or enterprise," wrote historian W. E. Woodward in his 1936 *A New American History*, ". . . they wandered about, looking over the country, and dreaming of gold mines."

5   But today the banks of the James River are yielding secrets hidden for nearly 400 years that seem to tell a different story. Archaeologists working at the settlement site have turned up what they consider dramatic evidence that the colonists were not ill-prepared dandies and laggards, and that the disaster-plagued Virginia Colony, perhaps more than Plymouth, was the seedbed of the American nation—a bold experiment in democracy, perseverance and enterprise.

6   The breakthrough came in 1996, when a team of archaeologists working for the Association for the Preservation of Virginia Antiquities (APVA) discovered a portion of the decayed ruins of the original 1607 Jamestown fort, a triangular wooden structure many historians were certain had been swallowed by the river long ago. By the end of the 2003 digging season, the archaeologists had located the fort's entire perimeter on the open western edge of the heavily wooded 1,500-acre island; only one corner of it had been lost to the river. "This was a huge find," William Kelso, chief archaeologist at the site, said shortly after the discovery. "Now we know where the heart is, the center of the colonial effort, the bull's-eye. We know exactly where to dig now, and

we will focus our time and resources on uncovering and analyzing the interior of the James Fort."

7   Since then, Kelso and his team have excavated the ruins of several buildings inside the fort's perimeter, along with thousands of artifacts and the skeletal remains of some of the first settlers. Only a third of the site has been excavated, and many of the artifacts are still being analyzed. Yet the evidence has already caused historians to reconsider some longheld assumptions about the men and the circumstances surrounding what Yale University history professor emeritus Edmund S. Morgan once called "the Jamestown fiasco." "Archaeology is giving us a much more concrete picture of what it was like to live there," says Morgan, whose 1975 history, *American Slavery, American Freedom: The Ordeal of Colonial Virginia,* argued that Jamestown's first years were disastrous. "But whether it turns the Virginia Company into a success story is another question."

8   The large number of artifacts suggests that, if nothing else, the Virginia Company expedition was much better equipped than previously thought. By the end of the 2003 season, more than half a million items, from fishhooks and weaponry to glassmaking and woodworking equipment, along with the bones of game fish and assorted livestock, had been recovered and cataloged. Many are now on display at the Jamestown Rediscovery project headquarters, a clapboard Colonial-style building a few hundred yards from the fort. "All of this flies in the face of conventional wisdom, which says that the colonists were underfunded and ill-equipped, that they didn't have the means to survive, let alone prosper," says Kelso. "What we have found here suggests that just isn't the case."

9   In a climate-controlled room down the hall from Kelso's sparsely decorated office, Beverly Straube, the project's curator, sorts and analyzes the detritus of everyday life and death in the Virginia Colony. Some of the more significant artifacts are nestled in shallow open boxes, labeled and carefully arranged on long tables according to where the items were found. From one box, Straube picks up a broken ceramic piece with drops of shiny white "frosting" attached to its surface. "It's part of a crucible," she explains. "And this," she says, pointing to the white substance, "is molten glass. We know from John Smith's records that German glassmakers were brought in to manufacture glass to sell back in London. Here we have evidence of the glassmakers at work in the Jamestown fort." From another box, she takes a broken ceramic piece with a cut-out hole and an ear-like protrusion. She compares it with a sketch of a ceramic oven, about the size of a toaster, used by 16th-century craftsmen to make clay tobacco pipes. Nearby are fragments of a glass alembic (a domed vessel used in distilling) and a ceramic

boiling vessel, known as a cucurbit, for refining precious metals. "These artifacts tell us that the colonists weren't just sitting around," Straube says. "When they were healthy enough to work, this was an industrious place."

10   In another room, Straube opens a drawer and pulls out a pitted piece of iron—round, with a point protruding from its center. It is a buckler, she explains, a shield used in hand-to-hand combat. It was found in a trench surrounding the fort's east bulwark. By 1607, she says, bucklers were considered largely obsolete as tools of war in Europe— which would seem to fit the traditional view that the Jamestown expedition was provisioned with castoff weapons and equipment. "But we believe these were deliberately chosen," Straube says, "because the settlers knew they were more likely to face guerrilla-type combat against Indian axes and arrows than a conventional war against Spanish firearms. So the buckler would have come in handy."

11   In the cellar of what had been a mud-walled building that extends outward from the eastern palisade wall, archaeologists have found pottery shards, broken dishes and tobacco pipes, food remains, musket balls, buttons and coins. The cellar had been filled with trash, probably in 1610 during a massive cleanup of the site ordered by the newly appointed governor, Lord de la Warre, who arrived at Jamestown just in time to prevent the starving colonists from abandoning the settlement and returning to England. Establishing the date helps show that the cellar's contents, which included the glassmaking and distilling equipment on display at the APVA headquarters, dated to the colony's critical first years. It is from such early artifacts that Kelso and Straube are revising the colony's history.

12   Sifting through cellars and trenches in and around the fort, Kelso and his team recently uncovered a surprisingly large quantity of Indian pottery, arrowheads and other items. These suggest that the colonists had extensive dealings with the Natives. In one cellar, an Indian cooking pot containing pieces of turtle shell was found next to a large glass bead that the English used in trade with the Indians. "Here we believe we have evidence of an Indian woman, inside the fort, cooking for an English gentleman," Straube says. While such arrangements may have been rare, Kelso adds, the find strongly implies that Natives occasionally were present inside the fort for peaceful purposes and may even have cohabited with the Englishmen before English women arrived in significant numbers in 1620.

13   What is known from Virginia Company papers is that the colonists were instructed to cultivate a close relationship with the Indians. Both documentary and archaeological records confirm that English copper and glass goods were exchanged for Indian corn and other foods, initially at least. But the relationship

didn't last long, and the consequences for both the English and the Indians proved deadly.

14   As grim as the first year was at Jamestown, the darkest days for the colonists were yet to come. In 1608, the settlement was resupplied twice with new recruits and fresh provisions from London. But when nearly 400 new immigrants arrived aboard seven English supply ships in August 1609, they found the colonists struggling to survive. In September, the former president of the colony, John Ratcliffe, led a group of 50 men up the Pamunkey River to meet with Wahunsunacock—better known as Chief Powhatan, the powerful leader of the Powhatan Indians—to bargain for food. The colonists were ambushed, Ratcliffe was taken prisoner and tortured to death, and only 16 of his men made it back to the fort alive (and empty handed).

15   That fall and winter in Jamestown would be remembered as "the starving time." Out of food, the colonists grew sick and weak. Few had the strength to venture from their mud-and-timber barracks to hunt, fish or forage for edible plants or potable water. Those who did risked being picked off by Indians waiting outside the fort for nature to take its course. Desperate, the survivors ate their dogs and horses, then rats and other vermin, and eventually the corpses of their comrades. By spring, only 60 colonists were still alive, down from 500 the previous fall.

16   The starving time is represented by debris found in a barracks cellar—the bones of a horse bearing butchery marks, and the skeletal remains of a black rat, a dog and a cat. To the west of the fort, a potters' field of hastily dug graves—some as early as 1610— contained 72 settlers, some of the bodies piled haphazardly on top of others in 63 separate burials.

17   In the conventional view of Jamestown, the horror of the starving time dramatizes the fatal flaws in the planning and conduct of the settlement. Why, after three growing seasons, were the men of Jamestown still unable or unwilling to sustain themselves? History's judgment, once again, has been to blame "gentlemen" colonists who were more interested in pursuing profits than in tilling the soil. While the Virginia "woods rustled with game and the river flopped with fish," according to The American Pageant, a 1956 history textbook, the "soft-handed English gentlemen . . . wasted valuable time seeking gold when they should have been hoeing corn." They were "spurred to their frantic search" by greedy company directors in London who "threatened to abandon the colonists if they did not strike it rich."

18   But Kelso and Straube are convinced the fate of the colony was beyond the control of either the settlers or their London backers. According to a landmark 1998 climate study, Jamestown was founded at the height of a previously undocumented

drought—the worst seven-year dry spell in nearly 800 years. The conclusion was based on a tree-ring analysis of cypress trees in the region showing that their growth was severely stunted between 1606 and 1612. The study's authors say a major drought would have dried up fresh-water supplies and devastated corn crops on which both the colonists and the Indians depended. It also would have aggravated relations with the Powhatans, who found themselves competing with the English for a dwindling food supply. In fact, the period coincides perfectly with bloody battles between the Indians and the English. Relations improved when the drought subsided.

19   The drought theory makes new sense of written comments by Smith and others, often overlooked by historians. In 1608, for example, Smith records an unsuccessful attempt to trade goods for corn with the Indians. "(Their corne being that year bad) they complained extreamly of their owne wants," Smith wrote. On another occasion, an Indian leader appealed to him "to pray to my God for raine, for their Gods would not send any." Historians have long assumed that the Powhatans were trying to mislead the colonists in order to conserve their own food supplies. But now, says archaeologist Dennis Blanton, a co-author of the tree-ring study, "for the first time it becomes clear that Indian reports of food shortages were not deceptive strategies but probably true appraisals of the strain placed on them from feeding two populations in the midst of drought."

20   Blanton and his colleagues conclude that the Jamestown colonists probably have been unfairly criticized "for poor planning, poor support, and a startling indifference to their own subsistence." The Jamestown settlers "had the monumental bad luck to arrive in April 1607," the authors wrote. "Even the best planned and supported colony would have been supremely challenged" under such conditions.

21   Kelso and his co-workers are hardly the first archaeologists to probe the settlement. In 1893, the APVA acquired 22.5 acres of Jamestown Island, most of which had become farmland. In 1901, the U.S. Army Corps of Engineers constructed a sea wall to protect the site from further river erosion; a few graves and the statehouse at the settlement's western end were excavated at the time as well. In the 1950s, National Park Service archaeologists found footings and foundations of 17th-century structures east of the fort and hundreds of artifacts, though they couldn't locate the fort itself; since the 1800s it was widely assumed to lie underwater.

22   Today, the site of the original colonial settlement is largely given over to archaeological research, with few visual links to the past. Kelso and a full-time staff of 10 work almost year-round, and they're assisted by some 20 student workers during the summer. Tourists wander the grassy site snapping pictures of Kelso's team toiling behind protective fences. Bronze statues of Smith and Pocahontas stand along the James River. There's a gift shop and a restored 17th-century church. And a $5 million "archaearium"—a 7,500-square-foot educational building that will house many of the colonial artifacts—is to be completed for the 2007 quadricentennial.

23   The surge in research at the original Jamestown can be traced to 1994, when the APVA , anticipating the colony's 400th anniversary, launched a 10 year hunt for physical evidence of Jamestown's origins and hired Kelso, who had excavated 17th-century sites near Williamsburg and was then conducting historical research at Monticello.

24   Kelso is unmistakably pleased with the revisionist spin his findings have given to the Jamestown saga. Yet rewriting history, he says, was not what he had in mind when he began the work. "I simply wanted to get the rest of the story," he says. Most of what is known of Jamestown's grim early years, he notes, comes from the writings of Smith—clearly the most prolific of the colony's chroniclers—and a handful of his compatriots, along with a few sketchy records from the Virginia Company in London. Such documents, Kelso says, are a "deliberate record" and often are "written with a slant favorable to the writer." Smith's journal, for example, frequently depicts many of his fellow colonists as shiftless and inept. But Smith's journal "is obviously slanted," says Kelso. "He comes out the star in his own movie."

25   An example is the tale of Smith's rescue by the Indian princess Pocahontas, which Smith first related in his writings in 1624, some 17 years after the incident. Because the story was never mentioned in his earlier writings, some historians now dismiss it as legend—though Pocahontas did exist.

26   Not that Jamestown's archaeological evidence is beyond question. Some archaeologists argue that it's nearly impossible to date Jamestown's artifacts or differentiate the founding colonists' debris from what later arrivals left behind. Retired Virginia archaeologist Ivor Noël Hume, the former director of archaeology at nearby Colonial Williamsburg, notes that the fort was occupied until the 1620s and was rebuilt several times. "It's hard to pin down what the original settlers brought with them and what came later," he says.

27   But Kelso and Straube say they can accurately date most of the artifacts and draw reasonable conclusions as to when certain structures were built and abandoned. "If we find a piece of broken pottery in a trash pit, and another piece of the same vessel in a nearby well," Straube explains, "we know these two structures existed at the same time." Moreover, she says, the appearance of certain imported items from Portugal, Spain or Germany indicate a period after the Virginia Company lost its charter in 1624 and the

colony's management was turned over to England's Crown. "It's really a different Jamestown in the later period," she says. Some historians still have their doubts. "What they are finding may require some adjustment to the views of historians relying solely on documents," Yale's Morgan concedes. But the reputation of Jamestown as a failure will be a hard one to shake, he adds: "It will take a lot more than a half million artifacts to show that the Virginia Company learned from its mistakes and made a go of it in the colonies."

28   Kelso is convinced that much more colonial history lies buried in the island's soil. During the 2004 digging season, excavators uncovered the footprint of a long and narrow building inside the fort. The presence of unusually fancy glassware and pieces of Chinese porcelain buried inside suggests to Straube that it was a place of high-style dining and entertaining, perhaps the governor's home, which written records indicate was built in 1611. In the cellar of another structure, a student volunteer uncovered wine bottles, intact but empty, that are believed to date to the late 1600s, when Jamestown was prospering as a tobacco and trade center.

29   "Were there gentlemen at Jamestown?" says Kelso. "Of course. And some of them were lazy and incompetent. But not all. The proof of the matter is that the settlement survived, and it survived because people persisted and sacrificed." And what began as an English settlement gradually evolved into something different, something new. "You look up and down the river as the settlement expanded and you find it is not like England. The houses are different—the towns, the agriculture, the commerce. They were really laying the roots of American society." Despite the agony, the tragedy, and all of the missteps, says Kelso, "this is where modern America began."

9

AFRICA AND THE SLAVE TRADE

BY OLAUDAH EQUIANO AND OMAR IBN SEID

Slavery, as an institution, was practiced from ancient times into the modern era. During the era of exploration and colonization, Europeans transported slaves to many locations to feed the intensive labor needs of their agricultural outposts. Stripped of their possessions, families, and dignity, Africans nonetheless carried their culture with them as they were forced into the hulls of ships and dumped on islands and marshy shores in the Americas.

In the English colonies, slavery took on an especially racist character as blackness became the stamp of bondage and the laws of private property were applied to the vibrant trade in human beings. Tobacco growing, and eventually cotton, required tremendous amounts of labor; Caribbean sugar producers had already shown the utility and possibilities in the exploitation of slaves.

As you read the following introduction and primary source documents, remember that the subjects are real people, not abstract images or units in a treatise on economics. Even Thomas Jefferson, author of the "Declaration of Independence," kept meticulous records of the production of his slaves, giving them little more recognition than that of stock animals, though now and again propagating his prodigy through a favorite house slave.

- *What were the main reasons that Europeans shipped Africans to the colonies as slaves?*
- *What was the middle passage?*
- *What were conditions like on slave ships?*
- *What were Olaudah Equiano's fears regarding the middle passage?*
- *What did some of the captured Africans on board the ship do to avoid being slaves?*
- *Who did Omar ibn Seid call infidels?*
- *Why do you suppose he called them infidels?*

INTRODUCTION

1   Although Moslem traders from north of the Sahara had carried on an extensive trade with the states of West Africa during the Middle Ages, Africa remained the "dark continent" to the light-skinned Christians of the North until the time of the discovery and exploitation of the Americas by the Europeans. Then, as the demand from the New World for cheap labor grew, the Europeans turned to Africa, and the West African coast from the Senegal River south to the mouth of the Congo began to swarm with ships intent on capitalizing on the trade in human beings.

2   Estimates of the number of Africans taken into slavery in the Americas range from nine million to 50 million, with the true figure probably close to the former. However, this figure does not include all the blacks uprooted from their homes. Millions died fighting in the wars to capture slaves, making

the arduous trek to the coast where the slave ships waited, or undergoing the devastating passage across the Atlantic.

3   As the control of the Atlantic slave trade passed successively through the hands of the Portuguese, the Dutch, the French, and the English (including the American colonists), the typical European cared little and knew less about the land from which the blacks were being taken. Until recent years, with the exception of a few studies of the trade itself, Europeans gave no serious thought to the history of West Africa prior to and during the trade.

4   Most of coastal Africa—the area with which the slavers dealt—was organized into states rather than into tribes or simple societies. Between the tenth and sixteenth centuries, in the interior, centered around the bend of the Niger River, the empires of Ghana, Mali, and Songhai flourished. These interior kingdoms had no direct contact with the Atlantic slave trade. The states of the West African coast were so strong and well fortified that the European traders were not able to penetrate the interior in order to capture slaves; instead, they had to depend on the coastal kings for their booty. These African political leaders competed for the monopoly on slaves with the various European traders. The blacks who were sold into slavery usually came from the area just behind the coast, and most were either captured in wars waged for the trade or collected by the coastal rulers as tribute from weaker states.

5   There is much controversy today about the effect of the slave trade on the coastal states. It is unclear whether the states benefited from the trade in terms of the improved standard of living that resulted from the increased commerce or whether the buying and selling of millions of people only brought about moral degeneration, which eventually led to the decline and virtual disappearance of the coastal kingdoms. The same questions might be asked, of course, of the individual traders and the countries involved in the trade. What is clear is that competition between the African states, fostered by the use of guns as trade goods by the European slavers, led to ruinous wars that weakened the states to the point that they could be taken over during the period of European colonization in the late nineteenth century.

6   Two of the main reasons Africans were so successfully used as slaves had to do with their physical resistance to European diseases and the high level of commercial organization they had achieved in West Africa. The American Indian population that had been enslaved by the Spanish in the New World was dying out at a startling rate because of the diseases introduced by the Europeans. The same diseases seem to have existed widely enough in Africa to allow the Africans to develop a certain immunity to them. Thus they were able to endure the conditions of slavery in the New World.

7   The African states' previous experience in commerce enabled them to adapt easily to dealing in human beings—the commodity then in demand— instead of in gold or salt. And the old trade routes into the interior began to yield the new trade item. Indeed, a high degree of commercial organization was needed to supply up to 100,000 people a year for the trade.

8   By the seventeenth century, most of the slave trade was carried on in standard commercial patterns. A ship would arrive off the coast of a trading station; depending on the particular arrangement, African businessmen would come aboard the ship to bargain or the ship's captain would go ashore. Customarily, there would be some haggling over the terms of the trade. European money had no value in Africa, so the blacks were usually bought with rolls of tobacco, rum, guns, or bars of useful metal, such as iron, copper, and brass. From time to time, cowrie shells, widely used in Africa as a medium of exchange, were introduced. After the deal was made, it was necessary to examine the goods. Only the best physical specimens were acceptable. Those who proved fit were branded with the mark of the trader, lest a substitution be made between the examination and the sailing.

9   When the time came to sail, the slaves were chained together and loaded into the ships. At this point there were many violent struggles. Sometimes the blacks would capture the ship; sometimes they would break away and dive overboard, preferring to face drowning rather than go as slaves to an unknown fate. The traders considered loading the ship the most dangerous part of the transaction.

10   Once under way, the traders would relax somewhat and begin the infamous "middle passage," so called because it was the second leg of the triangular pattern characteristic of the Atlantic trade during this period from Europe or New England to Africa, from Africa to the West Indies, from the West Indies to Europe or New England. Once the ship was at sea, speed was of the essence. The shorter the voyage, the fewer the slaves who would die on board. It has been estimated that one of every eight slaves died during this part of the trade. The quickest time between Africa and the New World was three weeks, but when winds were contrary or there was no wind at all, the voyage sometimes lasted over three months.

11   If weather permitted, the captives were kept on deck during the day and forced to exercise and eat. But when the weather was bad, they were kept chained for most of the voyage in incredibly cramped and poorly ventilated quarters below.

12   Upon arriving at its destination, the ship would disgorge its contents at a local slave mart, where the entire lot would be bid for on the basis of an average price. The purchaser was usually a slave dealer, who would either resell the slaves on the spot to individuals

who had been unable to participate in the initial bidding or transport the slaves elsewhere for resale.

13   The slave trade was so extensive that by 1850 one-third of the people in the world with African ancestry lived outside Africa, most of them in the Americas. This forced migration, one of the largest movements of people in the history of the world, had an incalculable effect on both Africa and the New World.

THE HORRORS OF THE MIDDLE PASSAGE[1]

THE INTERESTING NARRATIVE OF THE LIFE OF OLAUDAH EQUIANO

Olaudah Equiano

14   *Olaudah Equiano, the author of this selection, was from the Ibo country around Benin in what is now Nigeria. He was sold into slavery in 1756 to the British, who brought him to the New World. In 1766, he bought his freedom and went to England, where he worked as a barber and as a personal servant. He became actively involved in the anti-slavery movement in England and was interested in colonizing freed blacks in Sierra Leone. His autobiography, written in 1789, is one of the most informative of all such narratives by former slaves.*

15   *The portion of Equiano's narrative included here describes his experience of the "middle passage" from Africa to the West Indies. He recalled it as a horrifying example of man's inhumanity to his brothers. Included is a reference to the widespread fear among the captured Africans that they were to be eaten by the white men.*

16   The first object which saluted my eyes when I arrived on the coast was the sea, and a slave ship, which was then riding at anchor, and waiting for its cargo. These filled me with astonishment, which was soon converted into terror, when I was carried on board I was immediately handled, and tossed up, to see if I were sound, by some of the crew; and I was now persuaded that I had got into a world of bad spirits, and that they were going to kill me. Their complexions too differing so much from ours, their long hair, and the language they spoke (which was very different from any I had ever heard) united to confirm me in this belief. Indeed such were the horrors of my views and fears at the moment, that, if ten thousand worlds had been my own, I would have freely parted with them all to have exchanged my condition with that of the meanest slave in my own country.

17   When I looked round the ship too and saw a large furnace or copper boiling, and a multitude of black people of every description chained together, every one of their countenances expressing dejection and sorrow, I no longer doubted of my fate; and, quite overpowered with horror and anguish, I fell motionless on the deck and fainted. When I recovered a little I found some black people about me, who I believed were some of those who had brought me on board, and had been receiving their pay; they talked to me in order to cheer me, but all in vain. I asked them if we were not to be eaten by those white men with horrible looks, red faces, and long hair. They told me I was not; and one of the crew brought me a small portion of spirituous liquor in a wine-glass; but being afraid of him, I would not take it out of his hand. One of the blacks therefore took it from him and gave it to me, and I took a little down my palate, which, instead of reviving me, as they thought it would, threw me into the greatest consternation at the strange feeling it produced, having never tasted any such liquor before.

18   Soon after this the blacks who brought me on board went off, and left me abandoned to despair. I now saw myself deprived of all chance of returning to my native country, or even the least glimpse of hope of gaining the shore, which I now considered as friendly; and I even wished for my former slavery in preference to my present situation, which was filled with horrors of every kind, still heightened by my ignorance of what I was to undergo.

19   I was not long suffered to indulge my grief; I was soon put down under the decks, and there I received such a salutation in my nostrils as I had never experienced in my life: so that with the loathsomeness of the stench, and crying together, I became so sick and low that I was not able to eat, nor had I the least desire to taste any thing. I now wished for the last friend, death, to relieve me; but soon, to my grief, two of the white men offered me eatables; and, on my refusing to eat, one of them held me fast by the hands, and laid me across, I think the windlass, and tied my feet, while the other flogged me severely. I had never experienced any thing of this kind before: and, although not being used to the water, I naturally feared that element the first time I saw it, yet, nevertheless, could I have got over the nettings, I would have jumped over the side, but I could not, and, besides, the crew used to watch us very closely who were not chained down to the decks, lest we should leap into the water: and I have seen some of these poor African prisoners most severely cut for attempting to do so, and hourly whipped for not eating.

20   This indeed was often the case with myself. In a little time after, amongst the poor chained men, I found some of my own nation, which in a small degree gave ease to my mind. I inquired of these what was to be done with us? They gave me to understand we were to be carried to these white people's country to work for them. I then was a little revived, and thought, if it were no worse than working, my situation was not so desperate: but still I

feared I should be put to death, the white people looked and acted, as I thought, in so savage a manner; for I had never seen among any people such instances of brutal cruelty; and this not only shown towards us blacks, but also to some of the whites themselves. One white man in particular I saw, when we were permitted to be on deck, flogged so unmercifully with a large rope near the foremast, that he died in consequence of it; and they tossed him over the side as they would have done a brute.

21   This made me fear these people the more; and I expected nothing less than to be treated in the same manner. I could not help expressing my fears and apprehensions to some of my countrymen: I asked them if these people had no country, but lived in this hollow place (the ship)? they told me they did not, but came from a distant one, "Then," said I, "how comes it in all our country we never heard of them!"

22   They told me, because they lived so very far off. I then asked where were their women? had they any like themselves? I was told they had: "And why," said I, "do we not see them?" they answered, because they were left behind.

23   I asked how the vessel could go? They told me they could not tell; but that there were cloth put upon the masts by the help of the ropes I saw, and then the vessel went on; and the white men had some spell or magic they put in the water when they liked in order to stop the vessel, I was exceedingly amazed at this account, and really thought they were spirits. I therefore wished much to be from amongst them, for I expected they would sacrifice me: but my wishes were vain; for we were so quartered that it was impossible for any of us to make our escape.

24   While we stayed on the coast I was mostly on deck; and one day, to my great astonishment, I saw one of these vessels coming in with the sails up. As soon as the whites saw it, they gave a great shout, at which we were amazed: and the more so as the vessel appeared larger by approaching nearer. At last she came to an anchor in my sight, and when the anchor was let go I and my countrymen who saw it were lost in astonishment to observe the vessel stop; and were now convinced it was done by magic.

25   Soon after this the other ship got her boats out, and they came on board of us, and the people of both ships seemed very glad to see each other. Several of the strangers also shook hands with us black people, and made motions with their hands, signifying I suppose, we were to go to their country; but we did not understand them.

26   At last, when the ship we were in, had got in all her cargo, they made ready with many fearful noises, and we were all put under deck, so that we could not see how they managed the vessel. But this disappointment was the least of my sorrow. The stench of the hold while we were on the coast was so intolerably loathsome, that it was dangerous to remain there for any time, and some of us had been permitted to stay on the deck for the fresh air; but now that the whole ship's cargo were confined together, it became absolutely **pestilential**.

27   The closeness of the place, and the heat of the climate, added to the number in the ship, which was so crowded that each had scarcely room to turn himself, almost suffocated us. This produced copious perspirations, so that the air soon became unfit for respiration, from a variety of loathsome smells, and brought on a sickness amongst the slaves, of which many died, thus falling victims to the improvident avarice, as I may call it, of their purchasers.

28   This wretched situation was again aggravated by the galling of the chains, now become insupportable; and the filth of the necessary tubs, into which the children often fell, and were almost suffocated. The shrieks of the women, and the groans of the dying, rendered the whole a scene of horror almost inconceivable.

29   Happily perhaps for myself I was soon reduced so low here that it was thought necessary to keep me almost always on deck; and from my extreme youth I was not put in fetters. In this situation I expected every hour to share the fate of my companions, some of whom were almost daily brought upon deck at the point of death, which I began to hope would soon put an end to my miseries. Often did I think many of the inhabitants of the deep much more happy than myself, I envied them the freedom they enjoyed, and as often wished I could change my condition for theirs.

30   Every circumstance I met with served only to render my state more painful, and heightened my apprehensions and my opinion of the cruelty of the whites. One day they had taken a number of fishes; and when they had killed and satisfied themselves with as many as they thought fit, to our astonishment who were on the deck, rather than give any of them to us to eat, as we expected, they tossed the remaining fish into the sea again, although we begged and prayed for some as well as we could, but in vain; and some of my countrymen, being pressed by hunger, took an opportunity, when they thought no one saw them, of trying to get a little privately; but they were discovered, and the attempt procured them some very severe floggings.

31   One day, when we had a smooth sea and moderate wind, two of my wearied countrymen who were chained together (I was near them at the time), preferring death to such a life of misery, somehow made through the nettings and jumped into the sea: immediately another quite dejected fellow, who on account

pestilential: poisonous; marked by apparent ill will.

of his illness, was suffered to be out of irons, also followed their example; and I believe many more would very soon have done the same if they had not been prevented by the ship's crew who were instantly alarmed. Those of us that were the most active were in a moment put down under the deck, and there was such a noise and confusion amongst the people of the ship as I never heard before, to stop her, and get the boat out to go after the slaves. However two of the wretches were drowned, but they got the other, and afterwards flogged him unmercifully for thus attempting to prefer death to slavery.

32 In this manner we continued to undergo more hardships than I can now relate, hardships which are inseparable from this accursed trade. Many a time we were near suffocation from the want of fresh air, which we were often without for whole days together. This, and the stench of the necessary tubs, carried off many.

33 During our passage I first saw flying fishes, which surprised me very much: they used frequently to fly across the ship, and many of them fell on the deck. I also now first saw the use of the quadrant; I had often with astonishment seen the mariners make observations with it, and I could not think what it meant. They at last took notice of my surprise: and one of them, willing to increase it, as well as to gratify my curiosity, made me one day look through it. The clouds appeared to me to be land, which disappeared as they passed along. This heightened my wonder; and I was now more persuaded than ever that I was in another world, and that every thing about me was magic.

34 At last we came in sight of the island of Barbadoes, at which the whites on board gave a great shout, and made many signs of joy to us. We did not know what to think of this; but as the vessel drew nearer, we plainly saw the harbour, and other ships of different kinds and sizes; and we soon anchored amongst them off Bridge-Town.

35 Many merchants and planters now came on board, though it was in the evening. They put us in separate parcels, and examined us attentively. They also made us jump, and pointed to the land, signifying we were to go there.

36 We thought by this we should be eaten by these ugly men, as they appeared to us; and, when soon after we were all put down under the deck again, there was much dread and trembling among us, and nothing but bitter cries to be heard all the night from these apprehensions, insomuch that at last the white people got some old slaves from the land to pacify us. They told us we were not to be eaten, but to work, and were soon to go on land, where we should see many of our country people.

37 This report eased us much; and sure enough, soon after we landed, there came to us Africans of all languages. We were conducted immediately to the merchant's yard, where we were all pent up together like so many sheep in a fold, without regard to sex or age.

38 As every object was new to me, every thing I saw filled me with surprise. What struck me first was that the houses were built with bricks and stories, and in every other respect different from those I had seen in Africa: but I was still more astonished on seeing people on horseback. I did not know what this could mean; and indeed I thought these people were full of nothing but magical arts.

39 While I was in this astonishment one of my fellow prisoners spoke to a countryman of his about the horses, who said they were the same kind they had in their country. I understood them, though they were from a distant part of Africa, and I thought it odd I had not seen any horses there; but afterwards when I came to converse with different Africans, I found they had many horses amongst them, and much larger than those I then saw.

40 We were not many days in the merchant's custody before we were sold after their usual manner, which is this:—On a signal given, (as the beat of a drum) the buyers rush at once into the yard where the slaves are confined, and make choice of that parcel they like best. The noise and clamour with which this is attended, and the eagerness visible in the countenances of the buyers, serve not a little to increase the apprehension of terrified Africans, who may well be supposed to consider them as the ministers of that destruction to which they think themselves devoted.

41 In this manner, without scruple, are relations and friends separated, most of them never to see each other again. I remember in the vessel in which I was brought over, in the men's apartment, there were several brothers, who, in the sale were sold in different lots; and it was very moving on this occasion to see and hear their cries at parting.

42 O, ye nominal Christians! might not an African ask you, learned you this from your God, who says unto you, Do unto all men as you would men should do unto you? Is it not enough that we are torn from our country and friends, to toil for your luxury and lust of gain? Must every tender feeling be likewise sacrificed to your avarice? Are the dearest friends and relations, now rendered more dear by their separation from their kindred, still to be parted from each other, and thus prevented from cheering the gloom of slavery with the small comfort of being together, and mingling their sufferings and sorrows? Why are parents to lose their children, brothers their sisters, or husbands their wives?

43 Surely this is a new refinement in cruelty, which, while it has no advantage to atone for it, thus aggravates distress, and adds fresh horrors even to the wretchedness of slavery.

A Devout Moslem Sold to the Infidels[2]

Autobiography

Omar ibn Seid

44   *By the year 1100 the states of West Africa had come under the influence of Islam, and the rulers of Mali and Songhai were devout Moslems. It comes as no surprise, then, that many slaves brought to America were Moslem and spoke Arabic.*

45   *Omar ibn Seid, the author of the following sketch, was a member of the Fula tribe from what is now called Senegal. He was born about 1770. After being trained in Arabic and mathematics by his uncle, he became a merchant dealing primarily in cotton cloth. Subsequently, he was captured and sold into slavery in Charleston, South Carolina, by the **infidels**—in this case, the Christians.*

46   *He ran away from his master in South Carolina and was arrested in Fayetteville, North Carolina. While in jail, he began writing on the walls of his cell in Arabic, a feat that brought him to the attention of General James Owen, who purchased him. Although Omar was still a devout Moslem when bought by General Owen, he later converted to Christianity.*

47   *This brief autobiography is translated from the Arabic and begins with scattered selections from the Koran that Omar considered relevant to the story he had to tell.*

48   In the name of God, the merciful the gracious.— God grant his blessing upon our Prophet Mohammed. Blessed be He in whose hands is the kingdom and who is Almighty; who created death and life that he might test you; for he is exalted; he is the forgiver (of sins), who created seven heavens one above the other. Do you discern anything trifling in creation? Bring back your thoughts. Do you see anything worthless? Recall your vision in earnest. Turn your eye inward for it is diseased. God has adorned the heavens and the world with lamps, and has made us missiles for the devils, and given us for them a grievous punishment, and to those who have disbelieved their Lord, the punishment of hell and pains of body. Whoever associates with them shall hear a boiling caldron, and what is cast therein may fitly represent those who suffer under the anger of God.— Ask them if a prophet has not been sent unto them. They say, "Yes, a prophet has come to us, but we have lied to him." We said, "God has not sent us down anything, and you are in grievous error." They say, "If we had listened and been wise we should not now have been suffering the punishment of **the Omniscient.**" So they have sinned in destroying the

followers of the Omniscient. Those who fear their Lord and profess his name, they receive pardon and great honor. Guard your words, (ye wicked), make it known that God is all-wise in all his manifestations. Do you not know from the creation that God is full of skill? That He has made for you the way of error, and you have walked therein, and have chosen to live upon what your god Nasûr has furnished you? Believe on Him who dwells in heaven, who has fitted the earth to be your support and it shall give you food. Believe on Him who dwells in Heaven, who has sent you a prophet, and you shall understand what a teacher (He has sent you). Those that were before them deceived them (in regard to their prophet). And how came they to reject him? Did they not see in the heavens above them, how the fowls of the air receive with pleasure that which is sent them? God looks after all. Believe ye: it is He who supplies your wants, that you may take his gifts and enjoy them, and take great pleasure in them. And now will you go on in error, or walk in the path of righteousness. Say to them, "He who regards you with care, and who has made for you the heavens and the earth and gives you prosperity, Him you think little of. This is He that planted you in the earth, and to whom you are soon to be gathered." But they say, "If you are men of truth, tell us when shall this promise be fulfilled?" Say to them, "Does not God know? and am not I an evident Prophet?" When those who disbelieve shall see the things draw near before their faces, it shall then be told them, "These are the things about which you made inquiry." Have you seen that God has destroyed me or those with me? or rather that He has shewn us mercy? And who will defend the unbeliever from a miserable punishment? Say, "Knowledge is from God." Say, "Have you not seen that your water has become impure? Who will bring you fresh water from the fountain?"

49   O Sheikh Hunter, I cannot write my life because I have forgotten much of my own language, as well as of the Arabic. Do not be hard upon me, my brother.— To God let many thanks be paid for his great mercy and goodness.

50   In the name of God, the Gracious, the Merciful.— Thanks be to God, supreme in goodness and kindness and grace, and who is worthy of all honor, who created all things for his service, even man's power of action and of speech.

From Omar to Sheikh Hunter

51   You asked me to write my life. I am not able to do this because I have much forgotten my own, as well as the Arabic language. Neither can I write very grammatically or according to the true idiom. And

---

infidels: an unbeliever with respect to a particular religion, especially Christian or Islam.
the Omniscient: God.

so, my brother, I beg you, in God's name, not to blame me, for I am a man of weak eyes, and of a weak body.

52   My name is Omar ibn Seid. My birthplace was Fut Tûr, the two rivers. I sought knowledge under the instruction of a Sheikh called Mohammed Seid, my own brother, and Sheikh Soleiman Kembeh, and Sheikh Gabriel Abdal. I continued my studies 25 years, and then returned to my home where I remained six years. Then there came to our place a large army, who killed many men, and took me, and brought me to the great sea, and sold me into the hands of the Christians, who bound me and sent me on board a great ship and we sailed upon the great sea a month and a half, when we came to a place called Charleston in the Christian language.

53   There they sold me to a small, weak, and wicked man, called Johnson, a complete infidel, who had no fear of God at all. Now I am a small man, and unable to do hard work so I fled from the hand of Johnson and after a month came to a place called Fayd-il [Fayetteville]. There I saw some great houses (churches).

54   On the new moon I went into a church to pray. A lad saw me and rode off to the place of his father and informed him that he had seen a black man in the church. A man named Handah (Hunter?) and another man with him on horseback, came attended by a troop of dogs. They took me and made me go with them 12 miles to a place called Fayd-il, where they put me into a great house from which I could not go out.

55   I continued in the great house (which, in the Christian language, they called *jail*) 16 days and nights. One Friday the jailor came and opened the door of the house and I saw a great many men, all Christians, some of whom called out to me, "What is your name? Is it Omar or Seid?" I did not understand their Christian language.

56   A man called Bob Mumford took me and led me out of the jail, and I was very well pleased to go with them to their place. I stayed at Mumford's four days and nights, and then a man named Jim Owen, son-in-law of Mumford, having married his daughter Betsey, asked me if I was willing to go to a place called Bladen. I said, Yes, I was willing. I went with them and have remained in the place of Jim Owen until now.

57   Before [after?] I came into the hand of Gen. Owen a man by the name of Mitchell came to buy me. He asked me if I were willing to go to Charleston City. I said "No, no, no, no, no, no, no, I not willing to go to Charleston. I stay in the hand of Jim Owen."

58   O ye people of North Carolina, O ye people of South Carolina, O ye people of America all of you;

have you among you any two such men as Jim Owen and John Owen? These men are good men. What food they eat they give to me to eat. As they clothe themselves they clothe me. They permit me to read the gospel of God, our Lord, and Saviour, and King; who regulates all our circumstances, our health and wealth, and who bestows his mercies willingly, not by constraint. According to power I open my heart, as to a great light, to receive the true way, the way of the Lord Jesus the Messiah.

59   Before I came to the Christian country, my religion was the religion of "Mohammed, the Apostle of God—may God have mercy upon him and give him peace." I walked to the mosque before day-break, washed my face and head and hands and feet. I prayed at noon, prayed in the afternoon, prayed at sunset, prayed in the evening. I gave alms every year, gold, silver, seeds, cattle, sheep, goats, rice, wheat, and barley. I gave tithes of all the above-named things. I went every year to the holy war against the infidels. I went on pilgrimage to Mecca, as all did who were able.—My father had six sons and five daughters, and my mother had three sons and one daughter. When I left my country I was 37 years old; I have been in the country of the Christians twenty-four years.—Written A.D. 1831.

60   O ye people of North Carolina, O ye people of South Carolina, O ye people of America—

61   The first son of Jim Owen is called Thomas, and his sister is called Masajein (Martha Jane?). This is an excellent family.

62   Tom Owen and Nell Owen have two sons and a daughter. The first son is called Jim and the second John. The daughter is named Melissa.

63   Seid Jim Owen and his wife Betsey have two sons and five daughters. Their names are Tom, and John, and Mercy, Miriam, Sophia, Margaret and Eliza. This family is a very nice family. The wife of John Owen is called Lucy and an excellent wife she is. She had five children. Three of them died and two are still living.

64   O ye Americans, ye people of North Carolina— have you, have you, have you, have you, have you among you a family like this family, having so much love to God as they?

65   Formerly I, Omar, loved to read the book of the **Koran** the famous. General Jim Owen and his wife used to read the gospel, and they read it to me very much,—the gospel of God, our Lord, our Creator, our King, He that orders all our circumstances, health and wealth, willingly, not constrainedly, according to his power.—Open thou my heart to the gospel, to the way of uprightness.—Thanks to the Lord of all worlds, thanks in abundance. He is plenteous in mercy and abundant in goodness.

Koran: the sacred text of Islam, considered by Muslims to contain the revelations of Allah made to the Prophet Mohammed through the angel Gabriel.

66   For the law was given by Moses but grace and truth were by Jesus the Messiah.

67   When I was a **Mohammedan** I prayed thus: "Thanks be to God, Lord of all worlds, the merciful the gracious, Lord of the day of Judgment, thee we serve, on thee we call for help. Direct us in the right way, the way of those on whom thou hast had mercy, with whom thou hast not been angry and who walk not in error. Amen."— But now I pray "Our Father," etc., in the words of our Lord Jesus the Messiah.

68   I reside in this our country by reason of great necessity. Wicked men took me by violence and sold me to the Christians. We sailed a month and a half on the great sea to the place called Charleston in the Christian land. I fell into the hands of a small, weak, and wicked man, who feared not God at all, nor did he read (the gospel) at all nor pray. I was afraid to remain with a man so wicked and who committed so many crimes and I ran away. After a month our Lord God brought me forward to the hand of a good man, who fears God, and loves to do good, and whose name is Jim Owen and whose brother is called Col. John Owen. These are two excellent men.—I am residing in Bladen County.

69   I continue in the hand of Jim Owen who never beats me, nor scolds me. I neither go hungry nor naked, and I have no hard work to do. I am not able to do hard work for I am a small man and feeble. During the last 20 years I have known no want in the hand of Jim Owen.

Endnotes

1. From Olaudah Equiano, *The Interesting Narrative of the Life of Olaudah Equiano or Gustavus Vasa, The African,* Vol. 1 (New York, 1791), pp. 49–62.

2. From "Autobiography of Omaribn Seid, Slave in North Carolina, 1831," *American Historical Review,* Vol. 30 (July 1925), pp. 791–95.

Mohammedan: of or relating to Mohammed or Islam; Muslim.

10

BEARING THE BURDEN? PURITAN WIVES

BY MARTHA SAXTON

Documentation dealing with any one historical problem or event is usually presented in terms easily understood and generally agreeable to the people who possessed the power to present and record their interpretations. Our greatest handicap when dealing with the history of women is the immense dearth of materials that might otherwise enlighten us to their experiences. For centuries their story was told, in the main, by men. A woman might bear a child and suckle it, but inevitably a man hatched a tale of the birth and nursed the postnatal narrative along in his own words, not hers.

The story of the Puritans places unusual obstacles in the path of the thoughtful student. Their strong spiritual beliefs and desire to create and see the world in very narrow terms led to a male dominance in their community that at times exceeds our caricatures and stereotypes. Woman in Puritan society paid a dear price for entering this world as a female, and were held to exacting standards. Marriage was a spiritual partnership, an office to which a woman ascended and sustained with a deep sense of duty. She was obliged to both help her husband cleanse his life of spiritual impurities, while at the same time enduring the worst torments that he might shower upon her. Her efforts at motherhood could be manifested in no greater freedom than womanhood, and even while performing that office she was acting in the shadow of other forces.

Ironically, the greatest respect and recognition for a woman in Puritan society was earned by forfeiture of personal dignity and self-worth. Even this article, a sympathetic discussion of Puritan women, nonetheless relies upon testimony still smelling of the rich musk of long-deceased men.

- *How did Puritan beliefs define in defining the roles of men and women?*
- *What kinds of anecdotes help us to understand the status of women in Puritan life?*
- *What were some of the ironies faced by women in this world?*
- *What did such men as Cotton Mather believe to be the qualities of the best women in their community?*

1   Seventeenth-century American Puritans subordinated female to male wife to husband, and mother to father, insisting on obedience, modesty, and taciturnity for women. They justified this arrangement by emphasizing woman's descent from Eve and her innate irrationality, both of which made her more vulnerable to error and corruption than man. Because of this she was to view her husband as God's representative in the family. He would mediate her religious existence and direct her temporal one. She would produce children and care for them, but he would have the ultimate authority over them.

2   At the same time, the experience of Puritans of both sexes in the second half of the seventeenth century undermined this clearly defined system of authority in which the allocation of secular power flowed from a presumed moral and spiritual hierarchy. After 1660, women began outnumbering men in the churches, and by the end of the century the numerical difference was sufficient to prompt Cotton Mather to attempt to account for the demonstrated female proclivity for spirituality. Mather ascribed enhanced female religiosity precisely to that subordination that Puritan men insisted upon as well as mothers' suffering during childbirth.

3   Long before Mather published his conclusions to the end of the seventeenth century, other Puritan men anticipated his thinking about female virtue, and many identified its sources in female suffering. Men praised the patient endurance of wives with abusive husbands. Others granted to childbirth pain the power to enhance goodness. Some saw the sacrifices of mothering, rather than childbirth *per se*, as a source of virtue and testified to the moral significance of their mothers in the conduct of their lives. And still others simply acknowledged their mothers, wives, or other female relatives as inspirational or spiritually influential to them.

4   In the Puritan world then, women could and did earn respect for their moral stature in the family, and this was meaningful to women deprived of public recognition in a society run by men. It would be an important heritage to women of a later era. Pious women would pass on the idea that their principled expressions of conscience could shape morally, both family and society.

5   Before looking at the way women achieved moral authority, let us look at how Puritan men elaborated beliefs about the propriety of subordinating women to men. Jon Winthrop, Governor of Massachusetts, who was happily married to three submissive women, writing in the mid-seventeenth century put the ideal case:

> A true wife accounts her subjection her honor and freedom and would not think her condition safe and free but in her subjection to her husband's authority. Such is the liberty of the church under the authority of Christ, her king and husband; his yoke is so easy and sweet to her as a bride's ornaments; and if through forwardness or wantonness, etc., she shakes it off at any time, she is at no rest in her spirit until she take it up again; and whether her lord smiles upon her and embraceth her in his arms, or whether he frowns and rebukes her, or smites her, she comprehends the sweetness of his love in all, and is refreshed, and instructed by every such dispensation of his authority over her.

6   While not all American Puritans saw female obedience in such a cheerful light as Winthrop did, all agreed that it was essential to marital satisfaction and should exist regardless of the husband's comportment. John Cotton compared wifely obedience to the excellence and inevitability of the universe, the air we breathe, and the clouds that shower rain upon he earth. Benjamin Wadsworth, in a book published in 1712, wrote that a woman should 'reverence' her husband, as the Bible commanded. He was God's representative in the family, and even if he should 'pass the bounds of wisdom and kindness; yet must not she shake off the bond of submission but must bear patiently the burden, which God hath laid upon the daughters of Eve'. And Cotton Mather, writing before his final tempestuous marriage to Lydia Lee George would give these words a wistful ring, insisted that though the husband be 'ever so much a Churl, yet she treats him considerately'.

7   An important facet of this unanimous male insistence on female submission was the envy and fascination Puritan men felt for womanly meekness and obedience. Salvation demanded that men, as well as women, submit to God's will in all things. For women, submission to God's will and the will of the men around them made their lives, ideally, a continuum of obedience.

8   Men, however, enjoyed considerable social power during their lifetime as husbands and, depending upon their status, as community leaders. Submission and the self-suppression that it required, was, therefore, a more prickly and intractable issue for men than for women. Furthermore, as husbands, men determined how heavily or lightly the yoke of marriage would rest on their wives' shoulders. Men's direct responsibility for the suffering that their domination might cause women was likely to make them particularly alive to the issue.

9   Cotton Mather, who had openly linked woman's tendency to spiritual excellence with her subordination and suffering, wrote "But if thou has an Husband that will do so, [beat his wife] bear it patiently; and know thou shalt have –Rewards—hereafter for it, as well as *Praises* here . . . '. And Puritan men since the settlement of Plymouth had praised women for

remaining uncomplainingly with husbands who were violent and/or unfaithful. Mrs. Lyford, of Plymouth endured—and sometimes witnessed—her husband's sexual escapades for years in silence. Eventually, she testified against him. But, wrote the governor of the colony, William Bradford, approvingly, 'being a grave matron, and of good carriage . . . spoake of those things out of the sorrow of her harte, sparingly'.

10 The wife of Jared Davis submitted to years of her husband's cruelty, drunkenness, lies, scandalous behaviour, and indolence. He had, according to John Winthrop, neither compassion nor humanity toward his wife, insisted on sex with her when she was pregnant (which Puritans regarded as dangerous) and did not provide for her. The governor admired Mrs. Davis who, under all these provocations, continued to try to help her husband. As Winthrop had written elsewhere, Mrs. Davis was able to find in her husband's blows, God's love and correction. Winthrop and Bradford believed that the Christ-like acceptance of lengthy, undeserved abuse endowed women with a unique moral vantage point from which they might even venture to criticise their victimisers.

11 Men were also fascinated by—and implicated in—the crisis of child labour and delivery, which combined submission to physical suffering as well as the more difficult task: resignation to the possibility of death. Husbands were awed by their wives' apparent conquest of mortal fear.

12 Puritans believed that pregnancy rendered women more fearful than usual. The Reverend Peter Thacher wrote in his diary in February 1680, that his wife had fallen on a chair, and was 'soe frighted with it that shee had like to have fainted away' because she feared she had hurt the child in her womb. When normally timid women, rendered even more so by pregnancy, triumphed over the terror of death, they reassured the whole community of its ability to conquer its fear of the hereafter through submission to God. As Mather said at the funeral of 17-year-old Mrs. Rebeckah Burnel in 1724:

> But when it pleases Him, to take *children,* and those of that *Sex* which *Fear* is most incident and enslaving to; and make such *Babes* and *Sucklings* to triumph over the *Enemy,*—Oh! The *Wonderous Power* of our God! . . .

13 Thirteen years earlier, Cotton Mather's sister, Jerusha, decided when she was five months pregnant that it was time to get herself ready for death. She acknowledged that she was a fearful creature, and especially so because of her pregnancy, and wished to give herself up completely to God. She vowed that if God gave her an easy and short labour that she would dedicate herself to bringing up her child in fear of Him. She petitioned for a 'resigned will' and to be made fit for whatever God demanded for her. When her labour approached she prayed to be delivered from the sin of fear. As it happened, her labour was easy, but she and her baby died a short time later.

14 Mather, in recording his sister's death, assured his readers that Jerusha, while exceptionally joyous, said 'nothing that look'd at all Delirious', lest they discount the God-given courage with which she had faced her end. He quoted her saying that when she was healthy 'Death was a Terror to me. But now I know, I shall Dy, I am not at *all afraid of it. This* is a Wonderful *Work of God!* I know *that I am* going to Christ . . . I see things that are Unutterable!'. Her father, Increase Mather, asked her if she were not afraid of death. 'She replied with great Earnestness; "Not in the least! Not in the least! Not in the least!"' Mather ended his memoir with what he said were her last words, 'Eye has not seen, Ear has not heard, neither entered into the Heart of Man, the things which God has prepared for them that Love Him!'

15 Mather's text pointed out in many ways that if a frail, sickly and frightened (i.e. womanly) woman lived as a Puritan woman should, she would die blissfully; hence, ran the implicit parallel, how much easier would it be for a strong man to do the same.

16 Similarly, Barbara Ruggles, an inhabitant of Roxburg, was able, according to the Roxburg Church records, to 'shine in her life & death' because of the way she dealt with her afflictions, including a fatal delivery. She had a 'stone chollik in which sicknesse she manifested much patiens, and faith; she dyed in childbed . . . & left a godly savor behind her'.

17 When a woman lost the mortal battle of birth graciously, she acquired unhesitating male praise. When she won, her husband's admiration might be muted by feelings of competition or guilty ambivalence about the pleasure in which such suffering originated. In journal accounts, husbands often expropriated the religious significance of their wives' brushes with death to themselves. They mingled their admiration with a vision of their *own* sins as the origin of their wives' agonies.

18 When, in the late 1660s, God visited upon the wife of the Reverend Joseph Thompson of Billerica such a weakness as made the couple fear her pregnancy might end badly, Thompson took a lesson in submission to the Lord's will from his wife's peril. He acknowledged that nothing could happen without God's intervention. The Lord further let him see that he had not been sufficiently grateful for the health, companionship, and work of his wife. He therefore feared that God might punish him by taking her away—although one can imagine that Mrs. Thompson probably saw the punishment as hers. He prayed that the Lord would restore his wife's health and vowed perpetual gratitude for her. When his wife recovered, he charged himself with a return

to indifference toward his blessings in her and a 'vile hart'. Mrs. Thompson's near-death underlined to Thompson the sinful contrast between his unthankful acceptance of his spouse and his brief, divinely-inspired awareness of her value. And uncertainty and fear gave Thompson an all-too-brief reminder of the level of active, spiritual struggle on which he should be conducting more of his life.

19   The Reverend Thomas Shepard, in ruminating about the imminent birth of his child in the 1640s, wondered what would happen if the labour did not go well 'and her pains be long and [the] Lord remember my sin? And I began to trouble my heart with fear of the worst'. When he learned that his wife had delivered a baby safely, '. . . I saw the Lord's mercy and my own folly, to disquiet my heart with fear of what never shall be nor will be, and not rather to submit unto the Lord's will, and, come what can come, to be quiet there'.

20   Like Thompson, Shepard's wife's mortal risk made him acutely conscious of his own sins. When his fears went unrealized he attempted to learn the lesson of peaceful resignation to God's will. He could not avoid seeing that his wife, in giving herself up to miseries and uncertain outcome of travail, embodied this lesson.

21   In the same period the Reverend Michael Wigglesworth described his intimate involvement in his wife's labour. When she had pain, he:

> lay sighing, sweating, praying, almost fainting through weakness before morning. The next day, the spleen which enfeebled me, and setting in with grief took away my strength, my heart was smitten within me, and as sleep departed from myne eyes my stomach abhorred meat, I was brought very low and knew not how to pass away another night.

22   He then described feeling 'hasty and impatient', presumable with the excessive duration of their labour, and he prayed that the Lord make him want to 'stoop to his will'. His wife's endurance taunted him with the patience and submission he lacked. And although he portrayed his wife's labour as his own, it was she who demonstrated uncomplaining fortitude in the face of pains in which he likened to 'the pangs of eternal death'.

23   If women who were courageous in childbirth accrued complicated, competitive admiration from men, energetically religious mothering produced more straightforward praise. Sons whose mothers had toiled over their salvation knew from their own deep experience of maternal force what such efforts entailed. Unlike husbands who had impregnated their wives but been excluded from the redemptive suffering of labour, sons had been the object of mothers' strenuous efforts and sacrifices.

24   Cotton Mather described a good mother 'travail[ing] for her children more than once' to save them from the abominable sinfulness with which human birth had infected them. She was to work as hard as she could, instilling the principles of religion in her babies and catechizing them as soon as they could speak.

25   Perhaps the most fearsome aspect of a righteous mother was that she would rather see her children dead than living outside the grace of God. In Micheal Wigglesworth's famous epic, *The Day of Doom*, (1662) 'The tender mother will own no other/ of all her numerous brood/But such as stand at Christ's right hand/acquitted through his blood'. Mothers with this unique spiritual ferocity, who gave more importance to their children's salvation than to their physical lives, were exhibiting the highest form of human love a Puritan could imagine. And yet, it could engender the starkest fear.

26   Of all imagery pertaining to females, Puritans had the most positive associations with the lactating breast. In sermons, ministers used metaphors giving God, the father, the capacity to nurse his children. This potent symbol of security, warmth, and joy— the union of loving mother and nursing infant stood in stark contrast to the mother who would repudiate her unsaved offspring. In the eyes of a small child, the mother's immense power to give peace and happiness was paired with her ability to destroy forever the ease and hope of the unrepentant child.

27   The contrasting childhood images of perfect love and total terror persisted in the imaginations of children of such fervent mothers. In childbirth husbands saw wives resigned to God's will to sacrifice their own lives to create life. But the sons of deeply pious women remembered their mothers' seeming willingness to sacrifice *them* if their wickedness demanded it. Such fearsome, Janus-faced mothers undoubtedly contributed to men's admiration for female virtue at the same time that they implanted an abiding fear of powerful women.

28   Thomas Shepard recalled admiringly that his second wife cried and prayed in secret for her son, requesting that 'if the Lord did not intend to glorify himself by thee, that he would cut thee off by death rather than to live to dishonour him by sin'. His first wife, on the other hand, displayed the other ultimate motherly virtue.

29   In explaining to his son his mother's death, Shepard said that she 'died in the Lord, departing out of this world to another, who did lose her life by being careful to preserve thine, for in the ship thou wert so feeble and froward both in the day and night that hereby she lost her strength and at last her life'. The first Mrs. Shepard had sacrificed her life so that her child could live, and the second Mrs. Shepard was willing to sacrifice her *son* if his soul became corrupt. A mighty Puritan mother elicited both veneration and terror.

30   The sons of other spiritually influential women came up with more tranquil memories, formed from less terrifying maternal images. These men recalled prayerful women to whom love meant hawklike watchfulness for their sons' salvation. Thomas Shepard remembered that his own mother, who died when he was still young, bore 'exceeding great love to me and made many prayers for me'. In Increase Mather's *Autobiography* he called his mother, Cotton's grandmother, 'a very Holy, praying woman. She desired two things for him, he remembered; grace and learning. As a boy he learned to read from his mother. His father taught him to write, 'who also instructed me in grammar learning' in Latin and Greek. But, as Cotton later remembered, Increase's mother taught her son, his father, 'all that was good. . . among her Instructions . . . she mightily Inculcated the lesson of *Diligence*'.

31   Mather had often heard about his grandmother's potent combination of love and exhortation. He proudly recounted family lore: when Increase was very little his mother told him, that he was 'very much her *Darling*', and that all she wished for was to be a good Christian and a good scholar. She pleaded successfully on her deathbed that her 15-year-old son go into the ministry. She had been most 'honourable . . . for her *Vertue*, . . . that for which a *Woman* is most of all *to be Praised*'. She was Mather's model for his twice-travailing mother. He wrote 'She was a Woman of Uncommon Devotion, and in her Importunate Prayers for this her son, she . . . became *Twice a Mother* to him'. Mather's own mother had similar moral structure, challenging the family to live up to her example. Mather remembered her as 'a Godly, an Humble, and a Praying Woman, and one that often set apart *Whole Days* for prayer and Secret Interviews with Heaven'.

32   Frances Boland arrived in America from Scotland in 1682. In his journal he gave special thanks for the 'pious nurture and example of my godly mother . . . She was a praying woman and prayed much for her children'. He went on to say what a blessing it was for the young to have parents such as his.

33   John Dane, a surgeon in Ipswich, Massachusetts, remembered with respect that his mother had been a 'serious woman'. He recalled that she had once had a dream in which she heard a certain minister deliver a sermon; according to Dane's account she accurately foresaw the date, the place, and the text of that preacher's talk. Dane prudently did not praise his mother as a seer and mystic, which would have unsettled New World Puritans. Instead, he portrayed her as a sober student, indifferent to her gift of prophecy and desirous only to make 'good improvement of that sermon', which, thanks to her vision, she was able to enjoy twice.

34   The zealous mother was an exacting conscience to her children and, by extension, to the community.

Embedded in the Puritan notion of community was mutual moral responsibility and the notion that the sin of one member stained the whole society. Boys and girls both grew up cultivating the ability to spot a sin themselves and others. Cotton Mather wrote approvingly that his sister, Jerusha, recorded in her journal judgements on activities and behaviour of people in the community. He wrote that in her journal:

> She Remarks on the Dealings of God with Others; Especially if anything either Good or Bad were observable in the condition of the Town; But most of all what occur'd Joyful or Grievous, unto her nearest *Relatives*, and their Families; and she employes agreeable *Meditations* and *Supplications* there-upon.

35   Wives, in particular, were supposed to watch their husband's spiritual state. Benjamin Wadsworth had written that 'If Husbands that call themselves Christian, are vain, wicked, ungodly; their pious Wives (if such they have) should by a meek wining Conversation, indeavour their spiritual & eternal Good'. Christopher Lawson sued his wife for divorce in 1669, accusing her of failing in her duty as a converted Puritan to attend to the spiritual needs of her unconverted husband. 'The unbelieving husband', he wrote, 'should be wonn by the good conversation of the believing wife . . . '.

36   The Reverend John Ward praised his wife for being an 'accusing conscience' and letting him know when he was acting in an ungodly manner. Mather extolled Ward's wife who had lived happily with her husband for 40 years:

> Although she would so faithfully tell him of everything that might seem amendable to him . . . yet she ever pleased him wonderfully. And she would oft put him upon the duties of secret fasts, and when she met with anything in reading that she counted singularly agreeable, she would still impart it unto him.

The marriage of the Wards was an active spiritual partnership in which Mrs. Ward not infrequently gave her husband direction.

37   Women often achieved the role of conscience by becoming shadow ministers, absorbing, sometimes writing down (as Jerusha Mather did), and acting upon the weekly sermons of their husbands and/or pastors. Thomas Shepard commended his wife for her 'excellency to reprove for sin and discern the evils of men'. He went on to say that she loved the words of the Lord exceedingly and was, therefore, glad to read his notes for his sermons every week and ponder the thoughts therein.

38   Cotton Mather memorialized the second Mrs. Whiting for her 'singular piety and gravity', who prayed in her closet every day to God. He commended her for writing down the sermons that she heard 'on the Lord's days with much dexterity', while living by their messages all week.

39   Although Puritan traditions cast doubt on women's capacity for goodness and prohibited them from exercising concrete authority, Puritan women did achieve mortal stature from quietly enduring suffering, intense, dedication to the salvation of their children, and gentle correction of the behaviour of their spouses, and neighbours. The blessing Puritan men bestowed on notably virtuous women registered on the conflict in which it was born. Women had to criticise, suggest, and direct others—particularly men—with extreme caution as Puritan men were deeply alarmed when women presumed to judge them. Nonetheless, Puritan women, inclined to religious depth, would find respect and deference in their communities, no small treasures in a male-dominated world. And they would bequeath to later generations of women a tradition of moral criticism and the conviction that zealous effort on behalf of the salvation of others was part of their human responsibility. This belief would empower women to turn their moral energies upon their husbands, families, and in time, the world around them.

ROADS TO REVOLUTION

1 The change from dependency status to independent states was a slow, but a relentless process. It was an age when rapid communication was impossible. The fledgling North American colonies grew up quickly with little supervision. By the time the revolutionary period commenced in earnest, at the close of the French and Indian war in 1763, a new uniquely American character had already been formed. European wars over land rights merely hastened the process.

2 The dominant economic system of the seventeenth century was Mercantilism. Countries sought to acquire as much wealth as possible, at the expense of other nations. Colonial possessions were seen as aids in this endeavor. With this in mind, the Navigation Acts of 1651, 1660, 1663, and 1673 were passed. Briefly, these acts were designed to restrict colonial trade with all nations except Great Britain. Colonial commerce had to be routed through Britain. Transport had to be done on British ships with largely British crews. The point was simple: the colonies existed to help the "mother" country enrich herself.

3 Because of distance, bureaucratic inefficiency, and English preoccupation with domestic political concerns (*i.e.,* the king and Parliament arguing over who was in charge), the Navigation Acts were never strictly enforced. North American shippers did pretty much as they pleased. England had turned her back; the colonies prospered. . . .

4 In 1763 the situation changed. With their turf wars finally over, the British sought to solidify control over their North American possessions. But debt, to the tune of 137 million pounds sterling, plus distance, made this control virtually impossible. George Grenville, first Lord of the Treasury, moved quickly. Reasoning that the colonial tax load was light and that the colonies should naturally pay for the defense of their own property, Grenville enacted a series of measures designed to make the colonies more responsible. He also sought to renew crown authority in the area of colonial trade, an effort bitterly resisted by the colonies.

5 In the colonies, these efforts were seen as being similar to the actions of a long lost parent who suddenly needs help from his full-grown child. For most of the next 13 years, practically every effort by the British to raise money (taxes) or exercise control over the colonies was met with resistance by many in the colonies.

6 The British put forward the Royal Proclamation of 1763. This measure was designed to prevent colonial expansion west of the Appalachian Mountains, for the purpose of preventing Indian uprisings, and more expensive wars. Many colonials promptly ignored it. Parliament passed the Stamp Act in 1765, requiring the colonists to buy stamps to be fixed to printed matter and legal documents of many kinds: newspapers, pamphlets, almanacs, diplomas, leases, licenses, insurance policies, and the like. To the North American colonies, this was "taxation without representation," and protests up and down the Atlantic coast resulted. The act was repealed.

7 Boston became the hub of colonial discontent. Sam Adams organized the Sons of Liberty, a motley

group of ne'er do-wells bent on resisting British authority with a combination of economic intimidation and violence. Boycotts were the most effective message colonists could send to Parliament, but violence too was an option. On March 5, 1770 in Boston, British troops stationed in the city opened fire on a Boston mob, killing five. The attack galvanized radical support up and down the coast. Three years later, 15,000 pounds worth of British tea was dumped into the Boston Harbor in the famous Boston Tea Party.

8   King George III of England was an arrogant but bewildered man. Through a succession of prime ministers, he had sought a solution to the North American problem, but found none. By 1775, sporadic fighting had broken out. The goal of George III was clear: reassert royal control over the unruly North American colonists.

9   What was the purpose of fighting according to the colonial points of view? By early 1776, most colonists did not consider independence a viable option. The British crown, in the personage of George III, still had an almost mystical pull upon the back reaches of the collective colonial psyche.

10   Enter Mr. Thomas Paine. Paine wrote his famous pamphlet, *Common Sense*, in January, 1776, a time when most colonial citizens were not sure what they wanted, except to be left alone. Paine's accomplishment was to get the average "American" to think the unthinkable: they owed no allegiance to a man whose throne lacked legitimacy. Paine destroyed the king in the eyes of many colonial citizens. He also argued forcefully for independence, damaging the commonly held notion that the colonies still needed the "mother" country. Without allegiance to the king, and with no need for the mother country, Paine reasoned, why stay in the empire? Why not strike out on our own? To more and more citizens of North America, this began to make sense.

11

THE *REAL* FIRST WORLD WAR AND THE MAKING OF AMERICA

BY FRED ANDERSON

*It has taken us two and a half centuries to realize
just how important this conflict was*

The French and Indian War represented both the culmination and convergence of many strains of European colonization in America, as well as a departure from a trend toward multiple power competition in the American scene. The French were dealt a losing hand, though all colonial powers, including the English were going to fold in the years following the war. The Native populations were a key factor in the success or failure in European initiatives, but their gains in trade and connections were more than canceled out by losses from disease and European duplicity.

Fred Anderson identifies a number of ironies that pepper the story of the French and Indian War. None were so stark as that which befell Britain, victor in the war as that nation gained territory and prestige, but alternately a loser in European diplomacy as the fears and suspicions of other powers who allied in opposition to England's power. There was likewise a renewed vigor of a streamlined France stripped of the money-losing propositions of Canada and interior lands. Native tribes would stake their futures on England's power only to see it stripped away by the Colonials who had of late fought with their mother country against France but then turned on their masters.

The War with France set the stage for some of England's greatest challenges as a "imperial" power and forced their American subjects to decide whether or not they shared the English vision. The seductive allure of independence mixed with a sense of righteousness motivated the Colonials to act against their own mother country, and in the end cultivate the same imperial hubris, a natural inheritance bequeathed by the mother country to its spawn, and position the great Republic in line for the same sorts of historical setbacks that pained the English and similar empires.

- In what way is the word "imperial" used in the article?
- Where was the Ohio Valley in relation to tidewater colonies?
- Why did Europeans refer to the French and Indian war as the Seven Years War?
- What Native people were integral to events surrounding the war?

---

1   Two hundred and fifty years ago this winter, European courts and diplomats were moving ever closer to war. It would prove larger, more brutal, and costlier than anyone anticipated, and it would have an outcome more decisive than any war in the previous three centuries.

2   Historians usually call it the Seven Years' War. Modern Americans, recalling a few disconnected episodes—Braddock's defeat, the Fort William Henry "massacre," the Battle of Quebec—know it as the French and Indian War. Neither name communicates the conflict's immensity and importance. Winston Churchill came closer in *The History of the English-Speaking Peoples* when he called it "a world war—the first in history," noting that unlike the previous Anglo-French wars, this time "the prize would be something more than a rearrangement of frontiers and a redistribution of fortresses and sugar islands."

3   That prize was the eastern half of North America, and the war in which Britain won it raised, with seismic force, a mountain range at the midpoint of the last half-millennium in American history. On the far side of that range lay a world where native peoples controlled the continent. On the other side we find a different world, in which Indian power waned as the United States grew into the largest republic and the most powerful empire on earth. In that sense it may not be too much to give the conflict yet another name: the War That Made America.

4   Seeing what North America looked like on the far side of the Seven Years' War illuminates the changes the war wrought and its lingering influences. The traditional narrative of American history treats the "colonial period" as a tale of maturation that begins with the founding of Virginia and Massachusetts and culminates in the Revolution. It implies that the demographic momentum of the British colonies and the emergence of a new "American character" made independence and the expansion of Anglo-American settlement across the continent inevitable. Events like the destruction of New France, while interesting, were hardly central to a history driven by population expansion, economic growth, and the flowering of democracy. Indians, regrettably, were fated to vanish beneath the Anglo-American tide.

5   But if we regard the Seven Years' War as an event central to American history, a very different understanding emerges—one that turns the familiar story upside down. Seen this way, the "colonial period" had two phases. During the first, which lasted the whole of the sixteenth century, Indian nations controlled everything from the Atlantic to the Pacific, north of the Rio Grande, setting the terms of interaction between Europeans and Indians and determining every significant outcome. The second phase began when the Spanish, French, Dutch, and English established settlements in North America around the beginning of the seventeenth century, inaugurating a 150-year period of colonization and conflict by changing the conditions of American life in two critical ways. First, permanent colonies spread disease in their immediate vicinities; second, they radically increased the volume of trade goods that flowed into Indian communities. The results of this transformation were many, powerful, and enduring.

6   Epidemic diseases—smallpox, diphtheria, measles, plague—dealt a series of deadly blows to native populations. Ironically, the Indians nearest the European settlements, and who sustained the earliest and worst losses, also had the closest access to trade goods and weapons that gave them unprecedented advantages over more distant groups. As warriors raided for captives to prop up their dwindling populations and pelts to exchange for European weapons, wars among native peoples became ever more deadly. The Five Nations of the Iroquois, in what is now upstate New York, grew powerful in the mid-seventeenth century by trading with the Dutch at Fort Orange (Albany) and seizing captives from Canada to the Ohio Valley to the Carolinas. Iroquois power, of course, had its limits. Tribes driven west and north by their attacks forged alliances with the French, who supplied them with arms, and encouraged them to strike back.

7   The Iroquois were already under pressure when England seized New Netherland from the Dutch in 1664. This deprived the tribes of an essential ally when they could least afford it. Iroquois fortunes spiraled downward until the beginning of the eighteenth century, when the battered Five Nations finally adopted a position of neutrality toward the French and British empires.

8   The Iroquois soon found that this neutrality gave them a new form of power. They could play Britain and France off against each other in the wars that the contending empires fought during the first half of the eighteenth century. By the 1730s a half-dozen Indian groups—Cherokees, Creeks, Choctaws, Abenakis, and various Algonquians, as well as the Iroquois—were engaging in balance-of-power politics that made any maneuverings of the French, the British—and the Spanish too—indecisive. While it lasted, this balance permitted Indian and European groups to develop along parallel paths. When it ended, however, the whole edifice of native power came crashing down.

9   The Seven Years' War brought about that shift and, in doing so, opened a third American epoch, which lasted from the mid-eighteenth century to the beginning of the twentieth. The shift was not immediately perceptible, for from beginning to end the war reflected the importance of Indian power. The fortunes of war in North America ebbed and flowed according to when the Indian allies of the Europeans decided to engage or withdraw. When, in 1758, the

French-allied Indians on the Ohio chose to make a separate peace, Anglo-American forces could at last seize the Forks of the Ohio, the site of modern Pittsburgh and the strategic key to the trans-Appalachian West, bringing peace to the Virginia-Pennsylvania frontier. The following year the Iroquois League shifted from neutrality to alliance with the British, permitting the Anglo-Americans to take Fort Niagara and with it crucial control of the Great Lakes. In 1760 Iroquois diplomats preceding Gen. Jeffery Amherst's invading army persuaded the last Indian allies of New France to make peace, facilitating the bloodless surrender of French forces at Montreal.

The war was a momentous American turning point.

10   Recognizing the central role of Indians in the war certainly should not deny the importance of French and British operations in America or diminish the critical part played by the large-scale mobilization of the colonists. Those too were decisive and were part of the worldwide extension of the fighting. Britain's war leader, William Pitt, knew that the British army was too small to confront the forces of Europe on their home ground. He therefore used the navy and army together to attack France's most vulnerable colonies, while subsidizing Prussia and smaller German states to do most of the fighting in Europe. Similarly, from late 1757 Pitt promised to reimburse North America's colonial governments for raising troops to help attack Canada and the French West Indies, treating the colonies not as subordinates but as allies. This policy precipitated a surge of patriotism among the colonists. Between 1758 and 1760 the number of Anglo-Americans voluntarily participating in the war effort grew to equal the population of all New France.

11   Britain's colonists continued to enlist in numbers that suggest they had come to believe they were full partners in the creation of a new British empire that would be the greatest since Rome. Their extraordinary exertions made for a decisive victory, but one that came at a fearful cost. And that in turn had an impact that extended far beyond the Peace of Paris, which put an end to the hostilities in 1763.

12   Paradoxically, the war had seemed to damage the vanquished less than it did the victor. Despite the loss of its North American possessions and the destruction of its navy, France recovered with remarkable speed. Because the British chose to return the profitable West Indian sugar islands to France and to retain Canada, always a sinkhole for public funds, French economic growth resumed at pre-war rates. Because France funded its re-armament program by borrowing, there was no taxpayers' revolt. The navy rebuilt its ravaged fleet using state-of-the-art designs.

The army, re-equipped with the most advanced artillery of the day, underwent reforms in recruitment, training, discipline, and administration. These measures were intended to turn the tables on Britain in the next war, which was precisely what happened when France intervened in the American struggle for independence. (The expense of that revenge tempered its sweetness somewhat, but it was only in 1789 that King Louis and his ministers, facing a revolution of their own, learned how severe the reckoning would be.)

13   For Britain and its American colonies the war had complex, equivocal legacies. Pitt's prodigal expenditures and the expansion of the empire to take in half of North America created immense problems of public finance and territorial control. The virtual doubling of the national debt between 1756 and 1763 produced demands for retrenchment even as administrators tried to impose economy, coherence, and efficiency on a haphazard imperial administration. Their goal was both to control the 300,000 or so Canadians and Indians whom the war had ushered into the empire and to make the North American colonies cooperate with one another, take direction from London, and pay the costs of imperial defense.

14   The war's most pernicious effect, however, was to persuade the Crown that Britain was unbeatable. The extraordinary battlefield triumphs of the previous years made this inference seem reasonable, and the perilous conviction that Britannia had grown too mighty to fail contributed to the highhanded tone imperial officials now used to address the colonists and thus helped sow the seeds of revolution.

15.   Britain's American colonists had come to believe they were members of a transatlantic community bound together by common allegiance, interests, laws, and rights. Imperial administrators found this absurd. Even before the war they had been proposing reforms that would have made it clear the colonists were anything *but* legal and constitutional equals of subjects who lived in Britain. The outbreak of the fighting had suspended those reforms, and then Pitt's policies had encouraged the colonists to see the empire as a voluntary union of British patriots on both sides of the ocean.

16.   So when the empire's administrators moved to reassert the pre-war hierarchy, the colonists reacted first with shock, then with fury. What happened, they wanted to know, to the patriotic partnership that had won the war? Why are we suddenly being treated as if we were the conquered, instead of fellow conquerors?

17.   During the 12 years between the Peace of Paris in 1763 and the battles of Lexington and Concord the colonists clarified their beliefs, using language echoing the broad, inclusive spirit of equality that had rallied them during the late war. In time those ideas

became the basis of all our politics, but between 1763 and 1775 they were not yet founding principles. Rather, what took place in the postwar years was a long, increasingly acrimonious debate about the character of the empire, a wrangle over who belonged to it and on what terms and about how it should function. The dispute became so bitter precisely because the colonists believed they were British patriots who had proved their loyalty by taking part in a vast struggle for an empire they loved.

18   The irony here is intense and bears examining. The most complete victory in a European conflict since the Hundred Years War quickly became a terrible thing for the victor, whereas the defeated powers soon recovered purpose and momentum. Even a decisive victory can carry great dangers for the winner. Britain emerged from the war as the most powerful nation of its day, only to find that the rest of Europe feared it enough to join ranks against it; it confidently undertook to reassert itself in America only to unite its colonists in opposition to imperial authority. Finally, when Britain used its military might to compel the fractious colonists to submit, it turned resistance into insurrection—and revolution.

19   And what of the Indians? For them, the war's effects were transforming, and tragic. By eliminating the French Empire from North America and dividing the continent down its center between Britain and Spain, the Peace of Paris made it impossible for the Iroquois and other native groups to preserve their autonomy by playing empires off against one another. The former Indian allies of New France came to understand the tenuousness of their position soon after the war, when the British high command began to treat them as if they, not the French, had been conquered. They reacted with violence to Britain's abrupt changes in the terms of trade and suspension of diplomatic gift giving, launching an insurrection to teach the British a lesson in the proper relationship of ally to ally. By driving British troops from their interior forts and sending raids that once again embroiled the frontier in a huge refugee crisis, the Indians forced the British to rescind the offending policies. Yet by 1764, when various groups began to make peace, native leaders understood that their ability to carry on a war had become limited indeed. Without a competing empire to arm and supply them, they simply could not keep fighting once they ran out of gunpowder.

The war's effects were tragic for the Indians.

20   Meanwhile, the bloodshed and captive-taking of the war and the postwar insurrection deranged relations between Indians and Anglo-American colonists. Even in Pennsylvania, a colony that had never known an Indian war before 1755, indiscriminate hatred of Indians became something like a majority sentiment by 1764. When most native groups sided with the British in the Revolution, the animosity only grew. By 1783 Americans were willing to allow neither Indians nor the ex-Loyalists with whom they had cooperated any place in the new Republic, except on terms dictated by the victor.

21   In the traditional narrative mentioned earlier, the fate of native peoples is a melancholy historical inevitability; Indians are acted upon far more than they are actors. To include the Seven Years' War in the story of the founding of the United States, however, makes it easier to understand Indians as neither a doomed remnant nor as noble savages, but as human beings who behaved with a canniness and a fallibility equal to those of Europeans and acted with just as much courage, brutality, and calculated self-interest as the colonists. In seeking security and hoping to profit from the competition between empires, they did things that led to a world-altering war, which in turn produced the revolutionary changes that moved them from the center of the American story to its margins. No irony could be more complete, no outcome more tragic.

22   Finally, treating the Revolution as an unintended consequence of the Anglo-American quest for empire offers a way to understand the persistence of imperialism in American history. We like to read the rhetoric of the Revolution in such a way as to convince ourselves that the United States has always been a fundamentally *anti*-imperial nation. What the story of the Seven Years' War encourages us to do is to imagine that empire has been as central to our national self-definition and behavior over time as liberty itself has been—that empire and liberty indeed can be seen as complementary elements, related in as intimate and necessary a way as the two faces of a single coin.

23   Changing our thinking about the founding period of the United States by including the Seven Years' War can enable us to see the significance not only of America's great wars of liberation—the Revolutionary War, the Civil War, and World War II—but of the War of 1812, the Mexican War, the Spanish-American War, and all of the country's other wars for empire as well. Those conflicts are not exceptions to some imagined antimilitarist rule of American historical development; they too have made us who we are. To understand this may help us avoid the dangerous fantasy that the United States differs so substantially from other historical empires that it is somehow immune to the fate they have all, ultimately, shared.

12

THE FAMOUS TAX INCLUDED, TEA WAS STILL CHEAPER HERE

BY ROBERT CECIL

Did the American colonies win the American Revolution, or did the British simply lose it? In the following article, British historian Robert Cecil concentrates not so much on what the colonies did to win their independence, but upon the many blunders committed by the British to lose them.

This article details the political crisis leading up to the war in 1775. Since students of history most often receive the winning side's interpretation, they are seldom informed of the factors leading to the other side's defeat. Robert Cecil provides us with the opportunity to make comparative historical interpretations.

- *Were the colonials truly feeling repressed, or were they just feeling their oats?*
- *How does this British interpretation of the war differ from the traditional American viewpoint?*

---

1   In one way an Englishman's view of the Revolutionary War does not greatly differ from an American's. Our historians, in the main, agree with yours that the American colonies were lost through the mistakes and obstinacy of George III and Lord North and that the whole episode, whether regarded politically or militarily, is one of the most depressing in British history. It is at this point that the historians, and even more the ordinary readers, tend to part company. The Englishman, if he overcomes his reluctance to study the period at all, looks at it soberly and objectively and observes how hardly the imperial lesson was learned. Americans, on the other hand, very naturally regard the Revolution with the greatest enthusiasm as the starting point in a series of developments that led to the foundation of a **federal** republic unique in constitutional history, and to the remarkable political and economic expansion of the nineteenth century. The extraordinary later success of the United States, both in the economic and political sense, has to some extent led Americans to read their history backward and find in the Revolutionary War more signs and portents of a splendid future than were at that time apparent. This provides admirable material for July Fourth oratory, but stretches at places the fabric of history. After all, history is more than an ornamental garden, laid out with hindsight by teachers and historians; it is rather a jungle where living forces were once at work, and the reconstruction of this jungle is our real business if we wish to understand the past.

2   The first point that I want to suggest is that the conventional picture of the American colonists as a band of gallant pioneers oppressed by a tyrannous

---

federal: of, relating to, or being a form of government in which a union of states recognizes the sovereignty of a central authority while retaining certain residual powers of government.

government in London is a true one only if looked at through the eyes of a nineteenth or twentieth century democrat. The eighteenth century could have no inkling that the course of history would dictate that colonies in general should become self-administering and finally independent; indeed it was the shock of the American Revolutionary War that first began to teach that lesson. The eighteenth century regarded colonies as existing for the benefit of the mother country, with which, of course, the well-being of the colonies themselves was identified. **Adam Smith**, no enemy of the colonists, was the classic proponent of this theory. It is sometimes overlooked that the mother country accepted restraints on her own trade or agriculture in the interests of the colony, even if these restraints were of a less onerous character. For example, tobacco growing, although possible, was forbidden in Britain. Foreign produce, which was shipped via Britain, was cheap in the colonies, as duty had been paid by the British taxpayer. Adam Smith commented: "Parliament, in attempting to exercise its supposed right of taxing the Colonies, has never hitherto demanded of them anything which even approached to a just proportion to what was paid by their fellow subjects at home." To this very day, the British subject in the United Kingdom pays taxes at a much higher rate than any resident of the modern British colonies pays to his local administration.

3   Take next the question of defense. I quote again from Adam Smith: "If any of the provinces of the British Empire cannot be made to contribute towards the support of the whole Empire, it is surely time that Great Britain should free herself from the expense of defending those provinces in time of war . . . " The peace of 1763 had freed the colonists from the fear of attack by the French or Native Americans, and they naturally felt a greater degree of independence from the mother country. In Britain, however, the legacy of victory was a burden of debt and a strong feeling of dissatisfaction with the meager contribution, in men and money, that the colonists had made to their own defense. There was angry talk of contraband trade with the French in time of war. A particular grievance was that most colonies were reluctant even to provide adequate quarters for the British troops. This grievance had emerged even before the suspicion that the troops were more likely to be used against the colonists themselves.

4   When all this has been said, the fact remains that the British government acted with extraordinary stupidity. There was no settled policy of trying either to conciliate the colonists or to exert sufficient force to coerce them while it was still possible. The point I have tried to establish, however, is that the British acted within the framework of the accepted political and economic theory of the day and not out of some feeling of special animosity or desire to oppress the colonists. It is true that "no taxation without representation" was a political principle that many Britons had given their lives to affirm; but here again we are in danger of using hindsight in our interpretation of the word "representation."

5   England in the eighteenth century was not a democracy; it was an oligarchy, in which no practical politician, however liberal, seriously considered that all men had an equal right to elect the government that ostensibly represented them. A say in the government of the country was the privilege of those whose ownership of property and contribution to its greatness justified their claim. From this point of view a rotten borough in the hand of a great landowner was a way of ensuring that his contribution to the political and economic life of the nation received its due weight.

6   In the age of the **Whig oligarchy** and the rotten borough, there was little to convince Englishmen that the American colonists were being unjustly treated by not being represented at Westminster. It is clear to us today; it was a very debatable point in the eighteenth century. As a matter of fact, the colonists themselves, except the Pennsylvanians, did not take a very liberal view of the franchise for a good many years after the Revolutionary War. The British have never been strong on political theory; they could hardly be expected to realize that across the Atlantic the doctrine of John Locke and the Glorious Revolution of 1688 was believed more literally. Even less could they gaze into the future and divine that the course of the history of the next two centuries would vindicate the judgment of the American colonists. What they saw was a contumacious colony which paid less in taxes than they did, but would neither stand in arms to defend itself, nor pay for the mother country to do so.

7   Naturally the Americans objected to being taxed; we all do. They fought against the duties levied under the **Sugar Act of 1764**; the "non-importation" movement boycotted many English goods. The colonists objected even more strongly to an internal (that is, direct) tax, the Stamp Act of 1765, and justification for their position was found on constitutional grounds. **The Townshend Acts** then, in 1767,

---

Adam Smith: (1723–1790) Scottish political economist and philosopher who developed the theory of supply and demand.
Whig oligarchy: the elite leaders of the loyal opposition in eighteenth century England.
Sugar Act of 1764: tax on molasses.
Townshend Acts: (1767) levied duties on many items imported to the American colonies.

Boston Tea Party-Destruction of . . .

imposed a strong external (or indirect) tax, and this was resisted with equal, indeed memorable, vigor. What are we to say of the tea that was hurled into Boston Harbor? The tea had been exempted from the one shilling duty previously payable on transshipment in England and was taxed only threepence in the colonies. The same tea that cost an Englishman six shillings a pound cost the American only three. Yet John Adams wrote of the Boston Tea Party (1773): "Many persons wish that as many dead carcases were floating in the harbour as there are chests of tea." This is not the language of an oppressed people; it is the language of aggressive independence.

8   The plain fact is that the colonists believed (and events proved them right) that they were fully capable of managing their own affairs; they did not want any control, financial or otherwise. They were equally opposed to any restriction on the way in which they colonized the American continent. They had been made deeply apprehensive by the **Royal Proclamation of 1763**, which emphasized trade with the Native Americans and sought to protect them from the territorial encroachment of the whites. But the colonists themselves wished to colonize. Nobody had yet coined the phrase "manifest destiny," but the idea was there. If Britain was opposed, then freedom from Britain must be achieved.

9   This determination of the colonists to be free was scarcely understood in Britain; indeed their rapidly growing capacity to determine their own fate was lamentably underestimated in London. This explains the failure of the British government either to prepare for war or to make a settlement acceptable to the Americans. For it is probable that up to a very late hour a loose federation with George III as titular sovereign would have been acceptable to the Americans, provided that it carried with it full self-government. Meanwhile the British made no serious preparation. In 1774, at a time when General Thomas

---

Royal Proclamation of 1763: British attempt to prevent colonial expansion west of the Appalachian Mountains.

Gage in Boston was asking for 20,000 men, there were actually reductions both in the Army and Navy. In 1775, General William Howe and his brother Admiral Lord Howe were given the incompatible functions of Commissioners of Conciliation as well as commanders in chief. Inevitably the attack was not vigorously pressed for fear of prejudicing the **conciliation**; this at a time when George Washington was complaining of the spirit of the men under his command and the totally insufficient arrangements for supplying them. In 1776, Sir Guy Carleton with superior numbers trapped the American forces that had invaded Canada, but deliberately allowed them to escape, believing that a display of magnanimity might show them, as he put it, that "the way to mercy is not yet shut." Though the British were already making use of the Loyalists and the restless frontier tribes, who had long regarded the colonists as their principal enemy, the fighting continued to have some of the characteristics of a civil war; but this first phase was fast coming to an end. By July, 1776, German mercenaries were reaching New York in substantial numbers, and Jefferson, busy with his draft of the Declaration of Independence, referred with horror to their coming.

10   Meanwhile, in Paris, Silas Deane—and Benjamin Franklin not long after—was negotiating with the old enemy, the Catholic King of France. Lord Stormont, the British ambassador, had a shrewd idea of what was going on, but could not intervene openly. A steady stream of French, German, and Swiss volunteers was crossing in French vessels to the support of the American forces, while French loans and shipments of arms kept the new republic going during the desperate winters of 1776–77 and 1777–78, the winter of Valley Forge. That winter, even after the American forces that had taken part in the defeat of Burgoyne at Saratoga had joined Washington, the General estimated (in December, 1777) that he had only 8,200 fit men under his command. General Howe was unaccustomed, like all who learnt war in the European theater, to campaigning during the winter. He failed to realize that this was the decisive moment—before the French were finally committed to open intervention. Nothing was done and, in effect, the war was lost. It was lost because the limited, colonial war had become a renewal of the worldwide war with France that had merely been suspended in 1763. The French had used the interval to build up their fleet, and they were now able to concentrate it in Atlantic waters. Even before Spain with her Navy joined the Franco-American alliance in 1779, the British had virtually lost command of the sea, and this was bound to prove fatal.

11   In the first place, it was proving more and more difficult to protect trade and transport men and supplies to the American theater of war. Before the official French intervention took place in 1778, the depredation of American privateers, operating mainly from French ports, had already cost Britain 560 ships and losses equivalent to more than £1,800,000 at rates then current. In 1777, stores that had left England in March did not reach Howe till the end of May, and the summer campaign did not begin till August. Secondly, for their mobility the British forces in America relied to a very great extent on transport by water. Only on rare occasions were they able to operate effectively more than 15 miles from navigable water. Now all their movements were endangered. In 1778, when Clinton was evacuating Philadelphia, his entire army was almost intercepted at sea by a superior French fleet under D'Estaing. The sealing of Cornwallis' escape routes by the French fleet under De Grasse in 1781 was only the culmination. The capitulation of Yorktown that followed had been written on the wall three years before, for everyone but George III to see.

12   The retirement of General Howe in 1778 introduced a new handicap. While he was collaborating with his brother, Admiral Howe, relations between Army and Navy had been reasonably good. Afterward, however, old rivalries reasserted themselves. The British Navy was more interested in Rodney's operations in the Caribbean than in transport duty off the American coast. Howe's successor, General Clinton, quarreled with Admiral Marriot Arbuthnot, who had taken up command of the North American station in August, 1778. A British army officer bitterly observed of his brother naval officers: "They do not seem to think that saving the Army is an object of such material consequence." Cornwallis showed an incapacity for combined operations. Significantly enough, he later proved himself a capable general during the land struggle in India.

13   It is, of course, a truism that generals fight only as well as their opponents permit them to, and we must make every allowance for the genius of Washington, who not only kept his army together in the face of every difficulty but excelled in fighting the defensive war that circumstances imposed on him. He was one of the great leaders of irregular forces. Yet even so, the British generals were strangely inept. A contemporary commented: "This is an unpopular war and men of ability do not choose to risk their reputation." A shrewd contemporary observer regarded Benedict Arnold, in command of British forces, as superior to the *British* generals. The latter had been trained in the European school of set maneuver and siege warfare. Even their rigid discipline put them at the

---

conciliation: to overcome the distrust or animosity of; appease.

mercy of an irregular force, in which every man was his own company commander, if not his own colonel. The heavy equipment of the regulars immobilized them in the face of lightly equipped forces living off the land—their own land. The American terrain, thickly wooded and crisscrossed with streams and bogs, was unfamiliar to the British, and they failed notably to adapt themselves to it. Washington turned all these failings to good account.

14   What of the results of this **internecine** struggle? In the first place, of course, it welded the colonies into a union and equipped them with executive and legislative machinery and the means of defending themselves. This could have been accomplished so rapidly only under the pressure of war. The United States were now free not only to expand their commerce with any part of the world, but to populate the rich lands beyond the Alleghenies. In spite of a generous peace (1783), which astonished the French, relations with Britain did not fulfill the hopes of those in Britain who had always opposed **exacerbation** of the conflict. The War of 1812 reopened old wounds, and, as the nineteenth century continued, the scars still showed—more clearly perhaps in the United States than in the United Kingdom. I myself believe that some over-emotional and unhistorical presentations of the struggle constituted a real hindrance to harmonious Anglo-American relations. It is for consideration whether, even today, a fresh look should not be taken at some of the history textbooks of our two countries.

15   However that may be, any British view of the Revolutionary War must take into account what future generations of British statesmen learnt from it. Admittedly a generous offer of self-government in 1776, or even early in 1777, might conceivably have brought the war to an end while it could still be regarded as primarily a civil war; but the British did not formulate such an offer until too late. In February, 1778, Lord North was prepared to renounce the right to tax the colonists and to give them virtual autonomy in their own affairs; but by then the Continental Congress was unanimous for independence, and in May, 1778, the treaty with France was ratified. George III had clung too long to the contemporary idea of empire and his own concept of where his royal duty lay. Even a loose commonwealth connection might not have survived the strains and stresses of the Napoleonic Wars and Britain's blockade of Europe.

16   Leaving the field of speculation, we can be grateful that the American revolutionaries endowed with victory their great federal, republican experiment, without which the world would have been immeasurably poorer. We can rejoice, too, that Britain's failure in her first colonizing venture led thinking men to review the imperial relationship. Can anyone doubt that anything less than defeat could have caused the abandonment of Adam Smith's mercantile system, as applied to colonial territories? And but for this change of heart, the gradual transformation of a colonial empire into a commonwealth of self-governing, independent states could never have been accomplished.

---

internecine: of or relating to struggle within a nation, an organization, or a group.
exacerbation: to increase the severity, violence or bitterness of; to aggravate.

13

REVOLUTION WITH PEN & INK

BY WILLIAM C. KASHATUS

By January of 1776, the battles of Lexington, Concord, Bunker Hill, Montreal, and Quebec had been fought. Despite the bloodshed, there existed no consensus in the colonies as to why they were fighting. John Adams and Benjamin Franklin wanted independence. However, most British citizens in the 13 North American colonies favored reconciliation—a compromise with England.

On January 10, 1776, Thomas Paine published, anonymously, the pamphlet "Common Sense." Its impact was immediate and profound. Over 120,000 copies were sold, a runaway best seller by colonial standards. And it was influential. The writing was outrageous but persuasive. Simply put, Paine convinced Americans to think of themselves as just that: Americans. Previously, most "Americans" thought of themselves as British citizens and most still revered their king, George III. Paine changed that. He turned George III into an object of ridicule. He used words like "ruffian," "worm," and "ass." Paine wanted George III destroyed. Without that age-old relationship between king and citizen, between ruler and ruled, the last connection between England and America was removed.

Thomas Paine was a radical revolutionary. He hated George III for personal reasons, and authority in general for philosophical ones. Although he helped to set the tone for the American Revolution, the direction it took would soon pass him by. The historian Bernard Bailyn wrote: "The aim of Common Sense was to tear the world apart. (His) writing was not meant to reveal a future way of life . . . it was meant to overwhelm and destroy."

- *What was Paine's background? What qualified him for the role of radical revolutionary?*
- *Why was Paine's "American Crisis" so important to the Revolution?*
- *Why were the colonies "ripe for revolution" in the mid 1770's?*
- *How did Paine re-define the struggle with England?*
- *How was Paine different from the other "founding fathers?"*
- *What was the importance of "Common Sense" for the young revolution?*
- *Besides the British monarchy, what other forms of authority did Paine despise? Why?*
- *Why was Thomas Paine ignored when he died?*

---

1   By Christmas Eve 1776, the morale of the American troops has reached a low point. The British had forced General George Washington and his Continental Army to retreat from Brunswick to Trenton, New Jersey, and onto the western banks of the Delaware River in Pennsylvania. The British had set up camp on the rivers' east side. Once the Delaware froze hard enough for British forces to cross, Philadelphia itself would be within their grasp. If the British captured the patriot capital, all of

Pennsylvania, the keystone of the American states, would be vulnerable.

2 The American troops huddled around their campfires late in the afternoon of December 24. Dressed in shabby clothing and many with bandaged feet, they resembled little more than a ragtag band of backwoods fighters and forlorn militiamen. With the soldiers' spirits low and public support for American independence wavering, Washington feared for the Revolutionary cause. He resolved to make a stand, realizing that the clash would be a watershed in the colonial struggle for independence.

3 At nightfall, Washington ordered his officers to assemble the demoralized, poorly equipped, and greatly outnumbered troops and read to them Thomas Paine's *The American Crisis*. "These are the times that try men's souls," began the tract. "The summer soldier and the sunshine patriot will, in this crisis, shrink from the service of his country; but he that stands it NOW deserves the love and thanks of man and woman." Emboldened by Paine's words, Washington's men ferried across the ice-choked Delaware through a storm of hail and sleet on Christmas night and the following day they routed the Hessian mercenaries occupying Trenton. Paine's writing, once again, proved inspirational to the American cause.

4 Thomas Paine remains one of the most fascinating and enigmatic of all Revolutionary patriots. Born in Thetford, England, Paine lost his job as a poorly paid exciseman after trying to obtain better working conditions for his fellow workers. He left England and arrived in Philadelphia in November 1774 at the age of 37, carrying letters of introduction from Benjamin Franklin, whom he had met in London.

5 After the death of his first wife and an unhappy second marriage, Paine cared little about his appearance. His large, pendulous nose was the most striking characteristic of his ruddy face, which appeared hardened from years of drinking. Yet this unprepossessing individual would help instigate a great political revolution in America. A staunch idealist, Paine possessed a special gift for the inflammatory, using prose as his weapon. Historians have credited his 1776 pamphlet *Common Sense* with mobilizing popular support for the American cause. The pamphlet went through 25 editions and reached hundreds of thousands of readers in 1776 alone, making "innumerable converts" to independence. Similarly, his series of *American Crisis* essays restored the morale of the beleaguered Continental Army and the spirit of independence among a wavering American public at an important juncture in the Revolutionary War.

6 Paine's success rested with his unique ability to circulate among the highest and lowest orders of society. He worked hard to determine the political temper of the colonies, reading the newspapers of the day and frequently the taverns and coffeehouses of Philadelphia, to buttonhole anyone with an opinion. At the same time, Paine could express the ideas of the political elites in language that the uneducated masses understood, having arrived at many of the same conclusions out of his own experience.

7 Yet Paine could also be temperamental, obnoxious in his challenge to authority, and difficult to like. Where others restrained themselves from speaking openly of independence from Great Britain, Paine celebrated the concept of "revolution" and urged the colonists to follow suit. He was a radical gadfly who dedicated his life to the one and only thing he held dear—defending the God-given liberty of every man. No wonder John Adams, Congress's strongest advocate of American independence, both respected and feared him, remarking that "without the pen of Paine the sword of Washington would have been wielded in vain."

8 The North American colonies were ripe for revolution in the mid-1770s. After decades of loyalty to the Crown, the colonists' relationship with England was becoming strained. Saddled with a staggering £140 million debt from the Seven Years' War, Britain became financially dependent on the colonies and instituted a series of acts that used everything from tea to stamps to raise revenue. For the colonists, these acts, most of which restricted colonial trade, represented a sharp break with their long-held assumption that the British government would not interfere with the free pursuit of their economic interests. At the same time, Americans began to perceive Parliamentary policy as a systematic attack on their fundamental liberties as British subjects. The strongest resistance to these measures came from Massachusetts, where colonists boycotted British goods and destroyed tea in opposition to the new taxes.

9 On June 1, 1774, Parliament responded by closing the port of Boston until damages were paid. British lawmakers eliminated due process in colonial judiciary proceedings and gave the royal colonial governor the power to limit town meetings to as few as one a year. These so-called "Coercive Acts" were clearly designed to punish the Massachusetts colonists and intimidate any other colony that planned to resist imperial policy. Instead, the acts only served to unite the colonies in a common cause.

10 On September 5, 1774, delegates from 12 colonies convened in Philadelphia at the First Continental Congress. They declared the Coercive Acts void, urged Massachusetts to form an independent government, advised the people to arm themselves, and adopted economic sanctions against Britain. On October 14 the delegates passed their own *Declaration and Resolves*, which claimed for the colonial assemblies exclusive power of legislation subject only to royal veto. Their argument was, after all, against Parliament, not King George III. Nor did

they seek to alienate themselves from British rule, but to effect a reconciliation of differences by asserting their rights as British subjects. At least that was the colonial objective until Thomas Paine redefined their struggle.

11   When Paine arrived in Philadelphia, he found employment as an editor of the *Pennsylvania Magazine*. While the printer, Scotsman Robert Aitken, set the policies for the newspaper, ensuring that all articles would "avoid the suspicion of prejudice on the controversial issues of religion and politics, "Paine managed the operation's day-to-day business. He also submitted nearly a fourth of all published articles, going by the pseudonyms of "Atlanticus," "Aesop," and "Vox Populi."

12   Most of Paine's early contributions were light-hearted, informative essays that resulted in dramatic increase in circulation from 600 to more than 1,500 readers over a four-month period. Yet his best works were those in which he violated Aitken's policy by lashing our against England's rule. "When I reflect on Britain's involvement in the most horrid of all traffics, that of human flesh," Paine wrote in a March 1775 editorial attacking slavery. "I hesitate not for one moment to believe that the Almighty will finally separate American from Britain." Paine wasn't the first to raise the suggestion that the causes of American independence and abolitionism were closely related. Dr. Benjamin Rush, a prominent Philadelphia physician and member of the Continental Congress, has done so three years earlier. But Paine repeated the suggestion at a time when Americans were more receptive to those issues, making his writing more inflammatory as well as more relevant to American circumstances.

13   Following the British attack at Lexington and Concord in April 1775, Paine became even more vehement in his literary assault. Criticizing both King George and Parliament for sending troops "not for the defense of natural rights, but for the suppression of them," Paine urged Americans to "fight to defend their property as well as their political liberty."

14   Then Paine accused the British government of limiting the "social and political opportunities" of American women and encouraging Indians to attack innocent white settlers, making them the "tools of treachery and murder." He concluded with the prophetic statement, "the Almighty will separate America from Britain. Call it independence or what you will, it is the cause of God and humanity, and it will go on."

15   Aitken had read enough. He paid Paine for his last essay and told him to seek employment elsewhere. Nevertheless, the colonists wanted to read more. The British attacks on Lexington and Concord evoked greater sympathy for the American cause than had existed before. That is why Paine condemned the "obstinate American attachment to Britain" as well as those who hoped for reconciliation. "It was time to stir," he spoke up in the press. "Those who has long been settled has something to defend, those who had just come had something to pursue; and the call was equal and universal." Paine called for independence.

16   The writer saw America as an incubator for democracy where he could help champion the universal rights of all men. What's more, he eagerly wrote for public consumption what few of the delegates to the Continental Congress had dared to state in private, for fear of committing treason. Predictably, Congress's greatest advocates of an independent America-members like—Benjamin Franklin and Benjamin Rush—used Paine to test public opinion before making a definitive commitment themselves. They encouraged him to detail his arguments in a single pamphlet. Paine obliged by writing *Common Sense*.

17   From late autumn 1775 until the publication of the tract in January 1776, Paine spent his days in his rented rooms along the Philadelphia waterfront, writing about revolution. At nightfall, he visited taverns to engage in political debate and drink. Paine was a painstakingly diligent writer. A brief paragraph might take him days or even weeks, because he scrutinized each sentence and checked and rechecked his punctuation and spelling. When he needed money he contributed a short story or poem to one of the local newspapers. The editor would pay him a small sum, enough to survive a few days more, so he could work on his masterpiece.

18   Finally, on January 10, 1776, Paine published *Common Sense*, a 47-page pamphlet that advocated American independence in language the common man could understand and, ultimately, defend. He depicted King George as a tyrant, a co-conspirator with Parliament in an attempt to destroy the natural rights of the American colonists. Paine used strong, richly graphic images that aroused anger in his reader, comparing George to a "father-king" who relished his children, the Americans, as his main meal. "Even brutes do not devour their young," Paine exclaimed. "Out of fear for their freedom, many have fled England to America" in the hope of "escaping the cruelty of the monster."

19   Paine believed that monarchy was useless, having "little more to do than make war and give away places at court." He argued that "Americans should not feel any obligation to a crowned ruffian who sanctions war against them." Nor did Paine spare any criticism of the mixed constitution of Great Britain, considered at the time to be the most perfectly balanced form of government in the world with its divisions of King, Lords, and Commons.

20   "Why is the constitution of England so sickly?" Paine asked. "Because the monarchy hath poisoned the republic, the crown hath engrossed the commons." He believed a free America would do well to

learn from England's mistakes and draft a republican constitution with annual assemblies and a president who would be chosen each year from a different colony. A unicameral legislature would be empowered to pass laws, but only by a three-fifths majority. "Let this republican charter be brought forth placed on the divine law, the word for God," he urged. "Let a crown be placed thereon, so that the world may know, that in America THE LAW IS KING."

21   After his assault on monarchy and hereditary succession, Paine turned to the "present state of American affairs." He argued that the situation has become so intolerable that Americans must "cease negotiating for a repeal of the Parliamentary acts and separate from England." By declaring her independence, America would ensure a strong, lasting commerce, the happiness of its people, and protections from a hopelessly corrupt Europe. Almost like a preacher urging his congregation to embark on a divinely inspired mission, Paine urged his readers: "O! Ye that love mankind! Ye that dare oppose not only the tyranny but the tyrant, stand forth!"

22   *Common Sense* struck a resounding chord within the American conscience. The timing couldn't have been better. Only a few days before its release, King George delivered his opening speech to Parliament calling for suppression of the American rebellion. *Common Sense* gave the Crown a direct and unequivocal response. It proved to be an immediate success, being instantly copied, parodied, and translated into the language of every country that sympathized with the American cause. Nearly 120,000 copies were sold in the first three months after its release, and by the end of the year about 500,000 copies had found their way into bookstores, private libraries, and taverns in both Europe and America. The widespread distribution and huge readership of the tract resulted in the appearance of pamphlets, broadsides, and newspaper articles devoted to the controversial issue of American independence.

23   While some patriots, like Washington and Governor Edmund Randolph of Virginia, applauded Paine's work, there were some strong voices of opposition. John Adams, for example, feared the effect "so popular a pamphlet might have among the people." While he believed the work to be a "very meritorious production" and agreed with its call for American independence, Adams took great exception to Paine's plans for government. "Such a unicameral system," he warned, "was so democratic without any restraint or even an attempt at any equilibrium, that it must produce confusion and every evil work."

24   Paine wasn't a constitutional theorist. His task was tearing down governments, not creating them. While Congress eventually adopted his suggestion for a unicameral legislature and incorporated it into the Articles of Confederation, it proved to be a dismal failure, just as Adams had feared. Yet at the same time, *Common Sense* convinced many Americans who had previously been neutral on the subject of independence that a monarchy could no longer address their needs and that they should separate from England.

25   On July 2, 1776, when Congress voted for American independence, Paine's efforts were realized. He didn't seek personal fortune or fame, however, and downplayed his achievement, contributing whatever profits he made from the sale of his work to the Continental Army. Always restless as an observer, Paine yearned to be at the center of events. When the war turned against the Americans that year, Paine joined a ragtag group of Pennsylvania volunteers called the Associators in July 1776 and enlisted in the army where General Nathanael Greene took him on as his aide-de-camp.

26   While serving in the army, Paine worked to maintain its morale and secure foreign support for the patriot cause. Between December 1776 and April 1783 he wrote a series of 13 essays, later published collectively as the *American Crisis*. In these essays, Paine played upon the hatred of the British to stir the American public into greater support for the war as well as to attract a foreign military alliance. He reflected on the nature of the difficulties the Continental citizen-soldier experienced as he fought prolonged war over a wide expanse of territory. He also criticized those Americans who refused to take up the patriot cause, even if they based their noncompliance on religious scruples.

27   Appointed by Congress to its Committee on Foreign Affairs in 1777, Paine became embroiled in an incident known as the Silas Deane affair. Congress recalled Deane, an American agent in France, from his post in Paris after hearing allegations that he had become involved in private arms dealing before the signing of a French-American alliance. Paine proceeded to slander Deane in the newspapers, supporting his accusations by referring to confidential papers. In so doing, he not only compromised his position as a diplomat but also publicly revealed that France had, indeed, negotiated with the rebellious colonies while still at peace with Britain. Under pressure from the French ministry, Paine resigned his position on January 8, 1779.

28   Two years later, he made a much better impression on France when he traveled there with John Laurens, envoy of the Pennsylvania Assembly. They returned with both money and supplies for the Continental Army. Despite his success, however, Paine earned no recognition for his role in the mission.

29   Returning to England in 1787, he soon became embroiled in the political debate ignited by the French Revolution. His *Rights of Man*, which

defended the Revolution against the attacks of British Parliamentarian Edmund Burke, proved to be even more inflammatory than *Common Sense.* Charged with seditious libel for advocating an end to monarchy in Britain, Paine escaped to France, where electoral assemblies elected him to the French National Convention. Once again, however, he fell out of the good graces of the government and spent almost a year in prison. While living in France, he wrote his final great work, *Age of Reason,* attacking the basic principles of Christianity.

30   In 1802 Paine eventually returned to America a bitter, disillusioned man. The attacks on organized religion in *Age of Reason* caused waves of anger around the nation. Now considered "a person to be avoided, a character to be feared," he lived the final years of his life as an outcast. The 72-year-old writer died in New York City on June 8, 1809.

31   Today, Thomas Paine's *Common Sense* is widely regarded as a powerful expression of the American mind, just a step below the Declaration of Independence. His greatest legacy, however, was his faith in the ability of common people to determine their own political destiny. That faith allowed Paine to define a new vision of America as an asylum for universal freedom.

14

THE ROCKY ROAD TO REVOLUTION

BY JOHN FERLING

*While most members of Congress sought a negotiated
settlement with England, independence advocates bided
their time*

When the musical **1776** opened on Broadway when I was in fifth grade, my family
and I watched as our founding fathers sang their way to independence. The play had
its light, whimsical moments but it also told a more complex story of American independence than 57 men, who wholeheartedly agreed that the 13 colonies should
break away from Great Britain. The Continental Congress that met in 1775 and 1776
were men with various agendas and had different goals in mind when they met in
Philadelphia.

    The majority of the Congress were reluctant to dissolve their ties to the greatest
empire on earth. They had too much to lose. Not until Thomas Jefferson penned the
Declaration of Independence in June of 1776 did most congressional delegates support the break-up. Even then Jefferson's masterpiece was subjected to over 80 changes
by his fellow congressmen. He called those changes mutilations. The Declaration's
clause calling for the abolition of slavery was removed from the original document to
satisfy the southern delegation. By early July, the document met the approval of most
members and independence was declared. But as one delegate stated it was "a leap
into the dark" for all those involved.

- *Why did it take over a year to declare independence from Great Britain after the
  initial hostilities broke out?*
- *How was the Declaration of Independence a necessary instrument of
  propaganda?*
- *Why were most congressional delegates reluctant to break ties with Great
  Britain?*
- *Why did John Adams support a declaration of independence? Why did John
  Dickinson oppose independence?*
- *What were the issues that divided the Continental Congress?*
- *Why did the Reconciliationists differ from the pro-independence faction? How did
  the region where one lived affect one's position on independence?*
- *Why did proponents of independence believe that without a complete break-up
  with Great Britain, victory would be impossible?*

1   *We hold these truths to be self-evident, that all men are created equal, that they are endowed by their Creator with certain unalienable Rights, that among these are Life, Liberty and the pursuit of Happiness—That to secure these rights, Governments are instituted among Men, deriving their just powers from the consent of the governed . . .*

2   Laboring at his desk in the midst of a Philadelphia heat wave in June 1776, Thomas Jefferson hastened to complete a pressing assignment. A Congressional committee, recognizing his "happy talent for composition," had given the 33-year-old Jefferson responsibility for drafting a declaration of independence, a document that Congress needed almost immediately. Jefferson, one of Virginia's seven delegates to the Second Continental Congress, worked in his two-room apartment on the second floor of a tradesman's house at Market and Seventh streets, a heavily trafficked corner. He rose before sunrise to write and, after the day's long Congressional session, he returned to his lodging to take up his pen again at night. Toward the end of his life, Jefferson would say that his purpose had been to "place before mankind the common sense of the subject." Congress, he recalled, required an "expression of the American mind."

3   Jefferson well knew that America was at a defining moment in its history. Independence would sever ties with a long colonial past and propel the 13 states—and the new American nation to which they would belong—into an extremely uncertain future. Jefferson also knew that Congress wanted the declaration completed by July 1, less than three weeks after he was given the assignment.

4   No one appreciated better than he the irony in the sudden desire for haste. Jefferson had been prepared to declare independence perhaps as much as a year earlier, from the moment that war against the mother country erupted on April 19, 1775. Yet Congress had refused. In the 14 months since American blood had been shed at Lexington and Concord, American soldiers had also died at Bunker Hill, in the siege of Boston, and during an ill-fated invasion of Canada. In addition, the Royal Navy had bombarded and burned American towns, and the colonists' commerce had been nearly shut down by a British blockade. Still, Congress had not declared independence.

5   But not even Jefferson, passionate advocate of independence that he was, fully grasped the importance of the document he was preparing. Nor did his colleague, John Adams of Massachusetts, who had masterminded the arduous struggle within Congress to declare independence. Focused singlemindedly on that contentious undertaking, Adams regarded the actual statement itself as a mere formality—he would call it "a theatrical show"—a necessary instrument of propaganda. Jefferson, for his part, said little about his accomplishment. Not long after his work was completed, he would depart

Philadelphia to return to his responsibilities in the Virginia legislature. Still, he was more than mildly vexed that Congress had made revisions—or "mutilations," as he put it—to the language of his original draft. Historians now agree that Congress' alterations and excisions enhanced the Declaration's power. Jefferson's magisterial opening passage, and indeed, much of his original language, actually survived intact.

6   Today, the passage of time has dulled our memory of the extent to which many Americans, including a majority in the Continental Congress, were, for a very long period, reluctant to break ties completely and irrevocably with Britain. The creation of the document we have come to regard as the seminal expression of revolutionary ardor was by no means inevitable. More than two-and-a-quarter centuries after the Declaration was signed, this eloquent assertion of individual rights, reinstalled last September in a state-of-the-art glass encasement at the National Archives in Washington, D.C., can be assessed in all of its complexity—as the product of the protracted political debate that preceded its formulation.

7   By the summer of 1776, the patience of many congressmen had been sorely tried by bitter wrangling over the question of whether or not to declare independence. Many of the legislators thought it nonsensical to fight a war for any purpose other than independence, yet others disagreed. For month after bloody month Congress had sat on its hands, prompting John Adams to exclaim early in 1776 that America was caught "between Hawk and Buzzard," fighting a war it could not win unless it declared independence from Britain, thereby prompting England's enemies, most prominently France, to aid in the struggle.

8   America's war with the mother country had commenced when a British army of nearly 900 men, acting on orders from London, had marched from Boston to Concord, intending to destroy a colonial arsenal and, if possible, capture ringleaders John Hancock and Samuel Adams. The Second Continental Congress, which assembled in Philadelphia just three weeks later, had barely been gaveled to order when John Rutledge of South Carolina, a 35-year-old lawyer from Charleston, raised the critical question: "Do We aim at independancy? or do We only ask for a Restoration of Rights & putting of Us on Our old footing [as subjects of the crown]?" It would take Congress 14 months to answer that question.

9   Congress quickly divided into two factions. One felt that the British actions at Lexington and Concord in April required nothing less than a clean break from the motherland; they believed colonists would always be second-class citizens in the British Empire. This faction would have declared independence in May or June 1775. But a second faction, which comprised a substantial majority in Congress, yearned to

be reconciled with Britain. These delegates believed in waging war only to compel London to accept America's terms—Rutledge's "old footing"—to return to the way things were before Parliament tried to tax Americans and claim unlimited jurisdiction over them.

10   Opposition to Parliament had been growing since it enacted the first American tax, the Stamp Act of 1765. At the First Continental Congress, which met in Philadelphia in September 1774, some delegates wanted to force repeal of Parliament's repressive measures through a trade embargo. A more conservative faction had pushed for a compromise to provide American representation in Parliament. In the end, Congress adopted the trade boycott, and war had come. "Nothing," wrote John Adams, "but Fortitude, Vigour, and Perseverance can save Us."

11   Most who had attended the First Continental Congress now sat in the Second, where they were joined by several fresh faces. For instance, Hancock, who had escaped capture at Lexington thanks to Paul Revere's timely warning, was now a member of the Massachusetts delegation. Sixty-nine year old Benjamin Franklin, who had just returned to Philadelphia after a decade in London, had been named a delegate from Pennsylvania. Gone were those from the First Continental Congress who refused to countenance a war against Britain, prompting Richard Henry Lee of Virginia to observe that a "perfect unanimity" existed in the Second Continental Congress, at least on the war issue.

12   John Adams concurred that a "military Spirit" that was "truly amazing" had seized the land. Militiamen were "as thick as Bees," he said, marching and drilling everywhere, including in the steamy streets outside the Pennsylvania State House where Congress met. His cousin, Samuel Adams, believed an equally militant spirit gripped Congress and that every member was committed to "the Defence and Support of American Liberty." The Adams cousins soon discovered, however, that while all in Congress supported the war, sentiment for severing ties with Britain was strong only in New England and Virginia. Reconciliationists prevailed everywhere else.

13   John Adams counseled patience. "We must Suffer People to take their own Way," he asserted in June 1775, even though that path might not be the "Speedyest and Surest." He understood that to push too hard for independence was to risk driving conservative Americans back into Britain's arms. Thus, for most of 1775, the pro-independence faction never spoke openly of a break with Britain. Adams likened America to that of "a large Fleet sailing under Convoy. The fleetest Sailors must wait for the dullest and slowest." For the foreseeable future, he lamented, "Progress must be slow."

14   But Adams was confident that those who favored reconciliation would be driven inexorably toward independence. In time, he believed, they would discover that London would never give in to America's demands. Furthermore, he expected that war would transform the colonists' deep-seated love for Britain into enmity, necessitating a final break.

15   Reconciliationists were strongest in the Middle Atlantic colonies (New York, New Jersey, Pennsylvania, Maryland and Delaware) and in South Carolina, all of which had long since been drawn into the economic web of the Atlantic world. Before the war, the products of the backcountry—furs, hides and lumber—as well as grain, had moved through New York and Philadelphia to markets in the Caribbean and England. Charleston exported indigo and rice. In return, English-manufactured goods entered the colonies through these ports. Business had flourished during most of the 18th century; in recent years Philadelphia's merchants had routinely enjoyed annual profits of more than 10 percent.

16   The great merchants in Philadelphia and New York, who constituted a powerful political force, had other compelling reasons for remaining within the empire. Many relied upon credit supplied by English bankers. The protection afforded to transatlantic trade by the Royal Navy minimized insurance and other overhead costs. Independence, Philadelphia merchant Thomas Clifford asserted in 1775, would "assuredly prove unprofitable." The "advantages of security and stability," said another, "lie with . . . remaining in the empire."

17   And there was fear of the unknown. Some in Congress spoke of a break with Britain as a "leap in the dark," while others likened it to being cast adrift on "an Unknown Ocean." To be sure, many things *could* miscarry should America try to go it alone. After all, its army was composed of untried soldiers led, for the most part, by inexperienced officers. It possessed neither a navy nor allies and lacked the funds to wage a lengthy conflict. The most immediate danger was that the fledgling nation might lose a war for independence. Such a defeat could unleash a series of dire consequences that, the reconciliationists believed, might be avoided only if the colonies, even in the midst of war, were to negotiate a settlement *before* breaking absolutely with Britain. The reconciliationists held that it was still possible to reach a middle ground; this view seemed, to men such as John Adams, a naive delusion. Finally, the anti-independence faction argued, losing the war might well result in retaliation, including the loss of liberties the colonists had long enjoyed.

18   Even victory could have drawbacks. Many felt independence could be won only with foreign assistance, which raised the specter of American dependence on a European superpower, most likely autocratic and Roman Catholic France. But Adams believed that fear of anarchy accounted for most

conservative opposition to independence. More than anything, said Adams, it rendered "Independency . . . an Hobgoblin, of so frightfull Mein" to the reconciliationists.

19   Pennsylvania's John Dickinson soon emerged as the leader of those who sought rapprochement with Britain. Dickinson, who was 43 in 1775, had been raised on plantations in Maryland and Delaware. One of the few supporters of the war to have actually lived in England, where he had gone to study law, in London, he had not been impressed by what he found there. The English, he concluded, were intemperate and immoral; their political system was hopelessly corrupt and run by diabolical mediocrities. Returning to Philadelphia to practice law in 1757, he was soon drawn to politics.

20   Tall and thin, Dickinson was urbane, articulate and somewhat prickly. A patrician accustomed to having his way, he could be quick-tempered with those who opposed him. He had once brawled with a political adversary and challenged him to a duel. Early in the Second Continental Congress, following an incendiary speech by Adams, Dickinson pursued him into the State House yard and, in a venomous outburst, as recounted by Adams, demanded: "What is the reason, Mr. Adams, that you New England-men oppose our Measures of Reconciliation. . . . Look Ye," he threatened, "If you dont concur with Us, in our pacific System, I, and a Number of Us, will break off from you . . . and We will carry on the Opposition by ourselves in our own Way." Adams was infuriated by Dickinson's invective: the two never spoke again.

21   Dickinson had a distinguished record. In 1765 he had served in the Stamp Act Congress convened to protest that measure. Two years later, he published his cogent and illuminating *Letters from a Farmer in Pennsylvania*, America's most popular political tract before 1776, which assumed that Parliament, though possessed of the right to regulate trade, lacked authority to tax the colonists. That was the very stand taken by 1774's First Continental Congress, and a constitutional settlement along those lines—not independence—was what the reconciliationists hoped to achieve through war. Dickinson charged that London had launched an "inexpressibly cruel War." Its "Sword is opening our Veins," he said, compelling Americans to fight for their freedom.

22   But he also warned that a war for independence would be interminable. British prime minister Lord Frederick North had pledged an implacable fight to maintain "every Advantage" that Britain derived from its control of the colonies. Before any war for independence ended, Dickinson prophesied, Americans would have "tasted deeply of that bitter Cup called the Fortunes of War." Not only would they have to "wade thro Seas of Blood," but in due course, hostilities would bring on massive unemployment within the maritime trades, heinous cruelties along the frontier, slave insurrections in the South and the relentless spread of disease from armies to civilians. And even in the unlikely event independence was achieved, Dickinson argued, yet another catastrophe might well lie in store: France and Spain would destroy the infant United States. In contrast, a war for reconciliation would be short-lived. Confronted with "a bloody & tedious Contest attended with Injury to their Trade," Lord North's government would collapse. Its successor would be compelled to accept Congress' terms: American "Dependence & Subordination" on the Crown, but with it a recognition from London that Parliament's only power over the colonies was the regulation of American trade.

23   Given Dickinson's position as a longtime foe of Parliamentary taxation, it was only to be expected that he would emerge as a leader in Congress. Adams' rise, however, was a different story. When he became leader of the independence forces—what one contemporary observer, Dr. Benjamin Rush, described as the "first man in the House"—many were caught by surprise. Before his election to Congress in 1774, Adams was largely inexperienced in public life. He had served only one term in the Massachusetts assembly and had not even headed the Massachusetts delegation at the First Congress—cousin Sam had assumed that responsibility.

24   Forty years old in 1775, John Adams had grown up on a small farm just south of Boston, where his father moonlighted as a shoemaker to earn the money to send his oldest son to Harvard. Like Dickinson, Adams had practiced law, and also like him, had advanced rapidly. Within a dozen years of opening his law office, Adams maintained the heaviest caseload of any attorney in Boston. Unlike Dickinson, Adams was initially wary of the American protest against British policies, believing that the ministry had simply erred in its actions and might be expected to mend its ways. He had been converted to open support of the popular cause only in 1773.

25   Adams came to keenly desire a leadership role, but feared that his physical limitations—he was portly and balding—and irascible manner would frustrate his ambitions. Furthermore, he was no jovial backslapper. Gruff and argumentative, he was maladroit when it came to talking about what he regarded as the favorite topics of men: dogs, horses and women. Nevertheless, those who penetrated his churlish exterior discovered a good-natured, self-effacing and exceptionally bright individual. And he possessed the skills needed to be an effective legislator. He was tireless, a skilled debater, an incisive, if not flamboyant, orator and a trenchant thinker. He quickly won a reputation as the Congressional authority on diplomacy and political theory. His colleagues found him to be unfailingly well prepared, prudent, honest and trustworthy—in

26   short, just the man to follow in this high-stakes endeavor.

26   The first issue to truly divide the Second Continental Congress arose early on. In May 1775, as it considered the creation of the Continental Army, Dickinson insisted on petitioning the king with what he characterized as a "Measure of Peace." Adams privately branded it a "Measure of Imbecility" and raged that some delegates, at least those from the mercantile colonies of New York and Pennsylvania, were "selfish and avaricious." For those congressman, he charged, "a ship [was] dearer than" the lives of Continental soldiers. In October 1774, the First Continental Congress had petitioned the monarch; Adams feared that to do so again was to risk appearing weak. Franklin concurred. "It is a true old saying," he remarked, "that *make yourselves sheep and the wolves will eat you.*"

27   Nevertheless, the independence faction wanted no confrontation with Dickinson's at this crucial juncture of the war, and the Olive Branch Petition, as the peace measure was known, was approved, though only after a contentious debate over its wording. Richard Penn, a former governor of Pennsylvania, carried it to England. Franklin advised a London friend, a director of the Bank of England, that this was Britain's last hope for preventing "a total Separation" by the colonies. To another friend in England he wrote: "If you flatter yourselves with beating us into submission, you know neither the [American] people nor the country."

28   Soon after the debacle at Quebec, John Adams observed that there now existed "no Prospect, no Probability, no Possibility" of reconciliation. Late in February came still more stunning news. Congress learned that Parliament had enacted the American Prohibitory Act, shutting down all trade with the colonies and permitting seizure of colonial vessels. John Adams called the law "a Gift" to the pro-independence party. Virginia's Richard Henry Lee concurred, saying that it severed the last ties with the mother country. It was "curious," he stated, that Congress yet hesitated to declare independence when London had already "put the two Countries asunder."

29   As spring foliage burst forth in Philadelphia in 1776, ever larger numbers of Americans were coming round to independence. The "Sighing after Independence" in Massachusetts, said James Warren, speaker of the colony's House of Representatives, had become nearly "Universal." By mid- May every Southern colony had authorized its delegates to vote for breaking off ties with Britain.

30   Within Congress, emotions ran high. "I cannot conceive what good Reason can be assignd against [independence]," Samuel Adams railed in mid-April. He exclaimed that the "Salvation of the Country depends on its being done speedily. I am anxious to have it done." John Adams maintained that had independence been declared months earlier, America's armies would already possess French arms. Elbridge Gerry, a Massachusetts delegate, complained that "timid Minds are terrified at the Word Independency," while Franklin deplored those who clutched at the "vain Hope of Reconciliation." As for General Washington, he said he believed that Congress had "long, & ardently sought for reconciliation upon honourable terms," only to be rebuffed at every turn. He had long been of the opinion that "all Connexions with a State So unjust" should be broken.

31   Still, the reconciliationists held out, encouraged by a passage in the Prohibitory Act that authorized the monarch to appoint commissioners to grant pardons and to receive the grievances of colonists. Dickinson and his followers viewed the appointees as peace commissioners and held out hope that they were being sent to resolve differences. Many in Congress refused to budge until they learned just what the envoys had to offer. John Adams disdainfully predicted that this was "a Bubble" and a misbegotten "Messiah that will never come." Samuel Adams said that he was "disgusted" both with the "King & his Junto," who spoke of peace while making "the most destructive Plans," and with the reconciliationists who were willing to be "Slaves" to "a Nation so lost to all Sense of Liberty and Virtue." In May, as American newspapers published the text of Britain's treaties with several German principalities, authorizing the hiring of mercenaries, outrage toward the Crown skyrocketed. Many were now convinced, as Richard Henry Lee said, that the action proved Britain was bent "upon the absolute conquest and subduction of N. America." Nearly simultaneously, word arrived of yet more calamities in Canada. Congress had dispatched reinforcements following the failed attack in December, but smallpox and desertions soon thinned their ranks. With the arrival of British reinforcements in May, the American army commenced a long, slow retreat that lasted until mid-June. Now, said Lee, it "is not choice then but necessity that calls for Independence, as the only means by which a foreign Alliance can be obtained."

32   One final matter helped the slowest sailors in Congress catch up with the swiftest. Month after month had passed with no sign of the so-called peace commissioners. Then, in the spring, it was learned that, although some commissioners had been named, they had been ordered not to treat with Congress. That proved a final blow; all but the most ardent reconciliationists were persuaded that the king's envoys were coming for the sole purpose of dividing American opinion and derailing the war effort.

33   With the tide so turned, in mid-May, Congress declared that "every kind of authority under the . . .

Crown should be totally suppressed" and instructed each colony to adopt a new government suitable for providing for the "happiness and safety of their constituents and . . . America in general." John Adams, who called this the "last Step," believed this was tantamount to a declaration of independence. Even Maryland's Thomas Stone, a foe of separation, disconsolately allowed that the "Dye is cast. The fatal Stab is given to any future Connection between this Country & Britain." Only a formal declaration of independence remained, and that could not now be long in coming.

34   On June 7, three weeks after Congress urged changes in the provincial governments, Lee introduced a motion for independence: *"Resolved*, That these United Colonies are, and of right ought to be, free and independent States, that they are absolved from all allegiance to the British Crown, and that all political connection between them and the State of Great Britain is, and ought to be, totally dissolved."

35   Congress rancorously debated Lee's motion for two days. Several reconciliationists from the Middle-Atlantic colonies made their final stand, even threatening to "secede from the Union" if Congress declared independence. But their threats and recriminations no longer frightened the majority, including Oliver Wolcott of Connecticut, who recognized that America was in the "Midst of a great Revolution . . . leading to the lasting Independancy of these Colonies." On June 11, Congress created a five-member committee to prepare a statement on independence. Adams, Franklin, Jefferson, Roger Sherman of Connecticut and Robert Livingston of New York were given until July 1 to complete their work. Once again it was to Jefferson that a panel turned, this time for the fateful task of drafting the declaration.

36   Jefferson and his colleagues beat the deadline by two days, submitting on June 28 a document that explained and defended independence. By July 1, the final consideration of Lee's motion to declare independence was taken up. That day's session, John Adams told a friend in a letter written early that morning, would see "the greatest Debate of all." With the outcome no longer in doubt, he said that he prayed for "the new born Republic" about to be created.

37   When debate began midmorning on that hot, steamy Monday, Dickinson was first on his feet to make one last speech against independence. Speaking emotionally for perhaps as much as two hours in the stifling heat of the closed room (windows were kept shut to keep spies from listening in), Dickinson

reviewed the familiar arguments: America could not win the war; at best, it could fight Britain to a stalemate, and deadlocked wars often ended in partition treaties in which territory is divided among the belligerents; therefore, after all the killing, some colonies would remain part of the British Empire, while others would pass under the control of France or Spain.

38   It was John Adams—soon to be christened "the Atlas of Independence" by New Jersey's Richard Stockton—who rose to answer Dickinson. Striving to conceal his contempt for his adversary, Adams spoke extemporaneously in subdued tones. Once again, he reviewed the benefits of independence. Although his speech was not transcribed, he surely invoked the ideas he had expressed and the phrases he had used on many another occasion. Breaking ties with Britain, he argued, would ensure freedom from England's imperial domination; escape from the menace of British corruption; and the opportunity to create a republic based on equality of representation.

39   Others then took the floor. The speeches stretched past the customary 4 o'clock adjournment and into the evening. The business was "an idle Mispence of Time," Adams remarked sourly, as "nothing was Said, but what had been repeated and hackneyed in that Room an hundred Times for Six Months past." After the Congress reconvened the next morning, July 2, the delegates cast their momentous votes. Twelve states—the colonies would become states with the vote—voted for independence. Not one voted against the break with Britain. New York's delegation, which had not yet been authorized by the New York legislature to separate from the mother country, did not vote. (Dickinson and Robert Morris did not attend, and Pennsylvania cast its vote for independence by a three-to-two margin.)

40   Adams predicted that July 2 would ever after "be solemnized with Pomp and Parade, with Shews, Games, Sports, Guns, Bells, Bonfires and Illuminations from one End of this Continent to the other." He was wrong, of course, for July 4, the date that Congress approved the formal Declaration of Independence, would become the commemorative day. But Adams had made one prediction that would prove tellingly correct. With the Union intact after a 15-month battle for independence, and with the step finally taken that could secure foreign assistance in America's desperate war, Adams declared he could "see the Rays of ravishing Light and Glory" that would accompany military victory.

15

LETTERS OF ABIGAIL AND JOHN ADAMS

Through primary source documents—diaries, journals, and letters—we receive a glimpse into the thoughts and ideas of people in a different time and place. The past is not a neat package of people in consensus regarding the issues of the day. The letters of Abigail and John Adams provide an example of domestic conflict in the months immediately preceding the American colonial leaders declaring independence from Great Britain. Some colonists like Abigail Adams voiced their concerns that certain issues would be ignored by the future leaders of the new nation.

When Thomas Jefferson penned the words all men are created equal in the Declaration of Independence, did the word men incorporate women into the proposition of human equality? Or was men meant to be mutually exclusive of the female sex? Since women were excluded from being allowed to formally debate the issue of independence, Abigail Adams demanded to know the Second Continental Congress's intentions. Writing from her home in the outskirts of Boston, Abigail Adams sent numerous letters to Philadelphia where her husband John was a prominent delegate of the Second Continental Congress and a member of the Declaration committee. John was now forced to confront the issue of women's rights (at least with his wife) in the formation of the United States of America. (Abigail Adams's second letter was sent to Mercy Otis Warren, whose family was actively involved in the American Revolution. Both her husband and her brother James Otis were active in Massachusetts' politics and the independence cause. Warren's home became a common meeting place for revolutionaries.)

- *What are Abigail Adams's concerns about the cause for independence?*
- *What does John Adams mean by "the despotism of the petticoat?"*
- *When Abigail Adams writes to Mercy Otis Warren, what is the tone of her letter?*
- *How might colonists of Abigail Adams era have responded to: "we have it in our power not only to free ourselves but to subdue our Masters, and without violence throw both your natural and legal authority at our feet?"*
- *Were women remembered?*

(NOTE: The following letters were written in a time when there was no standardized spelling in America; thus, the letters remain in their original state.)

1776

ABIGAIL ADAMS TO JOHN ADAMS
31 MAR. 1776

1 I wish you would ever write me a Letter half as long as I write you; and tell me if you may where your Fleet are gone? What sort of Defence Virginia can make against our common Enemy? Whether it is so situated as to make an able Defence? Are not the Gentery Lords and the common people vassals, are they not like the uncivilized Natives Brittain represents us to be? I hope their Riffel Men who have shewen themselves very savage and even Blood thirsty; are not a specimen of the Generality of the people. I am willing to allow the Colony great merrit for having produced a Washington but they have been shamefully duped by a Dunmore.

2 I have sometimes been ready to think that the passion for Liberty cannot be Eaquelly Strong in the Breasts of those who have been accustomed to deprive their fellow Creatures of theirs. Of this I am certain that it is not founded upon that generous and christian principal of doing to others as we would that others should do unto us. . . .

3 I long to hear that you have declared an independancy—and by the way in the new Code of Laws which I suppose it will be necessary for you to make I desire you would Remember the Ladies, and be more generous and favorable to them than your ancestors. Do not put such unlimited power into the hands of the Husbands. Remember all Men would be tyrants if they could. If perticuliar care and attention is not paid to the Laidies we are determined to foment a Rebelion, and will not hold ourselves bound by any Laws in which we have no voice, or Representation.

4 That your Sex are Naturally Tyrannical is a Truth so thoroughly established as to admit of no dispute, but such of you as wish to be happy willingly give up the harsh title of Master for the more tender and endearing one of Friend. Why then, not put it out of the power of the vicious and the Lawless to use us with cruelty and indignity with impunity. Men of Sense in all Ages abhor those customs which treat us only as the vassals of your Sex. Regard us then as Beings placed by providence under your protection and in imitation of the Supreem Being make use of that power only for our happiness.

JOHN ADAMS TO ABIGAIL
14 APR. 1776

5 You ask where the Fleet is. The inclosed Papers will inform you. You ask what Sort of Defence Virginia can make. I believe they will make an able Defence. Their Militia and minute Men have been some time employed in training them selves, and

they have Nine Battalions of regulars as they call them, maintained among them, under good Officers, at the Continental Expence. They have set up a Number of Manufactories of Fire Arms, which are busily employed. They are tolerably supplied with Powder, and are successfull and assiduous, in making Salt Petre. Their neighboring Sister or rather Daughter Colony of North Carolina, which is a warlike Colony, and has several Battalions at the Continental Expence, as well as a pretty good Militia, are ready to assist them, and they are in very good Spirits, and seem determined to make a brave Resistance.—The Gentry are very rich, and the common People very poor. This Inequality of Property, gives an Aristocratical Turn to all their Proceedings, and occasions a strong Aversion in their Patricians, to Common Sense. But the Spirit of these Barons, is coming down, and it must submit. . . .

6 As to your extraordinary Code of Laws, I cannot but laugh. We have been told that our Struggle has loosened the bands of Government every where. That Children and Apprentices were disobedient-that schools and Colledges were grown turbulent—that Indians slighted their Guardians and Negroes grew insolent to their Masters. But your Letter was the first Intimation that another Tribe more numerous and powerfull than all the rest were grown discontented.—This is rather too coarse a Compliment but you are so saucy, I wont blot it out. . . .

7 Depend upon it, We know better than to repeal our Masculine systems. Altho they are in full Force, you know they are little more than Theory. We dare not exert our Power in its full Latitude. We are obliged to go fair, and softly, and in Practice you know We are the subjects, We have only the Name of Masters, and rather than give up this, which would compleatly subject Us to the Despotism of the Peticoat, I hope General Washington, and all our brave Heroes would fight. I am sure every good Politician would plot, as long as he would against Despotism, Empire, Monarchy, Aristocracy, Oligarchy, or Ochlocracy.—A fine Story indeed. I begin to think the Ministry as deep as they are wicked. After stirring up Tories, Landjobbers, Trimmers, Bigots, Canadians, Indians, Negroes, Hanoverians, Hessians, Russians, Irish Roman Catholics, Scotch Renegades, at last they have stimulated the to demand new Privileges and threaten to rebell.

"Charm by accepting, by submitting sway
Yet have our Humour most when we obey."

ABIGAIL ADAMS TO MERCY OTIS WARREN
BRAINTREE, APRIL 27 1776

8 He is very saucy to me in return for a List of Female Grievances which I transmitted to him. I think

I will get you to join me in a petition to Congress. I thought it was very probable our wise Statesmen would erect a New Government and form a new code of Laws. I ventured to speak a word on behalf of our Sex, who are rather hardly dealte with by the Laws of England which gives such unlimited power to the Husband to use his wife Ill.

9   I requested that our Legislators would consider our case and as all Men of Delicacy and Sentiment are adverse to Exercising the power they possess, yet as there is a natural propensity in Human Nature to domination, I thought the most generous plan was to put it out of the power of the Arbitrary and tyranick to injure us with impunity by Establishing some Laws in favour upon just and Liberal principals.

10   I believe I even threatened fomenting a Rebellion in case we were not considered and assured him we would not hold ourselves bound by any Laws in which we had neither a voice nor representation.

11   In return he tells me he cannot but Laugh at my extraordinary Code of Laws. That he had heard their Struggle had loosened the bands of Government, that children and apprentices were disobedient, that Schools and Colleges had grown turbulent, that Indians slighted their Guardians, and Negroes grew insolent to their Masters. But my Letter was the first intimation that another Tribe more numerous and powerful than all the rest were grown discontented. This is rather too coarse a complement, he adds, but that I am so saucy he wont blot it out.

12   So I have helped the Sex abundantly, but I will tell him I have only been making trial of the Disinterestedness of his Virtue, and when weigh'd in the balance have found it wanting.

13   It would be bad policy to grant us greater power say they since under all the disadvantages we Labour we have the ascendency over their Hearts.

14   And charm by accepting, by submitting sway.

ABIGAIL ADAMS TO JOHN ADAMS 7 MAY 1776

15   A Government of more Stability is much wanted in this colony, and they are ready to receive it from the Hands of the Congress, and since I have begun with Maxims of State I will add an other viz. that a people may let a king fall, yet still remain a people, but if a king let his people slip from him, he is no longer a king. And as this is most certainly our case, why not proclaim to the World in decisive terms your own importance?

16   Shall we not be dispiced by foreign powers for hesitateing so long at a word?

17   I can not say I think you very generous to the Ladies, for whilst you are proclaiming peace and good will to Men, Emancipating all Nations, you insist upon retaining an absolute power over Wives. But you must remember that Arbitary power is like most other things which are very hard, very liable to be broken—and notwithstanding all your wise Laws and Maxims we have it in our power not only to free ourselves but to subdue our Masters, and without voilence throw both your natural and legal authority at our feet—

16

JEFFERSON'S COP-OUT

BY JOSEPH J. ELLIS

Americans have usually been kind to their "founding fathers," treating them with a respect bordering on reverence. This group of men set up a framework of government that has, with the aid of two large oceans, endured for over 200 years. These men earned a reputation for being farsighted, idealistic, and selfless in the eyes of both historians and the American people.

At or near the top of the list sits the name of Thomas Jefferson. The Declaration of Independence, penned in large part by Jefferson, articulated the ideas of equality and freedom. His written and spoken views on the nature of government and individual liberty inspire not only Americans, but freedom seekers around the globe. The Declaration helped to inspire the French Revolution and the American Civil War.

This is both the popular and historical view of Jefferson. Less known about the man is his complicated and often contradictory views on the institution of slavery. Was he simply a hypocritical idealist, or a self-interested businessman whose views changed over time? In the article that follows, Joseph J. Ellis bores deep into the personal life of Thomas Jefferson, unearthing facts that will make many thoughtful Americans question their assumptions about the man.

- *What is, as the author puts it, the central dilemma of American History?*
- *How do the private and public lives of Thomas Jefferson personify this dilemma?*
- *In what ways could Jefferson's home Monticello be seen as a metaphor for his views on slavery and indeed for his entire life?*
- *How did Jefferson's complicated views on slavery evolve over time? What shaped his thinking in this area?*

---

1 Of all the gaps between his words and his actions, Jefferson's ownership of slaves is the most troubling. How did he manage the contradiction?

2 Thomas Jefferson was many things, but mostly he was a creature of paradox: the wealthy Virginia aristocrat who wrote the most famous statement of equality in American history; the sincere advocate of agrarian simplicity who worshipped the art and architecture of Paris; above all, the fervent believer in human freedom who lived his entire life as a slave owner. This last paradox has always seemed the most poignant, in part because Jefferson himself acknowledged the massive gap between his principled ideals and his personal reality, and in part because the paradox Jefferson lived was emblematic of the larger disjunction in American society—now generally regarded as the central dilemma of American history—between the promise of liberty and the fact of racial discrimination.

3 Jefferson never resolved the paradox. He went to his grave owning almost 200 slaves and just after drafting a last letter in which he paid tribute to the egalitarian principles of the Declaration of Independence. The question has always been: How did he manage this glaring contradiction? Granted, we all live lives that require us to straddle the space

between our fondest hopes and our imperfect actions. But in Jefferson's life that space was a yawning chasm that seemed to defy the customary internal compromises. How did he do it?

4   If we had access to a time machine, and were also allowed to bring along a tape recorder and lie detector, the obvious place to interrogate Jefferson would be at **Monticello**, preferably as he strolled along **Mulberry Row**, where his household slaves were quartered. We could walk alongside the master of Monticello, reading for the record several of his most uplifting public statements about human rights and individual freedom, then ask him to comment on the apparent contradictions between the lyrical rhetoric and the sordid reality of the scene.

5   Since we obviously can't interview Jefferson, the next best course is to recover as much of the surviving historical evidence as possible, acknowledge that it is unavoidably incomplete and fragile, then do all we can to interrogate that evidence with disciplined empathy. We must not be merely accusatory (*i.e.*, how could you do it?). We shouldn't search the past for trophies that satisfy our political agenda in the present. We must show, as Jefferson so famously put it, "a decent respect to the opinions of mankind"—including those of dead men whose opinions, shaped by conditions two centuries ago, differ from our own. We also need to be canny about the place and time from which we extract our historical sample. The obvious place is Monticello. The most revealing moment is the three-year period between 1794 and 1797:

6   Jefferson has retired to Monticello after serving four years as America's first secretary of state. His evolving attitude toward slavery is just reaching a crucial stage of its development. And, most helpfully for our purposes, he is surrounded by his slaves. We even have an intriguing historical clue to confirm we are looking in the right place, for Jefferson tells us what is in his mind at the time: "I have my house to build, my fields to farm, and "—here is the clue—"to watch for the happiness of those who labor for mine."

7   Precisely because Jefferson's most inspiring utterances about humankind's prospects seem capable of levitating out of any specific social context, floating above messy realities like balloons at a political convention, we need to bring our recovered Jefferson back to earth. That means Monticello.

8   Context is crucial to our pursuit. The most elemental fact confronting Jefferson upon his return to Monticello in 1794 was that he was heavily in debt. He owed about £4,500 to English creditors and another £2,000 to bankers in Glasgow. (Comparisons in modern-day terms are notoriously tricky to calculate, but can conservatively be estimated at several hundred thousand dollars.) He was not, as he liked to describe himself, an independent yeoman farmer but an indebted Virginia planter. His many statements about returning to the bucolic splendors of the agrarian life were unquestionably sincere, but they masked the more pressing reality that farming for Jefferson, now more than ever before, meant making money.

9   His landed assets were impressive, but deceptively so. Jefferson owned nearly 11,000 acres, about equally divided between estates surrounding Monticello in Albemarle County and western lands concentrated in Bedford County, about 90 miles away. This made him one of the largest land-owners in the state. One of the reasons he found it difficult to accept the full implications of his indebtedness was that he thought of wealth like an old-style Virginia aristocrat, in terms of land rather than money. For Jefferson, land was the best measure of a man's worth and, as he put it, "that of which I am the most tenacious." Despite the haunting presence of his English and Scottish creditors, he thought of himself as a landed and therefore a wealthy man.

10   Although Jefferson never fully grasped the intractability of his economic predicament, he had a sharp sense of the need to generate income. He described his thinking in a letter to a French correspondent in the spring of 1795:

> On returning home after an absence of ten years, I found my farms so much deranged that I saw evidently . . . that it was necessary for me to find some other resource in the meantime. . . . I concluded at length . . . to begin a manufacture of nails, which needs little or no capital, and I now employ a dozen little boys from 10 to 16 years of age, overlooking all the details of their business myself and drawing from it a profit on which I can get along till I can put my farms into a course of yielding profit.

11   Every morning except Sunday he walked over to the nailery soon after dawn to weigh out the nail rod for each worker, then returned at dusk to weigh the nails each had made and calculate how much iron had been wasted by the most and least efficient workers. Isaac Jefferson, a young slave at Monticello at the time, later recalled that his master made it clear that the nailery was a personal priority and that special privileges would be accorded the best nailmakers: "[He] gave the boys in the nail factory a pound of meat a week. . . . Give them that wukked the best a suit of red or blue; encouraged them

---

Monticello: Jefferson's home in Virginia
Mulberry Row: where slaves lived on the Jefferson plantation

mightily." Jefferson even added the nailery to his familiar refrain in the pastoral mode: "I am so much immersed in farming and nail-making," he reported in the fall of 1794, "that politicks are entirely banished from my mind."

12   From a financial perspective the nailery made perfect sense. But seen in the context of Jefferson's eloquent hymn to the bucolic beauties of the pastoral life, it was a massive incongruity. Jefferson himself gave no sign that he was aware of any contradiction: At times his obliviousness seemed almost calculated. There is no evidence that it ever occurred to him that his daily visits to the nail factory, with its blazing forges and sweating black boys arranged along an assembly line of hammers and anvils, offered a graphic preview of precisely the kind of industrial world he devoutly wished America to avoid.

13   At a more mundane level, Jefferson's dedication to the meticulous management of the nailery illustrates what compelled his fullest energies as master of Monticello. Both Madison Hemings, son of Sally Hemings, and Edmund Bacon, who was Jefferson's overseer for 16 years, recalled that Jefferson never showed much enthusiasm for agricultural pursuits. "It was his mechanics he seemed mostly to direct, and in their operations he took great interest," Hemings remembered. Jefferson spent little time in his fields, preferring to leave their cultivation to his overseers except at harvest time. He spent no time at all behind a plow and almost no time watching his slaves perform the arduous tasks of farming. What most fascinated him and commanded his fullest attention were new projects that demanded mechanical or artisanal skill of his laborers and that allowed him to design and superintend the entire operation. The nailery was the first of such projects, but it was followed by construction of a new threshing machine, plans for a flour mill, and an expensive canal along the Rivanna River.

14   But the biggest project of all was Monticello itself. He had been contemplating a major overhaul of his mansion ever since his return from France in 1789. From a financial point of view the idea of renovating Monticello, unlike his plans for the nailery, made no sense at all. But when it came to the elegance and comfort of his personal living space, Jefferson's lifelong habit was to ignore cost altogether, often going so far as to make expensive architectural changes in houses or hotels where he was only a temporary resident. His much grander plans for Monticello followed naturally from two idealistic impulses that seized his imagination with all the force of first principles: First, he needed more space, more than twice the space of the original house, in order to accommodate his domestic dream of living out his life surrounded by his children and grandchildren; second, his revised version of Monticello needed to embody

the neoclassical principles of the Palladian style that his European travels had allowed him to study firsthand. Since the expansion had to occur within severely constrained conceptions of symmetry and proportion, the new structure could not just spread out like a series of boxcars; but neither could it rise vertically, since Palladian buildings must present at least the appearance of a one-story horizontal line, preferably capped by a dome. What this meant, in effect, was that the original house needed to be almost completely torn down and rebuilt from the cellar up.

15   Monticello became a congested construction site replete with broken bricks, roofless rooms, lumber piles and, if some reports are to be believed, over 100 workmen digging, tearing and hammering away. The millions of 20th-century visitors to the mansion are the real beneficiaries of Jefferson's irrational decision to redesign and rebuild Monticello in the 1790s, though they would be mistaken to think the house in which Jefferson lived looked as it does now. It was in some state of repair or improvement throughout most of Jefferson's lifetime. More to our purposes, from 1794 to 1797 Monticello was part-ruin, part-shell and mostly still a dream.

16   Almost all the work, whether in the fields, the nailery or at the construction site for Monticello itself, was done by slaves. The total slave population on Jefferson's several plantations was a fluctuating figure, oscillating above and below 200 and divided between Albemarle and Bedford counties at the ratio of roughly three to two. Between 1784 and 1794, as Jefferson attempted to consolidate his landholdings and reduce his mounting debts, he had disposed of 161 slaves by sale or outright gift. But natural increase had raised the slave population on all his estates to 167 by 1796, and that number would grow gradually over the ensuing years. On his plantations in Albemarle County it would seem safe to estimate that Jefferson was surrounded by about 100 slaves during his three-year retirement. African-American slaves constituted the overwhelming majority of residents at Monticello.

17   If Jefferson had a discernible public position on slavery in the mid-1790s, it was that the subject should be allowed to retire gracefully from the field of political warfare, much as he himself was doing by retiring to Monticello. He wanted the whole controversy over slavery to disappear. This represented a decided shift from his position as a younger man, when he had assumed a leadership role in pushing slavery onto the agenda in the Virginia legislature and the federal Congress. His most famous antislavery formulations, it is true, were rhetorical: blaming the slave trade and the establishment of slavery itself on George III in the Declaration of Independence; denouncing slavery as a morally bankrupt institution that was doomed to extinction in *Notes on the*

State of Virginia. His most practical proposals, all of which were made in the early 1780s, envisioned a program of gradual abolition that featured an end to the slave trade, the prohibition of slavery in all the western territories, and the establishment of a fixed date (he suggested 1800) after which all newborn children of slaves would be emancipated. Throughout this early phase of his life it would have been unfair to accuse him of hypocrisy for owning slaves or to berate him for failing to provide moral leadership on America's most sensitive political subject. It would, indeed, have been much fairer to wonder admiringly how this product of Virginia's planter class had managed to develop such liberal convictions.

18   Dating the onset of a long silence is an inherently imprecise business, but Jefferson's more evasive posture toward slavery seemed to congeal in the 1780s with the publication of *Notes on the State of Virginia*. It was written in 1781 and 1782, when he was still reeling from charges of cowardice for fleeing a marauding British army in his last days as governor. *Notes* contained the most ringing denunciation of slavery Jefferson had yet composed, including an apocalyptic vision of racial war if emancipation were postponed too long. But these unquestionably sincere sentiments, written when he was emotionally exhausted and his customary protective shield was down, were not intended for public consumption. Jefferson never authorized the initial publication of *Notes* which appeared in a French edition in 1785, and only grudgingly agreed to an English edition two years later, when it was clear there was nothing he could do to stop it.

19   *Notes*, in fact, was the only book that Jefferson published in his lifetime, for he much preferred to convey his opinions on controversial issues in private conversations and personal letters, where he could tailor his views to fit his particular audience. The publication of *Notes* put him "out there" on the most controversial subject of the day without the capacity to modulate or manipulate his language to fit different constituencies in France and England or, most worrisome to Jefferson, his fellow slave owners in Virginia. From the moment that *Notes* began to circulate within the planter class of the South, Jefferson began to back away from his leadership role in the debate over slavery. His more passive and fatalistic position, which he maintained for the rest of his life, was that public opinion was not prepared for emancipation at present and must await enactment at some unspecified time in the future. In effect, he was abdicating his position as the uncrowned king of Virginia's most progressive planters.

20   Moreover, the more pessimistic racial implications of the argument he had made in *Notes* began to settle in and cause him to realize, for the first time, that he had no workable answer to the unavoidable question: What happens once the slaves are freed?

This was the kind of practical question that Jefferson had demonstrated great ingenuity in avoiding on a host of other major political issues. Indeed, one of the most seductive features of his political thinking in general was its beguiling faith that the future could take care of itself. Slavery, however, proved to be the exception to this larger pattern of inherent optimism. For one brief moment, in 1788, he seemed to entertain a bold if somewhat bizarre scheme whereby emancipated slaves would be "intermingled" with imported German peasants on 50-acre farms where both groups could learn proper work habits. But even this short-lived proposal only served to expose the inherent intractability of the postemancipation world as Jefferson tried to imagine it.

21   His fundamental conviction, one that he never questioned, was that white and black Americans could not live together in harmony. He had already explained why in *Notes*:

> *Deep rooted prejudices entertained by the whites, ten thousand recollections, by the blacks, of the injuries they have sustained; new provocations; the real distinctions which nature has made; and many other circumstances, will divide U. S. into parties, and produce convulsions which will probably never end but in the extermination of the one or the other race.*

22   Here was the single instance, with the most singularly significant consequences, when Jefferson was incapable of believing in the inevitability of human progress. Blacks and whites were inherently different, and, though he was careful to advance the view "as a suspicion only," he believed people of African descent were sufficiently inferior to whites in mental aptitude that any emancipation policy permitting racial interaction was a criminal injustice to the freed slaves as well as a biological travesty against "the real distinctions which nature has made." The unavoidable conclusion, then, was that slavery was morally wrong, but racial segregation was morally right. And until a practical solution to the problem of what to do with the freed slaves could be found, it made no sense to press for emancipation.

23   Finally, during the 1780s Jefferson became more intensely aware how much his own financial well-being depended upon the monetary value and labor of his slaves. As the depth of his own indebtedness began to sink in, there seemed to be three ways to raise large amounts of capital to appease his creditors: He could sell off land; he could sell slaves outright; and he could rent or lease the labor of his slaves to neighboring planters. He expressed considerable guilt about pursuing the latter two options, suggesting they betrayed his paternal obligations to the black members of his extended "family." He

gave specific instructions to his overseers that particular slaves who had been with him for some time should not be sold or hired out unless they wished it. But much as he disliked selling his slaves or temporarily transferring control over them to others, he recognized that such a course constituted his only salvation. In short, once he grasped the full measure of his personal economic predicament, the larger question of emancipation appeared in a new and decidedly less favorable light. It was now a matter on which he could literally not afford to be open-minded; nor, as it turned out, were the exigencies of this debt-induced predicament to change over his lifetime, except to grow worse.

24   The net result of all these influences was a somewhat tortured position on slavery that combined unequivocal condemnation of the institution in the abstract with blatant procrastination whenever specific **emancipation** schemes were suggested. The Duc de La Rochefoucauld-Liancourt, a French aristocrat fleeing the revolutionary bloodbath in Paris, captured the essential features and general flavor of Jefferson's slavery stance during his visit to Monticello in June of 1796:

> The generous and enlightened Mr. Jefferson cannot but demonstrate a desire to see these negroes emancipated. But he sees so many difficulties in their emancipation even postponed, he adds so many conditions to render it practicable, that it is thus reduced to the impossible. He keeps, for example, the opinion he advanced in his notes, that the negroes of Virginia can only be emancipated all at once, and by exporting to a distance the whole of the black race. He bases this opinion on the certain danger, if there were nothing else, of seeing blood mixed without means of preventing it.

25   If his position on slavery as a young man merits a salute for its forthright and progressive character, his position as a mature man invites a skeptical shaking of the head for its self-serving paralysis and questionable integrity. He saw himself, even more than his slaves, as the victim of history's stubborn refusal to proceed along the path that all enlightened observers regarded as inevitable. In that sense, he and his African-American charges were trapped together in a lingering moment, a historical backwater in which nature's laws would be sorely tested as both sides waited together for the larger story of human liberation to proceed with freed blacks finding a more suitable location with people of their own kind in Africa or the Caribbean. In this overly extended transitional moment, his primary obligation, as he saw it, was to serve as a steward for those

temporarily entrusted to his care and to think of his slaves, as he listed them in his Farm Book, as members of "my family," to be cared for as foster children until more permanent and geographically distant accommodations could be found.

26   Jefferson's sophisticated network of interior defenses allowed him to sustain this paternalistic self-image by blocking out incongruous evidence. For example, when forced by his creditors to sell 11 slaves in 1792, he ordered that they all be selected from his more remote Bedford plantations and that the sale itself be carried out in a distant location, explaining that he "[did] not like to have my name annexed in the public papers to the sale of property." Or, to take another example, in 1792 he approved the sale of Mary Hemings to Thomas Bell, a local Charlottesville merchant, claiming that the sale was justifiable "according to her desire." What he did not say was that Bell, a white man, was the father of Mary's two youngest children. The sale permitted the couple to live as common-law husband and wife.

27   Part by geographic accident, part by his own design, the organization of slave labor at Jefferson's plantations reinforced this shielding mentality in several crucial ways. Recall, first of all, that Jefferson's cultivated lands were widely distributed, half of them at Bedford several days' ride away. Until he completed his second house at Poplar Forest during his final retirement, Jefferson seldom visited those distant estates. Recall, too, that he seldom ventured into his fields at Monticello or Shadwell, leaving daily management of routine farming tasks to overseers. While he kept elaborate records of his entire slave population in his *Farm Book*, including the names and ages of all hands, his direct exposure to field laborers was limited. His cryptic notation on the division of slave labor is also revealing in this regard: "Children till 10 years of age to serve as nurses. From 10 to 16 the boys make nails, the girls spin. At 16 go into the ground or learn trades." The ominous phrase "go into the ground" accurately conveyed Jefferson's personal contact with that considerable majority of adult slaves who worked his fields. Except as names in his record books, they practically disappeared.

28   When Jefferson did encounter them, they were usually working on one of his several construction projects or apprenticing in the nailery. Most of his face-to-face contact with laboring slaves occurred in nonagrarian settings—the nailery, the sawmill, the construction site around the mansion—where he supervised them doing skilled and semiskilled jobs. Even the nailery, with its overtones of assembly-line monotony and Dickensian drudgery, allowed him to

---

emancipation: freedom for slaves

think about the work of the slave boys as an apprentice experience providing them with a marketable trade. In explaining Jefferson's compulsive tendency to launch so many mechanical and construction projects at Monticello, it is possible that they not only served as outlets for his personal energies, but also allowed him to design a more palatable context for interacting with his slaves as hired employees rather than as chattel.

29   All the slaves working in the household, and most of the slaves living along Mulberry Row on the mountain top, were members of two families that had been with Jefferson for over two decades. They enjoyed a privileged status within the slave hierarchy at Monticello, were given larger food and clothing rations, considerably greater latitude of movement, and even the discretion to choose jobs or reject them on occasion. Great George and his wife, Ursula, referred to as King George (a joke on George III) and Queen Ursula, were slaves in name only and effectively exercised control over management of the household. The other and larger slave family were all Hemingses, headed by the matriarch, Betty Hemings, whom Jefferson had inherited from his father-in-law, John Wayles, along with 10 of her 12 children in 1774.

30   It was an open secret within the slave community at Monticello that the privileged status enjoyed by the Hemings family derived from its mixed blood. Several of Betty's children, perhaps as many as six, had most probably been fathered by John Wayles. In the literal, not just the figurative sense of the term, they were part of Jefferson's extended family. All of the slaves that Jefferson eventually freed were descendants of Betty Hemings. If what struck the other slaves at Monticello was the quasi-independent character of the Hemings clan with its blood claim on Jefferson's paternal instincts, what most visitors tended to notice was their color. The Frenchman Liancourt left this account in 1796: "In Virginia mongrel negroes are found in greater number than in Carolina and Georgia; and I have even seen, especially at Mr. Jefferson's, slaves, who, neither in point of colour nor features, shewed the least trace of their original descent; but their mothers being slaves, they retain, of consequence, the same condition."

31   Since the members of the Hemings family were the front-and-center slaves at Monticello, most guests and visitors to the mountain top experienced the Jeffersonian version of slavery primarily as a less black and less oppressive phenomenon than it actually was. And, as overseer Edmund Bacon recalled, "there were no Negro and other outhouses around the mansion, as you generally see on [other] plantations," so the physical arrangement of appearances also disguised the full meaning of the slave experience. In short, Jefferson had so designed his slave community that his most frequent interactions occurred with African-Americans who were not treated like full-fledged slaves and who did not even look like full-blooded Africans because, in fact, they were not. In terms of daily encounters and routine interactions, his sense of himself as less a slave master than a paternalistic employer and guardian received constant reinforcement.

32   By the same token, if slavery was a doomed institution whose only practical justification was to preserve the separation of the races until the day of deliverance arrived at some unspecified time in the future, Jefferson was surrounded by rather dramatic evidence that it was failing miserably at that task. Racial mixing at Monticello was obviously a flourishing enterprise, much more so than his wheat fields. Several of Betty Hemings's grandchildren looked almost completely white, graphic testimony that whatever had begun with John Wayles had certainly not stopped back then. Jefferson's stated aversion to racial mixture had somehow to negotiate its visible examples all around him. In a sense, what he saw only confirmed his deepest fears about an amalgamation of the races, though his code of silence dictated that no mention of the matter be permitted in public. Despite his remarkable powers of avoidance, this is one topic we can be sure he brooded about, even if he never talked about it for the record. The eloquence of his silence provides the best evidence of what Monticello was like as a real place rather than an imagined ideal. If literary allusions afford the best mode of description, we need to dispense with Virgil's pastoral odes and begin to contemplate William Faulkner's fiction.

33   Of course, the story of Jefferson and his slaves at Monticello does not end in 1797. Twelve years later, after four years as vice president and eight years as president, he returned for his final encampment. During his declining years, especially after the Missouri crisis of 1820, Jefferson's public stance on slavery retreated even further from the leadership position of his youth. As a young revolutionary he had opposed the extension of slavery into the western territories. Now he reversed himself, advocating what he called "diffusion," the rather preposterous idea that the best way to end slavery was by allowing it to spread beyond the South. At the public level, diffusion was the most poignant and pathetic expression of his avoidance mentality, envisioning as it did the unpalatable evil of slavery conveniently disappearing in the misty expanses of the vast and uncharted lands of the West.

34   At the personal level, Jefferson's providential demise on July 4, 1826, spared him from witnessing the tragic end of the story. Only his spirit was present six months later when Monticello and all its possessions, including "130 valuable negroes," were put on the auction block and sold to the highest bidders. Jefferson was the invisible man that cold January

day when his surviving daughter and grandchildren cried as the slave families were split up and dispersed. His grandson "Jeffy" never forgot the sad scene, which he compared to "a captured village in ancient times when all were sold as slaves." The auction lasted five days, and when it was over the proceeds covered only a portion of Jefferson's monumental debt—by then, in modern terms, several million dollars—and the slaves he had vowed to protect disappeared "down the river."

35   His life had always been about promise. And his enduring legacy became the most resonant version of the American promise in the national mythology. But in his life, if not his legacy, there were some promises he could not keep, because there were some facts he had chosen never to face.

IV

EARLY AMERICA

1   Momentum increased for a complete break with England. Through the spring and summer of 1776, one colony after another pledged its support to the radical final step: independence and the formation of a new government. Thomas Jefferson summarized the sentiment of the time in his Declaration of Independence, penned in a three week period in June, 1776. The Declaration of Independence universalized traditional rights of English people and made them the rights of all humanity. It stated that "all men are created equal . . . they are endowed by their Creator with certain unalienable rights . . . among these are life, liberty, and the pursuit of happiness." With these words, America secured for itself the envy of oppressed peoples around the globe, then and now. Though it by no means assured American independence, it was an important first step toward a united front in the coming fight with the British; representatives from all 13 colonies signed the Declaration.

2   It was a long, grueling war. As historian Bruce D. Porter has noted, 25,324 were killed in the war, "nearly one percent of the population in 1780, and more than one in ten of all soldiers who served. As a percentage of the national population, the losses were three times higher than those of World War II and were surpassed only by the Civil War's." By 1780, Great Britain was in an imperial war against most of Europe as well as the 13 American colonies. Losses piled up—in India, the West Indies, and Yorktown, Virginia. In the Treaty of Paris in 1783, Britain recognized the independence of the 13 colonies. The United States were ceded all the territory between the Appalachians and the Mississippi River.

3   The war was over and the treaty was signed. Was the American Revolution complete? History is riddled with examples of "revolutions" that fail to replace old, corrupt political and social orders with new, more equitable ones. New systems of government had to be built from scratch. But colonial leaders were confronted by a seemingly insoluble dilemma: how to guarantee the very liberties that England was thought to have denied, yet still provide an orderly society where life and property are secure from internal and external threats. In other words, the question was this: How could they balance the need for both order and liberty?

4   It was a daunting challenge. If a society has total order, freedom necessarily is compromised. But if freedom is allowed to run amok, anarchy prevails. The solution to the dilemma is our Constitution, an admittedly imperfect but workable agreement between elites and the masses. The framers of the Constitution sought to diffuse the power of government in such a way as to minimize the possibility of tyranny coming from any one source. Thus, the power of the federal government is balanced by the local authority of individual states; the ability of the President to rule by force is checked by the Congress and the Supreme Court, and so on.

5   The beginnings of our present day governmental structure were thus established. But how would personal liberties be guaranteed? The first

10 amendments to the Constitution were approved four years after the Constitution was completed. Our most basic liberties—the rights that many Americans today take for granted—were included in this "Bill of Rights." In subsequent amendments during the past 200 years, the definition of democracy has been expanded, and the goal of equality has been begun to be addressed.

6   With the benefit of hindsight, what can the historian and the student of history conclude about the American Constitution? What are its strengths and weakness, its successes and failures? What are the key constitutional issues facing the country today? In a very real sense, the answers to these questions suggest the reality of an evolving America, a country constantly redefining itself.

17
CAPITAL IN CRISIS 1793

In the midst of a bitterly partisan feud between Republicans and Federalists that was polarizing the nation, the fledgling United States faced a terrifying and deadly crisis—Yellow Fever—that would decimate its capital, Philadelphia.

Mosquitos kill. They have wreaked havoc on human populations throughout history. Malaria, West Nile Virus, Yellow Fever. The Aedes Aegypti *mosquito is barely visible to the naked eye, but in 1793, these tiny flying insects brought the city of Philadelphia, Pennsylvania, then our nation's capital, to its knees. Men, women, and children, rich and poor, were caught in a vice of nature's creation. But try as they might, the more than 40,000 inhabitants lacked the knowledge to combat the disease effectively. By the end of that terrifying summer, thousands of Philadelphians had died, many needlessly.*

Doctor Walter Reed, a major in the Unites States Army during the Spanish American War, discovered the connection between the mosquito and yellow fever. His work saved thousands, perhaps millions of lives. But Dr. Reeds' efforts were over 100 years too late for the citizens of Philadelphia in the summer of 1793.

This story illustrates the power nature had, and still has, over vulnerable human populations. And it is also a testament to human beings' futile, sometimes foolish attempts to fight back.

- *What are the symptoms of yellow fever sufferers?*
- *What was the survival rate?*
- *Who was Doctor Benjamin Rush? What did he get wrong?*
- *Describe the scene on the waterfront of Philadelphia. How did this contribute to the onset of the epidemic?*
- *Why was it called "yellow" fever? What caused the patient to turn yellow?*
- *What was "Jesuits Bark"?*
- *What was the "heroic" bleeding that Dr. Benjamin Rush recommended?*
- *What were the reactions of George Washington, Alexander Hamilton and Thomas Jefferson to the Yellow Fever crisis?*

---

1   In the summer of 1793, Philadelphia was in the midst of a political crisis. Great Britain had declared war against revolutionary France, instantly polarizing American public opinion. Many favored France, whose political ideals seemed akin to our own. Others disagreed, pointing out the bloody massacres and other outrages that had recently convulsed Paris.

2   President George Washington's own cabinet split along party lines. Secretary of State Thomas Jefferson and his Republican Party were passionately in favor of France, while Secretary of the Treasury Alexander Hamilton and many other Federalists felt Britain was a bulwark of civilization against the rising tide of revolutionary anarchy. Nominally a Federalist, Washington tried to govern with fairness and impartiality. It was a difficult task, and sometimes even Washington's celebrated patience showed signs of cracking under the strain.

3   While the president grappled with partisan politics and the thorny issues of war and peace, a new threat was developing far closer to home. The spring of 1793 had been abnormally wet, but despite a bone-dry summer, stagnant pools of water remained in streets, alleyways and open fields, breeding insects by the millions. Diarists noted the presence of swarms of mosquitoes, little knowing the buzzing nuisances carried a deadly disease.

4   These mosquitoes spread the yellow fever virus, and within weeks Philadelphia, then the nation's capital, would suffer through the worst epidemic to plague an American city in the 18th century.

5   Philadelphia was the largest and most cosmopolitan city in the United States, boasting a population of more than 40,000 people. It was a city of monuments, many of them associated with the nation's beginnings. Congress met in Congress Hall, in the shadow of the Old State House (later Independence Hall), where the Declaration of Independence was signed and the Constitution was drafted.

6   Philadelphia's streets were paved with cobblestones and laid out on a grid plan that some visitors found unsettling. Used to the medieval jumble of avenues back home, a foreign traveler considered the right-angled streets "a mathematical infringement on the rights of individual eccentricity." The city's architecture injected a note of egalitarianism in an otherwise class-conscious age. Most homes were built of red brick in a colonial Georgian or the newly emerging "Federal" style.

7   Dolley Payne Todd lived in a house on Walnut and Fourth streets. She was charming, vivacious and beautiful, and her charismatic personality could not be contained by the straightjacket of Quaker convention. Her husband John Todd was a solidly middle-class lawyer whose sturdy, three-story red brick home was typical of the period.

8   Like many of his neighbors, John Todd conducted business from an office on the ground floor. While Todd and his clerks scribbled away on briefs and other legal documents, Dolley held court in the second-floor parlor. Known as a great entertainer, she was also the conscientious mother of two young sons. John Payne Todd was born on February 29, 1792, his brother William Temple in May 1793. Dolley managed an extended household that included her husband, sons, her 14-year-old sister Anna, at least one law clerk, a pet bird and a family dog named Pointer.

9   The Todds had some very distinguished neighbors. Dr. Benjamin Rush, for instance, lived a short distance away. Later known as the father of American psychology for his pioneering work in the treatment of mental illness, Rush also had an interest in politics. Elected to Congress in 1776, he had been one of the signers of the Declaration of Independence. He also was the preeminent physician of his generation, and he took his duties and responsibilities seriously. In addition to a large private practice, Rush was a professor at the University of Pennsylvania's Institutes of Medicine and Clinical Practice. His professional influence ranged far and wide, and it is estimated that more than 3,000 medical students took his classes from 1769 to 1813.

10   Rush was a compassionate man who advised his students to treat the poor and destitute. He was a leading light in the Pennsylvania Abolition Society, an antislavery group once headed by Benjamin Franklin. Rush was also stubborn and opinionated, ready to strike out at anyone who did not share his views. The great yellow fever epidemic would test his stamina and challenge his professional reputation.

11   The waterfront was the city's true heart, a raucous, bustling place where rich merchants rubbed elbows with sailors, small-business men, newly arrived immigrants and farmers fresh from the country. The broad Delaware River was an artery of commerce, its wind-dimpled surface crowded with merchant ships carrying goods from as far away as China.

12   Near the waterfront, a row of market sheds stretched down High Street, the barnlike structures sheltering vendors who sold fish, meat and produce to city dwellers far removed from the country. Farmers from southern New Jersey would cross the Delaware via Cooper's Ferry, arriving at the foot of Arch Street with carts loaded with vegetables. They would then wheel their burdens to the High Street market sheds. Young matrons like Dolley Todd would shop there frequently, baskets perched on their arms, for the family's needs. The market sheds became such a fixture that people began calling High Street "Market Street," a name that had stuck by the mid-19th century.

13   Water Street, which ran along the Delaware, was usually crowded with carts, drays and wagons of every description. The clip-clop of horses' hooves, the swearing of teamsters and the raucous cry of gulls combined with the singsong enticements of the various street vendors to produce a kind of cacophony of commerce. Water Street was filled with run-down warehouses, grog shops and cheap boarding houses. Taverns were everywhere, designed to accommodate a large, transient population of sailors, businessmen and newly arrived travelers.

14   The waterfront was not only crowded, but filthy. Philadelphia was considered a clean city, where refuse was picked up at least once a week. It was clean, but only by the loose standards of the 18th century. Noisome as well as noisy, the waterfront was littered with horse manure, rotting garbage and other detritus that created a loathsome stench each summer.

15   Despite the capital's burgeoning growth, bustle and prosperity, a dark shadow of pain, suffering and

death fell across the city during the summer of 1793. On August 4, Martha Washington sadly noted the passing of Polly Lear. Polly was the wife of Washington's chief secretary, Tobias Lear, and her loss was keenly felt. In her 20s at the time of her death, Polly had lived at the president's mansion at 190 High Street. More family member than the wife of an employee, the young woman had helped the aging first lady with the various entertainments that marked the official round. Her son had been born at 190 High Street, and now she was gone.

16   Polly Lear had died of a fever of a particularly virulent kind. The young woman's body had been wracked by alternating fever and chills, but her other symptoms were ignored in the emotion of the moment. Polly Lear was, in fact, one of the first victims of yellow fever in Philadelphia.

17   It was around this time that Dr. Rush was called in for a consultation. A fellow physician, Dr. Hugh Hodge, had a two-year-old daughter who was gravely ill with fever. Rush examined the child, but felt there was little to be done. After she died, Rush—a keen observer—noted the corpse had a yellowish tinge.

18   More and more cases of fever began to break out, and soon a pattern started to emerge. The fever seemed to cluster around Water Street, though scattered cases like Polly Lear's were cropping up all over Philadelphia. Victims displayed a wide variety of symptoms. Some were weakened by chills and a fever that might rise to 104 degrees; others fought violent nausea, hiccupping and vomiting. Toward the end of their often-fatal ordeal patients turned a sickly yellow.

19   Rush wrote down other symptoms in his voluminous notes, commenting that "a bleeding at the nose, from the gums . . . and a vomiting of black matter in some instances close the scenes of life." Modern science generally believes that yellow fever severely damages the liver, which brings on jaundice, a yellowing of the skin. Bleeding from the nose and other orifices is also a byproduct of liver damage, because it causes the loss of vitamin K, a blood-clotting agent.

20   On Monday, August 19, 1793, Rush met with Dr. Hodge and Dr. John Foulke at a boarding house on Water Street, just north of Arch Street. Mrs. Catherine LeMaigre, wife of a French importer, was terribly ill, racked with a high fever and vomiting large amounts of black bile. His medical colleagues were uncertain as to the nature of the strange malady, but Rush felt he had the answer. The disease that was killing Mrs. LeMaigre and so many others was a "bilious yellow fever."

21   Once they had mulled over his startling diagnosis, Hodge and Foulke concurred. But what was the source of the contagion? Dr. Foulke recalled that the sloop *Amelia* had arrived on July 24 with a cargo of coffee. Unfortunately the shipment had gotten wet,

and the beans started to rot. Anxious to rid the ship of its evil-smelling cargo, the captain had dumped the rotting coffee on Bell's Arch Street wharf. Soon the whole waterfront neighborhood was blighted by a sickening stench.

22   Rush was certain that the rotting coffee odor was the cause of the yellow fever. Like most physicians of his day, Rush believed that fever was caused by "noxious miasma-evil air caused by rotting matter, stagnant swamps or the breath of infected patients." In this case, he concluded, it was the rotting coffee beans, putrefying and noxious, that was the source of the contagion.

23   The authorities were notified, and the Philadelphia College of Physicians issued "guidelines" to help combat the spreading infection. Citizens should carry bottles of camphor or handkerchiefs dipped in vinegar, breathing these disinfectants frequently to ward off the fever. Rush advised "all the families I now attend, that can move, to quit the city."

24   In spite of these precautions; yellow fever was spreading to the "healthier" parts of town, well away from the disreputable waterfront. A man who lived on Walnut, between Second and Third streets, came down with the dreaded disease, scarcely a block from the Todds' house and just around the corner from Rush's own home. John Todd felt he could wait no longer; it was high time for his family to leave. Dolley, her two sons and her sister Anna joined the swelling exodus from the city. Like many other refugees, their destination was Gray's Ferry, a rural spot some three miles southwest of Philadelphia.

25   Todd elected to remain in Philadelphia. His parents refused to leave, and he felt a filial obligation. Another factor was the press of business. As the disease spread and the death toll mounted, there were wills to be drawn up and estates to be settled. Buried under a mountain of paperwork, Todd insisted his 23-year-old clerk Isaac Heston remain to help him with the workload.

26   Heston's legal work served as a nearly constant reminder of the terrible drama being played out on Philadelphia's streets. On September 19, Heston wrote his brother: "You cannot immagin [sic] the situation in this city. They are dieing [sic] on our right hand & on our left." Within days of penning this melancholy missive, Heston himself would come down with yellow fever.

27   Todd tried to nurse his stricken assistant as best he could, but the young man soon died. The lawyer's father, John Todd Sr., died on October 2, his mother soon after. Scores of people were succumbing each day, and as the death toll mounted, Philadelphia's medical community was divided over what cures were the most effective. The debate deepened when Secretary of the Treasury Alexander Hamilton and his wife, Betsey, came down with yellow fever.

28   Though Thomas Jefferson was a multifaceted genius, he exhibited the all-too-human trait of gloating over an enemy's misfortunes. Relatively safe at Gray's Ferry, he ridiculed Hamilton as being "timid in sickness." But Hamilton was ill, and he turned to a boyhood friend from the West Indies, Dr. Edward Stevens, for help and comfort.

29   Stevens prescribed wine, bark, small doses of oil of peppermint and compound spirits of lavender, as well as chamomile flowers. The "bark" was a drink made from a Peruvian tree. It was sometimes called "Jesuit's bark," but today we know it as quinine. Every two hours the secretary would stand in a tub while cold water was poured over his naked body. Between soakings Hamilton would sip brandy burnt with cinnamon, and also have flannel cloths impregnated with wine and spices applied to his stomach.

30   Hamilton and his wife seemed to respond to the treatments and survived the yellow fever. The secretary publicized his recovery and gave full credit to Stevens' "mild" regimen, but Rush hinted that such methods would end up killing, not curing, people. Convinced his own treatments were the only effective ones, Rush acidly commented that "Colonel Hamilton's remedies are now as unpopular in our city as his funding system is in Virginia. . . . "

31   In the early days of the epidemic, Rush also prescribed milder treatments for yellow fever patients—rest, mild stimulants and cool fluids. A grain of calomel (mercurous chloride) or the Mexican vegetable laxative jalap might also be administered. While many—though not all—of his patients died anyway, Rush pored over medical texts for guidance.

32   A Dr. John Mitchell had noted in 1744 that fever victims usually had large quantities of blood in their abdominal viscera. That was it! Extraordinary times called for extraordinary measures. In such a crisis, only "heroic" bleeding and purging would save a yellow fever victim from untimely death.

33   Rush believed the human body held around 25 pounds of blood, twice the actual amount. He recommended that 80 percent of a patient's blood—20 pounds or so—be drained away to effect a cure. Leeches were too slow for Rush; he urged doctors to use a surgeon's lancet to start the crimson flow. In similar fashion, Rush increased purging doses to 10 grains of calomel and 15 grains of jalap, at least 10 times the normal dose. The patient would produce copious black stools, the purges so violent that gastrointestinal bleeding would result.

34   Although detailed records do not remain, there can be no doubt that those violent purges and copious bloodlettings were deleterious at least, if not fatal, to his patients. When some patients recovered after his regimen, however, Rush was more convinced than ever that he was God's instrument to save Philadelphia from a terrible scourge. When many of his colleagues rejected his "depletion therapy" using words like "murderous" and "doses fit for a horse," the thin-skinned Rush dug in his heels and wrote vitriolic defenses against their "malice."

35   Rush's house on Third and Walnut streets became a kind of clinic, where victims were attended by the doctor himself or one of his five students or apprentices. Here bloodletting was the norm, with container after container of gore dumped into Rush's backyard in an unending scarlet flood. So much blood was spilled that the property was like a slaughterhouse. Flies swarmed, and the area was filled with a sickly sweet stench.

36   Though nobody knew it at the time, yellow fever is a virus transmitted by the feeding bite of the female *Aëdes aegypti* mosquito. Earlier that summer, around 2,000 French colonials had arrived in Philadelphia, refugees from a massive slave rebellion that had erupted at Sainte Domingue (now Haiti). Some of the refugees might have been sick, and it's also possible that infected mosquitoes—or their larvae—might have traveled aboard ship with the fugitives. Ships of the period had water casks, seepage puddles and other areas of dampness that could breed the insects. The *Aëdes aegypti* is a day feeder, and would find the crowded Philadelphia waterfront a movable feast.

37   The yellow fever epidemic was at its height during the months of September and early October. About half the population—around 20,000—fled the city. President Washington refused to panic and waited to leave Philadelphia until September 10 for his regularly scheduled trip to Mount Vernon. Congress had adjourned, the Supreme Court suspended deliberations and the State Department ceased to function. Secretary of State Jefferson wrote that "deaths are now about 30 a day. . . . All my clerks have left me but one, so that I cannot conduct business."

38   The hardworking clerks of the Treasury Department seemed to be made of sterner stuff; a skeleton crew managed to continue the nation's financial life. Mail delivery, one of the few federal functions that touched the lives of ordinary people of the time, ceased for the duration of the epidemic. Some have described Philadelphia as a ghost town in these difficult weeks, but its abandonment was more apparent than real.

39.   Most of the streets were deserted, save for the melancholy processions of carters hauling victims from their houses to the hospital. Thousands did remain but barricaded themselves within their homes for fear of catching the dread infection. A kind of siege mentality developed, and only dire necessity—like obtaining food—would persuade citizens to venture forth from their red brick "fortresses." The Wednesday and Saturday markets continued, though fewer farmers were willing to come in to sell their produce. Those who did demanded exorbitant prices.

40   Mayor Matthew Clarkson asked for volunteers to help him with the crisis, and a handful responded to his call. A kind of emergency headquarters was set up in the building at Fifth and Chestnut streets, recently vacated by the U.S. Supreme Court. Absalom Jones and Richard Allen, then lay preachers and leaders of Philadelphia's large free African-American community, worked tirelessly to help victims of the epidemic. Mayor Clarkson also used their Free African Society as a kind of relief organization.

41   Blacks were recruited to serve as nurses and to act as carters to carry victims to the hospital that was established at Bush Hill. Dr. Rush believed that people of African descent were immune to yellow fever. He was mistaken: 240 blacks died during the course of the epidemic. After the crisis was over, blacks were unjustly accused of extorting high wages, or even stealing from those they nursed. Jones and Allen later eloquently refuted these spurious charges. Absalom Jones became the first ordained African-American Episcopal priest, while Allen was to become the first bishop of the African Methodist Episcopal (AME) Church of North America.

42   The makeshift hospital at the Bush Hill estate was at first a place of horror and hopelessness where fever-wracked victims lay wallowing in excrement and vomit-stained pillows. Luckily, things changed. Steven Girard and Peter Helm were, like Absalom Jones and Richard Allen, heroes who emerged in the epidemic's darkest days. Girard, a French émigré businessman, became the general administrator of Bush Hill. Helm was a cooper who made barrels at his shop on Race Street and counted George Washington as one of his clients. Helm's responsibilities at the hospital included the transportation of patients, burying the dead and keeping the house and its grounds sanitary.

43   When John Todd was reunited with Dolley at Gray's Ferry, he was already exhibiting symptoms of yellow fever. Though the danger was obvious, Dolley refused to leave his bedside. In spite of her devoted nursing, Todd died on October 14. That same day her five-month-old son, William Temple, also died of the fever, leaving the grieving widow doubly devastated. Soon Dolley too began to suffer

the alternating fever and chills, with periods of prolonged delirium that were characteristic of the disease. She hovered between life and death, and it was said that only the thought of her surviving child, Payne, gave her the determination to live.

44   The yellow fever epidemic ended with the first frosts of late October. The death rate declined sharply, but people remained apprehensive. Washington returned from Mount Vernon, but as a cautionary move took up residence in Germantown, about seven miles from Philadelphia. On Sunday, November 10, he rode into the city against the advice of his associates.

45   The president was alone, without a retinue, and undoubtedly his sudden appearance was a reassuring sight to the few people who were in the streets. Calm and dignified as ever, he gracefully bowed to all he encountered. Symbolically, at least, Washington's visit signaled a return of normality to the federal city. People came back, businesses reopened and Congress reconvened in December.

46   Approximately 5,000 people died of yellow fever during the epidemic. Lives were forever altered by those few terrible months in 1793. If Philadelphia had been spared, Dolley Todd might have lived her whole life as the anonymous wife of an obscure Quaker lawyer. But the epidemic brought her both tragedy and a dramatically altered fate. In 1794 the grieving widow, lonely and with few financial prospects, married Representative James Madison of Virginia. As Dolley Madison, wife of the fourth president of the United States, she would later become one of the most colorful first ladies in the history of the nation.

47   Rush continued to practice medicine and teach until his death in 1813. He continued to insist his "heroic" methods had saved the city from even greater loss of life. Ironically, it seems that Rush's patients had survived in spite of his treatments, not because of them. We now know that yellow fever mortality rates don't go beyond roughly 50 percent. A modern analysis of Rush's patients showed that 46 percent survived, well within the statistical norm. Philadelphia would have smaller yellow fever visitations in 1794, 1796 and 1797, but none were as severe or traumatic as the terrible epidemic of 1793.

18

THE WHISKEY REBELLION

BY ROBERT S. KYFF

Most nation states have experienced some form of civil disobedience to one degree or another. The United States was born of violent action taken against its mother country, and while yet an infant state, it felt compelled to act against a nascent rebellion singeing the outer fringes of its frontier dominion. Not only has this country been occasionally forced to deal with the ironies of rebellious behavior from within, but likewise victim to terminology that betrays the more sordid notions of who has the privilege to claim moral propriety in their acts versus those who don't. One person may be labeled a rebel while another described as a rioter. In modern times the United States has suffered various urban disturbances resulting in deaths and property damage, and we have universally identified the events as riots. Notwithstanding that the same sorts of violence and resulting destruction took place in far-removed venues like frontier Pennsylvania, we nonetheless refer to them as rebellions. We discover, in our definitions, even subtler, more pervasive paradoxes, if not a historical hypocrisy, relating to race, class, and culture.

Distilling of whiskey had been an economic engine for the back country in Colonial America traceable to some of the earliest Scots-Irish settlers. By the time Alexander Hamilton, Secretary of Treasury in Washington's administration, went on the prowl for revenues to fund the new nation and pay off its debt, the distillation of spirits was a viable industry.

Unfortunately, the sectional nature of whiskey production brought about an acute awareness of the divisions that were already so clearly apparent in American life. The West sparred with the East over tangible realities like taxes and trade as well as philosophical positions that cleaved down to the root of American thought.

President George Washington was faced with the same dilemmas that would haunt his successors, and he set the precedent to which they would point when countering violence in their own times. The tax on whiskey was levied in a particularly irksome way, but the reaction to it would seem, on the surface, to have been overly violent, and then some.

Only after a full understanding of historical divisions between the parties, the skewed economic situations that existed by 1791, and a host of other real or imagined grievances can we come close to ironing out the Whiskey Rebellion. Like the events surrounding the acquittals of the police who beat Rodney King or the assassination of Reverend Martin Luther King, ensuing rebellions can not be isolated away from the greater historical trends that led to such human behavior on so grand a scale. Our ultimate challenge is to interpret these actions based upon a clear, reasoned look into the world in which they took place.

- *What was the history of distillation in the back country?*
- *Who numbered among the ranks of the Whiskey Rebels?*
- *How did this crisis reflect the nature of conflicts throughout early American history?*
- *What role did George Washington, as President, play in this sad episode?*

1   On August 1, 1794, a motley army assembled at Braddock's Field on the Monogahela River near Pittsburgh. Nearly 7,000 armed militiamen—some dressed in regimental uniforms, others wearing the yellow hunting shirts of Indian fighters—mustered on the plain where, 39 years before, British General William Braddock had been mortally wounded and his forces defeated during the French and Indian War.

2   To the casual observer the assembly might have appeared to be a celebration, given the holiday atmosphere that prevailed as military drums beat loudly, soldiers marched and countermarched, and riflemen took target practice, filling the air with thick gray smoke. But the purpose of the gathering was deadly serious. These were the "Whiskey Rebels"— backwoods citizens of Pennsylvania's four western counties (Allegheny, Westmoreland, Fayette, and Washington) who had assembled to demonstrate their defiance of the federal government's excise tax on whiskey and to coerce others into joining them in opposition. Many of the rebels advocated outright independence from the United States, and several of the units displayed a six-striped flag representing the six defiant counties of western Pennsylvania and Virginia.

3   The insurgents' immediate plan was to seize nearby Fort Fayette and then occupy and burn Pittsburgh, which in their eyes exemplified the haughty eastern patricians who had imposed this unfair tax. The rationale at the time, according to an 1859 defense of a key figure in the events, was that "as old Sodom had been burned by fire from heaven, this second Sodom should be burnt by fire from earth!"

4   The ardent force was led by "Major General" David Bradford, a wealthy layer who fancied himself the "George Washington of the West." As the troops assembled, Bradford, dressed in military attire and mounted on a "superb horse in splendid trappings," dashed across the field "with plumes floating in the air and sword drawn." The ostentatious Bradford (prudently deciding to bypass well-defended Fort Fayette) then led his forces eight miles west toward Pittsburgh for what was euphemistically described as a "visit." Relishing the upcoming plunder of Pittsburgh's fancy ships, one upcountry soldier twirled his hat on his rifle barrel and boasted, "I have a bad hat now, but I expect to have a better one soon."

5   The advance of such a lawless, anti-aristocratic mob terrified the citizens of Pittsburgh, even though many sympathized with the rebel cause. The residents' apprehension was heightened by an eerie apparition: a lone horseman riding through the streets holding a tomahawk above his head and warning that revocation of the excise tax would be only the beginning of a larger revolution. "A great deal more is yet to be done," he chanted ominously.

6   Fearing the worst, Pittsburgh's 1,200 citizens deployed a shrewd strategy to protect their town. Rather than greeting the insurrectionists with guns, they instead offered the soldiers hams, dried venison, bear meat, and, of course, casks of whiskey. Through these conciliatory actions, and by agreeing to banish known Federalist sympathizers from their limits, the Pittsburgh residents saved their town from destruction. Although the occupying force did burn a few farm buildings and steal some livestock, it soon dispersed, leaving "Sodom" largely undamaged and its populace shaken but unharmed.

7   The rally at Braddock's Field and the occupation of Pittsburgh marked the high point of what has since become known as the "Whiskey Rebellion." Perhaps because of its bibulous nickname—conjuring up images of comical, pop-gun skirmish involving moonshining hillbillies—the uprising, regarded by nineteenth-century historians as the most important national crisis between the Revolutionary and Civil wars, today is more often remembered as a minor bump on the road to national consolidation.

8   Such an interpretation, however, overlooks the true significance of the crisis, which, more than any in the nation's formative years, defined the nature of the new federal government and its relationship to its citizens. This single event embodied nearly all of the fundamental issues and conflicts facing the young American republic and its new Constitution: the clash between liberty and order in a democracy; western versus eastern interests; agriculture versus industry; the nature of taxation; the duties and rights of citizens; relations with European powers such as Great Britain and Spain; the influence of the French Revolution; the rise of political parties; and the meaning of the American Revolution itself.

9   While some historians have dismissed the suppression of the rebellion as "duck soup" for the federal government, the outcome of this Constitutional crisis was, in fact, far from a foregone conclusion. It might well have resulted in the establishment of new states, fully independent of the government in Philadelphia, or perhaps in the alliance of trans-Appalachian counties with British Canada to the north or New Spain to the south. Moreover, the uprising was fraught with fascinating ironies: the requirements of the excise tax that triggered the revolt were relaxed just prior to the largest protest against it; the insurrection itself seemed to be dying out just when the federal government decided to suppress it; and President Washington, who had led the American rebellion against British taxation, now found himself on the opposite side, crushing the revolt against a similar internal tax.

10   The roots of this complex and intriguing episode lay in the unique character of life on the western frontier during the 1780s and '90s. Separated from the coastal regions by vast stretches of rugged

wilderness, westerners lived an isolated and dangerous existence that was characterized by violence, economic uncertainty, and physical hardship.Despite frequent appeals to the federal government for protection, people all along the frontier lived in constant fear of massacre. Between 1783 and 1790 alone, 1,500 settlers in the Ohio Valley were killed, wounded, or captured by hostile Native Americans.

11 Many settlers who had moved west in pursuit of economic opportunity and personal liberty now found themselves living in lice-infested hovels and scratching out a bare subsistence on land owned by absentee landlords. Geography and politics made it difficult for farmers to ship their commodities to larger markets: overland transportation of goods to eastern cities was costly, while Spanish control of New Orleans prevented shipment via the Ohio and Mississippi Rivers. The settlers begged the federal government to negotiate with Spain for transportation rights, but by 1791 no agreement had been reached.

12 Amid such poverty and economic isolation, many backwoodsmen fell into a life of crudity and dissipation. Squalid living conditions, excessive drinking, and random violence were common. Head-strong settlers—many recently arrived from Scotland, Ireland, and Germany—grew increasingly frustrated by the disparity between their expectations of prosperity in American and the harsh realities of frontier life. Increasingly, they blamed their troubles on the presumed conspiracy between the federal government, which had proved unable or unwilling to control the Indians or to secure westerners access to Mississippi River trade rights, and the eastern elite.

13 It was against this background of economic impoverishment, political frustration, and social unrest in the trans-Appalachian West that, in March of 1791, the federal government imposed an excise tax on whiskey. Seeking to put the new nation on a sound financial footing, Treasury Secretary Alexander Hamilton convinced Congress and President Washington that the whiskey tax was needed to pay off the debts, now assumed by the federal government, that had been incurred by the former colonies during the Revolutionary War.

14 The new excise law required that each rural distiller pay either an annual rate of 0.60 for each gallon of his still's capacity or nine cents per gallon produced. Distillers also were expected to keep accurate records of production and to gauge and label each cask before shipment—stipulations that placed a particular burden on part-time, small-scale distillers not accustomed to such strict accounting. Federal excisemen were empowered to inspect stills and search property for contraband goods and illegal distilling operations. And, even more disturbing to westerners, the law called for accused tax evaders to be tried in federal courts at Philadelphia, necessitating a costly, time-consuming journey that could ruin the distiller financially even if he were found innocent.

15 The concept of an excise tax—an internal, direct tax on products produced—was especially odious to western Pennsylvanians. Numerous attempts to levy such taxes within the late colony of Pennsylvania had met with failure. Many recent immigrants from the British Isles had experienced first-hand the oppressive practices of the Crown's hated excise collectors, who often confiscated property and employed paid informers. And, of course, it had been an excise tax—the Stamp Tax—that had angered and turned American colonists against Britain, leading to the late war for independence. That the infamous tax of 1765 had been imposed by a government in which they enjoyed no representation, while the tax on whiskey was enacted by their duly elected representatives, mattered little to a populace not yet used to the federal system of government created only a few years before.

16 Finally, citizens feared that, once the federal government got its foot in the door with the whiskey tax, it would soon pass internal taxes on other goods. "I plainly perceive," a Georgian predicted, "that the time will come when a shirt shall not be washed without an excise."

17 On the nation's western perimeter, whiskey was more than a luxury item or an incidental distraction from the rigors of survival. It was the lifeblood of the backwoods economy and culture. Virtually cut off as they were from eastern markets and the Mississippi River trade, farmers found it more efficient to distill their rye grain into whiskey that could easily be sold or bartered. While the average pack horse, for instance, could carry only four bushels of grain, it could haul the equivalent of 24 bushels if that grain were converted into two casks of whiskey. Thus, in this more portable liquid form, "Monongahela Rye" became the "coin of the realm" in western Pennsylvania, used to pay hired workers or to buy everything from salt to nails to gun-powder.

18 But whiskey was much more than just commodity or currency on the frontier; it was a way of life. Whether sweetened with tansy, mint, or maple sugar or swallowed straight, whiskey lubricated nearly every rite of frontier existence. No marriage, baptism, contract signing, brawl, trial, election, meal, or funeral took place without generous helpings of the local brew. Doctors prescribed it for nearly every ill; ministers sipped it before services, field workers demanded it as refreshment; and the United States Army issued a gill each day to soldiers.

19 This insatiable thirst for whiskey rendered the still a "necessary appendage of every farm" that could afford it. "In many parts of the country," wrote

one observer, "you could scarcely get out of sight of the smoke of a stillhouse." While perhaps only 10 to 20 percent of western Pennsylvania farmers actually owned whiskey stills, many neighbors purchased stills together and shared their use. And, even those farmers who performed no distilling had a direct stake in whiskey production because they sold their rye grain to the local distillers.

20   Given the importance of whiskey on the frontier, it is not surprising that residents of the trans-Appalachian counties violently opposed the federal excise tax. The federal government in far-away Philadelphia—the same government that could not protect them from the Indians and could not secure them trade rights on the Mississippi—was asking westerners to shoulder a disproportionate financial burden by taxing their region's dominant product. Worse yet, in a society based on a barter economy, where coin and currency were scarce, the government demanded that its excise tax be paid not in whiskey or other commodities, but in hard specie.

21   It soon became clear that, in its search for the sweet honey of revenue, the federal government had stuck its hand into a beehive. Shortly after the whiskey tax went into effect on July 1, 1791, western Pennsylvanians responded with protest meetings, petitions, and outright assaults on revenue agents. In September 1791, 16 Washington County men dressed in women's clothing seized excise collector Robert Johnson, cut off his hair, then tarred and feathered him. When John Connor tried to serve warrants to those accused of the assault, he himself was whipped, tarred and feathered, and tied to a tree.

22   Mobs burned revenue collectors in effigy and attacked their offices and lodgings. To show that the backwoodsmen equated the excise tax with British colonial oppression, dissidents erected "liberty poles," familiar icons of the Revolutionary War, and set up committees of correspondence similar to those that had kept protestors informed of developments in the struggle against the former mother country.

23   Inspired by the French Revolution as well as the American tax resisters formed numerous democratic societies modeled after the Jacobin Clubs, righteously vowing to "erect the temple of LIBERTY on the ruins of palaces and thrones." These extralegal organizations particularly irked President Washington, who, with Frances upheavals in mind, viewed them as a direct challenge to Constitutional authority. They masked, he said, "diabolical attempts to destroy the best fabric of human government."

24   In May 1792, Secretary Hamilton, hoping to defuse the protests that rendered the whiskey revenue virtually uncollectible, persuaded Congress to reduce the tax rates and allow for monthly payments. When this failed to discourage the assemblies and quell the violence, Washington, in September 1792,

issued a proclamation ordering the dissolution of any organization or meeting designed to obstruct the enforcement of any federal law. This action, however, also effectively silenced the moderates who sought a peaceful solution to the controversy, thus leaving radical leaders free to pursue their violent tactics.

25   Sporadic attacks on revenue collectors continued through 1793, completely shutting down the collection of whiskey tax in all frontier regions. Meanwhile, the federal government in Philadelphia—already preoccupied by the Reign of Terror in France, Indian attacks on the frontier, and threats by Spain and Britain—was brought to a near-standstill by a yellow fever epidemic that killed more than 4,000 people in that city. Mistaking the federal government's distraction for lack of resolve on excise enforcement, tax protestors pressed their demands for its repeal.

26   In early 1794, radical leaders took a new tack. Instead of directing violence only against collectors and their offices, they now targeted anyone who complied with the tax or cooperated with its enforcement. Law-abiding distillers were visited by "Tom the Tinker" who "mended" their stills by riddling them with bullets. In Allegheny County, for example, mobs destroyed the 120-gallon still of William Cochran and dismantled the grist mill of James Kiddoe simply because both men had registered their stills with authorities as the law required.

27   Seeking to pacify the insurgents, Congress on June 5, 1794 further amended the excise law to provide accused tax evaders with local trials and small distillers with a special license for temporary operations. But on that same day, Congress passed a new revenue act extending excise levies to snuff and sugar—a move that confirmed protestors fears that the excise on whiskey would inevitably expand to other products.

28   When federal agents began serving arrest warrants on alleged tax evaders during the summer of 1794, violence erupted anew. At dawn on July 16, 40 rebels arrived at Bower Hill, the home of distinguished Revolutionary War officer John Neville, to demand his resignation as Inspector of Revenue for western Pennsylvania. Before his appointment as supervisor of excise collection, Neville—a wealthy whiskey producer whose clapboard mansion boasted such luxuries as mirrors, carpets, and an eight-day clock—had adamantly opposed the whiskey tax, leading rebels to suspect that he had taken a large bribe to assume his federal office. The once-respected Neville now was detested as a turncoat by the insurgents.

29   When the mob in his front yard ignored an order to disband, Neville fired into their midst, mortally wounding Oliver Miller. The rebels shot back and were closing in on the house when some of Neville's

slaves, armed in anticipation of attack, opened fire from the rear, wounding four more militiamen. After a 25 minute gun battle, the posse retreated.

30   The next day an army of five to seven hundred men led by Captain James McFarlane showed up at Bower Hill, which was now defended by 10 federal soldiers from Fort Pitt, under the command of Major James Kirkpatrick. After brief negotiations, the rebels set several of the estate's outbuildings on fire and began an exchange of gunfire with the defending troops. During the lull in the fighting, McFarlane, thinking he had heard a call to parley, stepped out from behind a tree and was shot dead by the regulars. Smoke and heat from the burning structures subsequently filled the house, forcing the soldiers to surrender. The insurrectionists pillaged Neville's home and estate, liberating the mirrors and fancy clock. But Neville, who had been secreted in a nearby ravine by the soldiers before the rebels appeared on his property, escaped, as did his family.

31   With the death of McFarlane—who was a respected Revolutionary War hero—the insurgents now had a martyr. Radical leader David Bradford denounced McFarlane's "murder" and called for the rendezvous of militia forces at Braddock's Field. As it turned out, this dramatic show of force on August 1 marked the rebellions zenith—and helped to provoke its violent suppression.

32   On learning of the rebels "visit" to Pittsburgh, President Washington and Secretary Hamilton decided that time for military action had come. The nascent federal government, they believed, could no longer tolerate such blatant defiance of its laws. Although most residents of upcountry Georgia, Kentucky, North Carolina, and Virginia also refused to pay the excise tax, the opposition in western Pennsylvania was more visible and violent than in these states, and its suppression would send a strong message to all of the dissidents.

33   Moreover, it was unthinkable to allow such treason to flourish in the very state that held the nation's capital. Exaggerated rumors of attacks on federal arsenals and invasions of towns by armed mobs swept through eastern cities. With Britain and Spain seeking to bully the young nation and France grappling with its revolution, this was no time for conciliation. At issue, Washington and Hamilton believed, was the very integrity and credibility of the federal government—perhaps even its survival.

34   Although he had made up his mind to wage war, Washington, hoping to appear conciliatory, in late August went through the motions of sending peace commissioners to seek a non-military solution. Thinking these negotiations legitimate, moderate leaders like Albert Gallatin, who himself later served as Secretary of the Treasury, persuaded many of the dissidents to cease their violence. Ironically, evidence suggests that opposition to the tax was waning just as Washington was preparing for military operations.

35   By early October, Washington had assembled a 12,950-man army from the state militias of Pennsylvania, New Jersey, Virginia, and Maryland. In many ways these forces were no more disciplined or well-organized than the dissidents they opposed. A curious blend of lower-class and gentlemen volunteers, the impromptu army suffered from high desertion rates, squabbles over chains of command, and persistent rumors that it was really being sent to fight Indians or seasoned British regulars.

36   But the militiamen's spirit was aroused when rebels derided their fighting prowess. "Brother, you must not think to frighten us," wrote one "Captain Whiskey" in a western Pennsylvania newspaper, "with . . . your watermelon armies from the Jersey shores; they would cut a much better figure in warring with the crabs and oysters about the Cape of Delaware." A "Jersey Blue" angrily retorted that the "watermelon army of New Jersey (had) ten-inch howitzers for throwing a species of melon very useful for curing a gravel occasioned by whiskey!" From then on this combined federal force would be known, both affectionately, and derisively, as the "watermelon army."

37   General Henry "Light Horse Harry" Lee, then governor of Virginia, commanded the force, whose ranks included the governors of Pennsylvania and New Jersey, Revolutionary General Dan Morgan, future explorer Meriwether Lewis, five nephews of President Washington, and Alexander Hamilton himself. The southern wing of the army marched northwestward toward Pennsylvania from Virginia and Maryland, while the right flank proceeded westward from New Jersey and eastern Pennsylvania.

38   On October 4, President Washington reviewed the northern contingent at Carlisle, Pennsylvania, and his charisma greatly boosted morale. Soldiers and townspeople alive gave the hero of the Revolution a royal welcome. One observer noted that "when I saw the President lift his hat to the troops as they passed along, I thought I caught a glimpse of the Revolutionary Scene."

39   After traveling to Fort Cumberland, Maryland, to review the southern wing of the army, the president returned to Philadelphia. Soon after, the two contingents converged in Bedford, Pennsylvania. Although Lee was left in charge of military operations, Hamilton served as the force's unofficial civilian leader. Officers familiar with Hamilton's ambition noted that the Secretary's tent was bigger than Lee's and that he sometimes gave orders directly to soldiers.

40   The army's march westward during those brilliant autumn days proved part picnic and part pogrom. As the column crossed the Alleghenies, the Whiskey Rebellion seemed to evaporate ahead of it.

Encountering no military opposition, the troops plundered plump chickens, butchered hogs, and imbibed generous portions of the notorious taxable liquid. The officers' diaries and letters read like tourist brochures noting for instance, that while Newtown was a poor place for acquiring hay it boasted "mountains of beef and oceans of whiskey."

41   But the army encountered—and inflicted— hardship as well. Because the huge force constantly out-marched its provisions, rations ran short. The troops' poorly made shoes disintegrated on cold, muddy roads. And the many liberty poles erected along the route served notice of the local citizens' hostility, which often manifested itself in taunts aimed at the soldiers or refusal of food or lodging.

42   In apprehending suspected leaders of the insurgency for interrogation, the troops could be brutal. On November 13in what came to be known as the "dreadful night," the New Jersey cavalry dragged 150 suspects from their beds, marched them—some half-clothed and barefooted—through snow and sleet and incarcerated them in a roofless outdoor pen. General Andrew White, dubbed "Blackbeard" for his cruelty, kept his 40 captives tied back-to-back in an unheated cellar for two days without food, then herded them like animals through 12 miles of mud and rain.

43   Because David Bradford and as many as 2,000 die-hard rebels fled westward into the wilderness, most of the suspects seized for questioning were not the ringleaders of the uprising. Hamilton and Lee, for instance, interrogated the moderate Hugh Brackenridge intensely for hours before concluding that their prisoner had been trying to temper the rebellion rather than incite it.

44   In late November, 20 obscure rebels—none of whom had actually been key figures in the uprising— were shipped to Philadelphia for trial. Paraded through the capital's streets on Christmas Day, the prisoners looked so wretched that even Presley Neville, son of the besieged excise inspector, felt sorry for them. Ultimately, only two suspects were found guilty of treason, and Washington, seeking to appear magnanimous, pardoned both.

45   Leaving 1,500 troops in Pittsburgh to maintain order, the bulk of the watermelon army began its return home in late November. The entire expedition had cost $1,500,000—about one third of the revenues raised by the whiskey tax during its entire life. But cost mattered little given the principles at stake. On January 1, 1795, a "gravely exultant" Washington proclaimed February 19 as a day of thanksgiving for "the reasonable control which has been given to a spirit of disorder of suppression of the later insurrection."

46   Indeed, Washington and the Federalists had much to be thankful for. With a relatively painless and largely bloodless military excursion, they had asserted the supremacy of the federal Constitution and ensured that the trans-Appalachian west would remain part of the United States.

47   The Whiskey Rebellion was a personal triumph for Washington as well. He had placed his political reputation and prestige on the line—and had prevailed. His actions would serve a precedent for John Adams in his handling of the Fries Rebellion in 1799, Andrew Jackson's response to the nullification crisis of the 1830s and Abraham Lincoln's reaction to secession in 1861.

48   Ironically, the defeat of western Pennsylvanians in the Whiskey Rebellion brought with it the alleviation of many of the region's problems. By spending so much money during its invasion, the watermelon army seeded western Pennsylvania with enough currency to germinate a prosperous commercial economy there. And in the single year following the rebellion, the Jay Treaty reduced Great Britain's Indian agitation and interference on the American western frontier, the Pinckney Treaty secured free trade on the Mississippi from Spain, and the Treaty of Greenville reduced the threat of Indian attack.

49   Finally, by dramatically defining the key political issues of the day—East versus West, agriculture versus commerce, plutocracy versus democracy, order versus liberty—the Whiskey Rebellion fostered the development of a two-party system in American politics. By 1801, with the election of Thomas Jefferson as president, the Republican Party, representing many of the principles advocated by insurgents, would gain control of the national government.

50   Thus, when the Republican Congress in 1802 repealed the hated excise that had started all the fuss, the Whiskey Boys could hoist their first untaxed jugs in 10 years and savor sweet victory.

19

THE MEASUREMENT THAT BUILT AMERICA

BY ANDRO LINKLATER

*The little-appreciated U.S. public-land survey not only
opened up our frontier but made possible our freedoms*

The United States enjoyed its blood-stained independence even as it suffered considerable debt incurred from the costly battle to achieve it. The one asset to which the young republic could turn for revenue was its western lands. The frontier was, by all accounts, an inexhaustible resource, though the means to exploit such vast wealth had yet to be devised by 1785. Linklater explains why he considers the Land Ordinance of 1785 as a threshold in American recognition of what the frontier would mean in the future, and something of definite spot to which to anchor Frederick Jackson Turner's "frontier thesis" when looking back from later perspectives.

Landmark transformations would evolve out of the order and process attached to the measuring out, titling, and disposition of contiguous, standard parcels of land. The Jeffersonian vision of an agrarian commonwealth was, ironically, subverted by the very land tenure on which it was planted and expected grow. Though land, along with concern for its protection and the rights born of owning it, spread the rule of law and a sense of concern for its use, the sheer magnitude of wealth associated with its disposition would ignite selling and consumption in ways that generated income and thus investment toward other ends than agriculture. Entrepreneurs came to use land as one of any sorts of medium of exchange by virtue of the assurance and stable value it carried with it.

In the midst of this march toward modern land usage, organized urban development, and economic values that prepped the nation for the free-for-all capitalism to come, ancient measuring techniques continued to mark the place. The spirit of old, Anglo-Saxon devotion to simple numbers and calculations left a stamp of archaic barbarism on the latest maps.

- *By what means was land measured?*
- *What was considered the "bottom ring" of land ownership?*
- *How did people physically measure a piece of land?*

---

1   LOOK OUT THE AIRPLANE WINDOW ON A flight from Los Angeles to Chicago, and you can see below one of the most astonishing man-made constructs on earth. It is more extensive than the Great Wall of China, yet it remains almost invisible unless you're looking for it. Once you begin to recognize it, however, the clues are everywhere: the checkerboard arrangement of the orchards and fields of California's

Great Central Valley; the rectangular farms in the canyons of the Sierra Nevada; the graph-paper grid of streets in Phoenix and Salt Lake City; the great plaid pattern of corn and soy across the prairies. All are aligned with the cardinal points of the compass, so that the lines run north to south and east to west.

2 These are the visible indicators of the United States public-land survey, a continuing project nearly as old as the nation itself. Since 1785 it has covered more than three million square miles from the Appalachians to the Pacific Ocean, shaping farms and cities and doing more to alter the American landscape in that time than wind or weather. But its invisible influence is more far-reaching yet. The survey created a structure of land ownership unlike any other in history and laid the foundation for the development of a society unique in its democracy and enterprise. And, almost incidentally, it ensured that the United States would be one of the last nations in the world to resist the metric system.

3 On September 30, 1785, Thomas Hutchins, the first official geographer of the United States, unrolled a 22-yard-long surveyor's chain on the west bank of the Ohio River. The government needed to raise money to pay off the mountain of debt it had accumulated in achieving its independence, and this land beyond the Appalachians was virtually its only asset. Before the sale could take place, however, the wilderness had to be measured out and mapped. This was Hutchins's job. The Northwest Ordinance that had been passed in May that year called for "disposing of lands in the western territory" and required him to lay out lines running east to west six miles apart; they were to be cut at right angles by north-south lines six miles apart. This would create a grid of squares, known as townships, each covering 36 square miles. The townships were to be divided into 36 one-mile-square sections, which would be sold at auction. Hutchins was performing a piece of magic, the transformation of wilderness into property.

4 The pattern of squares had been Thomas Jefferson's idea, proposed in 1784. The simplicity of the shape made it truly democratic. It was easily measured out, and its area could readily be checked by any potential buyer. In Jefferson's ideal society, based on a romantic idea of Saxon England populated by independent yeoman farmers, as many people as possible would own land. He wrote in *Notes on the State of Virginia* that "the proportion which the aggregate of the other classes of citizens bears in any state to that of its husbandmen [farmers], is the proportion of its unsound to its healthy parts, and is a good-enough barometer whereby to measure its degree of corruption." From the start, therefore, the survey was expected not simply to raise money but to shape a society.

5 The equipment was basic: a theodolite or a transit (at that date, little more than a telescope with built-

in compass), through which the surveyor could take a sighting on a distant mark to find its direction, and a Gunter's chain—a standard surveyor's chain exactly 66 feet long—to measure out the distance. Preceded by axmen who hacked a path through the trees, the foreman took the front end of the chain and marched toward the mark; when the chain was fully stretched, he cried, "Tally!," stuck a tally pin in the ground, and waited for the hindman to join him, gathering up the chain. So they moved across the country, like caterpillars, hunching up and stretching out, through forests, over swamps, up mountains, and down ravines.

THIS WAS WHAT UNDERPINNED THE LEGENDS OF THE FRONTIER, GUARANTEEING POSSESSION OF THE LAND, SUBSTANTIATING CLAIMS, SETTLING FEUDS.

6 "Before going a mile," one surveyor wrote of the hilly forests in eastern Ohio, "I discovered it was impossible to do accurate chaining in such a broken country, where the hills were so steep it was often with difficulty they could be climbed." William Burt, who ran part of the survey through the mosquito-infested swamps and prickly undergrowth of Michigan, was made of sterner stuff. "Dear Companion," he wrote to his wife, Phebe, in 1840, "I am now . . . about 40 or 50 miles from any Settlement in the midst of a swamp about twelve miles in diameter, but expect to get out tomorrow as I can see high Beech and maple Land to the North. My Coat and Pantiloons are most gone. If you could make me a frock [long coat] and a pair of Pantiloons of the strongest kind of Bedticking they would I think stand the Brush." In Kansas a young surveyor was taking a sighting in 1854, when, he reported, "a party of Indians fired on me and my men. A shell struck a tree against which I was leaning."

7 Despite the difficulties, by the end of the nineteenth century most of the country had been squared off into townships and sections, half-sections, and quarter-sections, down to a quarter-quarter section of 40 acres. Each parcel of land was identified on a surveyor's map, registered at a federal land office, and made available for purchase. This was what underpinned the legends of the frontier. The survey guaranteed the pioneers in their covered wagons legal possession of their land; it substantiated the claims of gold miners; it settled the feuds of cowboys and farmers; it financed the construction of the railroads. "The magnitude of the greatest land-measurement project in history is mind-boggling," wrote the geographer Hildegard B. Johnson in 1977. "One marvels at the determination with which these men threw and retraced their lines. Still their role is largely ignored in the history of the frontier."

8   In 1862 Lincoln introduced the Homestead Act, which gave anyone 160 acres so long as he or she built a cabin and worked the soil for five years. Parcels of land were given free to socially valuable people like Army veterans and teachers. State universities were founded on the proceeds of the sale of lands the federal government had given to the states, and railroad companies made their profits largely from the squares of land the government gave to them on either side of the track. In all, more than a billion acres entered private ownership.

9   The process had profound consequences. Most eighteenth-century Americans thought of those living on the frontier as one step removed from savagery—"our own semi-barbarous citizens" was how Jefferson described them—but early-nineteenth-century writers like James Fenimore Cooper began to extol them for their self-reliant enterprise, and a generation later they came to be taken as the very essence of what it meant to be American. In his famous 1893 essay "The Significance of the Frontier in American History," Frederick Jackson Turner argued that "the frontier promoted the formation of a composite nationality for the American people . . . that restless nervous energy, that dominant individualism working for good and for evil, and withal that buoyancy and exuberance which comes with freedom—these are traits of the frontier."

10   Turner's thesis has repeatedly been attacked on the grounds that the movement westward was too piecemeal and irregular to constitute the pushing back of a frontier. Far from being individualistic, it was usually communal. Yet his thesis refuses to die, because a distinctive American spirit did indeed arise from the expansion into the West. To contemporary observers, the origin of that spirit was obvious. It had little to do with the frontier family's experience in the wilderness and everything to do with its acquisition of landed property.

11   As early as 1813 the traveler John Melish commented approvingly, "Every industrious citizen of the United States has the power to become a freeholder . . . and the land being purely his own, there is no setting limits to his prosperity. No proud tyrant can lord it over him." Writing 20 years later from a less admiring viewpoint, Frances Trollope, the mother of the British novelist Anthony Trollope, expressed fear for the survival of civilized behavior when anyone could acquire land. "Any man's son may become the equal of any other man's son, and the consciousness of this is certainly a spur to exertion," she conceded in *The Domestic Manners of the Americans*. "On the other hand, it is also a spur to that coarse familiarity, untempered by any shadow of respect, which is assumed by the grossest and lowest in their intercourse with the highest and most refined."

12   It is easy to mock Mrs. Trollope, but if Jefferson's romantic view of the Saxons is discounted, the only model that history had so far provided for owning land was vertical, with the highest classes occupying the most, the lowest holding the least, and every social gradation from aristocrat to peasant determined largely by acreage. Now for the first time an entire society was being created, peacefully and legally, around a horizontal model of land distribution. In an era when land was the primary source of wealth and the key indicator of social class, the possibility that anyone could own it struck European visitors as revolutionary. In their eyes, that was what made America unique. A survey drawing from the 1780s shows its makers and their chain. Opposite, the chain itself.

13   Supporting evidence comes from an intriguing anomaly in Turner's thesis. He and his followers thought of the frontier as moving west, but in the early part of the nineteenth century, convoys of canvas-covered wagons also headed south, to Alabama, Mississippi, and Louisiana. By rights the frontier spirit should also have emerged there in the Deep South, with the same enterprising activity. Instead, a socially divided, hierarchical culture developed, markedly lacking in economic enterprise.

14   Most visitors blamed the South's idleness on its slave economy, but that wasn't the only thing that made the Southern frontier different. Throughout the region a nexus of fraud and corruption and the complications of earlier land grants made by French and Spanish governments prevented U.S. public land surveyors from establishing the kind of grid that was spreading into the Midwest. Surveys were forged, boundary markers moved, land officials bribed, and only those with deep pockets and smart lawyers could regard their titles to property as secure. In 1816 one local expert reckoned that "the titles in Kentucky will be Disputed for a Century to Come yet, when it's an old Settled Country." That lack of security kept the South from developing the sort of vigorous land market that flourished in the North, where financial institutions in New York and Boston created loans, bonds, and credit arrangements of ever-increasing sophistication to finance deals. And the Southern economy languished for much of the nineteenth century.

15   Significantly, one Southern state did escape the pattern. Stephen Austin, who brought hundreds of American families to Texas while it was still under Mexican rule, was so disgusted by the confusion of Kentucky's survey that he measured out the Americans' property accurately and in rectangles. As a result, much of Texas's public land came to be divided into plain, easily surveyed squares or oblongs that could be bought and sold without difficulty. When oil was discovered in Texas, late in the nineteenth century, real estate financing was available from institutions and individuals that had already done well in the land market.

16   The losers in all this were the American Indians. Almost every Indian war fought by the U.S. government from the Battle of Fallen Timbers in 1794 to the massacre at Wounded Knee in 1890 had its origins in the urge to pry ownership of land from its original occupants, and almost every Indian defeat was followed by a treaty in which they ceded territory to the U.S. government. Immediately afterward the surveyors would arrive with their chains and compasses, and in their wake would come the settlers. "It would be difficult to describe the avidity with which the American rushes forward to secure this immense booty," Alexis de Tocqueville wrote in *Democracy in America*. "Before him lies an immense continent and he urges onward as if time pressed and he was afraid of finding no room for his exertions."

WHAT JEFFERSON NEVER FORESAW WAS THAT THE SQUARED-OFF LAND WOULD BECOME A SOURCE OF CAPITAL, ENABLING SETTLERS TO BORROW, LEND, INVEST.

17   Yet, as Jefferson anticipated, the survey also gave even the farthest-flung pioneers an interest in a law-based society, for once their square parcels had been registered at the land office, the whole panoply of the law guaranteed their rights to them. And because they received their property from the U.S. government, they had a stake not just in their immediate society but in America itself, a sense of identification that immediately struck the English émigré Morris Birkbeck when he settled in Illinois in the 1820s. "Here, every citizen, whether by birthright or adoption is part of the government," he wrote, "identified with it, not virtually but in fact."

18   What Jefferson never foresaw was that the squared-off land would become a source of capital, enabling settlers to borrow, lend, and invest in other enterprises. A generation after Hutchins started measuring out its wilderness, the state of Ohio possessed "33 printing-offices, 27 banks, 12 cotton mills, 8 paper mills, 3 nail factories, an almost infinite number of stores, grist merchants and sawmills." This rural capitalism grew to fit in seamlessly with the industrial age in the 1850s and with the expansion of the railroad system across the country, financed by the federal government's lavish grants of public-survey squares that the railroad companies could then sell to settlers. Thus Jefferson's yeoman farmers inexorably became part of the capitalist world that went with the democratic distribution of land.

19   Equally inexorably, so too did the measurements used in the survey. Having decimalized the dollar, Jefferson enthusiastically proposed decimalizing American weights and measures. As a painless way of introducing the change, he argued that the survey's squares be measured in decimal units (a township would have measured 10 by 10 new decimal miles, each mile being about 6,086 old feet long, and subdivided into tenths, one-hundredths, and one-thousandths). It comes as something of a surprise to discover that George Washington, Alexander Hamilton, and James Madison all supported Jefferson's scheme for decimalizing.

20   But the measures that were eventually chosen for use in the survey, and that thus came to be adopted by every settler in the new Western lands, were archaic Saxon units based on the number four. The length of the standard surveyor's chain is usually described as 22 yards, but more important it was also four rods, each 16'/2 feet long. In sixth-century Anglo-Saxon England, the cultivation of an area measuring four square rods was reckoned as a day's work; 40 days' work made an acre, and 640 acres made a square mile. This ancient system was perfectly suited to the U.S. public-land survey because when it came to measuring out squares, a system based on four made life very simple.

21   The 640 acres that made up a section of a township could be divided into quarters, eighths, and sixteenths and still leave a whole number: 40, to be exact. This numerical neatness ensured that 40 acres became the basic unit on which Jefferson's great landed democracy was built. Owning a 40 was the bottom rung on the property ladder, and to a surveyor nothing could be easier to measure. A 40-acre square was merely 20 chains by 20. Railroads sold land by the 40-acre lot. After the Civil War freed slaves were reckoned to be self-sufficient with "40 acres and a mule." A nineteenth-century pioneer described how to pace it out on the prairie before the survey had even arrived: A walk 440 yards south, toward the midday sun, by 440 yards west, toward the setting sun, made a 40, and the claim could be registered later when the surveyor's map was drawn up. The heroes of John Steinbeck's *The Grapes of Wrath* were the dirt-poor farmers who scraped a living on dry, dusty forties in 1930s Oklahoma.

22   The survey was unified by running a number of carefully calculated north-south lines (known as principal meridians) and east-west lines (principal baselines) far enough to connect the work of one survey team with another. For example, the fifth principal meridian begins in Arkansas and runs all the way north to the Canadian border, connecting surveys in about 10 different states. Since the earth is not flat, the north end of a township is about 20 yards narrower than the 6 miles it is supposed to be. And the next township north is narrower still. The cure is to remeasure after four or five townships, bringing the distance back to 6 miles with a so-called correction line. In the Midwest, where roads tend to follow the survey lines, this produced a dead end and a sharp 90-degree turn after 24 or 36 miles of straight driving.

You can tell by the skidmarks that it takes drivers by surprise.

23   The surveyor's chain shaped urban America too. The average city block with surrounding streets covered five acres (five chains by 10), and in Philadelphia, Salt Lake City, and innumerable other cities, the central square measured 10 acres (10 chains by 10). When Ferdinand R. Hassler was authorized by Congress in 1836 to produce the first federally approved set of weights and measures, he publicly declared his preference for the 10-based metric system, but he conceded that the choice "of a set of standards in general depends upon the individual use made of them." For the United States, that could only mean the four-based measures that the survey had spread throughout the nation. Every attempt to replace the U.S. Customary System of weights and measures with the metric system has failed, so far, because that Customary System is built into the very structure and values of American society.

24   This is the significance of what you see from the airplane window, an enterprise so massive, so integral to the United States, that it almost disappears into the landscape.

V

TECHNOLOGY OF THE NINETEENTH CENTURY

1   When President Thomas Jefferson purchased the Louisiana territory from France in 1803, he envisioned a country that would slowly expand westward. Jefferson believed it would take up to 500 years before American settlers reached the Pacific coast line. A projected date for California statehood might well have been 2300! Hindsight shows that Jefferson was a better statesman than soothsayer.

2   By the end of the nineteenth century, the United States had developed into one of the world's giant industrial powers. Railroads travailed the landscape; factories produced more goods than Americans could possibly consume; and immigrants flooded into the United States hoping to escape persecution and find a better way of life. What factors contributed to this transformation of a predominantly agrarian nation into one of such enormous industrial output?

3   In the period following the War of 1812, Americans recognized the need to be more self-sufficient. Although two wars had been fought against their former "mother country" Great Britain, Americans remained reliant on London's manufacturing capabilities to turn the United States' raw materials into finished products. (In 1780, John Adams had predicted that America would not manufacture its own

goods for a thousand years.) It was an inefficient system. Why send England the cheaper timber, cotton, and tobacco leaves, while England received the greater profits from the higher-priced furniture, clothing, and stogies?

4   Invention is the mother of necessity. Invent something new and people will need it. Such was the case of Eli Whitney's cotton gin and the textile mills in Lowell Massachusetts. If you were a plantation owner, you couldn't survive without a gin and no community relied on homespun cloth like Martha Ballard and her daughters produced.

5   And the southern cotton gin and the northern textile mill were intricately connected. Cotton provided "the fuel" for the mills to make the clothing. Mass manufacturing had begun.

6   Commercial success was reliant on more efficient transportation. Canals were built linking rural areas to cities; inland trade would no longer be a barrier for commercial success. As late as 1820, it cost as much to ship a ton of goods 30 miles overland as it did to sent it across the entire Atlantic Ocean to Europe! By 1850, Americans looked back two generations and knew they would not be returning to that past except through front porch stories.

7   America's manufacturing capabilities allowed for domestic products to drive the economy. Many

workers were often enslaved to grow and produce materials without garnering sufficient wages. Profit remained in the hand of a selected few. Southern slaves received no monetary compensation and were forced to work until death did them part. Working class whites including many single women, and immigrants from Ireland and Germany might cite their personal freedom but northern mill labor was a source of rampant exploitation. Poor, uneducated children were forced to work at dangerous jobs too. Such workers huddled together in overcrowded, disease-ridden cities and suffered with starvation wages and no benefits. Add to this "melting pot," the Native Americans that were banished to barren foreign territory, and the human cost of an industrializing country left some Americans excited about the future, while excluding most individuals from deciding their own destinies.

20

ERIE CANAL: VIABLE EAST-WEST TRADE STARTED IN NEW YORK

BY DENNIS MAURIZI

The Erie Canal Song
I've got an old mule and her name is Sal
Fifteen miles on the Erie Canal
She's a good old worker and a good old pal
Fifteen miles on the Erie Canal
We've hauled some barges in our day
Filled with lumber, coal, and hay
And every inch of the way we know
From Albany to Buffalo
Low bridge, everybody down
Low bridge for we're coming to a town
And you'll always know your neighbor
And you'll always know your pal
If you've ever navigated on
The Erie Canal

A canal is a waterway dug across land for boats and barges to carry items from one place to another. What is the significance of a canal in the greater scheme of American history? And more specifically, why was the Erie Canal the most important one of its day?

The original 13 states were connected solely by the Atlantic Ocean. No one traveled overland from Georgia to New Hampshire. Trading goods required sending all items on the high seas. That scenario was fine for those huddled on the eastern seaboard but what about those settlers who ventured westward? How could they send their products from farm to market? Railroads were in their infancy and "interstate highways" consisted of ruts that often had tree stumps as high as two feet and you traveled at the "speed" of three miles per hour.

By the early nineteenth century, many in America saw canals as the solution to join the disparate states and territories. The construction of the Erie Canal in the Northeast connected communities that were isolated from each other. Trade routes were now open. Western towns grew in size and stature. Distance was no longer a barrier to one's commercial success.

- *What were the advantages in building a canal?*
- *What factors contributed to the building of the Erie Canal?*
- *Why was the Erie Canal called Clinton's Ditch?*

- *How did the Erie Canal change the way farmers grew food?*
- *This article deals with the rise of canals in America. What do you suppose led to the demise of canals?*

*(Note: **The Erie Canal Song** was composed in 1913—a post mortem setting—to protest the coming of the mechanized barge which would replace the mule that had been previously used.)*

---

1   Companies like Microsoft may be making millions off this whole internet thing, but I think I know where they may have gotten the idea—from a man by the name of DeWitt Clinton.

2   In the early 1800s, Clinton was governor of New York—twice actually. He was also the person pushing hardest for construction of the Erie Canal. A lot of non-believers pushed back.

3   The Erie Canal would need to cover over 360 miles, and would require eight years to build. Construction of the Erie Canal would cost in the very upscale neighborhood of $7 million. Critics laughed at the notion of "Clinton's Ditch," which may explain why critics are seldom put in charge of building canals.

4   A canal may not seem like big news today. Trips to outer space hardly seem like big news today. But if you look at a map of the United States you'll see how far it is from, say, Ohio to New York City. Do you see all those pesky mountains in between? Do you begin to see the problem?

5   Before the Erie Canal, east-west trade in this country was almost non-existent. Roads were little more than ruts, and were even worse when it rained. And as horrific as the logistics were, the costs were even worse. Freight rates ran a hefty $32 a ton per 100 miles, which was a prohibitive price for most commodities.

6   Shipping by water was not much easier, or less expensive. If farmers wanted to get their products to markets in the east, the only real choice they had was to first head south on the Ohio River to the Mississippi into the Gulf of Mexico, then around the tip of Florida and north again. Most farmers didn't bother producing more than they needed. What was the point?

7   The Erie Canal changed all that—it provided a water link between the interior of the country and the markets of the Atlantic seaboard. It's hard to overstate just what that meant.

8   On its back, a horse may be able to carry 400 pounds. In front of a wagon, that 400 pounds might go as high as 4,000 pounds. A horse who might struggle with 4,000 pounds could manage towing 50 tons loaded on a canal barge. That's 25 times more weight, without much more effort.

9   Farmers in western New York could get their goods to New York City using the Erie Canal. Just as important, manufacturers in New York City could get their goods to western destinations after construction was complete.

10   By any standard, the Erie Canal is an example of amazing achievement. Perhaps most amazing, though, was how long it took to get the darned thing off the ground. More than 100 years before construction on the canal was completed, in 1724, Cadwallader Colden, then Surveyor-General of what was New York Province, saw the canal as a great way to capitalize on some of the lucrative North American fur trade. Until that time, the European-bound business had belonged almost exclusively to Montreal, which had access to Atlantic shipping lanes via its position on the St. Lawrence River.

11   Colden knew a canal would have two advantages. One, it would be far easier to negotiate than the St. Lawrence, and two, it would be much less vulnerable to weather conditions. What the idea didn't have was public support. It would be 70 years before it got some. This time, it was the brain-child of New Yorker Elkanah Watson. Like Colden, Watson believed in the virtues of a water link between the Great Lakes Region and the Atlantic. Like Colden, he suggested following the Hudson north from New York. But unlike his counterpart, Watson decided against making a sharp left over to Lake Erie, and recommended continuing on to Lake Ontario.

12   He hoped the change in direction would help turn the tide. Unlike Colden's earlier plan, Watson's relied on improving existing rivers rather than digging a costly new canal. The idea had merit, but the results were mixed at best. Between cost overruns, the need to rebuild many of the wooden locks along the way, and the growing competition from the new wave of turnpikes, revenues from Watson's creation never covered expenses.

13   But New York diplomat Gouverneur Morris refused to give up the ghost, and did what he could to keep the notion of an east-west water link alive. "As yet," he implored, "we only crawl along the outer shell of our country. The interior excels the part we inhabit in soil, in climate, in everything."

14   What he said seemed to work. Public interest was rekindled. But still the question remained, should the link be a Lake Erie connection, or a revisited Lake Ontario version?

15   Finally, a determination was made. A Lake Erie route would need only half as many locks. It wouldn't require digging a special canal around Niagara Falls as an Ontario system would. And should trouble flare again with Britain, an Erie link would be far less vulnerable.

16   Alas, the vagaries of canal-building are many. After the federal government finally began a 10-year, $20 million program to overhaul the nation's transportation system, including construction of the Erie Canal, the War of 1812 broke out.

17   The Erie Canal project was put on hold. Even after the war, New York's neighboring states hoped it would stay that way. After all, they were working to improve their own transportation systems, and every delay for the Erie Canal meant increased opportunities for them to steal New York's thunder, as well as its trade.

18   The threat did not go unnoticed. "If you wish New York to remain, as now, the emporium of America," said one Erie backer to legislators in Albany, "suffer not the trade with the interior of your state be carried off triumphantly by the spirited and enterprising citizens of Philadelphia and Baltimore."

19   The Erie Canal's savior would turn out to be an ex-mayor, ex-governor, and ex-canal commissioner of New York named DeWitt Clinton. Ever since the powerful Tammany Society had put him out to pasture in 1815, Clinton had been looking for a way to regain his political footing. The canal gave him his chance.

20   The canal and Clinton both had no place to go but up. In Clinton's case, up meant a new political life via a trip to the governor's mansion for a second tour of duty. His passionate "Erie Canal Memorial," an agitated plea on the canal's behalf, supplied the magic.

21   "If we were to suppose all the rivers and canals in England and Wales combined into one, discharged into the ocean at a great city, after passing through the heart of that country, then we can form a distinct idea of the importance of the proposed canal." The Erie Canal, he proclaimed, would make New York the greatest commercial city of the world. History backs him up.

22   On July 4, 1817, ground was broken in Rome, N.Y. heralding the beginning of construction of the Erie Canal. After completion, the canal boasted 83 locks. It rises 565 feet from the Hudson River to Lake Erie and is 363 miles long. It measures 40 feet across at the water line, and is on average about four feet deep, tapering to a 28-foot-wide bottom. Aqueducts were built to carry it over intervening rivers. During the Erie Canal's heyday, mules and horses followed a tow-path along its bank.

23   Construction of the Erie Canal was completed in October of 1825, connecting Lake Erie at Buffalo to the Hudson River at Albany.

24   Oh, there are other canals—plenty of them. New Jersey has its Morris. Pennsylvania built the Delaware and Raritan. Ohio boasts two canals, the Ohio and Erie, between Portsmouth and Cleveland, and the Miami and Erie, from Cincinnati to Toledo. But the Erie Canal started it all. It is the Erie that led the way for a system of canals that helped unite our country when great distances and greater mountains threatened to keep its people apart.

21

WHEN OUR ANCESTORS BECAME US

BY JOHN STEELE GORDON

Until the nineteenth century, change took place slowly in most Americans' daily existence. "That's the way we've always done it" was the philosophy of an agrarian population. To live a modern life was to live a life of anxiety. Then why did people change the way they lived, if they felt comfortable in their present environment? Then again, perhaps they had little choice. According to John Steele Gordon, "our ancestors became us" by the middle of the nineteenth century.

- *What does the author mean that "our ancestors became us"?*
- *Why was there no need for the phrase "the good old days" before the industrial revolution?*
- *What factors led to the modernization of American lives?*
- *Did the common people view these changes for the better?*
- *Why did many people resist such changes?*

---

1   It is a commonplace that the American Revolution determined the political destiny of the country. Far less noted is the fact that the Revolution's consequences, profound as they were, had little, if any, impact on the daily existence of most Americans. The social structures and economic realities that had determined the everyday lives of the British subjects living in the colonies continued to determine the existence of the American citizens of the new Republic. Many still spent their whole lives within a few miles of where they had been born, and those who left home rarely returned. Most made their living by agriculture or commerce, and nearly all lived much as their parents and grandparents had lived before them.

2   It required another revolution, the industrial one, to shatter this timeless pattern of everyday life and bring into existence ways of living that are familiar to us today. The reality of day-to-day existence in the early Republic was not the idyllic picket-fence-and-cottage-garden image created by Currier & Ives and others in the middle of the nineteenth century. Far

from it. By modern standards the people of those days led lives that were overwhelmingly backward, dirty, drunken, and impoverished. And yet, when that life began to fade away, it evoked an intense nostalgia (a nostalgia Currier & Ives exploited most profitably).

3   At first the changes caused by the Industrial Revolution were hard to discern and affected most people only indirectly (just as the Information Revolution in our times began 30 years before the computer became a universal fixture about a decade ago). Then, beginning in urban areas in the 1820s and spreading out to the countryside, a series of developments turned people's ordinary lives upside down in a single generation. The railroad, good interior lighting, running water, central heating, cookstoves, iceboxes, the telegraph, and mass-circulation newspapers all became commonplace within a period of 30 years. In those same three decades the rapidly expanding middle class came to dominate American society.

4   To the people of that era the sudden transformation of their world was both exhilarating and profoundly disturbing: exhilarating because the quality of everyday life improved immensely; disturbing because the landmarks and rules of the old society vanished and a new, far more complex economic, social, and political universe emerged.

5   As early as 1844 Philip Hone, a mayor of New York City and the author of a vast diary that is indispensable to the study of his times, was utterly bewildered by the whirlwind of change that had come about in his lifetime. "This world is going on too fast," he wrote. "Improvements, Politics, Reform, Religion—all fly. Railroads, steamers, packets, race against time and beat it hollow. Flying is dangerous. By and by we shall have balloons and pass over to Europe between sun and sun. Oh, for the good old days of heavy postcoaches and speed at the rate of six miles an hour!"

6   Hone, by this time, was an old and deeply conservative man, and his use of the phrase "the good old days" is the earliest recorded. Before the 1840s there had been no need for such a phrase: the old days had been much like the present.

7   They never would be again.

A REVOLUTION RIDES THE RAILS

8   The new world that emerged during Hone's lifetime would not have been possible without the railroad, the seminal invention of the nineteenth century. Until the 1820's sustained land speeds over any great distance were limited to the pace of a brisk walk. In 1829, after Andrew Jackson had been elected President, he needed a full month to make his way by coach from Nashville to Washington for his inauguration. Until the age-old problem of overland transportation was solved, the benefits of the Industrial Revolution, which had begun half a century earlier, were limited by the markets the goods could reach. Before the late 1820s the only solution was the canal, and many canal projects were undertaken in the new United States. But while canals could move freight and passengers cheaply and in large quantities, they were expensive to build, could not operate in Northern winters, and were extremely restricted as to where they could be placed.

9   At the very turn of the nineteenth century, an Englishman named Richard Trevithick designed a practical locomotive around a new type of steam engine, and the railroad was born. Many engineering problems had to be solved before the railroad was a practical transportation system; it was only in 1829, the same year as Andrew Jackson's bone-bruising journey, that an engineer named George Stephenson built the Manchester and Liverpool Railway in England, the first commercially successful steam-powered railroad.

10   With the Manchester and Liverpool thriving, railroad projects blossomed in both Europe and America. Most were small, local affairs, designed only to break particular transportation bottlenecks or connect towns to the existing transportation system of river and canal. But soon much larger railroads were planned or came into existence by consolidation. By 1835 there were a 1,000 miles of railroad track in the United States. In 1840 there were 3,000. By the time of the Civil War more than 30,000 miles of railroads laced the country together.

11   The early trains were not comfortable in the least. In the summer they were extremely hot, and sparks from the woodburning engines were a constant menace. Returning from a trip to Montauk, George Templeton Strong, a New York lawyer and, like Philip Hone, the keeper of a remarkable diary, cursed the Long Island Railroad, as would countless millions after him: "Long detention, rain, smoke, dust, cinders, headache again, all sorts of botheration—home at half-past nine and went straight to bed doubting whether I should ever enjoy the blessing of a clean face again. . . ." Matters were no better in winter, when Strong complained that the cars "with their sloppy floors, red-hot stoves, and currents of chill air from opened doors and windows, are perilous traps for colds and inflammations."

12   The first coaches were linked together by nothing more complicated than lengths of chain, and the locomotive engineers delighted in trying to topple the stovepipe hats of the male passengers as the cars jerked suddenly into motion one by one. Indeed, much of what seems, to us, intrinsic to railroads was developed only later in the century. An adequate signaling system had to await the invention of telegraph signaling in 1851. Even the train whistle—that haunting, now nearly forgotten leitmotif of the steam age—did not appear before 1837.

13   But if the railroads were not comfortable, they were immensely practical from the very start. Until the coming of the railroad many people in the vast and undeveloped United States lived a week, even two weeks away from a major city. For people of modest means a visit to a big city might well be a once-in-a-lifetime event. Even the affluent were often trapped by walls of time and distance. In the early 1830s what became the Erie Railway was being considered for "the **sequestered** counties" of New York State. Philip Church, a nephew

---

sequestered: removed or set apart; segregated.

of Alexander Hamilton who had attended Eton and owned more than 100,000 acres of the Genesee Valley, was pushing hard for the railroad but had to make an extended, season-long trip to New York City to do it.

14   His daughter-in-law wrote to her father that "Mr. Church goes to New York for the winter, endeavoring to make interest for the railroad, which is now a topic of much feeling throughout the country. If they get it, it will be indeed annihilating all time and space. They talk most seriously of being able to go from Buffalo to New York in twenty-four hours. You may smile at this, but I assure you, it's all true."

15   Because railroads could carry passengers cheaply and quickly, they created traffic where none or little had existed earlier. In 1829 few people not elected to the Presidency could have undertaken a trip such as Jackson's. A generation later such a journey was a simple matter of perhaps three days, and people exploited the new mobility to the fullest. The Charleston and Hamburg Railroad in South Carolina began operations in 1830. One of the first in the country, it was on its completion the longest railroad in the world under one management, at 136 miles, and it almost immediately revolutionized travel patterns in the area. Travelers between the two South Carolina cities had previously relied on one stagecoach making three trips a week. Only five years later the railroad conveyed 15,959 passengers in six months, a fifty-fold increase.

16   Railroads quickly transformed the areas they reached, for they brought not only a great increase in personal mobility but also an equally vast increase in freight traffic. And it was the products of the Industrial Revolution that, more and more, were carried in their freight cars. As railroads widened the potential markets for factory goods, they helped lower the price of those goods, and that, of course, further stimulated demand.

17   As the railroads reached distant areas that had formerly been too remote to compete, older areas of the country often had to undergo wrenching economic readjustments. Once the railroads had connected the fertile fields of the Middle West with the Eastern seaboard, agriculture in the stony soil of New England became far less profitable. Many New England farmers migrated westward, and others gravitated to the textile mills that were springing up along New England's swift-flowing rivers. The great **diaspora** of rural New Englanders caused by agricultural decline and the influx of immigrants to the cities and new factories deeply disturbed the conservative, ethnically homogeneous society that had existed secure for two hundred years. It is no coincidence that the New England Historic Genealogical

Society, the oldest such organization in the country, was founded in 1845. It came into existence to keep alive the memories of the good old days of a vanishing New England.

18   Railroads also created markets where none had existed before. Until quick transport was available, fresh milk from rural areas could not be carried to the fast-growing cities. The rich could keep a cow or two in their stables or buy milk from nearby farmers who catered to the carriage trade. Less affluent city folk had to make do with what was called swill milk. Breweries kept herds of cows that were fed the mash after it had been fermented (and thus most of its nutrients extracted). The milk of these poor creatures was thin, bluish, and often contaminated with brucellosis and tuberculosis. The stench of overcrowded cow barns was often detectable half a mile away.

19   Then, in 1843, an agent for the Erie Railway had the idea of transporting milk from upstate Orange County to New York City. Lines a block long formed at the Erie terminal to buy all the milk offered for sale. Soon wholesome country milk was widely available for about two-thirds of the cost of swill milk and drove the latter from the market. The improvement in child care, public health, and quality of urban life was considerable.

20   But however practical railroads were, however great their effect on the quality and possibilities of everyday life and on the economy, it was their potential for speed that captivated the imagination of the people. Human beings had never been able to travel at even 10 miles an hour. Now it was possible to travel at two, even three times that speed for hour after hour, a thing inconceivable to anyone who had lived even a quarter of a century earlier. It is little wonder that the railroad almost immediately acquired a symbolic role for the early Victorians. It seemed to them the epitome of their newfound technological prowess and of the progress that they came to regard, with every good reason, as the hallmark of their new civilization.

21   Even Philip Hone, only 15 months after he had been yearning for the return of the good old days, was astounded at how news from Great Britain had been carried by ship to Boston and that "the distance from Boston [to New York], 240 miles, was traveled by railroad and steamboat in the astonishingly short time of seven hours and five minutes. What a change from the times when the mail stage left for Boston *once a fortnight*, and consumed a week in going to Philadelphia!"

22   As should be expected, the younger generation had none of Hone's occasional misgivings. "It's a great sight to see a large train get underway," George Templeton Strong wrote in 1839, when he was only

---

diaspora: a dispersion of an originally homogeneous entity.

19. "I know of nothing that would more strongly impress our great-great grandfathers with an idea of their descendant's progress in science. . . . Just imagine such a concern rushing unexpectedly by a stranger to the invention on a dark night, whizzing and rattling and panting, with its fiery furnace gleaming in front, its chimney vomiting fiery smoke above, and its long train of cars rushing along behind like the body and tail of a gigantic dragon—or like the d---l himself—and all darting forward at the rate of twenty miles an hour. Whew!"

THE NEW COMFORTS OF HOME

23   Before the Industrial Revolution the last major improvement in domestic technology had been the chimney, which came into use in middle- and upper-class households in the **high Middle Ages**. In the 1820s houses were still heated by fireplaces and lighted by candles. Water was hauled in by bucket from a well, spring, or **cistern**. Cooking was done on an open hearth, and storing perishable foods for more than a few hours in summer was usually impossible.

24   One of the earliest changes of the industrial era to affect people's daily lives was gaslight and the oil lamp. Before gaslight there were only candles and the light of the hearth to supply illumination after sundown. But candles were as expensive then, in real terms, as they are now. Only the rich could afford interior lighting in abundance; the poor went to bed with the dark.

25   Then, in the 1790s, a Briton named William Murdock developed a practical method of extracting in quantity a gas from coal that could be burned to produce a bright yellow flame. In 1813 coal gas was used to illuminate Westminster Bridge in London, and gas streetlights began to spread through British cities. Soon American cities were following suit. Gaslight had been demonstrated in Philadelphia in 1796, but it was Baltimore—where Rembrandt Peale maintained a museum lit by gas—that first passed an ordinance encouraging gas streetlights, in 1816.

26   In New York City the New York Gas Light Company was formed in 1823 and began to lay pipes for street lighting two years later. By the end of the decade Broadway was illuminated from the Battery to Grand Street, and soon all the major streets and avenues of the city, dark and dangerous since Dutch days, were brightly lit. Anne Royalle, an English resident of the city, was exhilarated in 1829 by "the profusion of lights to which I had long been a stranger."

27   Much as they appreciated the street lighting, people at first were very wary of letting gas into their homes, fearing explosions and fires, a fear by no means unjustified. By 1840, however, the advantages of gaslight had overcome their trepidation, and gas pipes were installed in more and more houses. By the 1850s its faint hiss and odd, dank smell filled the homes of the middle and upper classes. "Gas is now considered almost indispensable in the city," a New Yorker wrote in 1851. "So much so, that scarcely a respectable dwelling house is now built without gas fixtures."

28   Rural areas and towns too small to justify building a gasworks could not benefit from gaslight, of course. But beginning in 1830, the oil lamp, which burned whale oil, proved a cheaper and much superior alternative to candles. And by the 1860s oil lamps were more and more burning kerosene instead of oil from the fast-diminishing schools of whales. In both city and country, interior illumination was cheap for the first time in history and could be used in abundance.

29   Warmth as well as light entered the American household at this time. Although the Romans had had elaborate means of heating their villas and baths, the technology had vanished in the Middle Ages. Various means of central heating were rediscovered in the seventeenth and eighteenth centuries, and a few commercial establishments in Europe, such as greenhouses, employed them. The Bank of England had a hot-water heating system installed in its offices as early as 1792. But it was not until canals, and then railroads, had lowered the cost of coal, and the Industrial Revolution had drastically lowered the cost of ducting and pipes, by the 1840s, that central heating became possible for middle-class homes.

30   The first household furnaces used hot air. The early ones heated the air in a large brick vault about six feet by nine in the basement. The air was brought in from the outside by wooden ducts, and other ducts conveyed the warmed air to the rooms above. Big as they were, these furnaces could heat only the lower floors; upstairs bedrooms still relied on fireplaces.

31   While the early furnaces were a blessing, they were not always adequate to the job, and they often produced as much smoke and fumes as heat. On January 8, 1866—"the coldest day in sixty years"— George Templeton Strong complained that he could not get the temperature of his house

---

high Middle Ages (1300–1480): period in Europe when the church was the universal and unifying institution.
cistern: a receptacle for holding water or other liquid, especially a tank for catching and storing rainwater.

in New York above 38 degrees, despite the fact that both furnaces and all the fireplaces were roaring away.

32   Americans fell immediately in love with central heating. Englishmen visiting this country were horrified, just as they are today. "The method of heating in many of the best houses is a terrible grievance to persons not accustomed to it," wrote Thomas Golley Grattan, the former British consul in Boston, "and a fatal misfortune to those who are. Casual visitors are nearly suffocated, and the constant occupiers killed. An enormous furnace sends up, day and night, streams of hot air through apertures and pipes. . . . It meets you the moment the street door is opened to let you in, and it rushes after you when you emerge again, half-stewed and parboiled, into the welcome air." Hot-water systems and then steam, with all its technological, if not aesthetic, advantages, soon replaced the primitive hot-air furnaces, and by the 1860s the chill of winter was fast disappearing from middle- and upper-class American households.

33   Cooking had long been done on a fire in an open hearth. This chore was necessarily done largely on one's knees, and the need for constant adjustment of the coals meant that the cook stayed close to the fire for hours at a time. Benjamin Franklin invented a considerable improvement over the fireplace for heating in the 1740s with his Franklin stove, and it was not long before the possibility of a stove for cooking was considered.

34   But the cookstove didn't really catch on until the Industrial Revolution had begun to bring down the cost of cast iron and of shipping heavy freight. The cookstove, "that conserver of nerve and muscle, of woman's temper and woman's complexion," as one enthusiast termed it, was vastly more efficient, reliable, and easy to use than the hearth. Its arrival in American households was greeted by those who did the cooking with the same unbridled joy with which their descendants met the automatic dishwasher and clothes washer.

35   Just as furnaces and cookstoves provided heat, so the icebox provided cold. Ice had long been an item in American commerce, and the principles of insulation were well known. In the 1840s it became possible for small iceboxes to be made cheaply enough to become a feature of the middle-class kitchen, while the ice wagon on its regular rounds became a fixture in urban neighborhoods. A cold glass of milk in July became, in many American households, a marvelous reality, and the menace to health and the economic waste represented by spoiled food began to decline. By the 1850s ice—cut on ponds in the winter and stored in vast icehouses under tons of sawdust— was a major New England industry, employing upwards of ten thousand people. Some 150,000 tons of ice a year were shipped out of Boston as far as India,

and ice accounted for more freight tonnage than any other American item except King Cotton itself.

36   Houses fitted with the new technological marvels were a lot more comfortable than their immediate predecessors had been, but they still required a large number of servants to function efficiently. In the early years of the nineteenth century, affluent Americans had had a "servant problem" because only a small percentage of the population wanted employment as domestics and a large percentage wanted to employ them. But as people began to move off the farms, especially after the great Atlantic migration began in the 1840s, the price of servants began to tumble. To be sure, Europeans—especially the illiterate, primitive Irish immigrants fleeing the potato famine—were not much admired as domestic help; help-wanted ads often specified "American" applicants, a plain and simple code for "No Irish need apply." But servants were cheap and plentiful, and the latter half of the nineteenth century was to be the great age of domestic help in this country.

37   By mid-century a typical upper-middle-class urban household kept a cook, a waiter, and a maid, who cleaned the parlors and bedrooms. (The waiter not only waited on the table but also kept the china and silver in order and did such heavy chores as tending the furnace, hauling coal, and shoveling snow.) A wealthy family would have had not only these three but an upstairs maid, a laundress, a houseman (who did the heavy work), a coachman, and a governess for the children as well. Skilled domestic help (such as cooks) earned as much as six or seven dollars a week plus room and board, a decent wage then, for which they worked six days a week, generally rising an hour before the family and remaining on duty until dismissed for the night or the family went to bed. In many families favorite servants were an integral part of the household and were greatly loved and valued. Under these circumstances the life of a servant, especially for an unmarried female, could be a pleasant one. It was certainly a great deal more pleasant than most of the alternatives: a job in one of the new factories and a room—or, more likely, part of a room—in the teeming, noisome slums that were fast blighting American cities as immigration from abroad and from declining rural areas relentlessly accelerated.

THE MIRACLE OF CLEAN WATER

38   The Romans, of course, had developed elaborate means to supply Rome and other cities with water, but as cities decayed at the end of classical times, so did the technology needed to sustain them. It was

largely reinvented during the Renaissance. Because American cities were very small until the nineteenth century (even the largest, Philadelphia, had a population of only 42,444 in 1790), they could obtain the water they needed from local wells, streams, and, for the affluent, cisterns fed from house roofs. As the population of American cities began to swell in the first decades of the new century, the problem of water for drinking, cleaning, bathing, and cooking became acute.

39   People still bathed—when they bathed—in the kitchen. They used back-yard outhouses or chamber pots, whose contents as often as not were emptied into the streets. There rain or the herds of pigs that wandered around many American cities would, it was hoped, cope with the mess. Although it was not known at the time, water, grossly contaminated by this sewage, was the source of the frequent epidemics of waterborne diseases such as cholera and typhus that swept many American cities. Meanwhile, cisterns and water barrels provided ample breeding grounds for the mosquitoes that carried yellow fever and malaria.

40   American cities met the problem each in its own way and according to its local water resources. In 1830 Philadelphia opened the Schuylkill Water Works, and in 1832 the first houses in America to be built with bathrooms were supplied with water from this system. New York, with the greatest population and the greatest technical difficulties, did not get a reliable water supply until July 4, 1842, when the forty-five-mile-long Croton Aqueduct opened. Philip Hone, for one, was agog. Months later he reported in his diary that "nothing is talked of or thought of in New York but Croton water. . . . Fountains, aqueducts, hydrants, and hose attract our attention and impede our progress through the streets. . . . Water! water! is the universal note which is sounded through every part of the city, and infuses joy and exultation into the masses."

41   Soon the new cookstoves were fitted with water tanks, and hot running water, a luxury unimaginable a few years earlier, became a commonplace. To the middle and upper classes, this was nothing short of a miracle. The lack of running water was one aspect of the good old days that Hone and everyone else was more than happy to part with. Hone almost immediately had his mansion at Broadway and Great Jones Street fitted out with bathrooms. When George Templeton Strong's father had a bathroom installed in his house on Greenwich Street in 1843, his son became altogether carried away. "I've led rather an amphibious life for the last week," he wrote happily

in his diary, "paddling in the bathing tub every night and constantly making new discoveries in the art and mystery of **ablution**. Taking a shower bath upside down is the last novelty. A real luxury, that bathing apparatus is. . . ."

42   Of course, as with every major technological advance of the industrial era, there were those who saw the imminent collapse of Western civilization in the luxury of too frequent bathing. In 1845 the city of Boston, ever alert to the possibility that people might be enjoying themselves excessively, actually outlawed daily bathing except on a doctor's prescription. It is doubtful anyone paid the slightest attention.

43   In rural areas water from a hillside spring was often piped in to supply a farmhouse. In the 1850s the prefabricated windmill was developed to pump water to a tank in the attic, whence it flowed to kitchen and bathroom. In less affluent households the soon familiar farmhouse pump offered a vast improvement over hauling water by bucket.

44   As rapidly increasing demand brought down the cost of fixtures, the cost of having running water fell too. Bathrooms, originally built one to a household, were soon being built one to a floor and even one to a bedroom in the more prosperous houses. The American love affair with plumbing was on in earnest. As early as August 1846 the *New York Daily Tribune* was reporting that "the demand for water is so great in the present hot weather that it is found impossible to keep up the supply in the distributing basins as fast as it is taken out." New Yorkers were soon proud that they used as much water as London, then a city four times the size.

45   Within a few years new houses could not be sold unless they had **water closets** and bathrooms, and cities undertook crash programs of sewer and water-main construction. The drop in demand for well water often caused the local water table to rise alarmingly. This forced cities to construct storm and drainage sewers to overcome epidemics of flooded basements. Happily this also meant that the streets, once frequent quagmires of mud, now drained far more quickly after rainstorms.

46   By 1860 all major American cities had clean running water available in the areas inhabited by the middle and upper classes. As the amount of water used per person per day skyrocketed, the standards of personal hygiene and clean clothing soared as well. The stench of human existence that had been so pervasive as to go unnoticed now became socially unacceptable. (Servants, however, seldom rated a bathroom of their own and were certainly not

---

ablution: a washing or cleansing of the body, especially as a part of a religious rite.
water closet: a room or booth containing a toilet and often a washbowl.

allowed to use the family ones, at least when the family was in residence, so they were forced to continue to rely on the chamber pot and the kitchen hip bath. It was a common complaint for years in affluent households that other people's servants were a bit on the whiffy side.)

47   Far more important than the social niceties, however, the increasing availability of clean and abundant water in the 1840s and '50s dramatically reduced the number of deaths from waterborne diseases. It remains one of the greatest triumphs of public health in human history and an element in the increase in the average American life expectancy at birth, which was 39.4 in 1850 and rose to 48.8 by 1900.

EVERYONE (ALMOST) GETS RICHER

48   The Industrial Revolution generated wealth wherever it reached, and this new wealth, together with the new technology, now gave the middle class a standard of living that even the very rich had not known two generations earlier. The newly affluent were the most rapidly growing segment of the population. In 1828, when New York's population was 185,000, there were only 59 New Yorkers with property assessed at more than $100,000, a large fortune in those days. By 1845, when the city's population had more than doubled to 371,000, the number of citizens with property worth more than $100,000 had quintupled and the word *millionaire* had been coined to describe the very, very rich. The number of those who were, in the Victorian phrase, merely "comfortably fixed" far more than kept pace.

49   The relative ease with which new wealth could be created, not just in agriculture and commerce as before but now also in manufacturing, transportation, and finance, had profound consequences for human society. As early as 1828 the English social critic John Sterling wrote: "*Wealth! wealth! wealth! Praise be to the god of the nineteenth century! The golden idol! the mighty Mammon!* such are the accents of the time, such the cry of the nation. . . . There may be here and there an individual, who does not spend his heart in laboring for riches; but there is nothing approaching to a class of persons actuated by any other desire." Although Sterling was referring to England, his observations were equally true of the United States. Money—who had it and how much—was a subject of abiding interest to the early Victorians, an interest they made little, if any, effort to conceal. The cost of everything, even churches, was among the details regularly given in guidebooks to American cities.

50   The rapidly increasing middle class came to dominate society and taste in the 1840s and '50s, especially in the United States, which had no aristocratic tradition. The newly affluent, able to afford leisure, greatly increased the market for books and magazines while gaslight and oil lamps greatly increased the ease of reading and the time available for it. Publishers began to pour out new and inexpensive works of fiction and travel. (It is ironic that Charles Dickens, who deplored the Industrial Revolution and the capitalists who drove it, probably never realized that changes brought about by the Industrial Revolution had contributed mightily to his own immense income.)

51   The furnace and efficient stoves made entertaining and socializing much more pleasant in winter. The cookstove made elaborate cooking much easier in the middle-class kitchen and allowed meals to become as elaborate as those once served only in the wealthiest households. At the same time middle-class housewives, delighted to have vast sets of now-inexpensive matching china, flatware, and table linens (luxuries most of their mothers could only have dreamed of), naturally wanted to show them all off, and this further increased the trend toward elaborate meals.

52   The common obsession of the *nouveau riche* with manners, decorum, and proper behavior generated a big market for books and magazines dealing with etiquette, fashion, and "household management." The new preoccupation with proper behavior also ensured that the nineteenth century became the golden age of the euphemism. Thomas Bowdler gave his name to the language by carefully editing Shakespeare for a "family" audience, peopling the often bawdy plays with eunuchs and madonnas. Sexual matters and body parts—when their discussion was unavoidable—were wreathed in verbal cotton wool. Americans began referring to chicken as white meat and dark meat in order to avoid the all-too-suggestive breast and leg.

53   At the same time, the new technology profoundly affected decoration. High Victorian style has been traditionally ascribed to simple bad taste. In fact, it was largely determined by the wondrous capacities of gaslight, the easy availability of products of the Industrial Revolution, and the natural human tendency to go overboard with new possibilities.

54   In the mid-nineteenth century gilding and mirrors abounded to catch and multiply the twinkling glow of gaslight. Walls that had perforce been light-colored in all but the richest houses, to reflect what light there was, were now covered in the dark and often elaborately patterned wallpapers that newly invented presses were able to grind out by the acre. Floors were covered in equally elaborate wall-to-wall carpets, made possible by new looms developed in the 1840s. **Bric-a-brac**, china figurines, lithographs, and other ornaments once restricted to the rich now littered the tables, shelves, and walls of the

middle class. Conspicuous consumption was the order of the day.

THE BIRTH OF MASS CULTURE

55   Until the nineteenth century the speed of communication was, for the most part, limited to the speed of human travel. Although it had been realized as early as the 1720s that electricity could be conducted along a wire for a considerable distance and used to convey messages, more than a hundred years passed before the telegraph was a practical system. As with the railroad, the telegraph had many fathers, and no one can claim to have invented it. Samuel F. B. Morse put the whole thing together. He developed a practical single-circuit instrument, invented the remarkably efficient Morse code, and built, with money voted by Congress, a 37-mile telegraph line between Washington, D.C., and Baltimore. On May 24, 1844, his partner, Alfred Vail, in Baltimore, transmitted the words "What hath God wrought." The message arrived in Washington in about one-thousandth the time that any other means of communication would have required.

56   Once its practicality had been established, the telegraph spread quickly, often along railroad rights-of-way. By the 1850s all major American cities and many small towns were linked by telegraph, and in 1858 a telegraph cable between the United States and England was established. In 1861 a transcontinental line reached California.

57   Although the Atlantic cable failed in only four weeks and was not replaced until after the Civil War, America's profound isolation from Europe was coming to an end. At the turn of the nineteenth century, news from England had taken six to eight weeks to reach the United States. After the passage of less than a human lifetime, it could cross the Atlantic in as many minutes. The latest news from Europe and California involved matters that were happening *now*, not something that had transpired weeks or months earlier. "What hath God wrought?" was a question the early Victorians had occasion to ask themselves over and over again.

58   The telegraph was too expensive at first for most Americans to make use of it directly; transatlantic cables cost $1 a word with a 15-word minimum, nearly a week's wages for a skilled worker. Nonetheless, the technology had an immediate impact through the proliferating newspapers.

59   As the number of people and the percentage of the population above the subsistence level increased, their need and desire for information about their civilization, its perils, and its opportunities increased also. Until the 1830s there were few means to obtain it. Newspapers were expensive and targeted at specific audiences for specific purposes. Papers aimed at merchants supplied only news of the marketplace, prices, the arrivals and departures of ships. Political papers were the organs of particular factions and were hardly more than editorial pages wrapped in a little tendentious news.

60   Then, in the 1830s, the steam engine and new types of printing presses were combined, greatly lowering the cost per copy of newspapers and greatly increasing the number of copies that could be printed quickly. Suddenly newspapers could be afforded and read by the masses as well as the elite, and many intellectuals and politicians, such as Horace Greeley, of the *New York Tribune,* and Henry J. Raymond, of the *Times,* moved to exploit the new possibilities. But it was people like James Gordon Bennett and Benjamin Day, neither intellectuals nor politicians, who edited the first truly modern newspapers.

61   A newspaper, they thought, should not be an instrument of instruction or of political indoctrination; rather, it should be a window the people could use to look out onto the new industrial world—in all its splendor and misery—and form their own opinions. Their aim was to give the people what they wanted to read, not just what an editor thought was important or proper for them to know. It was Bennett, in the 1830s and '40s, who first printed stock tables and a sports page and first used the railroads and the telegraph to speed timely news from distant points to his readers. And it was the new newspapers that first exploited the insatiable appetite of the *nouveaux riches* for information on the life-styles of the rich and famous by introducing gossip columns and articles on the houses and clothes of the fashionable.

62   Americans responded immediately to this revolutionary brand of journalism. Long before Bennett's death his *New York Herald* had become the most successful paper in the world. He had made newspapers an essential part of daily life, and every day he printed nearly as many copies of the *Herald* as all the daily newspapers in the English-speaking world had printed at the turn of the century. The streets of every major city rang with the cries of newsboys hawking the latest issues. Weekly editions were taken by railroad to towns and villages throughout the country.

Bric-a-brac: small, usually decorative objects valued for their antiquity, rarity, originality, or sentimental associations.

63   "The daily newspaper," wrote the *North American Review* in 1866, only 30 years after the *Herald*'s founding, "is one of those things which are rooted in the necessities of modern civilization. The steam engine is not more essential to us. The newspaper is that which connects each individual with the general life of mankind."

64   The newspapers unified the Victorian age just as television unifies ours. They gave the people their sense of the world in which they lived, a world that had become in their lifetimes far wider and richer, far more interrelated and more complex than any known before. Ironically, it was the very richness and variety of the new world created by the proliferating technology that made so many yearn for the good old days.

65   More than anything else, the Industrial Revolution accelerated the rate of technological innovation. In 1790 the U.S. Patent Office issued three patents; in 1840 it gave out 458; and in 1860 there were 4,357. After 1867 no fewer than 12,000 were issued in any year.

66   At first the early Victorians had thought they were living in a singular age of transition from one period of order and regularity to another of equal predictability. It was only as the new miracles of technology continued to pile one on top of another and the social, political, and economic consequences of those miracles began to play themselves out that they came gradually to understand that the only thing now permanent was change itself.

67   By the Civil War the modern world had largely replaced the good old days in the developed areas of the country. While the pace of technological change would only continue to accelerate in future years, most later miracles, such as the electric light, the telephone, and the automobile, would only replace and improve upon the older ones, such as gaslight, the telegraph, and the railroad, that had come into being in the 30 years before the Civil War. And by that point, because of the Industrial Revolution, technological miracles had become a commonplace, and change a constant. The disconcerting sense of living through a discontinuity in the stream of time was lost.

68   To those who had lived through that discontinuity, however, it was the regularity and simplicity, certainly not the squalor, disease, and poverty, that they missed about the good old days. Through the softening haze of time—and with a good deal of help from the likes of Currier & Ives and Dickens—the good old days came to seem ever more appealing, compared with the "age of chaos . . . [this] heaving, tumbling age" (James Gordon Bennett's words) in which they now lived.

22
FROM UTOPIA TO MILL TOWN

BY MAURY KLEIN

*Eli Whitney's cotton gin increased the demand for southern cotton worldwide. South-
erners found it in their best interest to force Native Americans off of their lands in the
Southeast. The present day states of Georgia, Alabama, Mississippi and Florida were
cleared out to make way for the spread of the cotton kingdom. The cotton gin also set
the stage for industrialized thinking in the North: mass production.*

*The early 1800s witnessed changes in the workplace that drove a wedge be-
tween traditional, home-based family values and the economic realities facing many
rural Americans in the North. Technology was changing the way Americans lived,
worked and moved about. This had a profound effect upon us all, especially the
working woman.*

*Industrialization forced the production of cotton thread under one roof: the fac-
tory. The piece-work many rural women could previously count on for a little extra
cash was now available only in the towns—away from family, hearth, and home. It
was a difficult choice, but one that was made by thousands of rural New England
families. Many young women left their fathers and homes; others were forced to seek
the opportunities and risks of a factory job perhaps hundreds of miles away.*

- *Why did the young women choose mill work over other available jobs?*
- *What were their work schedules and living conditions like?*
- *What were the greatest difficulties faced in the mills?*
- *Why did the "associates" (owners) turn away from the idea of an "industrial utopia?"*
- *What was the LFLRA and what did it accomplish?*
- *Who finally ended, once and for all, the Lowell experiment?*
- *Why do you suppose "utopias" of this sort are seldom attempted in our modern
  age?*

---

1   The Boston Associates may have loathed Andrew
Jackson, but they spared no expense to honor his
visit to the utopian mill town they had built at
Lowell, Massachusetts. As Amos Lawrence en-
thused, "We will feed him on gold dust, if he will eat
it!" The lavish preparations began days before June
27, 1833, when the carriage bearing Jackson and his
vice president, Martin Van Buren, rolled into town
beneath welcome arches, bunting, decorations, and
two hickory trees planted for the occasion. Fifes
bleated and drums pounded martial airs, rifles
cracked inexpert salutes, and the overflow crowd
roared approval as Jackson endured the welcome
speech and went to the balcony of the Merrimack
Hotel to review the procession assembled in his
honor. Ranks of inept local militia stumbled past his
weary eye, followed by straggling files of local
officials.

2   Then came the girls.

3   They marched two abreast, 2,500 strong, clad in
white muslin dresses with blue sashes, their heads
crowned with parasols. Their line stretched two
miles and took half an hour to pass, yet Jackson's interest never faltered. The gallant old soldier bowed

to each pair as long as strength permitted, and exclaimed, "Very pretty women, by the Eternal!" The girls marched in corporation groups, the oldest companies coming first. At the head of each group a silk banner bore the company's name and proclaimed in bold letters the day's message: "PROTECTION TO AMERICAN INDUSTRY."

4   A year later that savvy frontiersman, Davy Crockett, feasted on the hospitality of the Associates, who wanted his vote in Congress for a high tariff. He ventured into the mills and talked to some of the operatives. "Not one expressed herself as tired of her employment, or oppressed with work," he reported. "All talked well, and looked healthy." His shrewd, practiced eye noticed that "Some of them were very handsome; and I could not help observing that they kept the prettiest inside, and put the homely ones on the outside rows."

5   The appearance of distinguished visitors soon became a commonplace event at Lowell, and one that the Associates encouraged for its advertising value. In promoting their mills as an industrial utopia they were quick to realize that the girls were the prime attraction, the trump card in their game of benevolent paternalism. As early as 1827 Captain Basil Hall, an Englishman, marveled at the girls on their way to work at six in the morning, "nicely dressed, and glittering with bright shawls and showy-colored gowns and gay bonnets . . . with an air of lightness, and an elasticity of step, implying an obvious desire to get to their work."

6   Observers who went home to rhapsodize about Lowell and its operatives as a model for what the factory system should become, trapped themselves in an unwitting irony. While there was much about the Lowell corporations that served later firms as model, the same did not hold true for their labor force. The young women who filled the mills, regarded by many as the heart of the Lowell system, were in fact its most unique element and ultimately its most transient feature. They were of the same stock and shared much the same culture as the men who employed them. This relative homogeneity gave them a kinship of values absent in later generations of workers. Benita Eisler has called them "the last **WASP** labor force in America."

7   The women who flocked to Lowell's mills came mostly from New England farms. Some came to augment the incomes of poor families, others to earn money for gowns and finery, to escape the bleak monotony of rural life, or sample the adventure of a fresh start in a new village. Although their motives were mixed, they chose the mills over such alternatives as teaching or domestic service because the pay was better and the work gave them a sense of

independence. Lucy Larcom, one of the most talented and articulate of the mill girls, observed that:

Country girls were naturally independent, and the feeling that at this new work the few hours they had of everyday leisure were entirely their own was a satisfaction to them. They preferred it to going out as "hired help." It was like a young man's pleasure in entering upon business for himself.

8   Leisure hours were a scarce commodity. The mill tower bells tolled the girls to work before the light of day and released them at dusk six days a week, with the Sabbath reserved for solemn observance. The work day averaged 12-and-a-half hours, depending on the season, and there were only three holidays a year, all unpaid: Fast Day, the Fourth of July, and Thanksgiving. Wages ranged between $2 and $4 a week, about half what men earned. Of this amount $1.25 was deducted for board, to which the company contributed another 25 cents. Meager as these sums appear, they exceeded the pay offered by most other mills.

9   The work rooms were clean and bright for a factory, the walls whitewashed and windows often garnished with potted flowers. But the air was clogged with lint and fumes from the whale-oil lamps hung above every loom. Since threads would snap unless the humidity was kept high, windows were nailed shut even in the summer's heat, and the air was sprayed with water. Delicate lungs were vulnerable to the ravages of tuberculosis and other respiratory ailments. More than one critic attributed the high turnover rate to the number of girls "going home to die."

10   The machines terrified newcomers with their thunderous clatter that shook the floor. Belts and wheels, pulleys and rollers, spindles and flyers, twisted and whirled, hissing and buzzing, always in motion, a cacophonous jungle alien to rural ears. At first the machines looked too formidable to master. One girl, in a story recalling her first days at Lowell, noted that:

she felt afraid to touch the loom, and she was almost sure she could never learn to weave; the harness puzzled and the reed perplexed her; the shuttle flew out and made a new bump on her head; and the first time she tried to spring the lathe she broke a quarter of the threads. It seemed as if the girls all stared at her, and the overseers watched every motion, and the day appeared as long as a month had at home. . . . At last it was night. . . . There was

---

WASP: White Anglo-Saxon Protestant.

a dull pain in her head, and a sharp pain in her ankles; every bone was aching, and there was in her ears a strange noise, as of crickets, frogs and jews-harps, all mingling together.

11   Once the novelty wore off, the strangeness of it all gave way to a more serious menace: monotony.

12   The boarding houses provided welcome havens from such trials. These were dwellings of different sizes, leased to respectable high-toned widows who served as housemothers for 15 to 30 girls. They kept the place clean and enforced the company rules, which were as strict as any parent might want. Among other things they regulated conduct, imposed a 10 o'clock curfew, and required church attendance. The girls were packed six to a bedroom, with three beds. One visitor described the small rooms as "absolutely choked with beds, trunks, bandboxes, clothes, umbrellas and people," with little space for other furniture. The dining room doubled as sitting room, but in early evening it was often besieged by peddlers of all sorts.

13   This cramped arrangement suited the Associates nicely because it was economical and reinforced a sense of group standards and conformity. Lack of privacy was old hat to most rural girls, though a few complained. Most housemothers set a good table and did not cater to dainty appetites. One girl reported dinner as consisting of "meat and potatoes, with vegetables, tomatoes and pickles, pudding or pie, with bread, butter, coffee or tea." English novelist Anthony Trollope was both impressed and repulsed by the discovery that meat was served twice a day, declaring that for Americans "to live a day without meat would be as great a privation as to pass a night without a bed."

14   The corporations usually painted each house once a year, an act attributed by some to benevolence and others to a shrewd eye for public relations and property values. Their zeal for cleanliness did not extend to bathing facilities, which were minimal at best. More than one visitor spread tales of dirt and vermin in the boarding houses, but these too were no strangers to rural homes. Like the mills, later boarding houses were built as long dormitory rows unleavened by strips of lawn or shrubbery, but the earlier versions retained a quaint charm for visitors and inhabitants.

15   Above all the boarding houses were, as Hannah Josephson stressed, "a woman's world." In these cluttered cloisters the operatives chatted, read, sewed, wrote letters, or dreamed about the day when marriage or some better opportunity would take them from the mills. They stayed in Lowell about four years on the average, and most married after leaving. The mill experience was, in Thomas Dublin's phrase, simply "a stage in a woman's life cycle before marriage." For many girls the strangeness of

it all was mitigated by the presence of sisters, cousins, or friends who had undertaken the same adventure.

16   Outside the boarding house the girls strolled and picnicked in the nearby countryside, attended church socials, paid calls, and shopped for the things they had never had. Dozens of shops vied with the savings banks for their hard-earned dollars and won more than their share of them. Those eager to improve their minds, and there were many, patronized the library and the Lyceum, which for 50 cents offered a season ticket for 25 lectures by such luminaries as Ralph Waldo Emerson, Horace Mann, John Quincy Adams, Horace Greeley, Robert Owen, and Edward Everett. Some were ambitious enough to attend evening classes or form study groups of their own in everything from art to German.

17   Above all the girls read. Their appetite for literature was voracious and often indiscriminate. So strong was this ardor that many slipped their books into the mills, where such distractions were strictly forbidden. It must have pained overseers to confiscate even Bibles from transgressors, but the large number that filled their drawers revealed clearly the Associates' determination to preserve the sharp distinction between the Lord's business and their own.

18   No one knows how many of the girls were avid readers, but the number probably exceeded the norm for any comparable group. Where so many read, it was inevitable that some would try their hand at writing. By the early 1840s Lowell boasted seven Mutual Self-Improvement Clubs. These were the first women's literary clubs in America, and the members consisted entirely of operatives. From two of these groups emerged a monthly magazine known as the *Lowell Offering* which in its brief life span (1841–1845) achieved a notoriety and reputation far in excess of its literary merits. The banner on its cover described the contents as *A Repository of Original Articles, Written Exclusively by Females Actively Employed in the Mills.*

19   No other aspect of Lowell rivaled the *Offering* as a symbol for the heights to which an industrial utopia might aspire. Observers at home and abroad were astounded at the spectacle of factory workers— women no less—capable of producing a literary magazine. Even Charles Dickens, that harsh critic of both English industrialism and American foibles, hurried this revelation to his readers:

I am now going to state three facts, which will startle a large class of readers on this side of the Atlantic very much. First, there is a joint-stock piano in a great many of the boarding-houses. Secondly, nearly all these young ladies subscribe to circulating libraries. Thirdly, they have got up among themselves a periodical . . . which is duly printed, published, and sold; and whereof I brought away from Lowell four hundred good solid pages, which I have read from beginning to end.

20   As the *Offering's* fame grew, the Associates were not slow to appreciate its value. Nothing did more to elevate their esteem on both sides of the Atlantic. Contrary to the belief of some, the magazine never became a house organ. Both editors, Harriet Farley and Harriott Curtis, were veterans of the mills who opened their columns to critics and reformers while keeping their own editorial views within more discreet and refined bounds. For their part the Associates were too shrewd not to recognize that the *Offering's* appeal, its effectiveness as a symbol of republican virtues, lay in its independence. To serve them best it must not smack of self-serving, and it did not.

21   Although the magazine's prose and poetry seldom rose above mediocre, the material offered revealing insights into every aspect of factory life. Inevitably it attracted authors eager to voice grievances or promote remedies. The editors trod a difficult path between the genteel pretensions of a literary organ and a growing militancy among operatives concerned with gut issues. Few of the girls subscribed to the *Offering* anyway; most of the copies went to patrons in other states or overseas. Small wonder that critics charged the magazine had lost touch with actual conditions in the mills or the real concerns of their operatives.

22   The *Offering* folded in part because it reflected a system hurrying toward extinction. By the 1840s, when Lowell's reputation as an industrial utopia was still at its peak, significant changes had already taken place. Hard times and swollen ranks of stockholders clamoring for dividends had dulled the Associates' interest in benevolent paternalism. It had always been less a goal than a by-product and not likely to survive a direct conflict with the profit motive. The result was a period of several years during which Lowell coasted on its earlier image while the Associates dismantled utopia in favor of a more cost-efficient system.

23   The self-esteem of the Associates did not permit them to view their actions in this light, but the operatives felt the change in obvious ways. Their work week increased to 75 hours with four annual holidays compared to 69 hours and six holidays for the much maligned British textile workers. To reduce unit costs, girls tended faster machines and were paid lower wages for piecework. That was called

speedup; in another practice known as stretch-out, girls were given three or four looms where earlier they had tended one or two. Overseers and second hands were offered bonuses for wringing more productivity out of the workers.

24   At heart the utopian image of Lowell, indeed the system itself, rested on the assumption that grateful, obedient workers would not bite the hands of their masters. When operatives declined to accept this role, factory agents countered with dismissals and blacklists. The result was a growing sense of militancy among the girls and the first stirrings of a labor movement. In 1834 and 1836 there occurred spontaneous "turnouts" or strikes in Lowell, the first protesting wage cuts and the second an increase in the board charge. Neither achieved much, although a large number of girls (800 and 2,500) took part. The Associates showed their mettle in one instance by turning a widow with four children out of her boarding house because her 11-year-old daughter, a **bobbin girl**, had followed the others out. "Mrs. Hanson, you could not prevent the older girls from turning out," the corporate agent explained sternly, "but your daughter is a child, and *her* you could control."

25   Between 1837 and 1842 a national depression drove wages down and quieted labor unrest at Lowell. When conditions improved and wages still fell, the disturbances began anew. In December 1844 five mill girls met to form the Lowell Female Labor Reform Association; within a year the organization had grown to 600 members in Lowell and had branches elsewhere in New England. Since unions had no legal status or power to bargain directly, LFLRA could only appeal to public opinion and petition the General Court (state legislature) for redress.

26   For three years the organization dispatched petitions and testified before legislative commissions on behalf of one issue in particular: the 10-hour workday. Led by Sarah Bagley and other women of remarkable energy and intelligence, LFLRA joined hands with workingmen's groups in the push for shorter hours. Their efforts were dogged, impressive, and ultimately futile. As their ranks swelled, they suffered the usual problems of divided aims and disagreement over tactics. More than that, the LFLRA failed in the end simply because it had determination but no leverage. Legislators and other officials did not take them seriously because they were women who had no business being involved in such matters and could not vote anyway. By 1847 LFLRA was little more than a memory. The 10-hour movement lived on, but did not succeed until 1874.

---

bobbin girl: worker that loads the spools of thread or yarn for spinning.

27   During its brief life LFLRA did much to shatter the image of Lowell as an industrial utopia. The Associates held aloof from controversy and allowed editors, ministers, and distinguished visitors to make their case. There were those who preserved Lowell as a symbol because they wanted to believe, needed to believe in what it represented. After several years of constant labor strife, however, few could overlook the problems pointed up by LFLRA: more work for less pay, deteriorating conditions in the mills and boarding houses, blacklists, and more repressive regulations. Lowell had lost much of what had made it special and was on the verge of becoming another bleak and stifling mill town.

28   Gradually the river and countryside disappeared behind unbroken walls of factory or dormitory. Nature approached extinction in Lowell, and so did the girls who had always been the core of its system. In 1845 about 90 percent of the operatives were native Americans, mostly farm girls; by 1850 half the mill workers were Irish, part of the flood that migrated after the famine years of 1845–46. The Irish girls were illiterate, docile, and desperate enough to work for low wages. They preferred tenements with their friends and family to boarding houses, which relieved the Associates of that burden. It did not take the Associates long to appreciate the virtues of so helpless and undemanding a work force. In these immigrants they saw great promise for cheap labor comparable to that found in English mill towns like Manchester.

29   So it was that Lowell's utopian vision ended where industrialism began. In time the Irish would rise up in protest as their predecessors had done, but behind them came waves of Dutch, Greek, and French Canadian immigrants to take their places in the mills. The native New England girls continued to flee the mills or shy away from them in droves, until by 1860 they were but a small minority. Their departure marked the emergence of Lowell as a mill town no different than any other mill town. One of the girls, peering from her boarding house window, watched the growing stories of a new mill snuff out her view of the scenery beyond and caught the significance of her loss. In her lament could be found an epitaph for Lowell itself:

> Then I began to measure . . . and to calculate how long I would retain this or that beauty. I hoped that the brow of the hill would remain when the structure was complete. But no! I had not calculated wisely. It began to recede from me . . . for the building rose still higher and higher. One hope after another is gone . . . one image after another, that has been beautiful to our eye, and dear to our heart has forever disappeared. How has the scene changed! How is our window darkened!

VI

CHANGES AND REFORM

1 By the middle of the nineteenth century, technology affected Americans in more ways than they could have imagined in 1800. In those 50 years, Americans no longer relied on doing things in the same ways that their ancestors had done. Manufacturing in the North and the cotton gin in the South transformed lives and occupations. Some yearned to hold on to the "good old days" as if they ever existed in the past. With change came concern that the new nation was heading toward chaos. Although Thomas Jefferson wrote in 1785 that rural folks were "the chosen people of God," many sought their livelihoods in towns and cities. They often had little choice to do otherwise.

2 In the early nineteenth century, one New Jersey iron manufacturer wrote numerous notations in his dairy stating that all hands were drunk. Drinking in America was a cause for concern as employers set new rules for the first generation of factory workers. America's morality monitors—primarily middle-class women and the clergy—attempted to stop others from drinking the hard stuff and led the temperance crusade. Their concern focused on keeping the family's breadwinner sober, so he could support his family on a meager wage. Rum led to ruin.

3 Traditional historians have labeled this era as "the age of the common man," although entire groups were excluded from this "age." Some upper-class women became so enraged at being neglected in a nation proclaiming, "all men are created equal," that they wrote their own declaration of independence. (They were simply not going to just bring up babies.)

Although their petition was ignored by the powers that be, they laid the groundwork for the women's movement for the next century and a half. Their advocacy for the rights of all people was summed up with the phrase "not for ourselves alone."

4 Eras of history are often separated by the different wars a nation has fought. The study of war's death and destruction fills volumes of our libraries, while little is written on diseases that destroyed a larger percentage of the population. As Americans began to live in closer proximity to each other, they became more susceptible to typhoid, cholera, and consumption; they succumbed to a variety of such ailments—many of which still plague our world today.

5 Not all people stayed on the eastern seaboard; many white Americans migrated to different regions of the continent in search of better opportunities and land. They left behind loved ones to pursue their fortune. No longer would they live in communities with white-steepled churches and established municipal laws. Searching for a semblance of order, many sought solace in newly established religious adventurers like the Shakers, Adventists, and Mormons.

6 As a new nation, America was seen abroad as a land of opportunity. Immigrants began arriving in large numbers during this time and they haven't stop coming since then. The Irish migrated by the thousands to escape the potato famine and British persecution. They may have suffered a hard lot in the cities of Boston, New York and Philadelphia but their fate in America was better than if they had remained in their homeland.

7   Reform did not occur as rapidly as the changes. While certain reform was not permanently achieved until the twentieth century—national rights for women and better sanitation to prevent cholera and typhoid, other reform was achieved and then abandoned—temperance led to prohibition but was later repealed. Most utopian religious societies that created isolated communities petered out, while the Mormons became powerful due to their isolation in the West. As for immigrants, America never welcomed them with opened arms but they were needed to do the hard and dangerous labor—such as building canals and working in the textile mills. It took time for much of America to recognize that a rising tide of reform lifts all people's boats.

23

THE TEMPERANCE MOVEMENT

BY DIANA ROSS MCCAIN

A strong puritanical element was present in post-World War I America, when the Eighteenth Amendment was added to the Constitution. This amendment prohibited "the manufacture, sale, or transportation of intoxicating liquors" within the United States. While "the drys" attempted to legislate morality by prohibiting the consumption of liquor, "the wets" argued that their constitutional rights were violated by removing their right to choose—or not to choose—fermented drinks.

The problem of "demon rum" dates back to the days of John Winthrop's Massachusetts Bay Colony. The temperance movement, started primarily by clergymen and women, "succeeded" by having the nation proclaim alcohol an illegal substance. In this article, Diana Ross McCain examines the temperance events of nineteenth century America that ultimately culminated with the ratification of prohibition.

- *What factors contributed to the rise of drinking in America?*
- *How did temperance reformers attempt to create a dry nation?*
- *Although prohibition became the law in 1919, why do you suppose the Eighteenth Amendment was repealed in 1933?*
- *What current movements in America attempt to change the way people live?*

---

1   America in the 1820s was a nation awash in alcohol. Each year an average of five gallons of hard liquor was guzzled for each person in the country, compared to just over two gallons per capita for every adult today. Even more alcohol was ingested in the average of 15 gallons of hard cider consumed by every man, woman—and child—in the land.

2   But the next four decades would see a momentous change in the nation's drinking habits, as millions of citizens cut back on their alcohol consumption or swore off intoxicating beverages altogether, and more than a third of the states passed prohibition laws. This dramatic drying out was the result of a campaign known as the temperance movement.

3   For nearly 200 years after the European settlement of America, alcohol lubricated every facet of

life. Each member of the average family, youngsters included, consumed it morning, noon, and night in the form of beer or hard cider. Wine and brandy graced the dining tables of the well-to-do. Everyone, from dignified clergyman to uncouth laborer, drank alcohol.

4   Any gathering, such as a barn raising or **husking bee**, was sure to include large quantities of rum or whiskey to help make the work proceed pleasantly. Alcohol aplenty was served at weddings, balls, and even funerals. Liquor flowed freely at the polls on election days, and many a vote was purchased for the price of a drink.

5   Taverns, which served as centers of community life, included all manner of intoxicating drink on their bills of fare. In these establishments men congregated to socialize, make business deals,

---

husking bee: a social gathering for husking corn.

discuss politics and current events, and swap stories. Here auctions, lottery drawings, and even court sessions were sometimes held, and much of this activity took place under the influence of intoxicants. After militia drill, worship services, or town meetings, men would retire to the local tavern to refresh themselves.

6   Alcoholic beverages were actually believed to play a crucial role in maintaining good health. Wine and brandy were ingredients in a number of concoctions prescribed by physicians. A Connecticut temperance speaker, Charles Griswold, declared in 1828 that, "the fashion has become almost universal, for new born infants, and their mothers to be constantly plied with strong doses of rum, brandy, gin, &c., under the denomination of sling, toddy, punch and flip, and advocates are not wanting who maintain strenuously that this practice is indispensable to health and quietness." Stiff belts of whiskey or rum were considered essential to sustain the strength of any man laboring at physically demanding outdoor tasks such as harvesting, and, reported Charles Griswold in the same 1828 speech, the custom existed among the laboring classes of "persuading, or, if necessary, of compelling young and promising children to receive regular **drams** with the father when at his work."

7   Alcoholic beverages were abundant and affordable. Cider, of course, could be made from the apples that were so plentiful. Farmers west of the Appalachians distilled vast quantities of grain into whiskey, which was easier to transport over the mountains. Whiskey cost as little as a quarter a gallon, so even the poorest could buy it.

8   Available non-alcoholic beverages were held in low regard. Clean, potable water was difficult to obtain, and some people actually considered water hazardous to their health. Milk, when available, was generally drunk by children and could be the source of the dreaded "milk sickness," contracted from the milk of cows who had eaten wild jimson weed, which contained a poison harmful to humans. Coffee and tea, which had to be imported, were often more costly than alcoholic beverages.

9   Although most Americans at the end of the eighteenth century considered alcoholic beverages a positive good, there were a few skeptics. One of these was Dr. Benjamin Rush of Philadelphia, perhaps the most prominent physician of his era, who in 1784 published *An Inquiry Into the Effects of Spirituous Liquors on the Human Body*. It proved to be an extraordinarily long-lived publication, with 170,000 copies printed by 1850.

10   Dr. Rush claimed that spirits—distilled beverages such as whiskey, rum, or gin, which typically had an alcohol content of nearly 50 percent—caused a host of diseases, including madness, palsy, **apoplexy**, and epilepsy, and aggravated many others. *"Spirituous liquors destroy more lives than the sword,"* the physician emphasized. Further, Dr. Rush declared, hard liquor was responsible for much human misery by leading men into debt, idleness, disgrace, and neglect of their families' welfare. The good doctor scoffed at the popular belief that spirits were necessary in very cold or very warm weather, or to sustain men working at hard labor, and acceded that there were only two instances in which spirits might be beneficial: "where the body has been exhausted by any causes, and faintness, or a stoppage in the circulation of the blood has been produced," and "when the body has been long exposed to wet weather, and more especially if cold be joined with it."

11   In place of spirits, Dr. Rush recommended the consumption of hard cider, beer, and wine—fermented beverages with a much lower alcohol content. He considered all three to be "wholesome" drinks.

12   Despite Dr. Rush's published opinions, widespread concern about the impact of spirits did not emerge until the early decades of the nineteenth century, when the first tremors of a temperance movement began to be felt in New England.

13   The timing was determined by several factors. Drinking to excess had increased dramatically in the period following the American Revolution and was still on the rise in the early 1800s. "Americans between 1790 and 1830 drank more alcoholic beverages per capita than ever before or since," notes W. J. Rorabaugh in his 1979 book, *The Alcoholic Republic: An American Tradition*. Inebriation was considered by many as a primary cause of crime, cruelty, poverty, lax morals, insanity, and the disintegration of many a family. In addition, alcohol-induced befuddlement often led to irreligion and endangered the drinker's chance for eternal salvation.

14   One reason cited for this rise in alcoholism was a great increase in the availability of inexpensive liquor, particularly western whiskey. Another was the boom in road building that took place following the Revolution and the consequent explosive increase in the number of taverns along those roads serving liquor—so many taverns, in fact, that it

---

dram: a unit of weight equal to ¹⁄₁₆ of an ounce.
apoplexy: sudden impairment of neurological function; a stroke.

proved impossible to enforce what laws did exist against excessive drinking.

15   This increase in imbibing occurred at a time when Americans were feeling the exhilaration of their young nation's successful experiment in democracy. This led many people to believe that in the land of liberty there existed a unique opportunity to raise humanity to a higher plane by ridding it of many of the evils that had plagued it for centuries. Simultaneously America was in the thrall of a fervent religious revival known as the Second Great Awakening which, according to Ian Tyrrell in the 1979 book *Sobering Up: From Temperance to Prohibition in Antebellum America, 1800–1860*, gave birth to the concept of "benevolence and service to mankind" as the duty of a true Christian. Thus were born movements to combat many sins and injustices: to abolish slavery, to win legal rights for women, to reform prisons—and to banish alcohol from the land.

16   The first attempt at a temperance campaign failed in the 1820s, largely because many people perceived it as an attempt by **Congregationalists** and **Federalists** to exert control over the population. But a subsequent effort, signaled by the founding in Boston in 1826 of the American Temperance Society, immediately sparked a tremendous reaction.

17   The American Temperance Society took an innovative approach to the alcohol problem, which included, according to Ian Tyrrell, "paid, full-time workers, a network of voluntary organizations, systematic financing, and the printed word as the basis of temperance propaganda." It focused on reforming the moderate drinker, devoting scant attention to rehabilitating the habitual drunkard. The society also included women in its ranks of volunteers—a novel step that greatly expanded its pool of potential workers and gave many females their first outlet beyond church and family for their talents and energies.

18   The result was phenomenal. Nine years after its founding, the American Temperance Society boasted more than 8,000 local societies and more than 1.5 million members, a figure which, according to Jack Blocker, Jr., in his 1989 book *American Temperance Movements: Cycles of Reform*, "represented about 12 percent of the free population of the United States and possibly as many as one in five free adults."

19   Temperance enjoyed its greatest victories in its native territory. Far fewer Southerners than New Englanders signed temperance pledges.

20   To be temperate meant to drink not a single drop of hard liquor. "We consider every temperate use of strong drink as an abuse of it," explained Charles Griswold in his 1828 Connecticut speech:

> because it can be proved to do no good to him that drinks it, and that it does more or less harm, in proportion to the quantity taken and the frequency with which it is taken—because this temperate drinking is always the first stage on the road to hard drinking, and because it is a perpetual encouragement to drunkards and others to continue in the habit of excessive drinking, and is particularly the most pernicious example to the rising generation.

Abstinence alone was the only way to prevent the abuse of spirits, Griswold claimed.

21   However, temperance advocates were permitted to consume the less potent wine, beer, and hard cider that Dr. Rush had condoned. These beverages' lower alcohol content, and the fact that they were not perceived as major causes of drunkenness, rendered them, in the opinion of temperance reformers, far less dangerous than spirits such as rum or whiskey.

22   That attitude changed when temperance crusaders undertook to rescue hardened drunkards from alcoholism. The observation that sips of wine or swigs of hard cider or beer were sufficient to draw reformed alcoholics back to their addiction, or could be the first step on a sober individual's path to the tippling of hard liquor and then on to chronic drunkenness, convinced temperance leaders of the evil of what previously had been considered innocuous beverages. And, ominously, consumption of beer, cider, and wine were on the rise in the 1830s.

23   As a result in 1836 the meaning of temperance was officially redefined by a convention of the American Temperance Union, the new nation-wide temperance organization, to require that one abstain from drinking any beverage containing the slightest amount of alcohol, including beer, wine, and hard cider. Total abstinence, called "teetotalism," was further advanced by the establishment, beginning in 1840, of Washingtonian Temperance Societies. These were groups of reformed alcoholics whose meetings featured emotional personal recountings by former inebriates of their slide down a slope rendered slick by alcohol into hell on earth, and of their redemption, via total abstinence, from the degradation of drunkenness. Their public confessions converted hundreds of

---

Congregationalist: one who advocates a type of church government in which each local congregation is self-governing.
Federalist: one who advocates a system of government in which power is divided between a central authority and constituent political units.

thousands of individuals, only a small percentage of them alcoholics, to teetotalism. Distaff auxiliaries, known as Martha Washingtonian Societies, involved thousands of women in the effort as well.

24   Temperance publications abounded, ranging from logical, reasoned discussions of the dangers of alcohol abuse and the benefits of sobriety to newspapers to songbooks to moralizing books for children to sentimental, saccharine tales of happy families destroyed by drink. One tear-jerker recounted the tale of a devoted father and husband who quaffed his first hard liquor when the deacon who ran the local general store offered it to him in place of three cents change owed on his bill. That single drink was the first step on the man's path to destruction, turning him into a drunk who physically and emotionally brutalized his family and neglected his livelihood until at last the destitute family was headed for jail. That degrading experience, from which the unfortunate family was rescued at the last minute only by a neighbor's kindness, proved to be the point at which the inebriate hit bottom. He vowed never again to let spirits pass his lips and kept the resolution thereafter, restoring love, harmony, and prosperity to his family.

25   Physicians began to echo Dr. Rush's recommendations of 40 years earlier and declare that alcohol not only had no curative or restorative powers, but in fact could aggravate and even cause disease. These pronouncements carried more weight with many Americans than did the moral arguments against alcohol.

26   One of the key targets of the temperance movement was the youth of America. Major efforts were made to prevent them from ever tasting that first potentially fatal drop of demon rum. Youngsters were enlisted in local chapters of youth temperance groups such as the "Cold Water Army," whose members signed the following pledge:

We, Cold Water Girls and Boys,
Freely renounce the treacherous joys
Of Brandy, Whiskey, Rum, and Gin;
The Serpent's lure to death and sin:

Wine, Beer, and Cider we detest,
And thus we'll make our parents blest;
"So here we pledge perpetual hate
To all that can intoxicate."

27   Still, it was no easy task to persuade Americans to abandon a tradition practiced for generations. The Congregational parsonage erected in the early 1830s in Middlefield, Connecticut, was, thanks to the influence of temperance advocate William Lyman, the first building raised in that community without rum being served to the laborers, according to Middlefield historian Thomas Atkins. But that landmark was not achieved without considerable struggle. "Good men in the church pleaded with tears for the old custom" of serving rum to the workers, reports Atkins, "and when they found that Mr. Lyman was immovable in his purpose, so many went home grieved, angry, disgusted, that the raising could not be finished that day."

28   Even among those who voluntarily embraced temperance, there was backsliding. The records of the Middletown, Connecticut, Sons of Temperance contain the names of many members who in the mid-1840s were expelled, suspended, or withdrew from the brotherhood, presumably for breaking their pledge not to drink. Some lapsed teetotalers returned to the fold, as indicated by the directive in the records that, "Bro. Shaddick's name be erased from the roll—and that he be again reinstated on resigning the pledge & paying a fine of one dollar."

29   Eventually, inevitably, the cry of "There oughta be a law" was raised. Between 1851 and 1855 a total of 11 out of the 31 states in the Union passed legislation that made the sale of alcoholic beverages illegal.

30   But it was just at its moment of apparent victory that the temperance movement began to collapse. Its fall, like its rise, was the result of several factors. There had for years been fundamental, divisive disagreement among temperance advocates concerning the methods and goals of the movement. The new state prohibition laws proved most unpopular and almost impossible to enforce. And the temperance movement's place in the public's attention was eclipsed by the drive to abolish slavery and the consequent increasing alienation of North from South that erupted into the Civil War in 1861.

31   Following the war Americans largely returned to their alcohol-soaked ways, a development countered by the rebirth of the temperance movement, this time led largely, at least at first, by women. The renewed crusade would culminate in the Eighteenth Amendment to the United States Constitution, which took effect in 1920, ushering in the notorious era of national prohibition that would last until the amendment's repeal in 1933.

24

ALL MEN AND WOMEN ARE CREATED EQUAL

BY CONSTANCE RYNDER

Owing to this nation's strong Protestant ethic, the early to mid-nineteenth century is remembered as the golden age of reform. Fervent Protestants believed that man was perfectible, and that by extension, society's injustices could and should be fixed. All manner of sins were attacked with a vengeance, and each crusade went by a particular name. The anti-slavery cause became abolitionism. The crusade to ban alcohol became the temperance movement. And the drive to secure for women the right to vote became the suffrage movement.

There was much more at stake in the women's suffrage crusade than acquiring the vote. During the 1840's women had no property rights, and the money they earned belonged to their husbands. Women could not sign legal documents or participate in legal proceedings. It was, indeed, not second-class citizenship; they were not citizens, in any legal sense of the world. To many women, this was the denial of equality and human dignity in the nation that was founded on the premise of guaranteeing both!

But the movement to secure women equal rights came up against every possible obstacle known. Men did not want to share the franchise; politicians did not want the idea even mentioned; even the movement itself would be fraught with disagreement and internal splintering. Owing perhaps to the centuries-old crusade to end slavery, women's rights took a back seat, both before and after the Civil War. When black men were finally given the franchise after the war, many women, who actively worked to end slavery, felt betrayed by a system that was stacked against them.

The leaders of the movement, Susan B. Anthony and Elizabeth Cady Stanton, among others, have been memorialized on coins and paintings and such. But like most efforts similar to these, this trivializes these women's accomplishments. The Seneca Falls Convention of 1848 not only started a crusade to get women the vote, it launched a world-wide movement to change people's attitudes about what a woman could and should do with her natural abilities. To this end, the movement continues today.

- *What event sparked the crusade for women's rights?*
- *What economic and legal rights were denied to women?*
- *At the Seneca Falls Convention, why was the suffrage resolution the most contentious?*
- *How did the press treat the convention in their stories?*

- *Why did some women jump ship on the movement?*
- *What was the connection between abolitionism and women's rights?*
- *How did passage of the 15th amendment divide the women's movement?*
- *What was Elizabeth Cady Stanton referring to when she wrote of the Victorian Double Standard?*
- *Why did Stanton advocate a reform of organized religion, and write The Woman's Bible?*

---

1   The announcement of an upcoming "Woman's Rights Convention" in the Seneca County Courier was small, but it attracted Charlotte Woodward's attention. On the morning of July 19, 1848, the 19-year-old glove maker drove in a horse-drawn wagon to the Wesleyan Methodist Chapel in upstate New York town of Seneca Falls. To her surprise, Woodward found dozens of other women and a group of men waiting to enter the chapel, all of them as eager as she was to learn what a decision of "the social, civil, and religious rights of women" might produce.

2   The convention was the brainchild of 32-year-old Elizabeth Cady Stanton, a noted abolitionist politician. Born in Johnstown, New York, Cady Stanton demonstrated both an intellectual bent and a rebellious spirit from an early age. Exposed to her father's law books as well as his conservative views on women, she objected openly to the legal and educational disadvantages under which women of her day labored. In 1840 she provoked her farther by marrying Stanton, a handsome, liberal reformer and further defied convention by deliberately omitting the word "obey" form her wedding vows.

3   Marriage to Henry Stanton brought Elizabeth Cady Stanton—she insisted on retaining her maiden name—into contact with other independent-minded women. The newlyweds spent their honeymoon at the World Anti-Slavery Convention in London where, much to their chagrin, women delegates were denied their seats and deprived of a voice in the proceedings. Banished to a curtained visitors' gallery, the seven women listened in stunned silence as the London credentials committee charged they were "constitutionally unfit for public and business meetings." It was an insult Cady Stanton never forgot.

4   Among the delegates was Lucretia Coffin Mott, a liberal Hicksite Quaker preacher and an accomplished public speaker in the American abolitionist movement, who was also disillusioned by the lack of rights granted women. A mother of six, Mott had grown up on Nantucket Island, "so thoroughly imbued with women's rights," she later admitted, "that it was the most important question of my life from an early age." In Mott, Cady Stanton found both an ally and a role model. "When I first heard from her lips that I had the same right to think for myself that Luther, Calvin, and John Knox had," she recalled, "and the same right to be guided by my own convictions . . . I felt a new born sense of dignity and freedom." The two women became fast friends and talked about the need for a convention to discuss women's emancipation. Eight years passed, however, before they fulfilled their mutual goal.

5   For the first years of her marriage, Cady Stanton settled happily into middle-class domestic life, first in Johnstown and subsequently in Boston, then the hub of reformist activity. She delighted in being part of her husband's stimulating circle of reformers and intellectuals and gloried in motherhood; over a 17-year period she bore seven children. In 1847, however, the Stantons moved to Seneca Falls, a small, remote farming and manufacturing community in New York's Finger Lakes district. After Boston, life in Seneca Falls with its routine household duties seemed dull to Cady Stanton, and she renewed her protest against the conditions that limited women's lives. "My experience at the World Anti-Slavery Convention, all I had read of the legal status of women, and the oppression I saw everywhere, together swept across my soul, intensified now by many personal experiences." A meeting with Lucretia Mott in July of 1848 provided the opportunity to take action.

6   On July 13, Cady Stanton received an invitation to a tea party at the home of Jane and Richard Hunt, wealthy Quakers living in Waterloo, New York, just three miles west of Seneca Falls. There she again met Lucretia Mott, Mott's younger sister, Martha Coffin Wright, and Mary Ann McClintock, wife of the Waterloo Hicksite Quaker minister. At tea, Cady Stanton poured out to the group "the torrent of my long-accumulating discontent." Then and there they decided to schedule a women's "convention" for the following week. Hoping to attract a large audience, they placed an unsigned notice in the Courier advertising Lucretia Mott as the featured speaker.

7   Near panic gripped the five women as they gathered around the McClintock's parlor table the following Sunday morning. They had only three days to set an agenda and prepare a document "for the inauguration of a rebellion."

8   Supervised by Cady Stanton, they drafted a "Declaration of Sentiments and Resolutions," paraphrasing the Declaration of Independence. The document declared that "all men and women are created equal" and "are endowed by their Creator with certain unalienable rights . . . ." These natural rights belong equally to women and men, it continued, but man "has usurped the prerogative of Jehovah himself, claiming it as his right to assign for her a sphere of action, when that belongs to her conscience and to her God." The result has been "the establishment of an absolute tyranny over her."

9   There followed a specific catalog of injustices. Women were denied access to higher education, the professions, and the pulpit, as well as equal pay for equal work. If married they had no property rights, even the wages they earned legally belonged to their husbands. Women were subject to a high moral code, yet legally bound to tolerate moral delinquencies in their husbands. Wives could be punished, and if divorced a mother had no child custody rights. In every way, man "has endeavored to destroy (woman's) confidence in her own powers, to lessen her self-esteem, and to make her willing to lead a dependent and abject life." Above all, every woman had been deprived of "her inalienable right to the elective franchise."

10   Eleven resolutions demanding redress of these and other grievances accompanied the nearly 1,000-word Declaration. When Cady Stanton insisted upon including a resolution favoring voting rights for women, her otherwise supportive husband threatened to boycott the event. Even Lucretia Mott warned her, "Why Lizzie, thee will make us ridiculous!" "Lizzie," however refused to yield.

11   Although the gathering was a convention for and of women, it was regarded as "unseemly" for a lady to conduct a public meeting, so Lucretia's husband, James Mott, agreed to chair the two-day event. Mary Ann McClintock's husband, Thomas, also participated. Henry Stanton left town.

12   When the organizers arrived at the Wesleyan Chapel on the morning of Wednesday, July 19, they found the door locked. No one had a key, so Cady Stanton's young nephew scrambled in through an open window and unbarred the front door. As the church filled with spectators, another dilemma presented itself. The first day's sessions had been planned for women exclusively, but almost 40 men showed up. After a hasty council at the altar the leadership decided to let the men stay, since they were already seated and seemed genuinely interested.

13   Tall and dignified in his Quaker garb, James Mott called the first session to order at 11:00 am and appointed the McClintocks' older daughter (also named Mary Ann) secretary. Cady Stanton, in her first public speech, rose to state the purpose of the convention. "We have met here today to discuss our rights and wrongs, civil and political." She then read the Declaration aloud, paragraph by paragraph, and urged all present to participate freely in the discussions. The Declaration was re-read several times, amended, and adopted unanimously. Both Lucretia Mott and Cady Stanton addressed the afternoon session, as did the McClintock's younger daughter, Elizabeth. To lighten up the proceedings, Mott read a satirical article on "woman's sphere" that her sister Martha had published in the local newspapers. Later that evening, Mott spoke to the audience on "The Progress of Reforms."

14   The second day's sessions were given over to the 11 resolutions. As Mott feared, the most contentious proved to be the ninth—the suffrage resolution. The other 10 passed unanimously. According to Stanton's account, most of those who opposed this resolution did so because they believed it would compromise the others. She, however, remained adamant. "To have drunkards idiots, horse racing rum-selling rowdies, ignorant foreigners, and silly boys fully recognized, while we ourselves are thrust out from all rights that belong to citizens, is too grossly insulting to be longer quietly submitted to. The right is ours. We must have it." Even Cady Stanton's eloquence would not have carried the day but for the support she received from ex-slave and abolitionist Fredrick Douglass editor of the antislavery newspaper, *North Star*. "Right is of no sex" he argued; a woman is "justly entitled to all we claim for man." After much heated debate the ninth resolution passed but by only a small majority.

15   Thomas McClintock presided over the final session on Thursday evening and read extracts from Sir William Blackstone's Commentaries on the Laws of England that described the status of women in English common law. Cady Stanton took questions before short speeches were given by young Mary Ann McClintock and Frederick Douglass. Lucretia Mott closed the meeting with an appeal to action and one additional resolution of her own "The speedy success of our cause depends upon the zealous and untiring efforts of both men and women, for the overthrow of the monopoly of the pulpit, and for securing to women of equal participation with men in the various trades, professions, and commerce." It, too, passed unanimously.

16   In all, some 300 people attended the Seneca Falls Convention. The majority were ordinary folk like Charlotte Woodward. Most sat through 18 hours of speeches, debates, and readings. One hundred of them—68 women (including Woodward) and 32 men—signed the final draft of the Declaration of Sentiments and Resolutions. Women's rights as a separate reform movement had been born.

17   Press coverings were surprisingly broad and generally venomous, particularly on the subject of female suffrage. Philadelphia's *Public Ledger* and *Daily*

Transcript declared that no lady would want to vote. "A woman is nobody. A wife is everything. The ladies of Philadelphia . . . are resolved to maintain their rights as Wives, Belles, Virgins and Mothers." According to the *Albany Mechanic's Advocate,* equal rights would "demoralize and degrade (women) from their high sphere and noble destiny . . . and prove a monstrous injury to all mankind." The *New York Herald* published the entire text of the Seneca Falls declaration, calling it "amusing" but conceding that Lucretia Mott would make a better President than some of those who have lately tenated the White House." The only major paper to treat the event seriously was the liberal *New York Tribune,* edited by Horace Greeley, who found the demand for equal political rights improper, yet "however unwise and mistaken the demand, it is but the assertion of a natural right and as such must be conceded."

18   Stung by the public outcry, many original signers begged to have their names removed from the Declaration. "Our friends gave us the cold shoulder, and felt themselves disgraced by the whole proceeding," complained Cady Stanton. "Many women sympathized with the convention's goals but feared the stigma attached to attending any future meetings." "I am with you thoroughly," said the wife of Senator William Seward, "but I am a born coward. There is nothing I dread more than Mr. Seward's ridicule." Even the McClintocks and the Hunts refrained from active involvement in women's rights after the Seneca Falls Convention.

19   But Cady Stanton saw opportunity in public criticism. "Imagine the publicity given our ideas by thus appearing in a widely circulated sheet like the Herald" she wrote to Mott. "It will start women thinking, and men, too." She drafted several lengthy responses to every negative newspaper article and editorial, presenting the reformers' side of the issue to the readers. Mott sensed her younger colleague's future role. "Thou art wedded to this cause," she told Cady Stanton, "that thou must expect to act as a pioneer in the work."

20   News of the Seneca Falls Convention spread rapidly and inspired a spate of regional women's rights meetings. Beginning with a follow-up meeting two weeks later in Rochester, New York, all subsequent women's rights forums featured female chairs. New England abolitionist Lucy Stone organized the first national convention, held in Worchester, Massachusetts, in 1850. Like Cady Stanton, Stone saw the connection between black emancipation and female emancipation. When criticized for including women's rights in her antislavery speeches, Stone countered: "I was a woman before I was an abolitionist—I must speak for the women."

21   Quaker reformer Susan B. Anthony joined the women's rights movement in 1852. She had heard about the Seneca Falls Convention, of course, and her parents and sister had attended the 1848 Rochester meeting. Initially, however, she deemed its goals of secondary importance to temperance and abolition. All that changed in 1851 when she met Cady Stanton, with whom she formed a life-long political partnership. Bound to the domestic sphere by her growing family, Cady Stanton wrote articles and letters; Anthony, who never married, traveled the country lecturing and organizing women's rights associations. As Cady Stanton later put it, "I forged the thunderbolts and she fired them." In time, Susan B. Anthony's name became synonymous with women's rights.

22   Women's rights conventions were held annually until the Civil War, drawing most of their support from the abolitionist and temperance movements. After the war, feminist leaders split over the exclusion of women from legislation enfranchising black men. Abolitionists argued that it was "the Negro's Hour," and that the inclusion of female suffrage would jeopardize passage of the Fifteenth Amendment to the Constitution, which enfranchised all male citizens regardless of race. Feeling betrayed by their old allies, Cady Stanton and Susan B. Anthony opposed the Fifteenth Amendment. Their protest alienated the more cautious wing of the movement and produced two competing suffrage organizations.In 1869, Lucy Stone, Julia Ward Howe—well known author of "Battle Hymn of the Republic"—and others formed the moderate American Women Suffrage Association, while Cady Stanton, Anthony, Martha Wright, and the radical faction founded the National Woman Suffrage Association (NWSA). Lucretia Mott, now an elderly widow, sought in vain to reconcile the two camps.

23   Both organizations sought political equality for women, but the more radical NWSA actively promoted issues beyond suffrage. Guided by the original Seneca Falls Resolutions, the NWSA demanded an end to all laws and practices that discriminated against women, and called for divorce law reform, equal pay, access to higher education and the professions, reform of organized religion, and a total rethinking of what constituted a "woman's sphere." Cady Stanton spoke about women's sexuality in public and condemned the Victorian double standard that forced wives to endure drunken, brutal, and licentious husbands. Anthony countenanced—and occasionally practiced—civil disobedience; in 1872, she provoked her own arrest by illegally casting a ballot in the presidential election.

24   By the time the two rival organizations merged in 1890 to form the National American Women Suffrage Association (NAWSA), much had been accomplished. Many states had enacted laws granting married women property rights, equal guardianship over children, and the legal standing to make contracts and bring suit. Nearly one-third of college students were female, and 19 states allowed women to vote in local

school board elections. In two western territories—
Wyoming and Utah—women voted on equal basis
with men. But full suffrage nationwide remained
stubbornly out of reach. NAWSA commenced a long
state-by-state battle for the right to vote.

25   NAWSA's first two presidents were Cady Stanton
and Anthony, by then in their seventies. Old age did
not mellow either one of them, especially Cady
Stanton. Ever the rebel, she criticized NAWSA's
narrow-mindedness and viewed with increasing
suspicion its newly acquired pious prohibitionist
allies. NAWSA's membership should include all
"types of classes, races, and creeds," she stated, and
resist the evangelical infiltrators who sought to mute
the larger agenda of women's emancipation.

26   Cady Stanton had long advocated reform of organized religion. "The chief obstacle in the way of
woman's elevation today," she wrote, "is the degrading position assigned her in the religion of all countries." Whenever women tried to enlarge their "divinely ordained sphere," the all-male clerical
establishment condemned them for violating "God's
law." Using the Scriptures to justify women's inferior status positively galled her. In 1895, she published *The Woman's Bible*, a critical commentary on
the negative image of women in the Old and New
Testaments. Even Anthony thought she had gone
too far this time and could do little to prevent conservative suffragists from venting their wrath. During the annual convention of NAWSA, both the book
and its author were publicly censured. Henceforth,
mainstream suffragists downplayed Cady Stanton's
historic role, preferring to crown Susan B. Anthony
as the stateswoman of the movement.

27   Elizabeth Cady Stanton died in 1902 at the age of
86, and Susan B. Anthony died four years later, also
at 86. By then a new generation of suffrage leaders
had emerged—younger, better educated, and
less restricted to the domestic sphere. The now-
respectable, middle-class leadership of NAWSA
adopted a "social feminist" stance, arguing that
women were, in fact, different from men and therefore needed the vote in order to apply their special
qualities to the political problems of the nation.

28   However, more militant suffragists, among them
Quaker agitator Alice Paul and Cady Stanton's
daughter, Harriot Stanton Blatch, continued to insist
upon women's absolute equality. They demanded a
federal suffrage amendment as a necessary first step
toward achieving equal rights. Paul's National
Woman's Party gained the movement valuable publicity by engaging in confrontational tactics, including picketing the White House, being arrested, and
going on hunger strikes while in prison.

29   Voting rights came in the wake of World War I.
Impressed by the suffragists' participation in the
war effort, Congress passed what became to be
known as the "Susan B. Anthony Amendment" in
1919. Following state ratification a year later, it enfranchised American women nationwide in the form
of the Nineteenth Amendment to the Constitution.

30   It had been 72 years since that daring call for fe-
male voting rights was issued at the Seneca Falls
Convention. On November 2, 1920, 91-year-old
Charlotte Woodward Pierce went to the polls in
Philadelphia, the only signer of the Seneca Falls
Declaration who had lived long enough to legally
cast her ballot in a presidential election.

25

DYING OF BREAST CANCER IN EARLY AMERICA

BY JAMES S. OLSON

No disease creates more fear and confusion for American women than breast cancer. Choosing to have a mastectomy—surgically amputating a breast—is an agonizing decision. Women ask: "Would a less radical procedure like a lumpectomy remove the cancer without losing the breast? Would chemotherapy eradicate the cancer cells in the breast tissue? Would radiation therapy stop the cancer without any surgery?" The early nineteenth century woman had only two choices: to have a radical mastectomy or to die.

In this story, we meet Nabby Smith and her famous family. We agonize with her as she discovers her breast cancer, as she makes her medical decision, and as she is operated on. From this narrative, we learn that the problems encountered by our American "ancestors" are strikingly similar to the ones we encounter today.

- *What factors contributed to Nabby Smith's breast cancer being a virtual death sentence?*
- *How did Nabby and her family react to the disease?*
- *Why was Nabby's surgery performed in such conditions?*

---

1   It was just a tiny dimple. On a man's chin it would have looked rugged and distinguished. On a woman's cheek it might have been called a "beauty mark." But this was a different dimple, a killer dimple. It was on her left breast and "Nabby" Smith wondered what it was. She had never noticed it before, nor had her husband William. Perhaps it was just another physical sign of age, they thought, an indicator that she was not a young woman anymore. It was a sign, to be sure, but not of old age. The dimple was as much a symbol of premature death as a skull and crossbones, and within a few years, it would turn Nabby into a virtual skeleton before killing her in a pain-wracked stupor. Actually the dimple itself was not really the problem. Beneath the dimple, buried an inch below the skin, a small malignant tumor was attaching itself to surface tissues and drawing them in, like a sinking ship pulling water down its own whirlpool. It was 1808 and Nabby was 44 years old. She had a husband and three children, but she did not have much of a life left.

2   At first Nabby did not give it much thought, only noticing it now and then when she bathed or dressed in the morning. Nor did she talk about it. Nabby Smith was a shy and somewhat withdrawn woman, quiet and cautious in the expression of ideas, more comfortable with people who guarded their feelings than with those who exposed them. She blushed easily and rarely laughed out loud, allowing only a demure, half-smile to crease her face when she was amused. She had a pleasant disposition and a mellow temperament, both of which endeared her to family and friends. Nabby was a beautiful woman, blessed with long, red hair, a round face, deep-blue eyes, and a creamy, porcelain complexion. She commanded respect, not because of an aggressive

personality but simply because of the quality of her mind and a powerful sense of personal dignity.

3   At least some of that dignity came from her background. Nabby Smith was a member of one of the most distinguished families in the United States. She was born in Quincy, Massachusetts, in 1766. Her parents named her Abigail Adams. They began calling her "Nabby" when she was little. Nabby had an extraordinary childhood. Her father was John Adams, the future president of the United States, and her mother was Abigail Adams, the most prominent woman in early American society. Her little brother John Quincy was destined to become president of the United States. From the time of her birth, Nabby's parents were busily engaged in colonial politics, eventually playing leading roles in the American Revolution and the War for American Independence. They raised her on a steady diet of dinner table and parlor political talk–animated discussions of freedom, liberty, rights, despotism, war, and foreign policy. Nabby absorbed it all; political philosophy in her family was not a mere abstraction. Her position in the family was secure.

4   She was the apple of their eyes. As an only daughter, Nabby enjoyed the special attentions of her father, who felt the need to protect her and pamper her. Abigail had always doted upon her, dressing her up in the latest fashions when she was little and counseling her when she was an adolescent. When Nabby grew up their relationship quickly evolved into a deep friendship. In spite of the devoted attentions of her parents, Nabby took it all in stride, never becoming spoiled or self-indulgent. She was even-handed, thick-skinned, and not afraid of responsibility—the daughter every parent dreamed of having.

5   When the War for Independence ended in 1783, Nabby was just 17 years old, but she was in for an adventure. Congress appointed her father to serve as the first United States minister to England, and in 1785 the family crossed the Atlantic and took up residence in a house on Grosvener Square in London. They were immediately caught up in the social and political life of the world's greatest city, meeting King George III at court and other prominent politicians and attending the whirlwind of parties, meetings, banquets, and festivals common to the life of an ambassador.

6   For the first few months in London, Nabby was somewhat depressed mostly because of homesickness but also because she had left behind a boyfriend who soon quit writing letters Her mood caught her parents offguard—it was uncharacteristic of her—and they tried to reassure her that soon she would be feeling better. They were right. Soon Nabby had noticed a young man who was part of the American diplomatic staff in London. Colonel William Smith, a young veteran of the Continental Army and secretary

to the American legation in London, had also noticed Nabby.

7   Smith was a dashing and handsome figure, racing around London in a two-seated carriage, something equivalent to a sports car today. He dressed well—a weakness for silk coats and shirts—and kept company with a variety of people in London's expatriate community, especially with Latin American liberals and radicals interested in securing independence from Spain. He was bold and impetuous, inspired by courage and limited by poor judgement. Because of his work with the American legation in London, and his role as secretary to Minister John Adams, Smith saw a great deal of the Adams family, and Nabby fell secretly in love with him. It was not long before he felt the same way, drawn to Nabby's beauty, grace, and intelligence. He proposed late in 1785 and they were married in June 1786, after a courtship which John and Abigail Adams felt was too short. They excused it because "a soldier is always more expeditious in his courtships than other men."

8   But Colonel William Smith was a soldier without a war, a dinosaur at the age of 28, and Nabby was in for a difficult life, an innocent victim of what her brother John Quincy called "fortune's treacherous game." Colonel Smith was not cruel. In fact, he always loved and cared for Nabby, and they had three children. With a stoicism that would have made the most devout Puritan proud, Nabby was more than willing to accept her financial fate and make a life for her family wherever Smith settled. The problem was that Smith never really settled down. He wasted his life away, always searching but never finding a place for himself, winning and losing political appointments, dabbling in Latin American *coup d'etats* and revolutions, dragging Nabby and the kids back and forth between New York and London trying to influence a new power broker or close another deal. He spent far more money than he ever earned, and Nabby was forever worrying about the bills and their reputation. By the early 1800s, Smith was trying to make his fortune in shady real estate schemes, hoping to profit from the desire of so many Americans to move west and get their own land, but he lost everything he had. He was bold but not shrewd enough for the life of an entrepreneur. In 1808, when Nabby first noticed the dimple, they were living on the edge of the frontier, in a small farmhouse along the Chenango River in western New York, where he spent the days behind an iron plow and a mule working a small plot of land. The Smiths were a long way, economically and geographically, from the heady world of Boston and London politics.

9   During the next year the dimple became more pronounced and more worrisome to Nabby, but it was not until late in 1809 that she felt a hard lump

beneath the skin. Nabby Adams was an intelligent, well-informed woman, and throughout her adult life the Adams family had been close friends with Dr. Benjamin Rush, the country's most prominent physician. Breast cancer was as much the dreaded disease in the early 1800s as it is today, something educated woman knew about and feared. Well-informed people had been aware of breast cancer for 2,000 years, since Greek physicians first called it *karkinos* (carcinoma), or crab, because of its tenacious ability to hold on, to defy all attempts to cure it or cut it out. In fact, breast cancer in women was really the first cancer human beings ever identified, probably because it was more visible than other deadly tumors. And they knew breast cancer started with a hard lump. No records exist describing Nabby Smith's initial reaction to the lump in her breast, but it is safe to say that the intermittent, low-key concern about the dimple was instantly transformed into a chronic, persistent worry that would never quite go away.

10   Like so many women then and today, Nabby tried to ignore the lump, hoping that in the daily, busy routines of running a small farm and household she would not have time to think about it. But cancer has a way of asserting itself, finally obliterating even the most elaborate attempts at procrastination and denial. Nabby's cancer was no exception. The lump underwent an ominous growth, in spite of the efforts of local healers who prescribed a dizzying variety of external salves and potions. She wrote home to John and Abigail Adams in February 1811 that her doctor had discovered "a cancer in my breast." As soon as they received the letter, her parents began urging their daughter to come to Boston for medical advice. Some things do not change. Even today, people suffering from cancer often head to the major cities where comprehensive cancer centers can treat them.

11   In June 1811, with the lump now visible to the naked eye, a desperate Nabby returned to Massachusetts. As soon as she arrived in Quincy, Massachusetts, Nabby wrote to Benjamin Rush in Philadelphia, describing her condition and seeking his advice. When Abigail Adams first looked at her daughter's breast, she found the condition "alarming." The tumor was large enough to distend the breast into a misshapen mass. John and Abigail took Nabby to see several physicians in Boston—Drs. Holbrook and Welsh and Tufts and Johnson—and they were cautiously reassuring, telling her that the situation and her general health were "so good as not to threaten any present danger." They prescribed hemlock pills to "poison the disease."

12   Soon after that round of reassuring examinations, however, the Adams family received a more ominous reply from Dr. Benjamin Rush. In her initial letter, Nabby told the famous physician that the tumor was large and growing, but that it was "movable"—not attached to the chest wall. Rush found the news encouraging, as do most cancer specialists today. Malignant tumors which are "movable" are better candidates for surgery, since it is more likely that the surgeon can get what is termed a "clean margin"—a border of non-cancerous tissue surrounding the tumor—reducing the chances that the cancer will recur or spread.

13   Knowing that Nabby had already travelled from western New York to Boston to seek more medical advice and to be cared for by her parents, Rush wrote a letter to John and Abigail Adams, telling them to gently break his news to Nabby. Dr. Rush wrote:

I shall begin my letter by replying to your daughter's. I prefer giving my opinion and advice in her case in this way. You and Mrs. Adams may communicate it gradually and in such a manner as will be least apt to distress and alarm her.

After the experience of more than 50 years in cases similar to hers, I must protest against all local applications and internal medicines for relief. They now and then cure, but in 19 cases out of 20 in tumors in the breast they do harm or suspend the disease until it passes beyond that time in which the only radical remedy is ineffectual. This remedy is the knife. From her account of the moving state of the tumor, it is now in a proper situation for the operation. Should she wait till it suppurates or even inflames much, it may be too late. . . . I repeat again, let there be no delay in flying to the knife. Her time of life calls for expedition in this business. . . . I sincerely sympathize with her and with you and your dear Mrs. Adams in this family affliction, but it will be but for a few minutes if she submit to have it extirpated, and if not, it will probably be a source of distress and pain to you all for years to come. It shocks me to think of the consequences of procrastination in her case.

14   Benjamin Rush knew that there were no home remedies or folk cures for breast cancer; Nabby Adams needed surgery—a mastectomy—and she needed it immediately.

15   Rush wrote to John and Abigail Adams, rather than replying directly to Nabby's inquiry, because he wanted them to break the news to her gently, to help her in overcoming the initial terror or she was going to feel about going "under the knife." Surgery in the early nineteenth century was a brutal affair. Cutting instruments were crude and there was no such thing as anesthesia. Patients were wide awake during the operation, and they had to be belted down and restrained from moving or screaming. It

was not at all uncommon for sick people to choose death rather than "the knife." And if they survived the surgery, they then faced the threat of massive infections. Nobody understood the principle of microscopic life, of germs which cause disease, or how careful, antiseptic procedures could prevent infections. Patients ran the risk of dying of massive infections within days of the operation. Surgery was always a last resort. But Benjamin Rush was convinced that Nabby's condition had reached the desperate point, and he wanted John and Abigail to talk her into it, to let her know that "the pain of the operation is much less than her fears represent it to be." Amputation of the diseased breast was her only chance.

16   They first had to convince their son-in-law. Fear of the "dread disease" had pushed William Smith into an advanced state of denial. When he learned of Rush's recommendation, he reacted indignantly, heading for libraries to learn whatever he could about the disease and its prognosis, hoping against hope to spare Nabby the operation. He talked and talked, trying to convince himself that maybe the tumor would just go away, that Nabby could probably live with it, that it was not so bad. Abigail Adams's mother had more faith in Rush and wrote to Smith: "If the operation is necessary as the Dr. states it to be, and as I fear it is, the sooner it is done the better provided Mrs. Smith can bring herself along, as I hope she will consent to it." She even asked her son-in-law, if Nabby agreed to the surgery, to be with "Nabby through the painful tryal." Smith finally acquiesced to Rush's opinion and Abigail's persistence. Nabby was also convinced that surgery was her only chance. They scheduled the operation for October 8, 1811.

17   There was nothing new about amputating a cancerous breast. Some surgeons in Europe had been performing the operation for more than a century, and the surgery was well known among Boston physicians. In 1728 Dr. Zabdiel Boylston amputated the breast of Sarah Winslow to remove a malignant tumor. The patient survived the surgery and lived another 39 years, dying in 1767 of old age, and local physicians were convinced that the operation had brought about the cure. Amputation was not, however, the treatment of choice for breast cancer in the late-1700s and early-1800s because the surgery itself was so harrowingly painful and the outcomes so problematic. Most patients undergoing surgery in the nineteenth century had to deal with the problem of massive post-operative infections. Surgery was always a last resort.

18   Nabby and William Smith, along with their daughter Caroline, and Abigail Adams travelled from Quincy to Boston the day before the operation. Late in the afternoon, they met with John Warren, widely considered to be the city's most skilled surgeon. Warren gave Nabby a brief physical examination and told her what to expect. It was hardly reassuring. In fact, his description of the surgery, of what Nabby was about to go through, was nightmarishly terrifying, enough to make Nabby, William, Abigail, and Caroline rethink the decision. But Rush's warning—"It shocks me to think of the consequences of procrastination in her case"—reverberated through all of their minds. Nabby had no choice if she ever hoped to live to see her grandchildren.

19   The operation was as bad as they had feared. John Warren was assisted by his son Joseph, who was destined to become a leading physician in his own right, and several other doctors who had examined Nabby back in July. Warren's surgical instruments, laying in a wooden box on a table, were quite simple. One was a large fork with two, six-inch prongs sharpened to a needle point. He also had a wooden-handled razor. A pile of compress bandages was in the box as well. In the corner of the room there was a small oven, full of red-hot coals, into which a flat, thick, heavy iron spatula had been inserted.

20   Nabby came into the room dressed for a Sunday service. she was a proper woman from the best family, and she felt obligated to act the part. The doctors were in professional attire–frock coats, with shirts and ties. Modesty demanded that Nabby unbutton only the top of her dress and slip it off her left shoulder, exposing the diseased breast but little else. She remained fully clothed. Since they knew nothing of bacteria in the early 1800s, there were no gloves or surgical masks, no need for Warren to scrub his hands or wash Nabby's chest before the operation or cover his own hair and beard. Warren had her sit down and lean back in a reclining chair. He belted her waist, legs, feet, and right arm to the chair and had her raise her left arm above her head so that the pectoralis major muscle would push the breast up. One of the physicians took Nabby's raised arm by the elbow and held it, while another stood behind her, pressing her shoulders and neck to the chair. Warren told Nabby to shut her eyes, grit her teeth, and get ready. Abigail, Caroline, and William stood off to the side to witness the ordeal.

21   Warren then straddled Nabby's knees, leaned over her semi-reclined body, and began his work. Like a father carving a Thanksgiving turkey, he took the two-pronged fork and thrust it deep into Nabby's breast. With his left hand, he held onto the fork and raised up on it, lifting the breast from the chest wall. He reached over for the large razor and started slicing into the base of the breast, moving from the middle of her chest toward her left side. When the breast was completely severed, Warren lifted it away from Nabby's chest with the fork. But the tumor was larger and more widespread then he had anticipated. Breast cancer often spreads to regional lymph nodes, and Warren discovered that Nabby already had

visible tumor tissue in the nodes of her axilla—under her left armpit. He took the razor in there as well and with his fingers pulled out nodes and tumor.

22 There was a real premium on speed in early nineteenth surgery. No wonder. Nabby was grimacing and groaning, flinching and twisting in the chair, with blood staining her dress and Warren's shirt and pants. Her hair was soon matted in sweat. Abigail, William, and Caroline had to turn their faces and eyes away from the gruesome struggle. With the patient writhing in pain and her family witnessing the spectacle, Warren wanted to get the job done as quickly as possible. To stop the bleeding, he pulled the red-hot spatula from the oven and applied it several times directly to the wound, cauterizing the worst bleeding points. With each touch, steamy wisps of smoke hissed into the air and filled the room with the distinct smell of burning flesh. Warren then sutured the wounds together, bandaged them, stepped back from Nabby, and mercifully told her that it was over. The whole procedure had taken less than 25 minutes. Abigail and Caroline quickly went to the surgical chair and helped Nabby pull her dress back over her left shoulder. Modesty demanded it. William helped her out of the chair and they all walked outside to the carriage. The two-hour ride to Quincy proved to be agony of its own for Nabby, with each bump in the road sending spasms of pain throughout her body.

23 Nabby had a long recovery from the surgery. Miraculously, she did not suffer from any serious post-surgical infections, but for months after the operation she was weak and feeble, barely able to get around. She could not use her left arm at all, and left it in a sling. Going back to the wilds of western New York was out of the question, so she stayed in Quincy with her mother, hoping to regain the strength she needed to return home. What sustained all of them during the ordeal of Nabby's recovery was the faith that the operation had cured the cancer. Within two weeks of the surgery, Dr. Benjamin Rush wrote John Adams congratulating him "in the happy issue of the operation performed upon Mrs. Smith's breast . . . her cure will be radical and durable. I consider her as rescued from a premature grave." Abigail wrote to a friend that although the operation had been a "furnace of affliction . . . what a blessing it was to have extirpated so terrible an enemy." In May 1812, seven months after the surgery, Nabby Adams felt well again. She returned home to the small farm along the Chenango River in western New York.

24 But Nabby Adams was not cured. Even today, breast cancer victims whose tumors have already spread to the lymph node do not have very good survival rates, even with modern surgery, radiation treatments, and chemotherapy. In Nabby's case, long before Dr. Warren performed the mastectomy, the cancer had already spread throughout her body. She was going to die, no matter what, and the horrific surgery in 1811 had served no purpose. Nabby suspected something was wrong within a few weeks of arriving home in New York. She began to complain of headaches and severe pain in her spine and abdomen. A local physician attributed the discomfort to rheumatism. The diagnosis relieved some of Nabby's anxiety, since she was already worried that the pain had something to do with cancer. Cancer patients grasp at straws, hoping against hope that there is an alternative explanation for their distress, something simple and common, like a cold or the flu or rheumatism, anything but a recurrence of the dread disease.

25 For Nabby Adams, however, it was not the flu or "the rheumatism." The cancer was back. That became quite clear in 1813 when she suffered a local recurrence of the tumors. When Warren amputated her breast and excised tissues from her axilla, he thought he had "gotten it all," removing the visible tumor tissue. But cancer is a cellular disease, and millions of invisible, microscopically tiny-malignant cancers were left behind. Some of them had grown into tumors of their own by the spring of 1813— visible tumors below the scar where Nabby's breast had once been and on the skin as well. Nabby's doctor in New York; then changed his diagnosis: her headaches and excruciating body pains were not rheumatism. The cancer was back and had spread throughout her body. Nabby Adams was terminal. She was going to die in a matter of months.

26 Nabby declined steadily in the late spring, finally telling her husband that she "wanted to die in her father's house." William Smith wrote John and Abigail Adams in May that the cancer had returned and that Nabby wanted "to spend her state of convalescence within the vortex of your kindness and assiduities than elsewhere." The colonel was back into denial, refusing to voice the certainty that his wife was going to die. Since the country was in the midst of the War of 1812, Smith told his in-laws, he had to go to Washington, D.C. to obtain a military appointment, and that he would return to Quincy, Massachusetts, as soon as the congressional session was over. John and Abigail prepared Nabby's room and waited for her arrival.

27 The trip was unimaginably painful—more than 300 miles in a carriage, over bumpy roads where each jolt meant stabbing pain. Her son John drove the carriage. When Nabby finally reached Quincy on July 26, she was suffering from grinding, constant, multiple-site pain. John and Abigail were shocked when they saw her. She was gaunt and thin, wracked by a deep cough, and her eyes had a moist, rheumy look to them. She groaned and sometimes screamed every time she moved. Huge, dark circles shadowed her cheeks, and a few minutes after she settled into

bed, the smell of death was in the air. Cancer cells not only divide rapidly, they also die rapidly, and when a patient has a body full of tumors, the body is also full of an increasing volume of dead, necrotic tissue. Those tissues are rancid and rotten, full of bacteria, and they give off a foul odor. Scientists today call the condition "cachexia"—he body seems to be feeding on itself—but in the early 1800s it was known as "the odor of death."

28   Nabby's pain was so unbearable, and her misery so unmitigated, that Abigail went into a depression of her own, a depression so deep she could not stand even to visit her daughter's room. It was her husband John Adams, the second president of the United States, who ministered to his dying daughter, feeding her, cleaning her and seeing to her personal needs, combing her hair and holding her hand. He tried to administer several recommended pain killers, but nothing seemed to help, not until she lapsed into a pain-numbing coma. Her husband returned from Washington, D.C., and the death-watch began. On the morning of August 9, Nabby's breathing became more shallow and the passage of time between breaths more extended. The family gathered around her bedside. She took her last breath early in the afternoon. A few days later, in a letter to Thomas Jefferson, John Adams wrote: "Your Friend, my only Daughter, expired, Yesterday Morning in the Arms of Her Husband, her Son, her Daughter, her Father and Mother, her Husbands two Sisters and two of her Nieces, in the 49th. Year of Age, 46 of which She was the healthiest and firmest of Us all: Since which, She has been a monument to Suffering and to Patience."

29   Except for a chosen few victims, breast cancer was a death sentence in the early nineteenth century, and the surgical treatment for it was almost as bad as the disease. From the moment she first noticed the lump, Nabby was doomed. During the rest of the century, physicians learned about anesthesia, which dramatically eased the trauma of surgery. They also learned about bacteria and started washing their hands before putting the scalpel to a patient's breast. They discovered that all tissue was composed of tiny cells, and that cancer was a disease process involving those cells. Around 1900, when surgeons developed the radical mastectomy—a new surgical procedure for removing a cancerous breast—patient survival rates increased. Seventy-five years after Nabby Adams died of breast cancer, women with the disease had a better chance of survival.

30   But even today, nearly 170 years after Nabby's death, breast cancer remains a frighteningly unpredictable disease. More limited surgical procedures, radiation therapy, and chemotherapy provide new treatments, but nearly 50,000 American women die of breast cancer every year. According to statistics released in 1993, one out of eight American women—a total of nearly 17 million people—will develop breast cancer during their lifetime. And according to existing survival rates, approximately 40 percent of them will die from it. The only real answer is early detection, hopefully from a mammogram examination when the cancer is tiny and curable. Nabby Adams did not have that option. We do.

26
THE EPIDEMIC 1849

BY CHARLES E. ROSENBERG

Cholera was the most terrifying disease to hit America in the nineteenth century. It did not kill nearly as many people as tuberculosis. But TB was (and is) a slow killer, taking years to waste away its victim. Cholera, on the other hand, strikes without warning and can kill within 24 hours. Americans feared cholera then, the way many fear AIDS today.

It came in three waves: 1832, 1849, and 1866. In the 1832 epidemic, Americans did not know what it was or what caused it. By 1866, health officials knew not only the cause, but also the preventative measures that communities could take to head it off. But in between, cholera killed tens of thousands, and put fear into millions.

- *What caused the disease?*
- *Where did it originate?*
- *What were some of the measures people took to prevent it?*
- *What were some of the explanations for the disease?*
- *Who was blamed? Why?*

---

1 Twenty-two days out of **Havre**, the packet ship "New York" dropped anchor at **quarantine** late Friday night, December 1, 1848. Early the next morning, New York's deputy health officer rowed out to inspect the new arrival and her 331 steerage passengers.

2 An alarmed captain greeted him with the report that seven immigrants had died below decks. Others were sick, exhibiting the unmistakable symptoms of cholera. It was no routine report which his deputy presented to Dr. John Sterling, the health officer. But it could have come as no great surprise.

3 Cholera, like revolution, had swept through Europe in 1848. Spreading outward from its **Ganges** homeland, the disease had, in a half-dozen years, visited almost every part of Asia, Europe, and the Middle East. In July, 1847, it was in Astrakhan, a year later in Berlin; early in October of 1848 it appeared in London. In the fall of 1848, as in the spring of 1832, cholera poised at the Atlantic.

---

cholera: an acute infectious disease of the small intestine, caused by the bacterium vibrio cholerae and characterized by profuse watery diarrhea, vomiting, muscle cramps, severe dehydration, and depletion of electrolytes.

Havre: Seine-Maritime Department in Northern France at the mouth of the Seine River, major seaport.

quarantine: enforced isolation or restriction of free movement imposed to prevent the spread of contagious disease.

Ganges: a river of northern India and Bangladesh rising in the Himalayan Mountains and flowing about 2,510 km generally eastward to the Bay of Bengal. The river is sacred to the Hindus.

4   Realistic Americans assumed that this barrier would not long protect the United States. The course of the epidemic was the same as it had been in 1832, except that the Atlantic was now crossed more rapidly, more frequently, and by larger ships. With cholera in London and Edinburgh in October, diarist George Templeton Strong commented resignedly, it would doubtless be in New York before the New Year.

5   By mid October, the medically sophisticated had already begun to notice forerunners of cholera in the atmosphere. Insects swarmed, **influenza** and diarrheas were epidemic, and the usual diseases of winter failed to respond to treatment. In this tainted air, the decades' accumulation of filth that polluted houses, streets, and yards was more than ordinarily **pernicious**. To allow the continued existence of such breeding places of pestilence seemed inexcusable, and moribund health boards and street-cleaning committees were attacked for their chronic inactivity. In Philadelphia the Board of Health, in Boston the City Council, and in Baltimore the Medical and Chirurgical Society had, by December, begun to prepare for the epidemic. Again, as in 1832, the reports of medical commissions filled hundreds of columns in newspapers and medical journals.

6   Though disquieting in their methodical description of agony and death, these reports provided some reassurance. They bore repeated testimony to the relative immunity of the well-nourished, the prudent, and the temperate. Nor, the reports agreed, did the disease seem as severe in this its second tour of Europe. New Englanders were especially soothed by a plausible new theory which held that cholera flourished only in areas underlain by limestone. Perhaps this explained how granite-bound New England escaped so lightly in 1832. Most reassuring of all was the unshaken conviction that the United States was the most prosperous, pious, and enlightened of nations. Cholera's ancestral home was India, its natural victims a dirty, ignorant, and fatalistic people.

7   There was little doubt in the minds of medical men, however, that cholera could thrive wherever there was sufficient filth. And no extraordinary sensibilities were required to see and smell the potential death in America's cities and villages. Few communities could provide their citizens with a reliable supply of water; sanitation and waste disposal were everywhere inadequate. Pigs, dogs, and goats still provided the only effective sanitation in many American cities. Pigs in the streets, like **Brother Jonathan** and the Indians, were an ineradicable part of the European image of the United States.

8   The hogs roamed everywhere. In New York pig-napping became a recognized trade (practiced by men who toured the city in wagons, scooping up unwatched pigs and selling them to butchers). In Little Rock, Arkansas, the porkers filled the streets and had, as one editor put it, begun to "dispute the side walks with *other persons.*" Such whimsy could not be shared by the parents of children killed or mutilated by foraging pigs.

9   New York had grown larger, but not cleaner, in the years between 1832 and 1849. Another generation's filth had merely been added to an already impressive accumulation. No American city was dirtier.

10   On the morning of December 2, 1848, the *New York* rode at anchor off Staten Island. Aboard were over 300 steerage passengers, all of whom had been exposed to cholera below deck. Prudence and public opinion alike demanded their quarantine.

11   But where? America's greatest port possessed no facilities adequate to quarantine 50, let alone 300, immigrants. After 15 years without cholera or yellow fever, New York's quarantine had become little more than an administrative gesture. Only the customs warehouses were large enough to accommodate so many people, and these were hurriedly converted into barrack-like hospital wards. Such improvisations were small improvement over the holds of the *New York*. Before the New Year, 60 of the immigrants had fallen ill; more than 30 had died. And over half of those originally quarantined had, as the health officer put it, "eloped ," scaling the walls and making for New York or New Jersey in small boats. Within a week, cases began to appear in New York City itself, in the most crowded and dirty of the immigrant boardinghouses.

12   Apprehensive interest turned suddenly to alarm, for it seemed that New York, like Moscow, might be scourged by cholera despite the cold of winter. Newspapers that printed cholera remedies were sold out within hours of publication. Both the New York Academy of Medicine and the Board of Health held special meetings within 24 hours of the discovery of the first cases. While the Academy of Medicine spent most of its time condemning the incompetence of the board, the board authorized the mayor to take whatever steps should be necessary to have the streets cleaned. A committee was also chosen to arrange for the establishment of cholera hospitals.

---

influenza: an acute contagious viral infection characterized by inflammation of the respiratory tract and by fever, chills, muscular pain and prostration.
pernicious: destructive, causing great harm.
Brother Jonathan: name for any patriotic American during or after the Revolutionary War.

13   For the moment these hospitals were not needed. The bitter cold of January brought the city a momentary reprieve, and there were no more new cases. For most New Yorkers, gold fever quickly replaced fears of cholera. But the more thoughtful realized that their city enjoyed only a respite. The warmth of the coming spring would certainly quicken the **dormant** seeds of the disease. New York had been fortunate in her freezing temperatures; the South was not so favored. On the sixth and eighth of December, vessels from Hamburg and Bremen brought cholera to New Orleans. In the mild New Orleans December, the disease spread rapidly among the unwashed and weary immigrants. These new arrivals quickly fanned out from New Orleans, and carried cholera with them to steamboat landings along the Mississippi, the Arkansas, and the Tennessee.

14   Winter temperatures limited the disease to the lower South. Few doubted, however, that spring and the opening of navigation would spread cholera throughout the Mississippi Valley. Quarantines had proved themselves useless; cleanliness alone seemed to offer protection. City council and local health boards were urged to have streets and houses cleaned and limed. "Another spring will bring the cholera among us," named a Milwaukee editor, "sweeping like the Angel of Death over our firesides."

15   Twenty Orange Street was not one of New York's fashionable addresses. Thirty yards from the front door was the Five Points, a focus of infection during the 1832 cholera epidemic, and still the most filthy and dangerous crossroads of a rough and sprawling port. A **tenement** two doors up from 20 Orange Street house had 106 hogs.

16   The poor and the criminal lived in Orange Street, and of these, only the most miserable tenanted its dark and oozing cellars. In the spring of 1849, James Gilligan, a laborer when he worked, lived with four women in a room 10 or 12 feet square in the rear basement of 20 Orange Street. The door had fallen front its hinges; the sashes of its two small windows were empty. There was no bed, no chair or table with the exception of two empty barrels, no movable furniture at all. Across these barrels the door was laid. This served as a table, and from it the five tenants ate the spoiled ham purchased at two or three cents a pound which was their usual fare.

17   Gilligan became ill on Friday, May 11. A habitual drinker, he thought little of his persistent cramps and vomiting. And by Saturday he felt better. On Monday the 14th, a local physician was notified that two of the women living in the cellar with Gilligan had sickened as well, complaining of severe cramps, vomiting, and diarrhea. Early Monday morning, Dr. Herriot made his way through the airless back yard which provided the only access to the rear basement of 20 Orange Street, lowered his head, and stepped down into the cellar. When his eyes had become accustomed to the dark, a scene **macabre** even for the Five Points confronted him. Three bodies, one male and two female, lay on the floor, a few rags separating them from the decaying earthen floor. Two of the three died before evening. By this time, another woman in the cellar had been taken ill, and she too died before morning.

18   Dr. Seth Geer, the city's resident physician, was notified early that morning. It was clear to him after he had visited 20 Orange Street—as clear as it had been to Dr. Herriot—that these unfortunates had died of cholera. And so he reported to the Board of Health. This was the 15th of May.

19   Most New Yorkers were not overly alarmed. It did not seem surprising to those more comfortably situated that such wretches should die "like rotten sheep." Degraded by rum and breathing impure air, they would have succumbed had cholera never existed. Testy old Philip Hone noted on Saturday the 19th that the cases thus far reported had all been in Orange Street, "where water never was used internally or externally, and the pigs were contaminated by the contact of the children."

20   The Board of Health was in a quandary. Despite intermittent efforts beginning in December, the board had not, by May, been able to establish even one cholera hospital. Fear and avarice had made it almost impossible to rent any sort of building. In desperation, Bedloe's Island, even steamboats and barges had been suggested as possible hospitals. But ship owners had proved as intractable as landlords: barges as well as houses would be permanently tainted in the public mind by their temporary use as cholera hospitals. By May, after five months of search, the only building which the board could confidently rely upon was the colored public school—and this prospective hospital possessed no sanitary facilities, not even facilities to heat water. On May 16, the day after hearing the report from Orange Street, the board established its first cholera hospital. It was the second floor of a tavern and ordinarily used for meetings and militia drills. Even this crude loft was obtained only at an exorbitant rent and after a mob, threatening to burn down the building, had been dispersed.

21   Before the epidemic had run its course, four of the city's public schools had been converted into makeshift hospitals, their desks ripped out and replaced by cots. But even these quasi-public buildings were not acquired without a struggle. The stigma of having

---

dormant: latent but capable of being activated.
tenement: a rundown, low-rental apartment building whose facilities and maintenance barely meet minimum standards.
macabre: suggesting the horror of death and decay.

once served as a cholera hospital could never be erased, trustees and teachers argued, while the children cast abruptly into the streets would lose interest in school and be exposed to the temptations of idleness and vile companions. They would serve only to increase the number of those susceptible to cholera.

22   The disease soon spread from the Five Points. Alarmed New Yorkers demanded that the Board of Health contain the disease before it invaded every part of the city. And by the end of June, the Board of Health had enacted what seemed to be a comprehensive **antechoir** program. The alderman and assistant alderman of each ward were authorized to hire four inspectors to help enforce the health ordinances—at a salary not to exceed $2 a day. The sale of fruits, vegetables, and fish from open carts was forbidden; and owners of filthy tenements were ordered to have them cleaned immediately.

23   At a hastily convened meeting on the 16th of May, the Board of Health chose a special Sanatory Committee, which was to meet daily and direct the city's campaign against cholera. This committee, chosen from among the members of the Board of Health, was invested with the board's full powers. The committee's first act was to appoint three prominent local physicians as medical councilors. Like the seven members of the Special Medical Council appointed in 1832, these three physicians had had no previous connection with the Board of Health. Their recommendations too were reminiscent of New York's earlier struggle with cholera. (Dr. Joseph M. Smith, chairman of the medical advisers, drew up a broadside summarizing his admonitions to the public. Aside from a few verbal changes, it was identical with the recommendations of the Board of Health during the 1832 epidemic.)

24   Still the disease spread. By June, many New Yorkers had deserted their homes for the pure air of the countryside. Those remaining provided themselves with **calomel**, **laudanum**, or perhaps those newer cholera remedies, sulphur pills and camphor "segars." Others turned to God, Catholics who had lived for years in mortal sin appeared again at Communion, and many of the city's Protestant churches held regular prayer meetings. June 28 had been set aside as a day of fasting and prayer by the General Synod of the Dutch Reform Church and the General Association of the Old School Presbyterians.

25   To the sorrow of clergymen, however, most New Yorkers seemed unmoved by this threatened judgment. "How small is the moral impression made upon the masses!" lamented one minister. The theaters "and other places of amusement and carnal pleasure," were "in full blast." The Sabbath itself was profaned by the illicit operations of over 500 **grogshops**.

26   It seemed inevitable that the mid-summer heat would force into luxuriant growth the already well-established rootings of the disease. (Even the air seemed to have lost its elasticity, one observer noted—as it had done in the summer of 1832.) And, editorialists commented acidly, there was little chance of cholera subsiding while the streets of New York were still covered with filth and garbage.

27   Such fears were soon justified. In July, the case rate began steadily and abruptly to rise. A week after the fourth, 85 new cases and 30 deaths were reported. The weather too had grown steadily warmer, and business declined as New Yorkers left and provincial merchants feared to enter the plague-ridden city. By the 14th of July, only one theater remained open. At least two dozen churches had, before the month ended, closed their doors as well. Though deaths increased, the city's streets were still filthy, still patrolled by pigs and dogs. Garbage still encrusted cellars and yards. It seemed clear that the city fathers were either ignorant or incompetent. As early as May 25, William Cullen Bryant's *Evening Post* had charged the municipal authorities with criminal neglect. *The Herald* too was quick to attack the "culpable neglect and imbecility" of the Board of Health.

28   Nor were such attacks unjustified. Things simply did not get done—despite the statutory power of the Board of Health "to do or cause to be done *any thing* which in their opinion may be proper to preserve the health of the City." The members of the Common Council who constituted the Board of Health were ill-prepared to implement such wide and ill-defined powers. Precedent and traditional **penury** determined that so vague a grant of power would be construed in the narrowest of fashions. New York **aldermen** were, moreover, notoriously immune to the promptings of civic morality. (A sardonic journalist suggested that the only way to have the city cleaned was to raise a fund and bribe the city councilmen— the standard procedure for getting things done in New York.) Even when the harried councilmen did attempt to enforce a regimen of strict cleanliness,

---

antechoir: preventative program designed to help stop the spreading of disease.
calomel: a colorless white or brown tasteless compound.
laudanum: a tincture of opium.
grogshops: shops that served alcohol (particularly rum diluted with water).
penury: extreme dearth; barrenness or insufficiency.
aldermen: members of the municipal legislative body.

they met with continual obstruction. Conflicts arose between city and state authorities, between the Board of Health and the Commissioners of the Alms-House, between the board and the president of the Croton Water Board. Equally discouraging was the **recalcitrant** attitude of the average householder. In an admission of impotence, the Board of Health finally resorted, as it had 17 years earlier, to requesting the city's clergymen to urge upon their congregations the sanitary regulations which the board had shown itself unable to enforce. Even the best of efforts, however, could not have overcome the inertia of generations.

29   Nowhere was the inadequacy of traditional practice more apparent than in the contract system of street cleaning. The contracts were political **manna** and it was assumed that the contractor would make no more than token efforts to fulfil the duties which he had agreed to perform. When during the cholera epidemic several of the contractors were forced to actually clean the streets, they begged to be released from their contracts, pleading that they could not fulfill them without incurring grave financial loss. A few contractors finally began to clean their appointed streets, but only after repeated threats. When the dirt was finally rooted up from streets and yards, it often lay uncollected for days or weeks in foul-smelling hillocks, seemingly more malignant than the same garbage or excrement left undisturbed. If gathered at all, such filth was dumped from the ends of city piers, frequently in places inaccessible to the swift tides of the river, where it lay impeding navigation and tainting the atmosphere. And it was no easy task to hire men for this dirty and unpopular work. Local hoodlums regularly stoned night-soil gatherers and sometimes shot their horses. Such arrangements were a permanent menace to the health of New York's inhabitants.

30   The city seemed unable even to bury its own dead. Bodies might lie for hours, in some cases for days, in the streets before they were started on their way to Potter's Field. After being unloaded from the **scows** that brought them to the city cemetery on Randall's Island, the dead were deposited in a wide trench some hundred yards in length, one body on top of another to within a foot or two of the surface. Fortunately, they were not allowed to lie thus and infect the city with the odor of their putrefaction. Thousands of rats swam each day from the city to the island, burrowed quickly into the hastily covered

trenches, and disposed of the excess flesh before it could mortify. Within the city itself land was at a premium, and churchyards permitted the burial of coffins two and three deep. Human bodies were not as numerous as the carcasses of the animals butchered each day in the city's **abattoirs**. During the epidemic, the bone-boiling establishments that normally disposed of these carcasses were ordered closed as menaces to the public health. As a result, the bones and **offal** of hundreds of animals were thrown each day into the river to putrefy, wedged against docks and slips by the returning tides.

31   Tempering the disgraceful with the absurd was the Sanatory Committee's campaign against the city's pigs. Despite the warnings of physicians, it was impossible to separate the poor from their pigs, a cheap and reliable source of garbage-fattened bacon and hams. Riots and subterfuge confronted the police when they attempted to move the hogs into the city's less crowded upper wards. The porkers had to be flushed out of cellars and **garrets**, where their fond owners had secreted them. Nevertheless, as a result of police persistence—and clubs—5–6,000 swine were being "boarded out" by the middle of June. But concentrated now in the northern wards they soon became a menace to the residents of these usually peaceful environs.

32   Despite such laudable efforts, the epidemic increased. By the end of July, business had almost ceased: hotels were empty; railroads and steamships arrived without passengers. The city's petty traders despaired, for many relied upon the custom of the provincial merchants who crowded into the city during ordinary summers. Local customers too had left the city and many small enterprisers were hard pressed to pay rents and buy fall goods. Few businessmen, however, went hungry. There were others who did; the working people were the most severely affected by the epidemic, unprepared as they were to undergo a protracted period of unemployment. Fortunately, the disease declined rapidly. The Centre Street Cholera Hospital had been closed and Niblo's Gardens reopened by the first of August. Two weeks later, businessmen were beginning to arrive in the city, and hotels and boarding-houses lost their desolate look. Boxes and bales again blocked sidewalks and carts filled the narrow streets, while newspapers felt called upon to attack the "reprehensible" cholera reports which the Board of Health continued obstinately to issue. Five thousand and seventeen New

---

recalcitrant: stubborn resistance to and defiance of authority or guidance.
manna: something of value that a person receives unexpectedly.
scows: large, flat-bottomed boats with square ends, used chiefly for transporting freight.
abattoirs: slaughterhouses.
offal: waste parts, especially butchered animals; refuse; rubbish.
garret: room on the top floor of a house, typically under a pitched roof.

Yorkers had died since May 16. And New York was lucky—other cities did not so easily escape.

33   April had been cruel, breeding cholera in dozens of American cities and villages. River and lake steamers sowed the disease at scores of landings, while the railroads, which already crisscrossed the Northwest, discharged cholera at points even more remote. The pestilence often flared up among immigrant barge and steamboat passengers, debilitated by long sea voyages, hungry, dirty, and huddled together on decks so crowded that even the sick could not lie down. Armed men discouraged attempts to land and bury the cholera dead. Bodies were lowered unceremoniously overboard, and drifted ominously past river and lake towns.

34   Gold-seekers carried the disease with them across a continent. Cholera waited in brackish streams and water holes, left by one party, to be passed on to the next group following across the plains. The route westward was marked with wooden crosses and stone cairns, the crosses often bearing only a name and the word "cholera." Nowhere could the disease have been more terrifying than on these trails, where men died without physicians, without ministers, and without friends.

35   By May, the disease had appeared as far north as Kenosha, Wisconsin. In hundreds of towns and cities, the outbreak of the first cholera case was expected daily. Newspapers in the smallest and most remote of communities were filled with demands for cleanliness, for the banishment of pigs, and for the establishment of hospitals. Managers of New England cotton mills distributed cholera tracts to their employees. Milwaukee built special bathhouses for arriving immigrants, while other town councils distributed chloride of lime to the poor.

36   It was in the infant cities of the West, with no adequate water supply, primitive sanitation, and crowded with a transient population, that the disease was most severe. St. Louis lost a tenth of her population. Cincinnati suffered almost as severely, Sandusky even more severely than St. Louis. Sextons, undertakers, even the horses in St. Louis were exhausted in the Sisyphean task of removing and burying the dead. Carts and furniture wagons served as makeshift hearses, and many of the dead came finally to an informal rest in the woods on Mississippi sand bars. In Sandusky, rough unfinished boards nailed hastily together served as coffins. Even such crude amenities were unavailable in San Antonio: here, in some cases, the dead were strapped to dried ox hides and dragged along on them, livid and purple, to their graves.

37   Few towns were sufficiently small or isolated to escape. Madison, Indiana, suffered eight to 15 deaths a day for several weeks. In Washington, another Indiana town, there were 60 deaths among the few hundred who had not fled. At the height of the epi-

demic, Belleville, Illinois, had 20 new cases a day. Every store closed; business ceased, and smoke from bonfires lit to purify the air continually shrouded the town. Of 350 persons at the camp of the United States Eighth Regiment, at Lavaca, Texas, 150 died. In the Rio Grande Valley as a whole, an army surgeon estimated that 2,000 out of 20,000 inhabitants had succumbed. It was calculated that the southern states had lost 10,000 slaves alone, and by September the price of Negroes had already risen in response.

38   There was little that could be done. Municipal health boards found their rudimentary powers insufficient to prevent or mitigate the epidemic. Indeed, many towns possessed no health board; in a greater number they existed more in statute than reality—except during epidemics. New York, like most states, had no public health legislation. The law providing for local boards of health, passed as an emergency cholera measure in June, 1832, had expired by limitation the following year. It took more than good intentions to clean a town or city; and cleanliness, physicians agreed, was the only guarantee of immunity from cholera.

39   Even the largest cities lacked administrative tools. Attempts to effect sanitary reforms were in many cities, as in New York, paralyzed by the politically expedient contract system. In Baltimore, a local physician remarked, the only effectual scavenger was a heavy shower. Not even Boston, well-governed by standards of the time, was able to thoroughly clean its narrow and ill-graded courts, lanes, and alleys. The filth disinterred from cellars and cesspools was piled in streets or dumped in rivers—and, to the horror of a Boston railroad man, on his tracks. Despite the menace of cholera, many communities were unwilling or unable to enact coercive legislation and to force citizens to clean their property. In Vincennes, householders were "earnestly urged," in Galena "earnestly requested," to clean and lime their premises. In even the most authoritarian of communities, the penalty for nonobservance of sanitary regulations was modest, at most a $50 fine or 30 days in jail. And even these mild penalties were rarely imposed.

40   Money too was lacking. Most Americans were unwilling to be taxed or otherwise inconvenienced at the behest of some health board. In a city as large as Chicago, unpaid volunteers enforced sanitary regulations. New York, like many other communities, entrusted city council members with much of the responsibility for enforcing such ordinances. But, as an early chronicler of Milwaukee commented: "human nature predominates in an Alderman—and self-preservation is the first law of nature."

41   Such a state of things could not be tolerated. Public meetings were called, to demand, to cajole, and to organize. Ward and district committees were chosen to aid sanitary inspectors ("Committees of Safety" they were called in New York). Once an epidemic

had begun, the sick were visited at home, and—less frequently—nursed in hospitals by volunteers. Ordinary citizens were, even in large cities, ready if necessary to assume the duties of a paralyzed municipal government. In St. Louis, the Board of Health completely abdicated responsibility and was soon replaced by a 12 member "Committee of Public Health," chosen at an open meeting. As a result of a bitter scuffle between regular and **homeopathic** physicians, the Cincinnati Board of Health, originally composed of medical men, was replaced by one containing a lawyer, an editor, a liquor dealer, a preacher, and a mechanic. Wherever officials had shown themselves incompetent or inefficient, editors urged fellow townsmen to call public meetings and form their own boards of health.

42   Those orphaned and made destitute had also to be cared for. And only the most radical questioned the responsibility of private charity for alleviating such misery. The need had only to be made known. In dozens of cities and towns, committees of "Christian gentlemen" collected and distributed food, clothing, money, even chloride of lime to the poor. Churches often allied themselves with these **ad hoc** committees, holding special collections for the sick and impoverished. One problem remained even after the epidemic had departed and business resumed its usual activity: What was to become of the orphans? Neither private persons nor informal committees were prepared to care permanently for these **waifs**. They were usually left to the churches, and in many cases it was the impetus of the cholera epidemic that allowed the establishment of much needed institutions for the care of dependent children. Such, for example, was the case in Chicago, Milwaukee, Sandusky, San Francisco, and St. Louis. Groups of Roman Catholics sponsored many of these orphanages, since their church possessed the trained and dedicated personnel necessary to staff and administer such institutions. (Catholics were, moreover, alarmed at the moral consequences of allowing Catholic children to be raised outside the church's influence.) Other such homes were established under secular or Protestant auspices.

43   Hospitals were the most immediate need in cholera-stricken communities, but a need not easily filled. Few communities had either the initiative or the financial resources necessary for their estab-

lishment before cholera appeared. And even with the presence of the disease lending urgency to their efforts, boards of health found it difficult to secure buildings for use as cholera hospitals. In Philadelphia, Rochester, New York, and many other cities, the rioting of the poor and the petitions of the genteel discouraged attempts to establish such "pesthouses." Threats of arson caused more than one landlord to refuse generous rents offered by health boards. Philadelphia, like New York, had to commandeer schools, rip out desks, and place cots in their stead. Indeed, the Quaker City Board of Health considered itself quite fortunate in being able to procure such large and airy buildings. In other cities, abandoned or little used hotels, taverns, or country houses were suddenly transformed into cholera hospitals.

44   Once established, the hospitals did not run themselves. Medicines, nursing, and medical care were almost always inadequate. In a New York cholera hospital, patients in extremis lay naked on cots, covered only with a much-used sheet. To many physicians, these wards served only as convenient depositories for patients already moribund. These pesthouses were administered so poorly that even physicians called for their abolition; house to house visitation—even tent colonies—would be preferable. In the popular mind, the cholera hospitals were cold and cheerless municipal slaughterhouses, where death was hurried by the ruthless experimentation of attending physicians. Only the poorest, the most wretched, those with no one to care for them died in cholera hospitals. No respectable family would allow even its servants to enter one. Its patients were the physically and morally abandoned, "the debased and **profligate**" of society. Cholera still seemed a disease of poverty and sin; lechery, gluttony, or alcoholism could as appropriately as cholera be entered on the death certificates of its victims. The deaths of the moral, the prudent, the respectable were usually ignored. They seemed **anomalous** and served only to increase alarm. In New York City, the *Herald* (July 17) noted that deaths by cholera "among the respectable, *including even ladies*, have all tended to produce an uncommon sensation in this city." By 1849, the connection between cholera and vice had become almost a verbal reflex. The relationship between vice and poverty was a mental reflex even more firmly established.

---

homeopathy: system for treating disease based on the administration of minute doses of a drug that in massive amounts produces symptoms in healthy individuals similar to those of the disease itself.

ad hoc: temporary.

waif: a homeless person, especially a forsaken or orphaned child.

profligate: recklessly wasteful.

anomalous: an apparent contradiction.

27

BURNED OVER: JOSEPH SMITH AND THE BOOK OF MORMON

BY TODD VELASCO

It has been said that the term "cult" is just a word used to describe someone else's religion. Joseph Smith would start a new church in 1830 that was so unique in its approach, and so unorthodox in its teachings, that many of its critics would use the derogatory term "cult" with impunity. Boasting around 10 million members world-wide in the present day, it is difficult to seriously consider a church that is so large and so popular a "cult". Considering the Mormons to be an original product of the times they were born into might be more accurate and fair. Regarding their prophet Joseph Smith as an original product of these times is a point that cannot be seriously debated.

During the Second Great Awakening questions about religious faith and spirituality were in plentiful supply. The answers to "higher" questions were not so common or easily agreed upon. Joseph Smith would attempt to answer all of these questions by unearthing a new truth. By bringing to the world a new volume of scripture called The Book of Mormon, Smith believed that with the publication of this work, all the spiritual confusion, doubt, and debate of the Second Great Awakening would be laid to rest.

Deeply engrained Christian traditions and doctrine were altered and twisted regularly by a swarm of radical preachers during this time. But no other spiritual leader would feel as certain that his new truth was the only truth to the extent that Joseph Smith held this conviction. Because of this adamant stance regarding his own ministry, there was a natural tendency for those that became aware of Smith and The Book of Mormon to regard his claims as either the long awaited answer or the ultimate deception—there was little middle ground.

The following article attempts to put Smith and his new scripture into an historical context. It also examines the strange and controversial story of how The Book of Mormon came into existence.

- *What elements in Joseph Smith's personal history and background might have affected his spiritual development?*
- *How did Smith's immediate environment (the Burned Over District) influence his life?*
- *In what ways was the religious fervor of the Second Great Awakening dramatically illustrated in both Smith's religious philosophy and in the activity of the Burned Over District?*

- *Why did the method of bringing forth The Book of Mormon naturally lead to criticisms and allegations of fraud?*
- *Why was the Mormon Church so attractive to some Christians during the Second Great Awakening? What did it offer that was unique and special?*

I distrust people who know so well what God wants them to do because I notice it always coincides with their own desires—Susan B. Anthony

PROLOGUE

1   In early 1830, a 24 year old New York man named Joseph Smith arranged for the publication of a new bible. Today, approximately six million Americans and another three to four million people around the world believe this book to be a holy scripture. However, too many of the questions regarding Smith and his new scripture lack the answers needed to satisfy the curious and even the converted.

2   The origin of the most uniquely *American* Christian church, The Church of Jesus Christ of Latter-day Saints (the Mormons), is inexorably tied to the mind, beliefs, mysticism, and passion of its founder and prophet; the most important event of Smith's early ministry being the coming forth of his new scripture: *The Book of Mormon*. The presentation of *The Book of Mormon* and the explanation of how it came into being was the beginning of a process known to Latter-day Saints as the "Restoration." In the Mormon tradition, Joseph Smith would be the instrument through which Jesus Christ's original and true church would be restored to the Earth.

3   The original Christian church, according to Mormon doctrine, was lost around the second century A.D. when early church leaders abandoned many of the teachings of Jesus and eliminated most of the of the old priesthoods. Mormons felt that existing Christian churches were apostate, but if they had faith, the apostates would be offered an opportunity to return to Christ's true church. This return could only be accomplished by accepting both *The Book of Mormon* as scripture and Joseph Smith as its prophet.

A BOY AND HIS CHURCH

4   Smith would achieve some level of notoriety from the time he was 14 years old and on. It was at this age that he first began to report mysterious visions and revelations. These testimonies would garner him attention and eventually a large following. They would also create scores of critics and naysayers. By the time he was 38, his name and portions of the story connected to it had spread throughout much of the United States. Not only was he known for being the arcane young preacher and prophet of the Mormons but also, in 1844, as an announced candidate for the U.S. presidency.

5   Some historians argue that Smith, despite the mystery and controversy that surrounded him, could have been a viable candidate in that strange election year. This, of course, is pure speculation as Smith was murdered by a fearful and angry mob in the Carthage, Illinois jail four months before the election. Carthage was a small town not far from the large Mormon settlement at Nauvoo, Illinois. Boasting between 15–20,000 Latter-day Saints, Nauvoo rivaled young Chicago in population during the early 1840s.

6   In 1839, the river town of Commerce, Illinois renamed Nauvoo by Smith, is where the prophet would dig his church in after episodes of persecution and scandal drove them from New York, Ohio, and Missouri. The sheer size of Nauvoo gave its unquestioned leader a political clout to accompany his perfunctory spiritual leadership. This was a fearful notion to several government officials and many of Illinois' citizens. Smith was granted extensive civic powers and jurisdictions when the Mormons first arrived. Soon, however, the tales of mysticism, magic, and polygamy that began to flow over western Illinois and far beyond changed this air of welcome to a cold burst of suspicion and resentment. Smith's position as prophet, president, mayor, sheriff, judge, and general of the 2,500-man "Nauvoo Legion" army put the focus of this fear almost solely on his head.

7   Clearly, it was the prophet's real political power that led most directly to his demise. Smith was a political kingmaker in the young state of Illinois. With around 20,000 votes at his command, he was feared by Illinois politicians of the time. Without Smith's endorsement, a statewide election would be hard-won for any candidate. Thomas Ford, the Governor of Illinois during Joseph Smith's tenure in Nauvoo ranked near the top of the preacher's

growing list of enemies. This was not the first time Smith and his group had fostered the resentment of a state's Governor. In 1838, the governor of Missouri, Lilburn W. Boggs, instructed his state's militia to drive the Mormons out of his state to "preserve the public peace".

8   This executive order is known today as the "Mormon Extermination Order." It followed a series of conflicts between Missourians and a group of self-styled Mormon "warrior-priests" known as the Danites. Later, after the Mormons were indeed driven from Missouri and resettled in Nauvoo, the governor of Illinois was fielding the same complaints from citizens and developing the same enmity for the Latter-day Saints. Polygamy, witchcraft, thievery, hooliganism, and heresy were charges leveled at the Mormons around every turn. But there were also the observations by outsiders that the Mormons were a hard-working, charitable, and Godly people who meant no harm. It's difficult to imagine that either of these descriptions could be completely true. It is clear, however, that in 1844, Governor Ford had found the end of his charity for the Mormons and their prophet. Ford was wise enough not to engage in the public spectacle that his Missouri counterpart Boggs had created. He would issue no executive orders and no public statements, but he would give at least his tacit approval for the Illinois militia to take a drastic step against Smith and his church.

9   A small number of disaffected Mormons had left the church and the Nauvoo settlement in early 1844. In cooperation with other anti-Mormon forces in western Illinois, they began to publish the *Nauvoo Expositor*. Smith viewed the embarrassing revelations from this newspaper (mostly about the Mormon practice of polygamy) as so damaging that the *Expositor* could not be allowed to continue publication. Along with his brother Hyrum whom he had named the "patriarch" of the church, the prophet broke into the offices where the *Expositor* was printed and destroyed the presses. Smith and his brother were subsequently arrested and jailed in nearby Carthage, Illinois. On June 27, despite the best efforts of the jailer, who moved the Smiths into his bedroom on the second floor of the tiny jail for their protection, the growing mob of disguised Illinois militiamen surrounding the jail would soon have their way.

10   Originally Joseph and Hyrum were placed in a cell with four other prisoners. The Smiths soon received visitors from Nauvoo—as well as two loaded revolvers that were smuggled in. Joseph seemed to know that his passion had played out and that he and his brother would never walk out of the Carthage jail alive. One of the other prisoners later told the story that, along with the guns, the visitors had also brought the prophet a bottle of red wine.

Smith had often preached against the evils of drinking and drunkenness but on this occasion he was willing to make an exception. After uncorking the bottle, he handed it to Hyrum and reportedly said, "Drink deep, my brother, for this is not for communion."

11   Joseph and Hyrum waited out the inevitable in the jailer's upstairs room. When the mob began to ascend the stairs, the Smiths opened fire. Two of the attackers lie dead as Hyrum tried to keep the door shut against the mob. A bullet was shot through the door killing Hyrum. As the mob squeezed into the room, Joseph Smith, now out of ammunition, jumped out the window. The combination of the bullets shot into his back as he leapt and the 15-foot drop to the ground insured the mob that the Mormon prophet was dead. No one was ever punished for any action undertaken that day in Carthage.

12   The bulk of the congregation (perhaps 85 percent) would accept the leadership of Joseph's friend (and head of the church's Quorum of the Twelve Apostles) Brigham Young. In 1846, two years after Smith's murder, they would begin to make their way out west, as persecution and disharmony would continue in Nauvoo. The remaining few stayed in Illinois and later went back to Missouri and formed the Reorganized Church of Jesus Christ of Latter-day Saints now known as the "Community of Christ".

13   Any map of the United States that attempts to detail its expansion westward will be peppered with the name Mormon from the Erie to the Great Salt Lake. So often forced to flee, they became important, but reluctant, pioneers. Although it is certainly not closely associated with the Latter-day Saints today, even Las Vegas, Nevada was originally an important Mormon settlement. The story does not begin in the Salt Lake area of Utah, where Brigham Young's contingent would settle and finally flourish; it begins in the small town of Sharon, Vermont where the future Mormon prophet Joseph Smith was born in December of 1805.

THE SEEKERS

14   Joseph's parents, Joseph, Sr. and Lucy Mack Smith would have nine children that survived into adulthood. Joseph, Jr. was their fourth child. He was born into very poor circumstances. The Smiths had recently lost their farm due to misguided business practices and roamed from tenant farm to tenant farm over the next several years with their growing family. Throughout much of this time they were struggling to survive; opportunities and time for the formal education of young Joseph and his siblings was almost nonexistent. When time did permit,

however, Lucy Smith took care to teach her children to read and write.

15   Smith was becoming a young man during the time known as the Second Great Awakening. This was a time (spanning roughly the first half of the nineteenth century) in which American Christianity was marked by an evangelistic fervor and an urgency to convert the world before the Messiah's eminent return. As with many American Christians of this era, in a spiritual context, the Smiths were regarded as "seekers". The family had no fixed religious affiliation. Through the years, they were known to have sampled and professed doctrines ranging from orthodox Christianity to the occult and even atheism. Some of the Smiths had been Presbyterian and also Congregationalist for a while, but Joseph rarely attended church. The Protestant ideal was dominant in this area and there were few Catholic churches. Which of the ever-growing number of Protestant groups to embrace was a question he began to consider with urgency.

16   At one point, Joseph had claimed membership in the Methodist church but quickly became disenchanted. Denominations such as the Baptists, Presbyterians, Methodists, Congregationalists, and their hundred-fold variations and sects were all claiming that their particular path was the only way to salvation. With the hardships of everyday life in these farming communities there was a natural inclination towards obsession with the rewards of the hereafter. Since the earthly life offered and promised little, the heavenly after-life became the focus. None of the Smiths appeared to contemplate such matters as much as young Joseph.

17   Shortly after the Smiths had moved to the town of Palmyra in western New York, Joseph started to develop a fascination with the spirit-world and the supernatural. It was at this time that he began to regularly use a "seer-stone." This was a common stone that was believed to give the user the power to "see" or sense certain things that could not be perceived with the natural eyes. The use of seer-stones was unusual but not particularly rare among people searching for something, or some answer, that was beyond their natural abilities to obtain. In the early nineteenth century, many individuals trusted the supernatural to provide answers to questions that natural science could not yet articulate. The local Christian churches rarely denounced the use of seer-stones or other means of supernatural divination. Some of the more prominent clergymen around Palmyra were known advocates and practitioners of the occult, constantly blurring the lines between mystic practice and church ritual.

18   There were those who felt that magical practices like the use of a seer-stone could provide men with wealth as well as wisdom. Rumors about buried treasure flew around western New York; pirates were said to have squirreled away gold in the multitudes all over the New York countryside. Smith would regularly employ a seer-stone to help him locate it.

19   This would be a work that Joseph would not only maintain, but would become rather infamous for locally; the term most often applied to this type of pursuit was "money-digging." Western New York had more than a few "money-diggers" and, universally, they would prove to be con-men. They would promise to ascertain, by supernatural means, the location of buried treasure for a fee. The fee would be rendered—but the treasure never found. Soon there was a crack down on this type of con-game and Joseph Smith would not escape untouched.

THE FIRE STARTERS

20   During the first two decades of the nineteenth century, the Second Great Awakening was heating up. Large-scale revivals would spring up time and again all over the country as the important Christian denominations competed feverishly for converts. At times, the movement seemed like an all-out war for the collective soul of America. In no other location was this phenomenon more evident than in western New York where the Smiths had settled. The region was most often referred to as the "Burned Over District." It was given that moniker due to the "fire and brimstone" ceaselessly flowing from the mouths of local preachers as they tirelessly fished for souls.

21   There was Mother Ann Lee, the English immigrant who founded the celibate Shaker sect. Mother Ann claimed to be a feminine reincarnation of the Christ. Her followers lived communally in villages scattered around New York, having fled persecution in New England. The Shakers, with their self-sufficient style of living and their rhythmic, ritualistic dances (for which they were nicknamed) were emblematic of the separatist millennial spirit of the age.

22   Other preachers in the Burned Over District would rival Mother Ann as a self-proclaimed Messiah. One such rival was the "Universal Friend" Jemima Wilkinson. Setting up shop in the aptly named village of Jerusalem, the "Friend" also professed her role as the "New Christ" and swore she would never die. Newspapers in Palmyra referred to her as an "Anti-Christ" and made much of a strange and somewhat sadistic practice she regularly engaged in.

23   The ritual involved an assistant that she referred to only as the "Prophet Elijah". He was a shuffling little homunculus who constantly followed the "Universal Friend" around like the gaze of a

gargoyle. At certain times, Wilkinson would wrap a girdle around Elijah's waist and tighten it to the point of extreme pain. In this compromised position, Elijah would be filled with the spirit of prophecy and begin to sputter out revelations from God. Despite her claims of immortality, the Universal Friend died in 1818. For years her body was left to decompose in the cellar of a Jerusalem home while her followers patiently waited for her earthly remains to be reanimated.

24   Isaac Bullard and his group of "Pilgrims" settled for a time in western New York. Bullard's group was, in at least two respects, the antithesis of Mother Ann Lee's Shakers. While the Shakers maintained a celibate life, Bullard's followers were advocates of free love and a few practiced plural marriage. Also, whereas the Shakers were the foremost proponents of the biblical ideal of "cleanliness is next to godliness," Bullard would preach that washing was a sin. He wore only bearskin coverings and bragged that neither he nor his clothes had been cleaned for several years.

25   The common thread running through all of these strange belief systems was the contention that the Earth's people were living in the "Last Days." They were sure the end of time was near, the millennium (not the chronological millennium, but the period of time following the return of Christ) was coming forth, and all must struggle to be in the number bound for heaven. All of the Burned Over sects taught that the day of Christ's second coming was very near. Although it is not widely remembered, the official name of the Shaker sect was "The United Church of Believers in Christ's Second Appearing." But perhaps no other Burned Over District group itched with the anticipation of the Messiah's return more than the Adventists. The word Advent means "arrival". Their founder William Miller was a charismatic Baptist preacher and biblical scholar who began preparing his church for the Advent (the return of Christ). Miller ardently studied scripture and boasted of a deeper understanding of its messages to the modern man. William Miller would convince thousands of "seekers" in New York and New England that he had accurately calculated (based on scriptural evidence) the *exact* date of Christ's return.

26   Miller set the date at March 21, 1843, the first day of spring. The Adventists surrendered all their worldly possessions to the church and awaited the day they would ascend to Heaven in the company of their Savior. It must have been a surrealistic scene that non-believers witnessed when the much-anticipated date finally arrived. The Adventists donned beautiful, royal-purple "ascension robes" and climbed to the highest points in their communities: the roofs of homes, the steeples of church buildings, the summits of small hills. They felt they would

surely be judged worthy of an eternity in Heaven if they served in the role of Christ's welcome-wagon. On high ground, wearing their loudly colored garments, they would have to be the first people Jesus would see as he was trumpeted back to Earth. All day long they gazed at the sky from their steeples and hilltops. Returning home that night, they wrestled with their bitter disappointment.

27   Miller recalculated. Again, the date was wrong. After a third try that failed, Miller stepped out of the pulpit. His successors explained his failed predictions away by claiming that cataclysmic events (unbeknownst to the mortals on Earth) had taken place in Heaven on the days in question and Christ's return had to be postponed (three times). In a more moderate incarnation of their doctrine, the Adventist church would teach their converts that the Advent was coming *soon*, but that no man could know exactly when. By adding this conservative tilt, the church would endure. Of the Burned Over District sects that survive to the present day, they are second only to Joseph Smith's Mormons in number. However, disappointment and tragedy would also endure for the evangelical Adventists—the most recent example being 1993's fiery tumult in Waco, Texas involving the Adventist Branch Davidians.

28   Surrounded by this eclectic mixture of faiths, Joseph Smith would begin his unique spiritual odyssey. The celibate Shakers, for refusing to reproduce, are gone; Wilkinson's and Bullard's groups only briefly existed; and the Adventists are fractured—but the strange little church formed by Smith in 1830 can brag of millions of dedicated members in the present day. Perhaps it is a testament to the power of print; for Joseph Smith would be the only one of these New York prophets to canonize new scripture on a grand scale. Smith had something tangible to hand his congregation; the book provided something concrete to lay their hands on, read, and study—it wasn't simply a nebulous vision that could easily be taken as genuinely inspired or left as obviously fraudulent. Neither would the book itself, to the great benefit of its prophet, be the typical rambling and personal religious manifesto common to cultish gurus; rather it was touted as another chapter of Christ's gospel sent directly—and materially—to Smith by messengers of God.

HEAVENLY VISIONS

29   In 1820, 14-year-old Joseph Smith was confused. The decision over which spiritual path to embrace had everlasting implications to him, and he would not take it lightly. He decided he would need the counsel of God to help him solve this problem. In the

early spring of that year, Smith is said to have received that counsel directly. Known as the "First Vision", this event and the subsequent revelations pertaining to it would be instrumental in transforming Joseph from a curious boy into a young man who believed he had been saddled with an awesome responsibility—the duty to deliver to the world the most important message it had received to date.

30   Much of the mystery and controversy surrounding Joseph Smith begins with this First Vision. The questions primarily stem from the fact that several differing accounts of the vision exist. However, all of the versions contain elements of the official church account, which is summarized as follows:

31   Smith purports to have gone into a grove of trees near his family's farm in New York to pray; he had done this on several earlier occasions. This time he went specifically to pray for guidance as to which church was true and which church he should then join. At this point he claims that the grove was filled with a blinding light. Then, suddenly, two glorious personages appeared before him. Both of them men clad in ethereal white garments—one older in appearance and one younger. The older personage identified himself as God the Father and introduced the other as his Son. The Son then told Joseph that *none* of the churches were true, but that he, Joseph, was to play a pivotal role in the restoration of the one true church that was lost many years ago.

32   Joseph would not record his official account of the First Vision until 18 years after he says it occurred. By this time Smith had started his new church and many new visions and revelations had taken place in the interim. When Joseph first told his story to his family and a few close friends in 1820, his tale was met with very hesitant acceptance. Strangely, over the next several years, Smith would begin to relate many different versions of his now famous vision (a total of nine variations would appear between 1820 and 1828). Possibly he was confused by the experience, but critics have suggested that Smith was developing and reverse-engineering his story to fit into and support his "Restoration" agenda.

33   If the "First Vision" was the *seminal* event in the restoration process, Smith's next extraordinary revelation was the most *crucial*—and certainly the most dramatic. Once again, Smith would report that a glorious herald would give him a cryptic and heavenly message. This event would occur on September 21, 1823, the first day of autumn. Smith's memory of this event was clearer; the various accounts recorded by him vary only slightly in content. At the end of this day, when he had retired to bed, a "resurrected personage" (sometimes referred to by Smith as an "angel") identifying himself as the spirit of a long dead man named Moroni, appeared (eerily floating in mid-air above Smith's bed) to give him some startling news.

THE ANGEL AND THE INDIANS

34   Joseph said that Moroni had informed him that, in mortal life, he, Moroni, had been the last surviving member of a transplanted group of ancient Hebrews called the Nephites. The spirit claimed this group of people and their tribal offshoots had inhabited the Americas in antiquity. Their history had been carefully compiled, abridged, and engraved onto golden metal plates by Moroni's father, a Nephite philosopher/ historian named Mormon. Moroni said that Joseph had been chosen to reveal Mormon's history of these ancient Americans to the world. An important and burdensome assignment to be sure, for this history would include an account of direct contact between these lost Americans and the resurrected Jesus Christ.

35   Like most religious scriptures, *The Book of Mormon* is a history. This factor has proved problematic for present-day Mormons. The book has suffered from increasing scrutiny and criticism through the years as more accurate methods of discovering the truth of the ancient past have been developed. The record is filled with inaccuracies and anomalies from beginning to end. The most glaring problem is a total lack of evidence known today to support the idea of transplanted Hebrews inhabiting ancient America at any time. Archeological and DNA evidence strongly suggests that all ancient Americans and their descendents are of *Asian* origin.

36   Most, if not all, scholars of Pre-Columbian American history (who are not members of the Mormon Church) feel that the "history" Smith revealed to the world was not a history at all. Rather, it was simply the fanciful musings of a clever, imaginative, and derivative writer of fiction. However, controversy over the historicity of *The Book of Mormon* was not a troubling issue for Smith in his lifetime. Very little was known about the history of ancient America in the early nineteenth century, so Smith would not have to worry about proving the book's historical accuracy. In 1830, when the book was first published, no one would have known the difference.

37   The next part of Moroni's message to Smith would prove to be the most examined, discussed, and debated episode in the world of Mormonism. Moroni explained to Joseph the manner in which he was to reveal the story. The ethereal visitor said that hidden under the ground on nearby Manchester Hill (later referred to by Mormons as Hill Cumorah) was a large stone box containing the aforementioned plates. The plates were bound together like a book by three large rings and inscribed with engraved characters. A small portion of the record was permanently sealed. The plates contained Mormon's history of the Nephites, their rivals the Lamanites, and other associated peoples (focusing on their relationship and interaction with a very watchful God)

as well as the all-important record of Christ's posthumous visit with them. The engravings on the plates were carved in a strange and heretofore unheard of type of hieroglyphics that Smith would call "Reformed Egyptian".

38   Because the plates were inscribed in a foreign and unknown language, Moroni informed Joseph that the Urim and Thummim would also be found with the plates. The Urim and Thummim was a legendary tool used in sooth-saying; it is mentioned a few times in the *Holy Bible*. The instrument consisted of two stones fixed into a frame resembling spectacles with the spectacles connected to a breastplate. By peering into the stones and holding the breastplate over his heart, Joseph would be able to translate the inscriptions on the plates into English. The presence of the Urim and Thummim in Smith's tale would give many of his critics and detractors fuel for their fires. Could this be Joseph Smith, once again, claiming to have powers of divination from a more elaborate form of "seer-stone"? Could this just be a specialized and, ultimately, much more profitable case of money-digging?

39   The spirit of Moroni told Joseph that when he had proven his worthiness, he would be allowed to obtain the golden plates and the Urim and Thummim and begin the translation. He was shown the location of the plates that night, but not allowed to obtain them. Moroni instructed him to return to that spot on that same date each of the next four years. At these meetings he would receive further instruction and testing. Reportedly, he would keep this covenant, but the next four years would hold much more for Joseph than just the annual sessions with the ghost of Moroni.

40   During this period of time Joseph met Emma Hale. Despite the disapproval of Emma's father, they were married. Emma's father Isaac was distrustful of Joseph from the beginning; he knew of Smith's money-digging activity and considered Smith shiftless and unreliable. The poor opinion that many would cultivate regarding Joseph's character got its most serious support in 1826. In this year, Smith was arrested and charged with deceptive theft in connection with a money-digging scam. Although he would receive little more than a stern lecture from the judge, Joseph promised Isaac Hale that his money-digging days were over. Perhaps they were, but Joseph still knew of one buried treasure that he must dig for.

41   The mysterious Indian burial mounds and ruined fortifications that haunted western New York endlessly fascinated Joseph. The identity of the mound builders was the subject of speculation by both amateurs and academics. Joseph had remarked on several occasions since his early childhood that discovering the secrets of this ruined and buried world would be a wonderful passage to fame and fortune. A popular (but completely unfounded)

theory that gained even more momentum during the Second Great Awakening identified the American Indians as descendents of the Lost Tribes of Israel. They were said to be ancient Hebrews who had made the trans-oceanic journey to the Americas in the distant past. Whether Hebrew or of some other origin, Smith guessed that such a sophisticated method of building fortifications and burying the honored dead could not be the province of "simple and savage" Indians. There must have been other civilizations that inhabited America in ancient times. Would the plates he would eventually claim to receive hold the proof?

42   He read and studied about the mound builders; there was semi-scholarship and pseudo-scientific speculation to be found in fairly good number. It is more than likely that by this time Smith had read what proved to be the most famous work published on the Hebrew theory of Indian origins: *View of the Hebrews*. This was a wildly speculative book written by a Vermont preacher named Ethan Smith (no relation). Ethan Smith was well known in the area and the subject matter of his book was a curiosity to almost all. The Palmyra lending library had several copies of the book. Many of the theories and ideas espoused in *View of the Hebrews* appear in different forms in *The Book of Mormon*. Much more importantly, several areas of *The Book of Mormon* narrative are so similar; that plagiarism of Ethan Smith's book was a charge leveled at Smith continually after his new scripture was made public.

43   It was shortly after midnight on September 22, 1827, when Joseph Smith gathered his wife and drove off to Manchester Hill. Joseph pulled the wagon far off the road and instructed Emma to wait for his return. Hours later, when he appeared out of the darkness, Emma reported that he seemed nervous, almost frightened, and was carrying something cumbersome under a cloth. Joseph told Emma that upon surrendering the golden plates to him, Moroni cautioned him to be vigilant in his charge of the record. He was to look after and protect it at all costs. The ghost said that no man (other than Joseph) was to see the plates save for three witnesses at a future time. In his final caution, the spirit warned that evil men would surely scheme against Joseph and try to wrest the plates from his care. Indeed, the rumors about "Joe Smith's Gold Bible" were already beginning to fly around the Burned Over District.

SPINNING GOLD INTO YARN

44   Joseph and Emma settled into a small house near her father's Harmony, Pennsylvania farm. It was here that Joseph would reportedly begin to translate

the golden plates. He would use a few scribes with Emma assuming this duty at first. She would take down his dictation as Joseph employed the Urim and Thummim to read the ancient record. Moroni's instructions to show the plates to no one at this time, extended even to Joseph's pretty and intelligent wife. They converted the tiny attic of the house into a "translation room". In this room, Joseph hung a large curtain to separate him from his spousal scribe. He warned her to never peer around the curtain. If she laid eyes on the plates or the Urim and Thummim, all would be lost. Despite her real affections for her husband, she was not without questions and doubts. However, her fears and doubts were allayed by her personal observations. Emma later wrote:

45   "No man could have dictated the writing of the manuscript unless he was inspired . . . when returning after meals, or after interruptions, he would at once begin where he left off, without either seeing the manuscript or having any portion of it read to him. This was a usual thing for him to do. It would have been improbable that a learned man could do this; and for one so ignorant and unlearned as he was, it was simply impossible."

46   Others were not inclined to believe this theory. Joseph might have been uneducated, but he was not illiterate or unintelligent. He could have easily had a copy of the *Holy Bible*, *View of the Hebrews*, a previously written manuscript—or, more likely, all three—behind that curtain.

47   Oliver Cowdery was a schoolteacher from Palmyra and a distant cousin of Joseph Smith. Because of their low pay, local citizens gave teachers free room and board. When it was the Smiths turn to quarter the young teacher, he struck up a close friendship with the family. Of course, he had heard the rumors about Joseph and his new bible. After a short time, Joseph, Sr. related the full story to Oliver. His curiosity overwhelmed him and he soon left for Harmony to offer his services as scribe.

48   With the assistance of the educated Cowdery, the translation process zipped along. Oliver transcribed hundreds of pages as the amount of time devoted to the task increased. By 1829, Joseph and Oliver had become fast friends. Cowdery had no doubt that Joseph was a prophet of God and Smith was more than impressed with Oliver's intelligence and insight. Taking occasional breaks from translating, the two would hold long discussions about the new church that would be formed when the scripture was complete.

49   On his initial trip to Harmony, Oliver Cowdery had stopped off briefly at the home of his friend David Whitmer. When Whitmer heard the reasons for Cowdery's trip to Harmony he asked his friend to evaluate the truth of Smith's story and report back to him at a later date. After receiving a favorable report from Oliver, David would volunteer free room and board to the prophet and his scribe for the honor of having the translation completed at his family's farm. The two eagerly accepted Whitmer's offer and departed for the farm in Fayette, New York.

50   David Whitmer was impressed with Joseph Smith much as his friend Oliver Cowdery had been. However, he was surprised to discover that the method of translation that the prophet used differed greatly from what had been previously reported. Joseph did not use the "Urim and Thummim" but employed his old seer-stone for translating. Whitmer would later give the following testimony about the way in which the plates were translated at his home:

51   "Joseph Smith would put the seer-stone into a hat, and put his face in the hat, drawing it closely around his face to exclude the light; and in the darkness the spiritual light would shine. A piece of something resembling parchment would appear, and on that appeared the writing. One character at a time would appear, and under it was the interpretation in English. Brother Joseph would read off the English to Oliver Cowdery, and when it was written down and repeated to Brother Joseph to see if it was correct, then it would disappear, and another character with the interpretation would appear. Thus *The Book of Mormon* was translated by the gift and power of God, and not by any power of man."

52   Of course, Smith was forbidden by Moroni to show anyone else the plates, but it would seem necessary for Joseph himself to see them when translating. Apparently, this was not true. It was reported by Whitmer and others that when Joseph would translate into his hat, the plates were either covered with a cloth or hidden away in another room.

53   The 275,000-word manuscript was completed in the summer of 1829. The lengthy narrative related the history of the Nephites, the Lamanites (who split from the Nephites), and other groups, focusing primarily on their dealings with God over a period of more than a thousand years. The story begins with the Nephites setting off, first by land, and then by sea from the Middle East on their long voyage to America. They were led on their trans-oceanic journey by their patriarch Lehi, who was aided by a God-given magical compass called the Liahona. This strange orb-shaped device was reportedly found by Smith in the same stone box that had contained the golden plates and the Urim and Thummim. Also stored in the box was another important *Book of Mormon* artifact known as the sword of Laban. With the record, the translators, the compass, and the sword all contained within the box unearthed by Joseph—the whole package appeared to be a sort of time capsule—an archive of Nephite history and culture.

54 Later editions of *The Book of Mormon* were divided up into chapter and verse in the same manner as the Holy Bible. However, the original manuscript was simply one long script separated only into "books." The portion of the scripture known as the Third Book of Nephi contained the all-important account (in what became chapters 11 through 28) of Jesus' appearance and ministry to these ancient Americans. Soon, the Nephite and Lamanite tribes began to ignore many of the words of God and warred constantly.

55 Ultimately, the Lamanites would destroy the Nephites. For their evil ways, the Lamanites were "cursed" by God with dark skin. According to the story, their descendants became the peoples known today as American Indians and were responsible for the aforementioned burial mounds and ruined fortifications. The last surviving Nephite (Moroni) would bury their engraved history and the other artifacts in A.D. 421 at the site of their last great battle with the Lamanites—Hill Cumorah (Manchester Hill). There the record would remain hidden for 1,400 years until it was imparted to Joseph Smith.

WITNESSING

56 Smith was well aware that if his book were to be accepted as a new gospel of Christ, he would have to provide the readers with some form of proof regarding the miraculous nature of its creation; there would have to be (as Moroni had said) three witnesses to the plates. In a revelation from God, Smith was told that Oliver Cowdery, David Whitmer, and another friend, Martin Harris were to be the three witnesses. Their testimony appears at the beginning of every copy of *The Book of Mormon*.

57 It is clear to the reader of this testimony, that what these men are describing is a *vision* and not an account of a physical experience. They do not say that they saw the plates and examined them, but that an angel displayed the plates before them. Martin Harris would later admit that he viewed the plates only with his "spiritual" eyes. Although Smith had been instructed to only allow for three witnesses to the plates, he believed that a more tangible encounter with the record must be sworn to; the vision of the angel recounted by the three men would not suffice. Smith felt that readers of the book must hear tell of men who saw the plates with their *natural* eyes. He quickly arranged for eight more witnesses to see the plates. Their testimony also appears in every copy of *The Book of Mormon*. Made up entirely of close friends and family, the eight witnesses claim to have physically seen and handled the plates.

58 Whether through fakery or through genuine inspiration—Joseph Smith's *Book of Mormon* mission was accomplished. The manuscript was complete; the testimonies to its authenticity were sworn out; and the plates were returned to Moroni as instructed. Whether it is a divinely revealed scriptural record or a cleverly engineered novel, the book has been the keystone of a church, a community, and a theology that not only endures, but continues to grow despite the plethora of questions and controversies.

EPILOGUE

59 *The Book of Mormon*'s appeal to Christians of the Second Great Awakening is ultimately not a great surprise. The book set Smith's church apart; by accepting it as scripture and a new gospel, a Mormon could feel they were a part of something very special; the restoration of Christ's church to the Earth. To many "seekers" of the Second Great Awakening this was the equivalent of hitting the spiritual jackpot. Because they were set apart, they stuck together. The tight-knit nature of the Mormon community, and the security that this provided during tough economic times, was one of its major attractions.

60 The book itself was also part of the charisma. While the book is, for the most part, a fairly dry and recitatious history, it is peppered with the necessary fables, parables, cautionary tales, and adventure stories to excite and inspire the reader. *The Book of Mormon* presented a mix of spiritual didacticism, epic biblical story-telling, and mystical Indian folklore that made it "fun" for some converts to read and study.

61 Certainly, the importance of the book's setting cannot be ignored either. To Americans, Christianity is, of course, a *foreign* religion. Its origins are traced back over 2,000 years to a location far away. Most American Christians will never step foot on the land that they consider holy. *The Book of Mormon* (if one accepts it as true) changes all of that. With the book telling of Christ's new gospel being delivered right here in the Americas, it made the Americas part of the "holy land." The book *Americanized* Christianity and brought it "closer to home."

62 Joseph Smith's role as prophet was a unique one and is the key to his iron-fisted control over the church. All prophets speak, in one form or another, *for* God. But Smith, if one believes (as his critics do) that he was the original writer of *The Book of Mormon* rather than the translator, gets to speak as God. Any doctrines or ideas that he wanted to introduce were simply put into the mouths of Jesus or God as he wrote the book. Therefore, the words spoken by Jesus or God or both in *The Book of Mormon* are

actually the words of Joseph Smith. However, if one believes (as the Mormon faithful do) that he was simply the translator of *The Book of Mormon*, then these words are actually coming from on high and cannot be questioned. If Smith's story of how *The Book of Mormon* came forth was accepted, then he could assume the much less dangerous role of "middle-man" rather than "source".

63   In late 1829, the faithful witness Martin Harris, mortgaged his farm for $3,000. He then gave this money to local printer E.B. Grandin. After the payment was made, Joseph gave the printer his

manuscript. In early 1830, the first 5,000 copies of *The Book of Mormon* were printed. By the dawn of the twenty-first century, The Church of Jesus Christ of Latter-day Saints was printing 15,000 copies a day.

64   Perhaps the most puzzling aspect of the entire Mormon saga is the fact that despite the *The Book of Mormon*'s status as "Another Testament of Jesus Christ" and a fifth gospel to the fifth largest church in America—the book, its prophet, and the church remain an enigmatic and largely unexplored subject by outsiders. Six million Americans, in many ways, remain strangers in our midst.

28
AMERICA'S WORST IMMIGRATION WAR

BY JON GRINSPAN

Walls on the Rio Grade, religious zealots, incomprehensible cultures, and terrorist threats to our way of life. Sounds like the fears of our own time. Actually, Jon Grinspan is describing another time in our nation's history: the 1840's and 1850's. The religion was different, and the threat to our way of life was exaggerated. But the solution (for many) was the same: keep the foreign element out.

In the mid-nineteenth century, the United States was primarily a Protestant country, a loose republic of self-governing states, counties and villages. In the mid-1840's, a huge influx of starving Irish, primarily Roman-Catholic, deluged eastern cities, especially New York. The Potato Famine in Ireland had driven them from their homeland. There existed among many Protestants a palpable resentment against the Catholic Church, and a fear that Roman Catholics would undermine democratic institutions by giving their first allegiance to Rome. These fears manifested themselves at the ballot box. The Democratic Party became the home of most Irish voters including those not even eligible to vote. Nativist elements came together in various political parties to counteract the perceived Catholic threat.

In time, the sectional crisis over the spread of slavery overshadowed the immigration issue. Issues of Protestant and Catholic were replaced by issues of North and South. But subsequent reactions to immigrants have proven that the issue will probably never go away. Ironically, Irish Catholics, the very group who were discriminated against in the 1850's, who would lead the charge to ban Chinese from this country. And in the 1920's, nativist groups, including the Ku Klux Klan, succeeded in closing America's doors to Catholics and Jews from Europe. Now, it is the Muslim who is feared, and the Mexican who gets punished. Perhaps the issue of immigration is the war that never goes away.

- *Why were the Irish resented?*
- *Who were the "Know-Nothings"? What did they do to the Irish?*
- *Why were the Irish accused of cheating on elections?*
- *What was the "purification of the ballot box"?*
- *Define each of these: Nativism and Xenophobia*
- *What was the other major issue of the 1850's?*
- *How does the history of the Know-Nothings shed light on our modern immigration debate?*

1   Americans are once again fighting over immigration, but our current dispute pales in comparison with past battles on the subject. A hundred and fifty years ago today, citizens not only debated immigration but voted, fought, and bled over it. And on November 4, 1856, a three-way presidential election pitted the Nativist "American" and Republican Parties against pro-immigration Democrats for control of our nation's borders, tenements, and very identity.

2   Though we often think of our era as polarized, the political climate of the 1850s was far worse. At the center of that decade's violence and vitriol were secret anti-immigration societies. Called "Know Nothings" because their members would play dumb if asked about the organizations, they considered themselves "Native Americans" opposed to increasing immigration. To combat "foreign" influence they tampered with elections, intimidated voters, and attacked immigrants. One popular Detroit Know Nothing even enjoined his readers to "carry your revolver and shoot down the first Irish rebel that dare insult your person as an American!" In the era before the Civil War, a startling number of Americans responded to the arrival of "Celt scoundrels" with firearms.

3   Know Nothings met in underground clubs because their beliefs went against traditional American attitudes toward immigration. At first the expanding republic broadly welcomed European refugees and fortune seekers, especially to help settle the Western territories. That began to change in the late 1840s, as conditions in Europe pushed many more poor people across the Atlantic. By 1856 three million Irish and German immigrants had arrived on American shores, driven by famine and unrest. With that many joining a nation of 23 million citizens, the proportion of foreign-born grew to be about the same as it is today.

4   Germans often took up farming on the frontier, but Irish immigrants congregated in the cities of the Northeast and Midwest. Exhausted by famine and oppression, few of them could afford life outside the slums. The Irish made up 30 percent of New York's population and accounted for 70 percent of the city's charity recipients and half its arrests. Life in midcentury American cities was grim, dirty, and tiring; most immigrants took jobs as day laborers, maids, and laundresses. The mortality rate in major cities actually rose by 33 percent between 1840 and 1855. As crowding, poverty, and violence soared in America's tenements, the "natives" took notice.

5   They responded with a wave of evangelical Protestant resentment. This wave had been surging before the rise in immigration and to its credit had also inspired the movement to abolish slavery, but it swelled into a tempest where Catholic immigrants were concerned. Few Catholics had lived in America before the Irish arrived, and the nation was at heart fundamentally Protestant. This meant not only bias against Catholic foreigners but also a belief that they were inherently opposed to democracy. Many Protestants considered their Christianity a personal "republicanized" faith that could be applied to politics—to oppose slavery, to ban liquor—without appearing undemocratic. Catholics were seen as mindless "emissaries of bloody and bigoted Rome," bishops' pawns incapable of voting their individual consciences.

6   Some of this bigotry stemmed from genuine election abuses. Many Irish voters were persuaded to support the Democratic Party in exchange for jobs as police and firemen. Some states even ignored the five-year legal wait for naturalization so that Irish immigrants could vote Democratic straight off the boat. These abuses say more about a political machine's manipulation of vulnerable immigrants than about the Irish themselves, but some Northerners began to see immigrants as a powerful tool of the mostly Southern Democratic Party. "Thrown upon our shores in swarms," new Americans were supposedly "dragged to the ballot-box with a vote in one hand and a glass of rum in the other."

7   By the mid-1850s gentlemen and thugs alike began to join the Know Nothings in droves. These "Natives" took the names of Indian tribes, calling their lodges the "Choctaws" or the "Oneidas" and their leaders "sachems." They joined forces with street gangs—in New York the Plug Uglies and Rip Raps and Bowery Boys—and launched vicious attacks on immigrants. Gang members dressed in stovepipe hats, red shirts, and leather boots and vests and poured into slums brandishing revolvers, Bowie knives, and clubs. They battled Irish gangs, burned churches, and brutalized Catholic clergymen, especially on election days. For all the tension of our modern elections, imagine if each November the Bloods, Crips, and Latin Kings took to the streets to make war for the Republicans or Democrats.

8   The Nativists were most threatening when they struggled for "the purification of the ballot box." They were too secretive to run directly as the Know Nothings, but their American party did extremely well in the 1850s. As the traditional Whig and Democratic parties grew weaker, elections became multiparty contests. The Americans ran on an openly xenophobic platform, calling for a 21-year waiting period before naturalization, literacy tests for voting, and a ban on Catholics serving in government.

9   In 1854 and '55 the American party experienced great success throughout the Mid-Atlantic, Midwest, and New England. Combining their hatred for Catholic immigrants with an evangelical drive against slavery, the Know Nothings claimed two thirds of the congressmen elected to oppose the slavery-accommodating Kansas-Nebraska Act. By 1855 more

than a million voters were casting Know Nothing ballots, where just a handful had two years earlier. Leaders of other parties complained about their obsession with Irish immigrants, because, in the words of one Massachusetts Republican leader, "the people will not confront the issues we present, they want a Paddy hunt & on a Paddy hunt they will go."

10   And the rise in Nativism was larger than the American party alone. Many in the nascent antislavery Republican party supported the Know Nothings' xenophobia. Top Republican leaders, including Salmon P. Chase and David Wilmot, who wrote the antislavery Wilmot Proviso, either were Know Nothings themselves or owed their power to nativist backing. Abraham Lincoln and the future secretary of state William Seward were practically alone among the Republican leadership in their abhorrence of the Know Nothings.

11   Coming into the 1856 presidential election, American voters had three major parties to choose from, each intertwining the immigration and slavery issues. The American Party ran the proslavery ex-President Millard Fillmore, to the chagrin of its mostly antislavery base. The Republicans, in their first presidential election, ran John Frémont, a California adventurer who opposed slavery and privately endorsed the Know Nothings' 21-year naturalization initiative. Frémont's handlers cleverly kept his Nativism quiet, thus attracting the support of many Midwestern German immigrants. And the Democrats, unhappy with the shifting national discourse, ran James Buchanan, an ineffectual moderate who had the backing of proslavery and immigrant voters.

12   This fractured political climate became even more confused when northern Know Nothings, unhappy with Fillmore's stance on slavery, formed the North American Party and nominated John Frémont as well. Now four parties squared off for the Presidency, two of them running the same man. That realignment, made in February 1856, marks the moment when slavery overtook immigration as *the* issue in American politics.

13   On November 4 each party trotted out its voters, with Know Nothing and immigrant gangs playing their parts. The results were predictable. Though the American Party did surprisingly well, winning a fifth of the popular ballots and Maryland's electoral votes, Buchanan won 45 percent of the popular vote and Frémont just 33 percent. Counting both the sizable portion of Frémont's support that came from Nativists and the American party's 20 percent of the vote, probably more than a third of the electorate opposed immigration. Slavery split the nativist bloc; the American, North American, and Republican parties, working together, could have easily won the Presidency. Some Republicans kicked themselves for refusing to accept a Know Nothing as Frémont's running mate, citing it as the "fatal error" that gave Buchanan the win.

14   The slavery debate had proved decisive, but American nativism was slow to disappear. In Massachusetts voters endorsed literacy tests for voting rights. Elsewhere gangs continued to persecute Catholics, burning the cathedral in Philadelphia and rioting in Baltimore. But as other issues seized the nation's attention and Irish immigration slowed, the Know Nothings began to weaken. They could no longer count on millions of voters or control of two parties. Meanwhile Irish and Catholic citizens began to gain wider acceptance in American society. Catholicism is now America's largest religious denomination. A majority of the current Supreme Court justices are Catholic. So much for "war to the hilt on Romanism."

15   But immigration riles us still. Americans scream at one another, wave flags, build walls, and struggle to decide what place the foreign-born have in a nation of immigrants. What our recent debates have seen very little of is violence, outright bigotry, or secrecy on anything like the scale of past quarrels. Even the Minutemen who "patrol" our Southern border bear no comparison to the Plug Uglies or Rip Raps of the 1850s. Regardless of hurtful rhetoric, no one has raided Mexican neighborhoods or tried to enforce an impossibly long waiting period for citizenship or ban immigrants from public office. History can sometimes be uplifting in its bleakness, putting our own time in encouraging perspective. The simple truth of our tense struggle with immigration is that, 150 years on, we can all be proud to declare that we no longer "know nothing."

VII

MOVIN' WEST

1 From the earliest European incursions into the Americas, one motive has drawn them ever more resolutely into the interior: wealth and land. Many high-minded individuals surely lent different justifications to the great invasion, but none could completely cloud the greed and hunger that drove the westward quests of immigrants and adventurers.

2 Among Native Americans, there was an ever increasing awareness of the intent of Europeans to take over the west, even if they didn't fully understand the motives for this drive. In recognition of the realities of the Europeans' tendency to contest over their prizes, many Native American tribes established alliances and sought to achieve the sorts of delicate balances that would keep one European group ascending over another. This was a misguided hope, however, since in the end first the English, and then Americans, came to dominate North America.

3 Many leaders among native groups would rise up in an attempt to stem the tide of European expansion. Pontiac led the Ottawas against encroaching settlers in the 1760s, and Tecumseh fought with the British in the War of 1812; both were futile efforts that were condemned to failure. By the 1830s, even the southern tribes, especially the Cherokee, were under siege. Their entire tribe was stripped from their ancient acreage and forcibly moved to the Indian Territory in Oklahoma. Andrew Jackson, a politician who built his career on exploitation of the frontier, ordered an Indian removal program that has since been called the "trail of tears."

4 As the century progressed, expansion came to play a greater part in the political life of the country. Land speculators, plantation owners, and small-time farmers fought over banking and finance, while pro-slave and abolitionist forces staked out their opposing positions on the issue of slavery in the territories. The heated debate over this issue was manifested in the compromises struck between the two major political parties over the seized territory. In 1820, a compromise creating Missouri as a slave state in exchange for allowing Maine in to the nation as a free state pointed to the degree of hostility spawned by this issue.

5 By 1845, many Americans were eying the lands to the Southwest governed by the recently independent nation of Mexico. As war stirred the blood of politicians and the imaginations of average Americans, John O'Sullivan penned his great moral justification for American expansionism, labeling the unbridled rush to grab Texas and the rest of Northern Mexico as "Manifest Destiny."

29

THE AGONY OF REMOVAL

BY STANLEY W. HOIG

In 1828, two men were elected to lead their nation's people. Their respective goals were diametrically at odds with each other and would ultimately result in the end of one nation's sovereignty. John Ross became the first Principal Chief of the Cherokees under their new republican constitution, which was written by Ross in 1827, and modeled after the United States Constitution. When John Ross took the oath of office, he swore to: "faithfully execute the office of Principal Chief of the Cherokee Nation and will, to the best of my ability, preserve, protect and defend the Constitution of the Cherokee Nation."

While John Ross became the Cherokee's Principal Chief, Andrew Jackson was elected President of the United States. During the 1828 presidential campaign, Jackson promised to remove the Cherokees west of the Mississippi River if elected. Jackson's constituents—the common man—wanted the southeast land all to themselves. Also in 1828, gold was discovered on Cherokee land in Dahlonega, Georgia. Ten thousand white men invaded. The Cherokees' sovereignty was broken by the invaders' greed. And Jackson delivered on his promise, with his first presidential act—pushing the Indian Removal bill through Congress.

The state of Georgia passed numerous laws against the Cherokees. All Cherokee laws were declared null and void. Georgia law was established as the supreme law of the land. Cherokee land was unlawfully usurped by Georgia and sold by lottery, where no Cherokee could participate. The Cherokees could not even dig for gold on their own land. Despite the Supreme Court's ruling that Georgia's acts were unlawful, President Jackson refused to enforce the law.

Few Native American groups attempted to acculturate into United States society as much as the Cherokees. Many became literate in English, converted to Christianity, and even kept slaves to cultivate their crops in the region of Tennessee, Alabama, and Georgia. They were adopting the white man's ways and saw themselves as allies not foes of the U.S. government.

In December of 1835, John Ridge leader of a Cherokee "treaty party" signed a document with the U.S. government in New Echota, which ceded all Cherokee lands east of the Mississippi river in return for western lands and other considerations. "The treaty" was without authority of the Cherokee Nation. All who signed it, received payment and land. Subsequently, Principal Chief John Ross carried a protest petition to Washington with 15,000 signatures—90 percent of all Cherokees. The petition fell upon deaf ears. The Cherokee never ceded title to their land, but were thrown off by the American government.

The following article is from a chapter in Stanley W. Hoig's book "The Cherokees and Their Chiefs: In the Wake of Empire." It is a narrative account of the Trail of Tears or in Cherokee "Nunna-da-ul-tsun-yi," Trail where they cried the forced removal of the Cherokees from their homeland.

- *Why were the Cherokee people divided against themselves?*
- *How were the Cherokees removed from their homeland?*
- *How did John Ross attempt to save his people? Why did he fail?*

- *What were conditions like along the forced march west?*
- *What can be learned about the U.S. government and the public character of that time?*
- *The article concludes that the Cherokee nation was grievously infected by an epidemic of deadly acrimony. How would that acrimony affect future generations of Cherokees and their relationship to the United States?*

1   The decade of the 1803s would prove to be a period of great stress for the Cherokee Nation. Its upheaval and removal west was an ordeal of enormous magnitude. Not only would the leadership of John Ross and others be tested severely, but the whole fabric of Cherokee society would be wrenched with such violent passion as virtually to destroy the Cherokees' sense of tribal being. They arrived in the West, in truth, a people fiercely divided against themselves.

2   A federal census taken in 1835 provides a statistical overview of the Old Nation Cherokees on the eve of its dissolution in the East. The total population was 16,542, with slightly more females than males. Nearly half the females were under age 16, and half the males under 18. A slave population of 1,592 existed in the nation, and 201 whites were intermarried into the tribe.

3   Considering the number of mixed-blood leaders, the nation as a whole contained a surprising number of people of pure Cherokee descent. Of the total population, 12,463 were full blood and nearly 3,000 were either one-half or one-quarter blood. Literacy had gained a significant foothold, with 1,070 who could read in English and 3,914 who could read in Cherokee. There were 19 schools in the nation, but only 292 schoolchildren.

4   Though wealth was distributed unevenly between the richer and the poorer tribesman, in comparison to other tribes the Cherokees were well off, with 22,405 cattle and 7,628 horses. Their 8,184 houses provided more than adequate shelter. However, there were but 130 wagons in the entire nation—a scant number to carry more than 16,000 people westward.

5   The New Echota treaty stipulated that the Old Nation Cherokees were to be removed by May 23, 1838. As soon as the treaty had been ratified by Congress, President Andrew Jackson issued a proclamation that the United States no longer recognized the existence of any government among the Old Nation Cherokees. Ross was warned that any further resistance to removal would be put down by the U.S. Army.

6   Jackson was passionate in his determination that removal of the Cherokees would be underway before his term of office ended in the spring of 1837. He was rewarded in this when a Treaty party group became the first to migrate in response to the Echota agreement they had helped manipulate. The 600 or more people who gathered at New Echota in January 1837 represented the wealthy elite of the Cherokee Nation. Some of them, such as Major Ridge, had received handsome compensation for their relinquished land, property, and stock. The fine carriages in which the warmly dressed families rode, the stout wagons loaded with personal goods, the finely groomed horses, the fatted oxen, and the numerous black servants were in great contrast to the desperately poor, captive emigrants who would follow. As planned, this group arrived at their new homesites in time to plant spring crops.

7   In order to attend the wedding of his daughter, Major Ridge dropped out of this first 1837 migration. However, he along with Stand Watie, accompanied the second contingent of 446 Cherokees, which departed Ross's Landing on March 3. There were few wealthy people in this party. Some of them had been virtually shanghaied or tricked into leaving their homes. Most had been lured into migrating by the expense money paid them by the government—money that was soon thrown away in gambling and drunken revelry while waiting to leave.

8   This government-supervised group departed with great sadness at leaving their homeland. Eleven flatboats loaded with people, their possessions, and foodstuff—cornmeal, flour, and bacon—set afloat on a water route that followed the Tennessee, Ohio, Mississippi, and Arkansas Rivers. Elijah Hicks accompanied the group as an interpreter; Dr. C. Lillybridge, who kept a diary of the journey, went along as attending physician. The agonizingly long and slow course was fraught with navigational hazards that caused delays. Exposure to cold, rain, and snow in the open boats contributed to numerous colds, pleurisy, fever, and diarrhea. Despite these hardships, the Cherokee party finally reached its boat destination of Fort Coffee, Indian Territory, on March 28 without having lost a member. Most of this group moved on north to the Grand River and Honey Creek region.

9 Criticism and protest were widespread from the many who saw the Treaty of New Echota as a sham concocted by the administration to achieve its purpose of Indian removal. Among the critics was Gen. John Ellis Wool, who then commanded troops assigned to the removal. Finding it impossible to protect the Cherokees from whites in Georgia and Alabama, he resigned his post in dismay, citing the "white men, who, like vultures, are watching, ready to pounce upon their prey and strip them of everything they have or expect from the government of the United States."

10 The task was equally distasteful to Brig. Gen. R. G. Dunlap, head of the Tennessee Volunteers. During the summer of 1837 his volunteers were assigned to the building of stockade enclosures, only partially roofed, in which to detain the Cherokees who were to be rounded up at bayonet point and sent west. He, too, saw the Echota treaty as a fraud against the will of the majority of the Cherokees. When he and his Tennessee men, who had long been associated with Cherokee people, found the task of dragging peaceful families from their homes too distasteful to continue, Dunlap also resigned.

11 Still another migration party of 365 members had departed from the Calhoun, Tennessee, agency on the northward overland trail. Almost immediately they became ravaged by dysentery and fever. The journal of B.B. Cannon, conductor of the expedition, from October 14 through December 28, 1837, is filled with entries of wagon breakdowns, severe rains, roads that were quagmires, and the 15 burials made along the way.

12 The John Ridge and Elias Boudinot families, along with the William Lassley family and a woman named Polly Gilbreath, departed Creek Path, Alabama, during mid-October 1837 headed for the Indian Territory. They, too, took the northern route through Nashville, where Ridge paid a courtesy visit to former President Andrew Jackson at his Hermitage home.

13 Despite these early removals, by the end of the year less than 2,000 Cherokees had migrated, leaving over 16,000 who still held firm behind Ross. His standing among these Old Nation Cherokees was extremely high. One newspaper noted that "a more popular man with his own people does not live than John Ross."

14 After accompanying the Western delegation to Washington, Ross remained in the capital until after the inauguration of President Martin Van Buren. Eventually he secured an audience with the new chief executive. Van Buren, however, was a strong disciple of Jackson's Indian policy, and the Cherokee chief made no headway with him. Ross returned home in March 1837 and was pleased to learn that some of his tribal archenemies had already departed.

15 During August, special agent John Mason Jr. was sent to meet with the Cherokee council at Red Clay in an attempt to persuade Ross and his followers to accept removal. Ross not only ignored the combination of pleas and threats presented by Mason, but also immediately led another delegation to Washington to strongly protest the removal. This time Van Buren refused to even see him.

16 The determined Cherokee leader remained in the capital through the winter, doing his best to get a new treaty written. He eventually managed to persuade Van Buren to agree to a two-year delay in the removal deadline, but political pressures caused the chief executive to renege on his promise. Ross and his followers suffered still another defeat when a memorial plea signed by more than 15,000 Cherokees was rejected by Congress.

17 Incensed that reports that the Cherokees were making no plans to leave, Van Buren placed some 7,000 army and state troops under the command of Maj. Gen. Winfield Scott, with firm orders to remove the Cherokees by the treaty deadline. On May 10 Scott issued a proclamation warning the Indians to begin preparing for emigration to the West. He also put his troops to rounding up the Cherokees.

18 Scott admonished the soldiers to use "every possible kindness" in carrying out their task. The ensuing invasion of the Cherokee Old Nation homeland and the capture and imprisonment of more than 15,000 Cherokees, however, became an orgy of nefarious behavior by the army. Families were dragged from their homes on the spot, others were hunted down; property was taken from rightful owners at gunpoint; innocent people were abused and degraded; some were killed; and many were caused to die from exposure or illness.

19 The public press of the day was virtually silent on the behavior of Scott's troops in the roundup, and it is apparent that the country at large had little awareness of how badly the Cherokees were being treated. It was left to the missionaries to report the sordid details of Cherokee capture and incarceration during their roundup of May and June 1838. The private diaries and letters, some of which were published in missionary organs, provide the harsh truth of the event.

20 The daily journal of missionary Daniel S. Butrick tells of a deaf and dumb man who was shot and killed when he failed to obey a soldier's command; of fathers seized away from their homes and not permitted to return to their wives and children; of mothers dragged away leaving behind children who were still hiding in fear in the forest; and of virtually all the Cherokees being forced to leave behind all of their worldly possessions—clothes, cattle, horses, furniture, bedding, pots and pans—everything except the clothing they wore. Butrick was at the Ross's Landing collection camp on May 31.

21   *A little before sunset a company of about 200 Chero-*
kees were driven into our camps. The day had been
rainy, and of course all, men, women, and children,
were dripping wet, with no change of clothing, and
scarcely a blanket fit to cover them. Mothers brought
their dear little babes to our fire, and stripped off their
only covering to dry, their little lips, blue and trem-
bling with cold.

22   At Calhoun Agency on June 16, 1838, the outspoken Evan Jones wrote in his journal.

The Cherokees are nearly all prisoners. They have been
dragged from their houses, and encamped at the forts and
military posts, all over the [Cherokee] nation. In Georgia,
especially, multitudes were allowed no time to take any
thing with them except the clothes they had on. Well-
furnished houses were left a prey to plunderers, who, like
hungry wolves, follow in the trail of the captors. These
wretches rifle the houses and strip the helpless, unoffend-
ing owners of all they have on earth. Females who have
been habituated to comforts and comparative affluence are
driven on foot before the bayonets of brutal men. Their
feelings are mortified by the blasphemous vociferations of
these heartless creatures. It is a painful sight.

23   Once captured, the Cherokees were driven like
brute animals into the stockade pens. Horses
were taken away from those who had brought
them and sold at auction to whites for virtually
nothing. Many of the poorly fed and ill-cared-for
prisoners were stricken with debilitating illnesses. Already beset with grief from losing their
homes, they huddled in fear and confusion. Even
so, they had no way of knowing that the worst
was yet to come. The bedazzled mass of Cherokee people remained crammed into 23 stockade
pens without bedding, cooking utensils, extra
clothing, or adequate sanitation facilities. They
were, as one white minister put it, "prisoners,
without a crime to justify the fact."

24   The few boards and bark that served as the
only shelter were wholly inadequate. Most of the
Cherokees had only the clothes on their backs during
three months of captivity, and these garments did
little to protect against the burning heat of summer
or the incessant rains and falling temperatures of
autumn. Some Indians drank themselves into stupors
with smuggled whiskey; guards used liquor and
other treats to lure Cherokee girls into the bushes.

25   Bad sanitation conditions to the extreme, lack of
washing or bathing facilities, foul drinking waters,
and the inadequate, unhealthy food soon led to general poor health and sicknesses. It has been estimated
that as many as 2,500 Cherokees perished while
being brought in or while being held in the cramped,
disease-ridden stockades.

26   Always present around the confinement camps
were whiskey peddlers, unscrupulous whites who
married Indian women to profit from government
compensations, and those who, as a Tennessee paper
declared, strove to destroy every vestige of virtue
and morality of the captive Cherokees. One observer
noted: "Already have the Shylocks, who hovered
over this territory while there remained food for
them to prey upon, fixed their gluttonous eyes upon
the frontier, and will speedily follow the 'last Indian'
to his new home."

27   Later it was revealed how soldiers marched
through the mob of stunned Cherokees and grabbed
up enough to load a steamboat and forced them
aboard, often dividing husbands and wives, parents
and children. Some families were never reunited.
Upon arrival at the mouth of the Grand River, the
refugees were put ashore among the canebrakes in
burning summer heat without shelter or food other
than a barrel of moldy crackers that was knocked
open and strewed about on the ground.

28   Three groups of Cherokees were sent west in
June 1838. Under escort of Lt. Edward Deas, a
party of nearly 800, the first to be forcibly emigrated,
embarked from Ross's Landing by double-decked
keelboats on June 6. However, by the time the
group reached Paducah, Kentucky, more than 300
of Deas's charges had disappeared. Two other detachments followed soon after. An uncounted
group left Ross's Landing by keelboat down the
Tennessee River, and another was sent overland
to Waterloo, Alabama, before being put on boats.

29   A severe drought curtailed further removal of
the remainder of the summer. It was reported that
it was impossible to procure water through the
Cumberland Mountains, and many of the rivers
were too low for boat travel. By fall the stage was set
for one of the blackest chapters in U.S. history, the
Cherokee removal over what has become known
today as the "Trail of Tears."

30   The main body of Cherokees was still in the
stockades when Ross returned home in July. He
was shocked to find how his Cherokee Nation had
been ravaged by Scott's troops and white citizens.
Ghostly homes and towns sat uninhabited except
for scavengers who scurried about looting the
houses, fields, and even graves. Earlier in Washington, Ross had pad a visit to Scott. He presented
the Cherokees' case, winning the general's admiration and respect. Now upon seeing the pathetic situation of his people, Ross went to meet Scott again
at the Calhoun, Tennessee, agency. Arguing that
the Cherokees could best manage their own removal, Ross persuaded Scott to provide an allowance of $65 per person. He further arranged the
appointment of himself as superintendent of removal and subsistence.

31   When the retired Andrew Jackson learned of this
at his Hermitage home in Nashville, he howled in
fury. Though feeble of hand, the old warrior penned

a scathing letter to Atty. Gen. Felix Grundy demanding that the contract with Ross be terminated and asking, "What madness and folly to have anything to do with Ross . . . Why is it the scamp Ross is not banished from the notice of the administration?"

32   In August, Ross was permitted to meet with other Cherokee leaders to work out plans for the removal. It was determined that the emigration would begin during September in detachments led by Cherokee conductors and monitored by Cherokee Light Horse police. The land route was preferred, though those who were ill would be transported by boat. Ross submitted a request and won approval for compensation of $60 a person. Lewis Ross, brother of the chief, made arrangements with contractors for food and other necessities to be supplied at depots along the way. General Scott agreed to provide wagons, horses, and oxen. And when Ross requested a postponement because of the drought, Scott permitted a delay for the start of the final great removal. The delay was, indeed, necessary; but as a result, the Cherokees remained in their sweltering camp prisons through the summer, undergoing much suffering. On August 1, Ross assembled his Cherokee followers and let them in a pledge that, despite the loss of their homeland, the Cherokee Nation would never die.

33   The rains came in late September as the mass of Cherokee people were brought to the assembly area at Rattlesnake Springs, near present Charleston, Tennessee. The imprisoned Cherokees named the accumulation camp "Aquohee" or "Captured." On the cold, drizzling morning of October 1, 1838, the first group of wagons pulled into position and the loading began. The chiefs had divided the nearly 12,000 pro-Ross Cherokees (by official postremoval estimate) at Calhoun into 10 groups of equivalent size. An 11th detachment to form at the Tennessee agency comprised some 650–750 Treaty party members. This dissident group would follow their own southern route directly westward to the Indian Territory.

34   Another Tennessee-based overland party organized under Richard Taylor at Ross's Landing would follow the northern route. Butrick and his wife, he on horseback and she in a one-horse carryall, were members of this wagon train. His diary—the only daily record of the Trail of Tears yet found—described the difficulties, disturbances, and deaths of the detachments as it traveled up the Sequatchie Valley and turned west across Walden's Ridge onto the northern route followed by the ten groups from Calhoun Agency.

35   Still another party, made up of 1,200 or more Cherokees at Fort Payne (the former Will-stown), Alabama, would make up a 13th overland contingent. The party was led by John Benge, assisted by George Lowrey, second chief of the nation. On September 29, Benge and Lowrey wrote to Ross to say that on the next day they would move out the first of 1,090, with three families yet to come. They commanding officer at Fort Payne had told them to leave by the first of October, at the fort's issuing officer would cease to distribute rations as of that date. There were only 83 tents for the entire group. Two-thirds of the detachment were in a destitute condition, many being in want of shoes, clothing, and blankets as well as tents. It was hoped that additional supplies could be picked up at Huntsville. Following down the northerly flow of the Tennessee River, the Alabama Cherokees reached Reynoldsburg, Tennessee (no longer existing, but then situated directly east of Camden), on October 8.

36   There had been a good deal of sickness among the emigrants. The entourage crossed the Tennessee River at Reynoldsburg and moved on for the Iron Banks near Columbus, Kentucky, where it could be ferried across the Mississippi. After looping through the southeastern corner of Missouri, the Alabama Cherokees drove directly west across northern Arkansas, from Smithville to Fayetteville and on to the Indian Territory.

37   The tragic exodus of the pro-Ross Cherokees by the northern overland route was the portion of the removal that saw the greatest suffering and did most to create the infamous repute of the Trail of Tears. The human misery, deaths, and brutality of this sorry episode of American history are overwhelming, reflecting both upon the U.S. government and the public character.

38   William Shorey Coodey, a scholarly Cherokee with Scot blood who had already moved west in 1834, wrote with deep compassion of the removal. He noted that the "pangs of parting are tearing the hearts of our bravest men at this forced abandonment of their dear lov'd country" and recalled how he had felt at his "last lingering look upon the brow of Lookout [Mountain] dimly fading in the distance as the current bore us away, forever." Having returned east to witness the great exodus of 1838, he observed the teams and loaded wagons that stretched at great distance through the forest; the knots of people around each wagon quietly saying their sad farewells; the stately, white-headed form of the aged Beloved Man Chief Going Snake atop his pony, still ready to lead the way. Behind them the flames and smoke rose high from the temporary camp, to which the soldiers had put the torch—a cruel reminder that there would be no going back ever to the life they once knew. Coodey could not restrain the bitterness he felt. "Wretched indeed," he commented, "must be that individual who can fold his arms and look with composure upon scenes like these. I envy not such a being, but despise, aye, loathe him from my very soul whether white or red."

39   Many Cherokees had become resigned to their fate. Conductor George Hicks expressed his people's sorrow at being forced to quit the land of their childhood, "but stern necessity says we must go, and we bid a final farewell to it and all we hold dear." They would go, he added, "If the white citizens will permit us, but since we have been on our march many of us have been stopped and our horses taken from our Teams for the payment of unjust and past Demands."

40   Two famous old chiefs of the Cherokees were still alive to make the trip west. Going Snake, once speaker of the Cherokee council, would he honored by having a district in the new land named for him before he died. Chief White Path, the full blood who in 1838 had attempted to lead a rebellion against the ways of the white man, would fail to make it to the new land.

41   The first Tennessee detachment was under the lead of conductor Hair Conrad, who because of illness was replaced by Daniel Colston. This group had started earlier but was recalled because of the drought. When the sad farewells had been said and the wagons were ready to roll, John Ross stood on a wagon and spoke a prayer in the Cherokee tongue wishing the party God's guidance. A bugle sounded, and the procession began on what would be a fateful journey for all and a deathly one for many.

42   Scott had set a course that would use essentially the same route as that taken by Cannon. The overland processions would follow down the Hiwassee River from the Aquohee stockade to Blythe's Ferry on the Tennessee River, then west across Tennessee, then "via Nashville, Colcondo [Golconda, Kentucky], Cape Girauce [Cape Girardeau, Missouri], and the ridge roads of Missouri [westward]." It was Scott's choice, but some blame must be given Ross for agreeing to this much longer northern route that was far more perilous than the direct southern route used by the Treaty people.

43   The second group under Elijah Hicks departed only three days after the first and soon overtook and passed it. Only a portion of Hick's group of scantily clad people even had wagon covers to protect them from the wet, cold weather. After two weeks of hard travel, most had grown weary and despondent, and illness had set in. By the time they reached Nashville, they dying had already begun. Four or five Cherokees were buried there, and a week alter near Hopkinsville, Kentucky, Chief White Path succumbed to age and illness. He was buried beside the trail, his grave marked with a wooden slab, which had been painted to resemble marble, and a tall pole bearing a white linen flag.

44   These first two detachments were followed in line from the Calhoun area by nine other Ross groups during the rest of the month and into November. In order, they were Jesse Bushyhead, with 48 wagons and 135 people; Situwakee, 62 wagons and 1,250 people; Captain Old Field and later Stephen Foreman, 49 wagons and 983 people; Moses Daniel, 52 wagons and 1,035 people; James D. Wofford (Chooalooka), 58 wagons and 1,150 people; James Brown, 42 wagons and 850 people; George Hicks, 56 wagons and 1,118 people; Richard Taylor, 51 wagons and 1,029 people; and Peter Hildebrand, 88 wagons and 1,766 people. These counts included a number of slaves who endured the journey alongside their owners. The last overland departure was made on November 7.

45   The obstacles and misfortunes encountered on the northern route by the 11 overland wagon trains were virtually unending. It would be hard to devise a more difficult scenario or a more tragic one. The situation of moving the elderly and ill many miles along an area with poor roads, which were made increasingly rutted and torn by use and weather; the shortage of adequate transportation, food, clothing, bedding, or shelters; the severe lack of medical care of byway facilities; the need to push forward in disregard of their circumstances and long delays at the ice-clogged Mississippi; the victimizing of the Indian caravans by whites who charged exorbitant fees for provisions and services, including some who committed outright robbery; and excessive tolls to cross land and streams. These things were all exacerbated by weather conditions that ranged from inclement to raging blizzard, by fatigue, by the despair of seeing loved ones perish, and by a sense of lost hope.

46   A citizen of Maine who was traveling through western Kentucky at the time provided our most poignant account of the Cherokee march. In a letter that appeared in the New York Observer on January 26, 1839, he described the plight of a large number of Cherokees he saw encamped in a grove of woods by the roadside. He estimated that there were 60 wagons, 600 horses, and some 40 pairs of oxen. A heavy rain with driving winds had hit the area, and the Indians had only their canvas wagon covers for a shield. They were already weary from the trail, and several of the older ones were suffering badly. Some were quite ill.

47   Later the New Englander, met another group of 2,000 Indians, plus that many animals, that filled the road for more than three miles in length. Inside the wagons were the sick and feeble, many near death. A few of the Indians rode horses, but the majority of them, even old women, were on foot carrying heavy packs. Many of the Cherokees had no shoes to protect them from the frozen ground they trod. The observer was told that at virtually every stopping place 14 or 15 people were buried. He told of a woman whose youngest child was dying in her arms:

She could carry her dying child a few miles farther, and then she must stop in a stranger-land and consign her much loved babe to the cold ground, and that too without pomp or ceremony, and pass on with the multitude. . . . .

When I past the last detachment of those suffering exiles and thought that my native countrymen had thus expelled them from their native soil and their much loved ones, and that too in this inclement season of the year in all their suffering, I turned from the sight with feelings which language cannot express and wept like childhood then.

48   It has been estimated generally that of nearly 18,000 Cherokees rounded up by Scott's troops, 1,500 of them are believed to have perished en route to the West, making a total of nearly 4,000 who died while being brought in, held at Aquohee and other camps, or on the trail. One Cherokee scholar, however, calculated that the figure was probably closer to 8–10,000 for the five-year period of removal from 1835 to 1840.

49   In great contrast to Ross-allied caravans was an October group of 700 Treaty party members who, permitted excesses far beyond those allowed others, traveled in comfortable style, drove their own horses and carriages, and enjoyed the benefit of their slaves. This contingent followed its own course, taking a directly westerly course from Calhoun to Ross's Landing to Winchester and Memphis, Tennessee, and from there directly across Arkansas to Little Rock. Having shipped much of their baggage by boat, they moved at a leisurely pace. It took them 21 days from Memphis to Little Rock, a distance of 137 miles, or less than seven miles a day. They still reached the Indian Territory in some 65 days on January 7, 1839.

50   Like the captain of an ill-fated ship, Ross did not leave his beloved Old Nation until the last group of 228 set forth in November 1838. They soon caught up with and joined and 1,613-member company of Peter Hildebrand, which was busy with four boats ferrying its 79 or so wagons and carriages across the Tennessee River. Ross wrote to General Scott, reporting that other detachments were spread along the road to Nashville and that so far things were going well except for some sickness. Soon, however, the weather would turn bad and the road would be filled with broken wagons and hapless people.

51   Ross's wife, Quatie, was already ill when she set forth in their wagon from the head of the Coosa River in Georgia. Her son James McDonald was now 24, Allen was 21, and daughter Jane was 17. They could tend themselves; but Silas was only nine, and George eight. Quatie gave them all the care she could. Yet by the time they reached Kentucky, the rigors of the trail had made her condition worsen into pneumonia. Though she did not complain, Ross became greatly concerned for her. At Paducah, Kentucky, he left the wagon caravan and took his family aboard the Victoria, which was carrying the last small group of Cherokees from Alabama under the charge of John Drew. During January 1839 the steamer made its way down the icy Ohio and Mississippi Rivers, then up the Arkansas to Little Rock. There on February 1, Quatie died. Ross buried her in a shallow grave dug from the frozen ground, then moved on upriver to the new home of the Cherokee Nation in what is now eastern Oklahoma. Eventually he would establish his home at Park Hill, near present Tahlequah. Behind him lay defeat and the ashes of the world he and his people had once known.

52   Ross's great contest with the government of the United States over the Old Nation lands was done. But there still remained the task of keeping alive a nation that was grievously infected by an epidemic of deadly acrimony.

30

George Catlin's Obsession

BY BRUCE WATSON

No artist devoted himself more passionately to a single subject than George Catlin. An exhibition at the Renwick Gallery in Washington, D.C. asks: Did his work exploit or advance the American Indian?

George Catlin was the first great painter to travel beyond the Mississippi to paint the Indians. "If my life be spared, nothing shall stop me from visiting every nation of Indians on the Continent of North America." Native Americans, and their way of life, were dying off, the victims of disease, alcohol, and "civilization". George Catlin was absolutely determined to preserve, through his paintings, what he believed to be the color and nobility of these people.

He was just seven years old in 1803 when Thomas Jefferson sent Lewis and Clark on a three-year expedition to explore the newly acquired Louisiana Purchase. That same year, his mother and grandmother were kidnapped by Iroquois Indians. As a young man he studied law, but soon gave it up to pursue his dream of painting the Indians. In 1830, Catlin made his initial pilgrimage to St. Louis to meet William Clark and learn from him all he could of the western lands he hoped to visit. In that same year, the Indian Removal Act commenced the 12-year action that would remove the remaining Indians from land east of the Mississippi. Within a few years, the Mandan would be decimated by smallpox; with in a few decades, the number of buffalo would drop from millions to a few thousand.

By the time he was finished, Catlin had painted over 2,000 portraits and landscape scenes, and collected a wide variety of Indian artifacts. He had exhibited his collection in major American cities, and in 1839 he crossed the Atlantic to display his Indian Gallery in London and eventually Paris and Brussels as well.

- *What did Catlin mean by a "collection of Nature's dignitaries"?*
- *How did he view the term "savage"?*
- *Was he exploiting the Indians? Why or why not?*
- *How many tribes would he visit?*
- *What happened to Catlin and what happened to his work?*

---

1 One day in 1805, a nine-year-old boy exploring the woods along the Susquehanna River in south central New York came face-to-face with an Oneida Indian. The boy froze, terrified. Towering over him, the Indian lifted a hand in friendship. The boy never forgot the encounter or the man's kindness. The experience may well have shaped George Catlin's lifework.

2 Today Indians from nearly 50 tribes are gathered in the Renwick Gallery of the Smithsonian American Art Museum in Washington. There are Sioux, Crow, Kickapoo, Comanche, and many more, resplendent

in full tribal dress. The faces of famous chiefs mix with those of young women and medicine men. A huge tepee sits in the middle of the gathering, and the sound of stampeding buffalo wafts through the galleries. Hundreds of paintings adorn the walls, accompanied by displays of artifacts—a buffalo headdress, arrows, beaded garments. At the center of it all is a lone white man—part showman, part artist—who devoted his life to preserving, in his words, "the looks and customs of the vanishing races of native man in America."

3   In "George Catlin and His Indian Gallery" (through January 19, 2003), hundreds of stark, simple portraits stare impassively at visitors. The show, which also includes Catlin's renderings of Indian rituals and landscapes of the prairie he traveled by steamboat, horseback and canoe in the 1830s, marks the first time in more than a century that Catlin's paintings and the items he collected have been exhibited together in the manner he displayed them (1837–1850) in salons along the Eastern Seaboard and in London, Paris and Brussels. The artist, who was both heralded and criticized while he was alive, died in 1872 wondering what would happen to his gallery. "In his time, Catlin was considered a B-Painter, but he was a complex and fascinating figure," says the exhibit's co-curator George Gurney. "His collection is the largest of pre-photographic material of Native Americans. It's an incredible record."

4   Though not the first artist to paint American Indians, Catlin was the first to picture them so extensively in their own territories and one of the few to portray them as fellow human beings rather than savages. His more realistic approach grew out of his appreciation for a people who, he wrote, "had been invaded, their morals corrupted, their lands wrested from them, their customs changed, and therefore lost to the world." Such empathy was uncommon in 1830, the year the federal Indian Removal Act forced Southeastern tribes to move to what is now Oklahoma along the disastrous "Trail of Tears."

5   Catlin had little or no formal training as an artist, but he grew up hearing tales of Indians from settlers and from his own mother, who at age seven had been abducted, along with her mother, by Iroquois during a raid along the Susquehanna in 1778. They were soon released unharmed, and Polly Catlin often told her son about the experience.

6   Despite a talent for drawing, Catlin (the fifth of 14 children) followed the importunings of his father, Putnam Catlin, and studied law. In 1820, he set up a practice near Wilkes-Barre, Pennsylvania, where he had been born in 1796 (though the family moved to a farm 40 miles away in New York when he was an infant). But he found himself sketching judges, juries and "culprits" in court, and after a few years he sold his law books and moved to Philadelphia to try his hand as an artist.

7   He earned commissions to paint the leading figures of the day, including Sam Houston and Dolley Madison, but struggled to find a larger purpose to his work. "My mind was continually reaching for some branch or enterprise of the art, on which to devote a whole lifetime of enthusiasm," he wrote in his memoirs. He found it circa 1828, when a delegation of Indians stopped in Philadelphia en route to Washington, D.C. Captivated by "their classic beauty," Catlin then began searching for Indian subjects. He felt that "civilization"—particularly whiskey and smallpox—was wiping them out, and he vowed that "nothing short of the loss of my life, shall prevent me from visiting their country, and of becoming their historian." Although recently married to Clara Gregory, the daughter of a prominent Albany, New York, family, Catlin packed up his paints in 1830, left his new wife and headed west. (The Catlins, by all accounts, adored each other, and Catlin was constantly torn between devotion to his family, which in time would include four children, and his artistic ambitions.)

8   St. Louis was then the edge of the Western frontier, and Catlin wasn't there long before he wrangled a meeting with the city's most illustrious citizen, Gen. William Clark. Having already explored the Louisiana Purchase with Meriwether Lewis, Clark was then the government's Superintendent of Indian Affairs for Western tribes. Catlin presented his early portraits to the general and asked for Clark's assistance in making contact with Indians in the West. Clark was skeptical at first, but Catlin convinced him of the sincerity of his quest. That summer, Clark took Catlin some 400 miles up the Mississippi River to Fort Crawford, where several tribes—the Sauk, Fox and Sioux among them—were having a council. Surrounded by gruff soldiers and somber Indians, whose customs were largely a mystery, Catlin took out his brushes and went to work. He would stay in the West six years, though he returned most winters to his family.

9   During those years, he painted 300 portraits and nearly 175 landscapes and ritual scenes. Back in New York City in 1837, he displayed them salon-style, stacked floor to ceiling, one above the other—row after row of faces identified by name and number—an arrangement to which the Renwick has been largely faithful. More than a century and a half later, there remains something startling and immediate about the faces. At first glance, they seem condemning, as if daring us to look at them without guilt. But after contemplating them awhile, they appear less forbidding. Catlin called his gallery a "collection of Nature's dignitaries," and dignity indeed makes certain individuals stand out. A stately Chief Kee-o-kuk of the Sauk and Fox proudly holds tomahawk, blanket and staff. La-dóo-ke-a (Buffalo Bull), a Pawnee warrior, poses commandingly in full

ceremonial paint. Catlin's landscapes are equally evocative, depicting virgin rivers and rolling hills as if from the air.

10   Throughout Catlin's career, journalists tended to praise his work even as some art critics dismissed him as an "American primitive," calling his artistry "deficient in drawing, perspective and finish." More controversial was his attitude toward people most Americans then regarded as savages. Catlin denounced the term, calling it "an abuse of the word, and the people to whom it is applied." He praised Indians as "honest, hospitable, faithful . . . " and criticized the government and fur traders alike for their treatment of natives. Indian society, he wrote, "has become degraded and impoverished, and their character changed by civilized teaching, and their worst passions inflamed . . . by the abuses practiced amongst them."

11   If Catlin alive stirred controversy for his championing of Native Americans, today he is as likely to be seen as an exploiter of them. "A native person is challenged, I think, not to feel on some level a profound resentment toward Catlin," says W. Richard West, director of the Smithsonian's National Museum of the American Indian and himself a member of the Cheyenne and Arapaho tribes. "His obsession with depicting Indians has an extremely invasive undertone to it." As for Catlin's relentless promotion of his gallery, West adds, "There's no question . . . he was exploiting Indians and the West as a commodity. On the other hand, he was far ahead of his time in his empathy for Indians. Catlin swam against the tide to bring to light information about the Indians that depicts them accurately as worthy human beings and worthy cultures."

12   And what did the men and women who posed for Catlin think of their portraits? Reactions to Catlin's work varied from tribe to tribe. Sioux medicine men predicted dire consequences for those whose souls he captured on canvas, yet Blackfoot medicine men readily allowed themselves to be painted. The Mandan, awed by Catlin's ability to render likenesses, called him Medicine White Man. Sometimes his portraits stirred up trouble. Once among the Hunkpapa Sioux on the Missouri River, he painted Chief Little Bear in profile. When the portrait was nearly finished, a rival saw it and taunted, "[The artist] knows you are but half a man, for he has painted but half of your face!" The chief ignored the affront, and when the portrait was done, he presented Catlin with a buckskin shirt decorated with porcupine quills. But the insult led to an intertribal war that claimed many lives. Some Sioux blamed Catlin and condemned him to death, but by then he had moved farther upriver.

13   In his six years on the prairie, Catlin survived debilitating fevers that killed his military escorts. (He later touted his travels in long-winded accounts published as travelogues.) Though most of his early work was undertaken within a few hundred miles of St. Louis, one journey took him to a place few white men had gone before. In the spring of 1832, he secured a berth on the steamboat *Yellowstone*, about to embark from St. Louis on a journey 2,000 miles up the Missouri River. Steaming into each Indian settlement, the *Yellowstone* fired its cannon, terrifying natives, who fell to the ground or sacrificed animals to appease their gods. Catlin was mesmerized by the "soulmelting scenery." He watched great herds of buffalo, antelope and elk roaming "a vast country of green fields, where the men are all red." In three months on the Upper Missouri, working with great speed, Catlin executed no fewer than 135 paintings, sketching figures and faces, leaving details to be finished later. In July, near what is now Bismarck, North Dakota, he became one of the few white men ever to observe the torturous fertility ritual of the Mandan tribe known as O-kee-pa, which required young men to be suspended from the top of the medicine lodge by ropes anchored to barbs skewered in their chests. When displayed five years later, Catlin's paintings of the ceremony drew skepticism. "The scenes described by Catlin existed almost entirely in the fertile imagination of that gentleman," a scholarly journal observed. Though Catlin was unable to corroborate his observations—smallpox had all but wiped out the Mandan not long after his visit—subsequent research confirmed his stark renderings.

14   In 1836, despite the vehement protests of Sioux elders, Catlin insisted on visiting a sacred, red-stone quarry in southwestern Minnesota that provided the Sioux with the bowls for their ceremonial pipes. No Indian would escort him, and fur traders, angry about his letters in newspapers condemning them for corrupting the Indians, also refused. So Catlin and a companion traveled 360 miles round-trip on horseback. The unique red pipestone he found there today bears the name catlinite. "Man feels here the thrilling sensation, the force of illimitable freedom," Catlin wrote, "there is poetry in the very air of this place."

15   Except for his run-in over the quarry, Catlin maintained excellent relations with his various hosts. They escorted him through hostile areas and invited him to feasts of dog meat, beaver tail and buffalo tongue. "No Indian ever betrayed me, struck me with a blow, or stole from me a shilling's worth of my property . . . ," he later wrote. By 1836, his last year in the West, Catlin had visited 48 tribes. He would spend the rest of his life trying to market his work, leading him to the brink of ruin.

16   On September 23, 1837, the New York *Commercial Advertiser* announced the opening of an exhibit featuring lectures by Catlin, Indian portraits, "as well as Splendid Costumes—Paintings of their villages—Dances—Buffalo Hunts—Religious Ceremonies, etc." Admission at Clinton Hall in New York City

was 50 cents, and crowds of people lined up to pay it. When the show closed after three months, the artist took it to cities along the East Coast. But after a year, attendance began to dwindle, and Catlin fell on hard times. In 1837, he tried to sell his gallery to the federal government, but Congress dawdled. So in November 1839, with Clara expecting their second child and promising to join him the following year, Catlin packed his gallery, including a buffalo-hide tepee and two live bears, and sailed for England.

17   In London, Brussels, and at the Louvre in Paris, he packed houses with his "Wild West" show. He hired local actors to whoop in feathers and war paint and pose in tableaux vivants. In time he was joined by several groups of Indians (21 Ojibwe and 14 Iowa) who were touring Europe with promoters. Such luminaries as George Sand, Victor Hugo and Charles Baudelaire admired Catlin's artistry. But general audiences preferred the live Indians, especially after Catlin convinced the Ojibwe and the Iowa to reenact hunts, dances, even scalpings. In 1843, Catlin was presented to Queen Victoria in London, and two years later, to King Louis-Philippe in France. But renting halls, transporting eight tons of paintings and artifacts, and providing for his Indian entourage—as well as his family, which by 1844 included three daughters and a son—kept the painter perpetually in debt. In 1845, in Paris, Clara, his devoted wife of 17 years, contracted pneumonia and died. Then the Ojibwe got smallpox. Two died; the rest went back to the plains. The next year his three-year-old son, George, succumbed to typhoid.

18   In 1848, Catlin and his daughters returned to London, where he tried to drum up interest in installing his gallery on a ship—a floating "Museum of Mankind"—that would visit seaports around the globe. But his dream came to nothing. He lectured on California's gold rush and sold copies of his paintings, using the originals as collateral for loans. In 1852, his funds exhausted, the 56-year-old Catlin was thrown into a London debtor's prison. His brother-in-law came to take Catlin's young daughters back to America. The dejected artist later would write that he had "no other means on earth than my hands and my brush, and less than half a life, at best, before me." He again offered to sell his gallery (which Senator Daniel Webster had called "more important to us than the ascertaining of the South Pole, or anything that can be discovered in the Dead Sea . . . ") to the U.S. government. But Congress thought the price too steep, even when Catlin lowered it from $65,000 to $25,000. Finally, late that summer, Joseph Harrison, a wealthy Pennsylvania railroad tycoon for whom Catlin had secured a painting by the American historical artist Benjamin West, paid Catlin's debts, acquired his gallery for $20,000 and shipped it from London to Philadelphia. It sat there

in Harrison's boiler factory, while Catlin—who had repaired to Paris with a handful of watercolors and a few copies of his originals that he had hidden from his creditors—set out to rebuild his life, and his gallery. From 1852 to 1860, he bounced between Europe, the Pacific Northwest and South and Central America painting Indians from the Amazon to Patagonia. Or did he? Some scholars, dubious because of the wildness of the accounts and the lack of documentation, doubt that he left Europe at all. In any case, by 1870 the dogged artist had completed 300 paintings of South American Indians and had recreated from sketches some 300 copies of his original Indian Gallery portraits. "Now I am George Catlin again," he wrote his brother just before returning to America in 1870. He exhibited his "Cartoon Gallery," as he called the copies and his South American and other later works, in 1871 in New York City, but it did not draw crowds. The show, however, earned Catlin a powerful ally when it moved to the Smithsonian Institution later that year.

19   Although Smithsonian Secretary Joseph Henry thought Catlin's paintings had "little value as works of art," he needed them: a fire had just destroyed most of the Smithsonian's collection of Indian paintings (works by John Mix Stanley and Charles Bird King). Henry offered Catlin both support and a home. For nine months, the artist, in his mid-70s, white-bearded and walking with a cane, lived in the Smithsonian Castle. In November 1872, Catlin left Washington to be with his daughters in New Jersey. He died there two months later at age 76. Among his final words were, "What will happen to my gallery?" Seven years after his death, Harrison's widow gave the works acquired by her husband (some 450 of Catlin's original paintings and enough buckskin and fur, war clubs, pipes, and more, to fill a third of a freight car) to the Smithsonian. The gallery was displayed there for seven years starting in 1883—the last comprehensive public show of both artifacts and paintings until this fall. Most of the works now at the Renwick are originals, but there are also some copies from his Cartoon Collection, which was eventually returned to his daughters and later purchased by collector Paul Mellon, who gave most of it to the National Gallery of Art.

20   Catlin's reputation remains as mixed today as ever. "He may end up being regarded as a B-Painter," says co-curator Gurney, "but his best portraits contain a vitality and directness that equal almost anyone's." His greater contribution, undoubtedly, was his signal role in helping to change the perception of Native Americans. "Art may mourn when these people are swept from the earth," he wrote, "and the artists of future ages may look in vain for another race so picturesque in their costumes, their weapons, their colours, their manly games, and their chase."

31

THE GREAT MIGRATION

BY GREGORY M. FRANZWA

Imagine, if you will, the decision families had to make in the past. How many of us would even remotely consider walking barefoot over 2,000 miles, facing the threats of cholera, drowning, starvation, even buffalo stampedes? Can we even imagine walking for five months, 10–20 miles a day, through heat, cold, rain and drought? What of the unknown dangers like Indians? (Turns out, native peoples were the least of their worries.)

Much has been made of the trans-Pacific and Atlantic immigrant journeys, of the risks and rewards our ancestors took on to settle the Americas. And justly so. But many Americans have forgotten the trek taken by those who came before: the half-million or so who crossed this continent on the Oregon Trail. They headed west, always west: to Oregon, for the rich farmlands, to California for the land and gold, to Utah for religious freedom.

What was missing on the way out there? Things to do! The trail was often incredibly boring. Today we get stir-crazy being in a car or a plane for a few hours. These people faced the monotony of days or weeks at a time with nothing to vary the routine. Many of the emigrants never saw Indians, and those they did see rarely threatened them. One of the challenges of the journey was fuel—for cooking and heat. Wood was scarce. When they could find wood, they usually used it for repairs—usually of their wagons. So to cook, the travelers used buffalo "chips", a gentle term used to describe the beast's droppings. The chips burned slowly with no smell (buffalo are vegetarians). It was an ideal solution.

The selection that follows, written by Gregory Franzwa, provides a good overview of the day-to-day conditions faced by emigrants on the Oregon Trail.

- *Why did most emigrants prefer oxen over mules?*
- *What supplies do you suppose they had to take?*
- *What factors determined the departure date? Why was the date crucial?*
- *Describe their contacts with Indians. How had they been misled?*
- *How many miles made for a "good day" of travel?*
- *What was the top priority for the travelers, except of course for survival?*
- *What percentage of people who made the trip died along the way?*
- *Why do you suppose tough discipline of the wagon trains proved to be an advantage?*

---

1   This year marks the 150th anniversary of the first significant emigration of pioneers and covered wagons to the Northwest via the overland route known as the Oregon Trail.

"Having sold my farm and am leaving for Oregon Territory by ox team, will offer . . . all of my personal property to wit:. . . "

2   That's the way the sale bills started, and the fence posts of the Midwest were studded with them after 1843. Otherwise solid, stable farm families were pulling out, leaving for Oregon on a highway about which they had heard but never had seen; people who had through three or four generations moved from the Eastern Seaboard over the Alleghenies, then jumped into Ohio, maybe Kentucky, Illinois, Missouri, Iowa Territory, or Arkansas. They had labored with strength we scarcely can imagine today—to cut the forests and build their log cabins, to force their plows through prairie turf that fought back stubbornly.

3   And now they were leaving. The barrier of the Great Plains—called the Great American Desert—had been breached, and the way to the Promised Land lay clear. They had been assured that wagons holding the essential possessions of farm families could reach the valley of the Willamette River in western Oregon, where the government was parceling out sections of land to those who dared make that perilous transit and settle.

4   It became the greatest and most concentrated migration in U.S. history. Before movement along the trail slacked off during the Indian troubles of the 1860s and finally gave way to the transcontinental railroads, upwards of 400,000 men, women, and children made the toilsome four- to five-month journey to the American West.

5   Interest in the Pacific Northwest, which had begun to build with the 1806 return of Meriwether Lewis and William Clark from their famous expedition to the region, continued to grow with the tales of fur traders, missionaries, and adventurers during the next 35 years. Inspired by what they had heard, a wagon train of settlers led by John Bidwell and John Bartleson set out from Westport, Missouri in the spring of 1841. The emigrants soon joined up with a party of Jesuit missionaries and their guide Tom Fitzpatrick, accompanying it as far as Soda Springs in Idaho. There on August 10 the group split. About 30 men plus one woman and her baby turned southwest with Bartleson and Bidwell toward California—finally reaching the San Joaquin Valley after experiencing enormous hardships and abandoning their

wagons in present-day Nevada. Meanwhile the missionaries and at least 23 of the pioneers continued toward Oregon. They made it, too, but also had to leave behind their wagons. The next year 125 more intrepid travelers followed. These first Oregon-bound pioneers had started a movement that in 1843 became the so-called "Great Migration" over what would become known as the Oregon Trail.

6   During the hard winter of 1842–43, interest in overland emigration surged as thousands of midwestern farmers attended meetings of emigration societies to learn more about the 2,000-mile trail and the lush valley to which it led. Newspaper editors had printed letters arriving from Oregon via Cape Horn—letters glowingly encouraging, for the writers were desperate for company. Potential emigrants eagerly sought advice from the few men in the States who had been west.

7   Young Edward Henry Lenox, who had homesteaded in Missouri's Platte Purchase, accompanied his father, Thomas, to a meeting in Platte City to hear an Oregon enthusiast named Peter H. Burnett speak of the road to the Pacific Northwest.

8   *Mr. Burnett hauled a box out into the sidewalk, took his stand upon it, and began to tell us about the land flowing with milk and honey on the shores of the Pacific. . . . He told of the great crops of wheat which it was possible to raise in Oregon, and pictured in glowing terms the richness of the soil and the attraction of the climate. And then, with a twinkle in his eye, he said 'they do say that out in Oregon the pigs are running about under the great acorn trees, round and fat, and already cooked, with knives and forks sticking them so that you can cut off a slice whenever you are hungry.*

     Father was so moved upon by what he had heard . . . that he decided to join the company that was going west to Oregon.

9   Hundreds of other families also made that decision in 1843. They reinforced small, light farm wagons to withstand the jolting journey; made lists of vital household goods to take; studied and restudied packing strategies; and selected strong young cattle to pull the load—usually two span of oxen for each wagon, plus a couple of spares.(*) Many emigrants also picked a milk cow or two and possibly a favorite riding horse. Families wealthy enough to do so could ship furniture, kitchen ranges, or pianos to the West Coast via Cape Horn, but emigrants absolutely could not take such heavy items overland.

10   Having sold their land and disposable belongings, the travelers bid tearful farewells to their relatives

and neighbors. In most instances they never would be reunited. Then many of the emigrants traveled overland to St. Louis, where they booked passage on shallow-draft steamboats for the 300 mile, four- to six-day voyage up the Missouri to the booming frontier town of Independence. Before boarding the boats, those who had brought their own wagons knocked them down, piling the running gear into the wagon boxes to obtain a lower shipping rate.

11   Independence lay only a few miles inside the western border of the United States, and for 16 years it had served as the head of the Santa Fe Trail [see map on pages 34–35]. Now it experienced a burst of visitation the likes of which it never had seen. Travelers began congregating there as early as April; by June about 1,000 Oregon-bound pioneers had passed through the area and were on their way west.

12   Most of the emigrants left the steamboats at Independence Landing. They snaked their teams and wagons up the hill to the high ground, then traveled about three miles south to the town square to make final preparations for the journey. Those who had brought only cash and belongings were able to buy good rigs around the bustling square at surprisingly reasonable prices.

13   A few travelers from St. Louis stayed on the boats for another half-day's voyage upriver to Westport Landing (now downtown Kansas City). They, too, faced a three-mile southward journey before arriving at the border town of Westport, from which they soon spread out toward the rendezvous to wait until the grass on the prairies greened.

14   In 1843 that rendezvous point happened to be Fitzhugh's Mill on Indian Creek, about five miles south of Westport and just a few hundred yards inside the Missouri border. Here the emigrants waited and watched the prairie from campsites containing more than 120 covered wagons. The journey could not begin until the grass stood at least several inches high and could sustain the emigrants' oxen and livestock. But a late start, the travelers realized, could mean arriving in the western mountains after the onset of winter.

15   The greening took longer than usual that year. The annuals of 1842 had grown tall, died, and covered the ground with a thick layer of matted thatch. The cool, damp spring of 1843 delayed the germination of the seeds, and, once sprouted, the bluestem fought to poke up to daylight.

16   Eventually nature cooperated, and during the third week of May some 875 emigrants loaded their tents, bedding, and cooking utensils onto their heavily laden wagons and broke camp. Just a few minutes of travel carried the excited pioneers across the

Missouri border and out of the United States—they were on their own now, away from the protection of the Constitution and the body of law governing the young republic.(**)

17   At the head of the caravan rode Captain John Gannt, a plainsman the travelers had recruited as pilot for $800. Gannt was heading for California and would be leaving the emigrant train when it reached Fort Hall (in present-day Idaho). Fortunately, another expert on the overland trail would be available for the next leg of the journey. Dr. Marcus Whitman the well-known missionary—had returned east the previous year from his station on the Walla Walla River. Now planning to head back west, Whitman had met with the group's leaders and promised to catch up with the caravan after conducting some business in Missouri.

18   Among the throng now heading west were the families of the Applegate brothers—Jesse, Charles, and Lindsay—with a large herd of cattle and a number of horses.(***) Near the front of the procession rumbled the wagon of Peter Burnett, who though now Oregon-bound would become the first governor of the state of California. Another future leader, James M. Nesmith—destined to be a U.S. senator from Oregon—also was in the party, as was John M. Snively, who had recruited dozens of potential emigrants for the trip, only to see all but six back out.

19   Emigrant jaws dropped in awe as the wagons rolled across a boundless prairie that billowed like an ocean as far as the eye could see. Never before had the travelers seen anything like it—wildflowers to the horizon and not a tree in sight.

20   Men, women, and children walked beside their wagons(****) as they proceeded southwest over a faint trace that eventually joined the well-beaten Santa Fe Trail. Almost totally bare of vegetation, that broad highway, hammered by heavily laden freight wagons for more than two decades already, lay as flat as a billiard table and as wide as today's U.S. highways.

21   On the day after leaving Fitzhugh's Mill, the Oregon-bound pioneers left the Santa Fe Trail near present-day Gardner, Kansas, crossing Bull Creek and turning due west. (By the mid-1840s a simple sign stood at this junction—"The Road to Oregon.") After 20 more miles of travel, the emigrants encountered their first obstacle—the Wakarusa River. The river's steep banks and lack of natural crossing points rather than its moderate size hindered these and subsequent travelers, who usually had to spade ramps through the soft earth down to the water, then cross and spade their way back out of the declivity.

22   Once on the other side, the emigrants continued northwest to strike the Kansas or Kaw River, which they followed for nearly 30 miles before locating a decent fording place. Rarely was the water shallow enough to roll the wagons across, especially in the spring. Sarah Hill reported that the leaders built rafts to ferry the wagons across the swollen stream. She also recalled that friendly Indians helped save a wagon that had capsized in the river. It took five days for the big train and its trailing livestock to cross.

23   From the beginning the travelers realized that strong leadership and a military-type structure were needed to preserve orderly governance of the free spirits heading west. Now, after this brief shake-down period, they paused long enough to choose a governing council and to elect Peter Burnett captain and James Nesmith "orderly sergeant."

24   Because the loose cattle moved more slowly than the ox-drawn wagons, causing friction between the stock owners and those who had none, the emigrants now agreed to divide the caravan into two halves. Travelers with only a few head of stock per family moved ahead in one group, while the others formed a separate "cow column" that proceeded at its own pace under the leadership of Jesse Applegate.

25   Applegate later wrote a colorful account of the overland journey, and portions of his description of the daily routine [abridged here] are worth quoting:

26   *It is four A.M.; the sentinels on duty have discharged their rifles—the signal that the hours of sleep are over—and every wagon and tent is pouring forth its night tenants. Sixty men start from the corral, spreading as they make through the vast herd of cattle and horses that make a semicircle around the encampment, the most distant perhaps two miles away.*

27   *The corral is a circle one hundred yards deep, formed with wagons connected strongly with each other; the wagon in the rear being connected with the wagon in front by its tongue and ox chains. It is a strong barrier the most vicious ox cannot break, and in case of an attack of the Sioux would be no contemptible intrenchement.*

28   *From 6 to 7 o'clock is a busy time; breakfast is to be eaten, the tents struck, the wagons loaded and the teams yoked and brought up in readiness to be attached to their respective wagons. All know when, at 7 o'clock, the signal to march sounds, that those not ready to take their places in the line of march must fall into the dusty rear for the day.*

29   *There are sixty wagons. They have been divided into fifteen divisions or platoons of four wagons each, and each platoon is entitled to lead in its turn.*

The leading platoon today will be the rear one tomorrow. . . .

30   *The pilot, by measuring the ground and timing the speed of the wagons and the walk of his horse, [has selected] the nooning place, as nearly as the requisite grass and water can be had at the end of five hours' travel. The wagons are drawn up in columns, four abreast, the leading wagon of each platoon on the left. This brings friends together [for the noon rest] as well as at night.*

31   *It is now one o'clock; the bugle has sounded, and the caravan has resumed its journey. It is in the same order, but the evening is far less animated than the morning march; a drowsiness has fallen apparently on man and beast. . . .*

32   *The sun is now low in the west, and at length the painstaking pilot is standing ready to conduct the train in the circle which he has previously measured and marked out. The leading wagons follow him so nearly round the circle that but a wagon length separates them. Each wagon follows in its track and so accurate the measurement and perfect the practice that the endmost wagon of the train always precisely closes the gateway. Within ten minutes from the time the leading wagon halted, the barricade is formed, the teams unyoked and driven out to pasture.*

33   *Everyone is busy preparing fires to cook the evening meal, pitching tents and otherwise preparing for the night. All able to bear arms have been formed into three companies, and each of these into four watches. Every third night it is the duty of one of these companies to keep watch and ward over the camp.*

34   *Before a tent a violin makes lively music, and some youths and maidens have improvised a dance upon the green; in another quarter a flute gives its mellow and melancholy notes to the still night air. It has been a prosperous day; more than twenty miles have been accomplished of the great journey.*

35   The emigrants slept in bedrolls or tents, either beneath the wagons or outside the circle. A nagging fear of Indians persisted during this and later migrations, despite the fact that natives rarely attacked the well-protected trains. The indigenous population more likely approached the caravans seeking trinkets and goods; many emigrants saw them more as beggars than warriors.

36   The spectacle of the prairie itself excited the travelers, but the Kansas thunderstorms—among the most violent on the continent—elicited even more awe. These usually formed in the afternoon, when

cumulonimbuses to the west developed their distinctive anvil tops. A slight breeze began popping the wagon canvas as faint thunder rolled over the prairie. Then low rolling clouds swept across the sky, obscuring the sun, and the breeze became a driving wind.

37   If the captain concluded that a violent storm lay in store, he corralled the wagons and ordered the stock moved inside, because nothing generated a stampede like a bolt of lightning. The technique later backfired on at least one train, when 250 cattle charged over and through the fence of wagons.

38   Travelers often climbed into their wagons when the rainstorm began in earnest, realizing nevertheless that the painted canvas tops protected against a torrent for only so long. Soon water oozed between the threads, and before long a second rainstorm drenched the wagon's interior.

39   The caravan now headed west from the area of present-day Topeka to a difficult crossing at the Red Vermilion River—another waterway with steep banks into which emigrants had to spade ramps. Thirty-two miles to the northwest lay the crossing of the Black Vermilion, and another dozen miles brought the travelers to one of the most idyllic camping spots on the Oregon Trail—Alcove Spring on the east bank of the Big Blue River.

40   Edwin Bryant, traveling with the Donner Party three years after the Great Migration, described the gushing spring as being "as cold and pure as if it had just been melted from ice. . . . We named this 'Alcove Spring,' and future travelers will find the name graven on the rocks, and on the trunks of the trees surrounding it."

41   The emigrants continued northwest into today's Nebraska, smoothing and deepening the trace that guided them. Each day fairly resembled the last as they followed the Little Blue River until it made a U-turn south. Then they headed out across the undulating prairie to a ridge of sand hills. From its crest they caught their first view of the Platte River, which would guide them for the next 600 miles.

42   A number of previous travelers had commented on the view of the river from the sand hills. Benjamin E. Bonneville, the American explorer-spy Washington Irving idolized, arrived there on June 2, 1832 and found a braided stream 2,200 yards wide and from three to six feet deep.

43   The emigrants always sought campsites with three requisites—firewood, grass, and water. The Platte was hospitable, providing an ample water supply, albeit often muddy. And grass generally grew along its riverbank. Some of the islands on the river boasted willows and cottonwood trees, but wood nevertheless often remained scarce.

44   So the emigrants followed the mountain men's advice—they gathered buffalo chips from the prairie. This task often fell to the children, who at first handled the chips gingerly with two fingers. Later they took to sailing the dry, remarkably unoffensive dung like modern-day frisbees. Women gathered the chips in their aprons. This natural, abundant fuel burned hot and slowly, and with absolutely no unpleasant odor.

45   Where the emigrants found buffalo chips, they found bison, which supplied ample quantities of meat along the river. John A. Stoughton reported that the great beasts were so abundant that the caravan often had to resort to gunfire to prevent the huge herds from trampling the wagons.

46   Bison stampedes frightened men and cattle alike. The first intimations of danger drifted across the plain as a distant, continuous rumble, much like thunder. Then clouds of dust rose on the horizon, and soon the black mass of thousands of the animals moved into sight. If the stampede appeared to be headed toward the wagon train, men on horseback rode out and fired into the thundering herd, trying to divert it one way or another. Stoughton reported that one stampede missed the 1843 train by only a half-mile: "Their hoofs sounded like thunder and we could hear the rattle of their interlocked horns for miles." Edward Henry Lenox reported that a stampede of 3,000 animals passed within 200 yards of the caravan before tumbling headlong over a 20-foot embankment and into the river.

47   As the caravan continued west along the Platte, the travelers watched the land change before their eyes. Prairie became sand hills; sand hills became foothills and picturesque rock/clay formations. They passed the future site of Fort Kearny, established on the south bank five years later to protect and assist the growing numbers of emigrants. On the wagons lumbered, past the future stations of the overland stage line and the Pony Express—and past places of concealment where in future years Indians would attack westbound emigrants.

48   After about a week's travel upstream, the emigrants passed the forks of the Platte. Although they knew they eventually would have to follow the North Platte drainage, the topography wouldn't permit turning north yet. So they continued on for the present along the south side of the South Platte.

49   The wide, normally shallow river could be practically dry in some places but a raging torrent in others. So muddy that some observers said it flowed "from the bottom side up," the Platte easily could claim oxen and mules in its quicksand if handlers weren't extremely careful.

50   By this time Dr. Whitman had joined the caravan. The migrants welcomed the missionary doctor's guidance. In essence he told them, as Applegate later recorded, that "nothing is wise that does not help you along; nothing is good for you that causes a moment's delay."

51   Four days west of the forks the travelers found a fording place that appeared practical. But the river remained perilously high due to heavy spring rains and the snow melt from the mountains to the west. One 1843 diarist reported an eight-day delay at the crossing. Another wrote that the actual passage over the stream took four days.

52   To accomplish the dangerous crossing, men at Dr. Whitman's suggestion removed the running gear from some of the wagons and chinked their boards with tar and oakum to convert them into boats. The emigrants then chained or roped together most of the wagons. Men also fashioned "bull boats" from buffalo hides stretched over willow ribs, which they used to ferry across supplies and lighten the wagons. Some of these virtually unnavigable craft capsized, but all of the wagons eventually made it to the north bank.

53   Once across the river the caravan scaled the rise that future emigrants would dub "California Hill" to reach the high plateau between the forks. And there began discomfort that bedeviled the caravan for most of the trip's remainder. On that high, dry bench, wheel hubs screamed on their axles for lack of lubrication; the wooden wheels dried and shrank; and the iron tires loosened and fell off.

54   But the versatile pioneers knew adversity well by now. They built huge fires to heat and expand the three-inch iron tires; shimmed out the wheels; and then hammered the hot iron back into place. And when supplies of axle grease ran out, the travelers resorted to buffalo tallow to lubricate the wheels.

55   The high ground ended suddenly 22 miles northwest of the ford at one of the most daunting points on the trail—"Windlass Hill." Unhitching the oxen on the brink of the precipice, the travelers led the beasts down. Then they locked the wagons' brakes, dug in their heels at the end of short ropes, and laboriously lowered the wagons into Ash Hollow and the bank of the North Platte River. The descent was described by one diarist as breaking the monotony; also the legs of the horses, mules, and oxen, and the arms of the teamsters.

56   But at the foot of the slope lay the ideal campground—plenty of water from the Ash Hollow Spring, abundant wood from the ash grove, and enough grass to satisfy the livestock.

57   Now the tempo of the journey began to quicken. If the scenery sometimes seemed tedious along the Platte, soon it overflowed with wonders. Forty miles northwest, on the left bank of the river, rose the stark geological formation the Mormons later called the Ancient Bluff Ruins. A half-day later the emigrants saw a distinctive natural structure on the western horizon that they dubbed Court House Rock. Next to it stood a smaller rock, which they named Jail Rock. The formations lay about four miles south of the trail, but the magnifying effect caused by heated air rising off the sand made the distance seem more like four blocks. Many emigrants who already had walked 15 to 18 miles that day hiked or rode horses another eight to the Courthouse and back, just to get a closer look. Those who climbed to the top of that landmark spotted the tall spire of Chimney Rock on the western horizon 14 miles distant. That called for another visit, but fortunately the formation lay within two miles of the trail.

58   Emigrant diaries mention Chimney Rock more often than any other landmark along the trail. Noted Dr. A. H. Thomasson's journal entry of 1850: "We went up it about 4 hundred feet then it became so steep they was feet holts cut in so we could clime up about 25 feet further then we could see where some had cut noches and drove little sticks to clime about 20 feet further but did not venture up that I suppose that there is not less than 2 thousand names risen in difrin places."

59   Here also Sarah Hill wrote that many of her family's animals mingled with bison herds and were lost.

60   Within sight of Chimney Rock, the last of the region's three great geological "curiosities Bluff— loomed over the western horizon, hugging the south bank of the river so closely that wagons could not pass that way. This landmark forced a detour to the south over what came to be known as Robidoux Pass."

61   Entering present-day Wyoming, the emigrants now headed for Fort Laramie, the first semblance of civilization since leaving the States. En route, they visited Fort Platte, started in 1839 to compete with the American Fur Company's nearby Fort John, which, however, everyone knew as Fort Laramie, after the nearby river.

62   The inhabitants of Fort Platte welcomed the travelers; on July 14, John Boardman wrote that he went to a "dance, where some of the company got gay. Pleasant."

63   Travelers had to wait until Fort Laramie, however, to obtain needed services. Its six-foot thick, 15-foot high adobe walls sheltered a trading post where supplies could be replenished at outrageous

prices; a blacksmith shop; and a form of post office. An old trader, James Bordeaux, ran the post and kept peace with the Indians. Some 2,500 Oglala and Brule Sioux lodges stood nearby.

64 Eight miles west of Fort Laramie the trail passed a tall sandstone and white chalk bank that travelers nicknamed Register Cliff. One needed only a nail to incise one's name in the chalklike rock, and thousands of those inscriptions and dates survive to this day. Three miles farther the wagons of the Great Migration left faint tracks over a sandstone hill. Today those tracks, deepened by tens of thousands of subsequent wagons, cut nearly four feet into the hillside.

65 A few days later, the Great Migration suffered one of its few tragedies. As the caravan neared La Prele Creek, the nine-year-old son of A. J. and Nancy Hembree was doing something dangerous—riding on the tongue of his family's wagon, balancing between the oxen. Perhaps the wagon lurched into a rut. "He fell off waggon tuna & both wheels run over him" recorded an eyewitness. The accident happened on July 18, and the company continued into camp on La Prele Creek with the unconscious boy, who died there the next day.

66 James Nesmith, traveling two days behind the ill-fated family, reported seeing "a fresh grave with stones piled over it, and a note tied on a stick, informing us that it was the grave of Joel J. Hembree, who was killed by a wagon running over [his] body. At the head of the grave stood a stone containing the name of the child, the first death on the expedition.

67 The grave is on the left hand side of the trail close to [La Prele] Creek."(*****)

68 Considering the record of succeeding wagon trains, the emigration of 1843 seems to have been comparatively lucky. During the years, about one emigrant in 20 perished along the trail—thousands to accidents; thousands of others to diseases that included cholera and dysentery. Most who died were buried right on the trail, so that the wheels of following wagons would obliterate the sight and scent of the grave. Without this precaution, hungry wolves were likely to unearth the corpse.

69 The emigrants finally rejoined the North Platte near present-day Casper, Wyoming, to head due west along its south bank. Here, tying the wagons together with ropes and chains, they forded the river without incident at a point where Brigham Young would establish the Mormon Ferry in 1847.

70 As the travelers headed over Emigrant Gap, they encountered a new danger—alkaline springs. Arriving at Poison Spring, which later caravans could identify from the carcasses of livestock that surrounded it, the teamsters had to beat their thirsty oxen to keep them from drinking the water. The Great Migration had to continue 16 miles south to Willow Spring to find a campsite with good water.

71 Shortly thereafter, the caravan reached Independence Rock—that great landmark the travelers believed marked the halfway point on the long trail to Oregon. In fact, Independence, Missouri lay only 814 miles behind them, and the weary travelers still faced more than 1,100 miles of hardship. But the sight of the rock thrilled the pioneers nevertheless. Thought to have been named for a fur trader's July fourth celebration there in 1824, the oval-shaped 128-foot-high granite boulder was the "Register of the Desert," holding the name of just about everyone who passed by.

72 William T. Newby reported that his wagon reached the rock about 10 A.M. on July 28. Most caravans in subsequent years tried to reach this point by the Fourth of July, but the Great Migration had pushed off nearly a month later than planned.

73 Recounted James Nesmith of his two days at this notable stop: ". . . had the pleasure of waiting on five or six young ladies to pay a visit to Independence Rock. I had the satisfaction of putting the names of Miss Mary Zachary and Miss Jane Mills on the southeast point of the rocks, near the road, on a high point. Facing the road, in all the splendor of gunpowder, tar and buffalo greese, may be seen the name of J. W. Nesmith, from Maine, with an anchor. Above it on the rock may be found the names of trappers, emigrants, and gentlemen of amusement, some of which have been written these ten years."

74 Just after passing the rock the caravan made the first of nine Sweetwater River crossings, and six miles farther west the travelers saw an awesome slash through a rock that towers nearly four hundred feet high. The Sweetwater River had chiseled this gargantuan gash known as Devil's Gate.

75 Split Rock—actually a mountain with a deep cleft in its top—next loomed into view. Then came the "Three Crossings," where the caravan thrice forded the Sweetwater in a gate-like canyon about two miles long. The chiselers continued their work, leaving names as high as six hundred feet up the walls.

76 Despite the difficulty of the journey, the thrills continued for the awestruck pioneers. A dozen miles ahead lay Ice Slough, where water collected beneath an insulating layer of peat and froze during the harsh winters. It stayed frozen through July; the emigrants needed only to dig a foot or so to find a shelf of pure ice. The treat was so rare in the intense July heat that some packed and preserved the ice in blankets to celebrate their subsequent arrival at South Pass with mint juleps.

77   A party of fur traders traveling east from Oregon had discovered that great pass—a saddle in the Wind River Range fully 29 miles wide—in 1812. Moountain men subsequently rediscovered it in 1824. This gateway, perhaps more than any other topographical feature on the frontier, made possible the pioneers' settling of the Pacific Northwest. Wagons could negotiate the gently sloping gap in the continental divide, meaning that families could travel the distance on wheels.

78   Tallmadge B. Wood remarked that the pass "was so gradual that the traveler would scarcely perceive that he was ascending were it not for the great change in the atmosphere." For that matter, most travelers remained unaware that they had scaled a 7,412-foot summit at all. Not until they arrived at Pacific Springs—the first water they encountered that flowed toward the Pacific Ocean—did they realize they had crossed the continental divide into Oregon Territory The ground of the soggy marshland less than three miles west of South Pass shook when emigrants stepped toward the pool the little spring branch formed on its journey to the great western sea. The travelers rejoiced; the voyage lay downhill from this point forward.

79   About four days into Oregon Territory the emigrants arrived at the Green River, a deep, treacherous stream. Here again, tight military discipline paid off, and the river that was destined to take so many lives in succeeding years failed to claim even one from the Great Migration.

80   On Monday, August 14, the travelers arrived at a trading post near Blacks Fork of the Green, which Jim Bridger and Louis Vasquez, two veteran mountain men, had established some years earlier. The pioneers found the post sadly lacking in supplies. Recounted John Boardman, "Arrived at Bridger & Vasquez's Fort, expecting to stay 10 or 15 days to make meat, but what our disappointment to learn the Sioux and Cheyenne had been here, run off all the buffalo, killed 3 Snake Indians and stolen 60 horses."

81   Having come too far to allow this frustration to weaken their resolve, the emigrants turned north at Bridger's fort. On the road for three months now, the veteran travelers were well toughened for the daunting final stages of the journey. In the green valley of the Bear River they crossed first Smith's Fork, then Thomas Fork (just into present-day Idaho) and arrived at the fantastic Soda Springs, noted for their iron-laden, carbonated waters. Government explorer John Charles Fremont, by this time traveling with the Great Migration on another of his frontier surveys, described the most famous one, Steamboat Spring: "In an opening on the rock, a white column

of scattered water is thrown up, in form like a jet-d'eau, to a variable height of about three feet. . . . It is accompanied by a subterranean noise, which, together with the motion of the water, makes very much the impression of a steamboat in motion; and, without knowing that it had been already previously so called, we gave to it the name of Steamboat Spring."

82   Young Jesse A. Applegate, then about nine years old, and some of his friends decided to test the Steamboat's entertainment potential. One of the boys placed his hat over the puffing opening to see if he could contain the force, which blew off the crown, sending Applegate and his companions into fits of laughter.

83   The wagons rolled northwest to Fort Hall—built by entrepreneur Nathaniel Wyeth in 1834—arriving in late August. At this trading post the caravan found the remains of wagons abandoned during the much smaller migration of 1842, when Captain Richard Grant of the Hudson's Bay Company dissuaded the Oregon-bounders from further wagon travel.

84   Whitman, certain that Grant was wrong and that a large source of manpower could overcome the hurdles barring earlier caravans, convinced the emigrants that they should attempt to reach the Columbia in their wagons. They cannibalized the 1842 wagons to repair their own and pulled out for the final, agonizing leg of their journey.

85   Although the trail from Fort Hall coursed down the left bank of the Snake River—a tributary of the Columbia—the water remained all but inaccessible to the cattle. The river had carved a deep trench in the scoria, and the lava walls rarely boasted a break wide enough to allow animals passage to the water far below. Fremont described the land well: "A melancholy and strange looking country—one of fracture, and violence, and fire."

86   A difficult crossing of the Snake was eased by the presence of two islands, which enabled the caravan to ford the river in three stages. Fremont, by now three weeks behind the column, reported the river as 1,000 feet wide and six to eight feet deep. An Indian in the vicinity told him that the emigrants had "placed two of their heavy wagons abreast of each other, to oppose a considerable mass against the body of water."

87   The road continued across a barren desert to the Boise River, then followed its left bank to the Hudson's Bay Company's Fort Boise, located near the confluence of the Boise and Snake rivers. The emigrants once again made a difficult crossing of the old adversarial Snake in much the same manner as their previous crossing.

88   Although the present state of Oregon now lay beneath the emigrants' feet, hardships still plagued the travelers. They arrived at the Malheur River, where a few turned off to head south for California. Then the main body trudged northward; after two days they reached a point called Farewell Bend, which provided their last view of the river that had guided them for nearly 320 miles. The Burnt River now afforded a narrow pathway to the north, where the pioneers finally traversed some flat land called Virtue Flat by later travelers. Then, coming abreast of what subsequent voyagers dubbed Flagstaff Hill, they gazed over a precipice with mixed emotions. Spread below them lay the Baker Valley (named 30 years later), and on the horizon loomed the most formidable range of mountains the Great Migration had encountered so far. Although the emigrants thought they now faced the Blues, in fact that mountain range lay yet ahead; this impressive obstacle was the Wallowas.

89   Entering Ladd Canyon Hill, a precipitous descent over a rocky road, the caravan faced its toughest transit yet—la grande ronde, a saucer-shaped ring of mountains blocking the way to the destination. At the bottom a beautiful, fertile valley—destined for settlement soon after the Willamette Valley filled with homesteaders—spread itself before the weary pioneers, who then climbed back out and left the lush landscape behind. Now, at least, the worst really lay behind them.

90   They turned north at the so-called "Cayuse Post Office," following a trail into the present state of Washington, to camp about four miles beyond Waiilatpu, the Whitman Mission. The doctor already had returned, having left the caravan in la grande ronde to hurry ahead to his mission.

91   The emigrants now encountered another Hudson's Bay Company post, Fort Walla Walla. Complained Nesmith: "prospect is dreary . . . near to the fort are sand banks not possessing fertility enough to sprout a pea. . . . At the fort we could procure no eatables . . . . country looks poverty stricken."

92   At this desolate site the train split, one faction continuing to Wallulu in dugouts, canoes, rafts, or batteaux via the Columbia, under Jesse Applegate's guidance. This contingent floated to the Celilo Falls and then portaged to The Dalles, herding the cattle over an Indian trail near Mount Hood. The remaining emigrants completed their journey down the Columbia on horseback.

93   Now, so near the end of the journey, the Applegate families ironically became victims of the expedition's most heart-rending tragedy. The Columbia at one point measured 58 yards wide with 25-foot walls. Young Jesse Applegate was in one boat with his parents, his Uncle Jesse and Aunt Cynthia, and a hired Indian pilot. A second boat held two of Jesse's brothers, 11-year-old Elisha and nine-year-old Warren; his cousin Edward Applegate (also about nine); two unrelated young men; and Alexander McClellan, about 70.

94   The boats rounded a bend and Uncle Jesse saw "breakers ahead extending in broken lines across the river, and the boat began to sweep along at a rapid rate." He and his companions watched in horror as the pilotless companion boat veered into dangerous water near the opposite bank.

95   "Presently there was a wail of anguish, a shriek, and a scene of confusion in our boat that no language can describe," Jesse remembered. "The boat we were watching disappeared and we saw the men and boys struggling in the water. Father and Uncle Jesse, seeing their children drowning, were about to leap from the boat to make a desperate attempt to swim to them, when mother and Aunt Cynthia, in voices that were distinctly heard above the roar of the waters, commanded, 'Men, don't quit the oars, if you do we will all be lost.'"

96   All watched helplessly as a whirlpool claimed the stricken boat. Elisha swam to safety. The two young men grabbed bed ticks to push ashore. McClellan tried to hold Edward on a pair of oars but his strength gave out, and both were lost. Warren also vanished beneath the foaming waters, never to be seen again.

97   One by one, the emigrants arrived at Fort Vancouver, the most important Hudson's Bay trading post west of the Rockies, where the towering Dr. John McLoughlin, chief factor for the company, reportedly received them well. Said Boardman, McLoughlin "charged nothing for the use of his boat sent up for us, nor for the provisions, but not satisfied with that sent us plenty of salmon and potatoes, furnished us house room, wood free of charge, and was very anxious that all should get through safe."

98   After recovering from the arduous passage down the Columbia, the travelers crossed the river to the mouth of the Willamette, hugging the shore for about 20 miles until they reached Oregon City, the little village on the east bank built just below the Falls of the Willamette. At last the pioneers were home.

99   In this classic pattern families settled the Pacific Northwest. As the Willamette Valley filled, new arrivals moved north into present-day Washington state and south into Oregon's central valleys. Within two decades, three generations of American wanderlust ground to a halt. Energy formerly devoted to traveling now turned to making a living—breaking prairie

in those fertile valleys, building cabins, proving out staked claims.

100   Those who made the trip had realized that they were experiencing a great adventure. For this reason, to the great benefit of posterity, at least 2,000 of them remained awake every night along the way to record the day's events in their diaries.

101   And as they lived out their remaining years in their new Pacific Northwest homes, the overland emigrants joined pioneer associations to reminisce; earned seats of honor at community and church gatherings; and responded to the eager requests of grandchildren for story after story of the cross-country adventure.

102   And though those heroes may not have cast off their Apollonian wreaths, their diaries prove it— most of them had had the time of their lives.

103   The Oregon-bounders of the Great Migration— and those who followed year after year for decades thereafter—all have long since returned to the dust that lay beneath their weary feet at trail's end. But in the Pacific Northwest their memory lives on.

(*) Some overland travelers chose mules to pull their wagons, but most preferred the patient and durable ox. Although covering less ground in a day than a mule, the ox was an easy keeper, did not fight the mud or quicksand at river crossings, cost less to buy, and required no expensive harness.

(**) The United States by 1843 included 26 states, with Missouri taking the nation to its westernmost limit.

(***) The size of the Applegates' herd—usually cited as 4,000 head of cattle and 1,000 horses—may have been exaggerated. The difficulties involved and the number of horsemen needed to drive that many loose stock over the 2,000-mile route have led some historians to challenge these figures.

(****) Contrary to lore, virtually all but infants and the sick walked the majority of the distance to Oregon.

(*****) In December 1961 a rancher collecting rocks for a dam he was building found a dolomite boulder on the north bank of La Prele Creek. On the rock's flat face, a chiseled inscription read "1843. J. Hembree." The "4" was reversed. The curious landowner ran an article in a local newspaper in the hopes of obtaining more information. Paul Henderson of Bridgeport, Nebraska, an authority on the Oregon Trail, identified Joel Hembree. Because the new dam threatened to inundate the gravesite, Henderson and a team of experts excavated the grave (finding the perfectly preserved skeleton of the unfortunate lad, partially covered by an oak dresser drawer); placed the remains in a new pine box; and reburied them on higher ground.

32

SANTA FE TRAIL

BY ERIC NIDEROST

In early 1822, William Becknell returned home from a trading trip with a smile on his face and money in his pocket. He had made the long journey to New Mexico, and succeeded in setting up a relationship that would, eventually, net $145,000.00 annually in trade between the United States and Mexico. The trade was done by horse and wagons-hundreds of them-over a 900 mile trip between Becknell's native Missouri and the old Spanish frontier city of Santa Fe. This trade would reach its high-water mark in the 1830's, and remain active until the establishment of rail links into the Southwest in the 1880's.

Trade transforms lands and peoples, like disease or war. Mexican money and Mexican mules did much to change frontier Missouri. The silver peso was, for several decades, the principal medium of exchange in the West, much preferred to the unstable, inflated paper currency issued by state banks. More than half the goods freighted down the trail from the United States were destined for the northern Mexican cities of Chihuahua, Durango, and Zacatecas, mining towns where a great deal of silver was in circulation. And the stubborn but nearly indestructible Mexican mules that came back with the traders soon became the most important work animal of the nineteenth-century West. Before long Missourians were importing jackasses of their own to use as breeding stock.

The Oregon Trail earned, rightfully, a place in American lore as a prototypical American success story. While not as fabled or as influential as that trail, the trade on the Santa Fe Trail was nevertheless important. It set the stage for what would, a couple decades later, become the rapid incursion into Mexican lands by Americans of all stripes. This would lead to a war between the two nations, and one of the biggest landgrabs in American history.

- *What was William Becknell's goal in going to Santa Fe?*
- *Who were the "leather soldiers"?*
- *Describe Santa Fe's location and geographical disadvantages.*
- *What is the author's view of Spanish colonial policies? Why?*
- *Why were common manufactured goods so costly in Santa Fe?*
- *The author refers to Indian "depredations". How are the native people in the area depicted in this article?*
- *What were the fears of the traders? What were the realities?*
- *Describe the culture clash between the American traders and their Mexican hosts.*
- *What were the long-term results of the trade?*

1   When Mexico gained its independence from Spain in 1821, the remote province of New Mexico opened its distant doors to American can traders and their much desired goods.

2   On September 1, 1821, William Becknell left Franklin, Missouri, with four companions on an expedition to trade with the Comanche Indians on the Great Plains. The venture seemed dangerous and quixotic, because the Comanche were elusive and notoriously warlike. The Americans were also venturing into Spanish territory, and the Spanish always kept a weather eye open for foreigners. If caught, they could expect arrest, confiscation of goods and imprisonment.

3   Becknell was a typical borderlands pioneer of the period, semi-literate but wise in the ways of wilderness survival. He was a veteran of the War of 1812, accustomed to weapons and not squeamish about using them. His companions were evidently men of the same stripe, inured to hardship and able to defend themselves. Nevertheless, trade, not trouble, was the primary objective of the journey.

4   By November, the Becknell party had yet to encounter a single Comanche, and the whole enterprise must have seemed a fiasco. Then, on November 13, their bad luck got seemingly worse when they met a party of Spanish dragoons. These were most probably the famed *soldados de cuera*, or "leather soldiers," guardians of the Spanish frontier. They were formidable-looking fighting men and probably sported their customary quilted hide armor, sleeveless jerkins that were made of several layers of oxhide. These jerkins, plus the oval shields they carried, were designed to be proof against Indian arrows. The *soldados de cuera* carried lances, but they had muskets, too, so Becknell had reason to be concerned.

5   It was an uneasy moment; a vast cultural as well as political chasm yawned between the two groups of horsemen. If the Americans were captured, their fates would be in the hands of Spanish authorities not usually kindly disposed toward foreigners. And Spanish justice was anything but swift; Becknell and his companions might find themselves incarcerated in a flea-ridden jail for months, possibly years. But the dragoons were happy to see the Americans and eager to impart a startling bit of intelligence: Mexico was now independent of Spain. The Mexican revolution had been raging for more than a decade, ever since Father Miguel Hidalgo rang the tocsin of revolt by uttering his *Grito* [Cry] *de Dolores.* After much bloodshed and political intrigue, pro-independence factions had coalesced around one Agustin de Iturbide. Spanish rule had ended by the summer of 1821.

6   The dragoons urged Becknell to accompany them to Santa Fe, capital of the now Mexican province of New Mexico. Long starved of civilized goods, the New Mexicans would be more than eager to buy whatever the Americans were carrying on their pack horses. Becknell and his party needed no further coaxing; the Santa Fe market was far more promising than trying to track down free-roaming bands of elusive Comanche.

7   Although the Americans had entered Mexican territory illegally Governor Facundo Melgares was in a mood to be pragmatic. He had served the Spanish crown much of his adult life, but was ready and willing to trim his sails to the prevailing political wind. Once Becknell and the other Americans arrived in Santa Fe, the governor made them feel welcome.

8   Becknell and company had a limited number of goods with them, but apparently turned a tidy profit. After about a month's stay, they returned to Missouri and spread the news: New Mexico was now open to American trade. A story is told—probably apocryphal—about how Becknell's men excited a crowd by dramatically slicing their saddlebags and letting a golden stream of coins spill to the ground.

9   Hispanic New Mexico had been founded by Juan de Onate in 1598, when the latter led a great entrada, or colonizing expedition, into the area. The Spanish had soon dominated the region's Pueblo Indians and set about creating a little enclave of Hispanic culture on the frontier. The capital city of Villa Real de la Santa Fe de San Francisco de Asis (Royal Town of the Holy Faith of Saint Frances of Assisi), or "Santa Fe" for short, had been established by Don Pedro de Peralta, third governor of the province, in the winter of 1609–10.

10   By the early 19th century, Santa Fe was literally an outpost of empire, a speck of civilization in a vast wilderness. Much of the colony clustered around the Rio Grande, but this stretch of the river was hardly an artery of commerce like the Mississippi. It provided water, but little else, and was unnavigable. Santa Fe's only link to the outside world was a thin and tenuous trail that led south to Ciudad Chihuahua, and thence to Mexico City, some 1,500 miles distant.

11   If commerce is the lifeblood of nations, Santa Fe was anemic. The thin trickle of goods that filtered up from Mexico City was barely enough to sustain its economic heart. Colonists hungered for things that would brighten their drab, isolated lives and provide them with some comforts and amenities. Middlemen merchants in Ciudad Chihuahua, some 600 miles to the south, capitalized on this desire by supplying goods at exorbitant rates. Even historians, normally objective, have characterized the Santa Fe—Chihuahua trade as "pure extortion."

12   Physical isolation and Spanish intransigence combined to make New Mexico a bucolic backwater, rich in sheep, horses, mules and products like pinon nuts, but poor in material goods. Spanish policy, a hidebound compendium of suspicion and

mercantilist theory forbade any industry that might compete with the mother country. Colonies like New Mexico existed solely for Spain's parasitic exploitation. Foreign trade was anathema, lest outsiders get a piece of the economic "pie."

13   Spain jealously guarded its frontiers, ever vigilant for signs of foreign presence on its soil. In the 18th century a few French trappers had wandered in, and while the locals generally welcomed them, Spanish authorities usually had imprisoned them or sent them packing. The first American in Santa Fe may have been one James Purcell, a Kentucky carpenter who arrived in 1805 and was permitted to stay, which he did until 1824.

14   The most famous American incursion into Spanish New Mexico had been by Lieutenant Zebulon Pike. The real motives behind Pike's 1806–07 trip are obscure and mired in controversy. In any case, Pike and his men had been arrested, escorted to Santa Fe under guard, and given a decidedly chilly reception. After first being sent to Chihuahua, they had then been escorted through Texas and released. Pike's accounts of his New Mexico sojourn might have whetted a few expansionist appetites, but real interest in the Southwest remained dormant until 1821.

15   By 1822, the Santa Fe trade had begun in earnest. Everyone now realized, as one enthusiastic but not overly literate observer put it, that "the Mackeson [Mexican] province Has de Clared Independence of the mother cuntry and is desirous of a traid With the people of the United States." Becknell was the first to sing the praises of the Santa Fe trade, but he wasn't content merely to publicize the commerce; he intended to practice what he preached. That spring he advertised in a St. Louis newspaper for 70 men to come West for the purpose of trading for horses and mules and catching wild animals of every description."

16   "Captain" Becknell and others grasped an essential truth: The legacy of Spain, coupled with geographical isolation, had made even everyday manufactured goods scarce and costly. Goods that were comparatively cheap in the United States could command high prices in New Mexico. Becknell organized a trading expedition that set out for Santa Fe in August 187.2 with 21 men and three heavily laden ox-drawn wagons. His party was joined at the Arkansas River by one John G. Heath, who himself was leading a small group of men and animals. But as the traders trekked across the Kansas plains, Becknell entertained grave doubts about the route he had followed the previous year. Oxen were surefooted, but it was doubtful the beasts could haul heavy wagons up the steep mountain trail. Becknell and his party decided to take a more direct route, leaving the Arkansas River to strike out into the arid reaches of the present-day Oklahoma Panhandle and eastern New Mexico.

17   The shortcut, later called the Cimarron Cutoff, nearly proved fatal to man and beast alike. Although not a true desert, the region was arid enough to produce ovenlike temperatures that sapped strength and eroded the will. When their water was gone—or so the story goes—the men came upon the freshly killed carcass of a buffalo. Slicing open the animal's stomach, they were able to get enough water to survive. Becknell's expedition made it to Santa Fe, and after successful trading, the men again ventured on the Cimarron Cutoff, though by a slightly different route. The 50-mile-long cutoff would remain risky for the unwary or unprepared, but it proved to be a viable alternative to what would become known as the Mountain Branch of the Santa Fe Trail.

18   Several other groups journeyed to Santa Fe in 1822, and all seem to have earned enough money to make further ventures attractive. Among the Santa Fe-bound traders the following year were Stephen Cooper and Joel Walker, who led an expedition of 30 men. Each man led two pack animals carrying an average of $200 worth of goods on their backs.

19   The Cooper-Walker party ran into some bad luck when Osage Indians made off with most of their horses. Undaunted, the traders simply went back to Missouri for additional horseflesh, then returned to the trail. They reached Santa Fe safely, and when they returned to Missouri in October 1823, they brought with them more than 400 "jennies, jacks, and mules." Some historians thus credit Cooper and Walker with introducing what later became the fabled Missouri mule.

20   By 1824, there were mounting problems as well as profits. Indian depredations became a serious concern, as when a group led by John McKnight was ambushed by Comanche. McKnight was killed and the rest of his party forced to flee. Many would-be entrepreneurs had second thoughts about the Santa Fe Trail. But a practical solution was found—banding together in large parties for mutual protection.

21   On May 5, 1824, men gathered in Franklin, Mo., to adopt traveling rules and elect a captain for a proposed caravan to Santa Fe. There are conflicting reports as to the size of the expedition that left on May 25, but there were at least 78 men, 23 carriages and wagons, and about 200 horses. They were apparently well armed; they may even have had a small cannon. The expedition carried more than $30,000 worth of goods, and returned with a reported $190,000 in furs, gold and silver—a healthy profit by any definition.

22   One of the residents of Franklin who took note of these westbound caravans was an apprentice saddlemaker named Christopher Houston ("Kit") Carson. Destined to become one of the West's most famous frontiersmen, young Kit Carson hooked up with a trade wagon train and ran off to New Mexico in 1826. But Franklin, sometimes only a nominal

jumping-off point for Santa Fe, was soon replaced by Independence, Mo., a new town founded in 1827. Since Franklin was some 931 miles from Santa Fe, and Independence about 800 miles, the Santa Fe Trail was duly shortened. Franklin was soon gone anyway, wiped out by the flooded Missouri River in 1828. By that year, the Santa Fe trade had passed through infancy and was entering a fairly robust adolescence.

23   There were still problems to be addressed, however, including the constant threat of Indian depredations. In fact, Indian attacks—or at least the threat of them—may well have caused a temporary decline in the trade in 1829. But influential politicians such as Senator Thomas Hart Benton of Missouri did all they could to promote the trade and nurture its growth. Official trail surveys were conducted, and with some measure of success, but the Indians were another matter. Treaty negotiations with various tribes assumed a degree of political sophistication and cohesion the native Americans of the Plains did not possess. Roving bands of Osage, Kiowa and Comanche might be friendly or hostile, as circumstances or whim dictated. One band of Indians might trade peacefully; another try to run off livestock, and a third try to kill lone travelers. Many whites responded to Indian depredations by the indiscriminate killing of any native that fell into their hands. Finally President Andrew Jackson ordered Secretary of War John Eaton to provide military escorts for the Santa Fe caravans.

24   In accordance with this presidential directive, Captain Bennet Riley was dispatched with four companies of the 6th Infantry. Riley was ordered to accompany caravans to the Mexican border in the Arkansas River region. Because of the international complications that might result, Riley had no authorization to go beyond the United States-Mexican border, even if he received word that a caravan was under Indian attack. The captain's task was rendered even more difficult because he commanded infantry—and the Plains Indians were some of the finest horsemen in the world.

25   In some respects, the 1830s marked the apogee of the Santa Fe trade. In 1831, the amount of merchandise funneled into New Mexico doubled to about $250,000 worth of goods. Once-sleepy Santa Fe had become a bustling commercial center, and its plaza an enormous open bazaar. Many people were reaping profits, including such entrepreneurs as Charles and William Bent. The Bents would later become famous for the Bent's Old Fort trading post they established on the Arkansas River in what is now Colorado.

26   Josiah Gregg enters the story at this point, and it is fortunate the trade found a chronicler just as it was entering its mature phase. Gregg was sickly, an invalid in fact, and his doctors felt a change in climate might do more good than a wagonful of patent medicines. The 24-year-old Gregg responded with alacrity; Santa Fe seemed a worthy destination, since his brothers Jacob and John had already been on some trading expeditions to New Mexico.

27   The adventure began in the spring of 1831. Although in some ways Independence was the "official" jumping-off point of the Santa Fe Trail, caravans did not fully assemble until they reached Council Grove, some 35 miles distant. The ailing greenhorn left Independence May 15, 1831, so sick he couldn't mount a horse, but had to travel in a Dearborn carriage.

28   For the most part, caravans used the so-called Pittsburg wagon, modified cousin of the more famous Conestoga. The wagons were drawn by mules or oxen; although oxen could crop prairie grasses as they went, Gregg maintained they weakened when natural fodder became drier and shorter. Mules seemed to have had more stamina in the (literally) long haul.

29   Gregg's caravan was a typical one for the period, consisting of nearly 100 wagons crammed with a combined total of $200,000 worth of merchandise. "Captain" Elisha Stanley, the duly elected leader of the party presided over some 200 able-bodied men, some invalids like Gregg, and even a few women, in this case Mexicans returning home.

30   Once on the trail, each day followed a predictable routine. Travelers rose, gobbled a quick breakfast, then harnessed their animals to their wagons. Mules often lived up to their cantankerous reputations; Gregg reports seeing one stubborn animal being dragged to the harness, his splayed feet plowing four furrows into the prairie. The captain would shout only "Stretch out!"—his words giving order to apparent chaos—and then they would be on their way.

31   Contrary to movie depictions, a large party of wagons moved in four parallel divisions, not single file. That way, if danger threatened, each division could quickly form one side of a defensive square. The square was also formed at night; it provided not only a defensive wall but also a corral to pen animals. Smaller parties marched in two lines, forming an oval during nightly halts.

32   Once Gregg's caravan reached the Arkansas River, the wagons paralleled the waterway for more than 100 miles before they struck south along the Cimarron Cutoff. Gregg noted the abundance of wildlife, even though the rumbling and creaking of the wagons and the crack of the seamsters' whips shattered the stillness of the prairies. There were antelope, and buffalo were both a novelty and a source of food. Gregg saw "some thousands" of buffalo along the route.

33   There were also Indians, and a growing anxiety about being attacked. These fears seemed realized

when a party of some 80 Sioux appeared. At first, the warriors were so far off they were mistaken for buffalo, but as they drew nearer, the shrill cry of "Indians!" rang through the camp. But the Sioux were friendly and displayed an American flag as a symbol of their peaceful intentions.

34   Another encounter occurred on June 19 as the caravan descended into the Cimarron Valley. A band of warriors appeared, precursors of a huge host of Indians. The caravan was thrown into a panic, as greenhorns fumbled with their weapons, only to find rifles empty, powder wet, or ramrods broken. The traders formed a ragtag battle line, then advanced to the martial strains of fife and drum. The Indians were delighted, not cowed, by this display of bravado, and probably thought the parade was staged for their entertainment. A chief came forward, dressed in a rough red coat and smoking a *calumet*, or ceremonial pipe. The Indian leader offered the pipe to Captain Stanley who took a puff in a gesture of peace, then told the chief by sign language to withdraw his warriors. Most of the warriors did withdraw, but only to join their wives and children, who now appeared on the scene. The Indians set up camp, which Gregg estimated had between 2,000 and 3,000 individuals.

35   The caravan finally managed to shed its Indian admirers and proceeded up the Cimarron Valley to Willow Bar. After a brief skirmish with some hostile Indians, the traders reached Upper Spring on the last day of June. Then came the Rabbit Ear Mounds, so called because of the way these curious hillocks looked from eight or 10 miles away They were now in present-day New Mexico, but still some 200 miles from Santa Fe. The caravan encountered a *cibolero,* or Mexican buffalo hunter. He was a colorful figure, with his low straw hat, leather jacket and pants, and quiver of arrows, and he was eager to sell them some supplies. Soon, other Mexicans appeared, trading buffalo meat and bread to the Americans.

36   Refreshed by the meat, and by the assurances of a friendly reception, the caravan stopped at Round Mound, yet another hill that broke the monotonous flatness of the prairies. To the south, they could see the prairies stretching to the horizon, and to the north, the snow-mantled peaks of the Rocky Mountains. Gregg's party met a cluster of Mexican customs agents en route, well guarded by a cavalry escort. Ostensibly the Mexicans were there to provide safe conduct for the American visitors, but the real purpose was to keep an eye on the "Yanquis," and to prevent smuggling. At long last the caravan reached San Miguel del Vado, at a point where the trail crosses the Pecos River and gingerly skirts around the high mountains to loop into Santa Fe. Gregg and about a dozen men left the main party to press on to the New Mexico capital. When they reached a high ridge, they could see Santa Fe spread

before them: a collection of flat-roofed adobe buildings nestled under the looming shadows of the Sangre de Cristo Range.

37   For the New Mexicans, the arrival of an Anglo caravan was an occasion for rejoicing, a time of color and excitement that broke up the daily routine. The teamsters and wagon merchants were also looking forward to Santa Fe, and not just for making money They knew about the Mexican women, who had a well-deserved reputation for beauty. The wagoners shaved, spruced up and put on their "Sunday best." eager to make a good impression. As the wagons entered the 250-foot-square main plaza from the east, crossing Francisco Street, the hooves of the draft animals and the wheels kicked up little swirls of dust along the narrow streets.

38   First stop was the columned custom house, where the Mexican government exacted more than the usual "pound of flesh" in high tariffs. But once that onerous duty was over, the Missouri traders could set up shop without delay. Santa Fe citizens greeted the sight of the wagons with acclamations, and shouts of *"La entrada de la caravana!"* and *"Los Americanos!"* Much of the business was conducted in the main plaza, where the Governor's Palace and other important buildings were located. The Missouri merchants brought a cornucopia of goods, all eagerly sought after. There were shawls, felt hats, cotton hose and bolts of calico. Santa Fe residents hungered for glass; clear or opaque, it made no difference. Well-prepared Missourians made sure they had plenty of bottles, window panes and mirrors. Manufactured goods were in short supply, and Americans sold such commonplace articles as nails, axes, adzes, hoes and hunting knives.

39   Anglo-Americans like Gregg experienced something of a culture shock in New Mexico. The Spanish chatter, the fragrant smell of cooking chile and the whitewashed adobe houses all assaulted the senses of first-time visitors. There were religious as well as cultural differences; Protestants like Gregg tried hard to be objective, but still considered the Catholicism they found there gross superstition. Santa Fe was a town of some 4,000 inhabitants in the 1830s, and it possessed both the amenities and vices of civilization. After the hardships of the trail and with money burning holes in their pockets, Americans wanted entertainment. The La Fonda Inn catered to foreigners, making sure that the alcohol was free-flowing and that the gambling lasted all night.

40   The senoritas of Santa Fe exuded a particular fascination. By day, their facial charms were hidden under a flour paste or the red juice of a plant called alegria. The end result was a hideous mask, but the main object was to protect delicate skin from the sun. When evening came, the masks were washed off to reveal an often stunning beauty. Colorful

rebozos enveloped their heads, and calf-length skirts—daring by Anglo standards—revealed slim ankles. But Gregg frowned upon the almost universal habit of women smoking cigars!

41   The Santa Fe trade lasted until 1848, when the United States acquired much of the Southwest as part of the Mexican cession that ended the Mexican War (which began 150 years ago, in 1846). The impact of the Santa Fe Trail traders extended far beyond the world of commerce, of course. Men like Josiah Gregg had publicized the region, revealing its fertile valleys, abundant resources and friendly non-Indian population. In an era of Manifest Destiny and expansionism, land-hungry Americans needed to hear no more. The trade also had exposed Mexico's weak grip on the Southwest. Frontier defenses were weak; some Mexican troops carried 17th-century blunderbusses that were virtual antiques. Such reports—and they were true—had made the region seem a ripe plum for conquest. And the native Hispanic population—with a few exceptions—held no really strong loyalties to a neglectful Mexican government 1,500 miles away.

42   But trade, not conquest, was the original intention of the American merchants. The Santa Fe trade should be remembered not merely as a precursor of Manifest Destiny but also as an example of two cultures, Hispanic and Anglo-American, meeting and interacting to the benefit of both.

33

AMERICA'S FORGOTTEN WAR

BY ROBERT W. JOHANNSEN

The United States had been interested in procuring Texas from the moment that Jefferson purchased the Louisiana Territory. In 1836, Texas became an independent Republic, though its principal leaders would strategize to gain admission to the United States. The greatest political obstacle to accepting Texas outright was slavery, and principally the extension of that institution into the west and the territories. Indeed, Johannsen points out that the greatest irony to sprout from the Mexican War was the ill-will sowed between the North and South from the gaining of the vast new territory, and the inevitable product of such, the Civil War.

The Mexican War was a huge effort, and required a national mobilization on a gigantic scale. The number of men sent to fight on multiple fronts insured that most Americans would have some contact with the war. Johannsen points out that this was a "literate" war, and thus given first billing in the newspapers of the land.

This war was fought by large numbers of volunteers, apparently shipped out with little training, and attached to regular armies. Though frowned upon by the professional soldiers, they were nonetheless in the thick of all of the major campaigns. They represented a paradox in that they were never fully integrated into the war effort, but were instrumental to the eventual military victories enjoyed by the United States.

- *What were the three fronts along which war with Mexico was fought?*
- *To what degree did volunteers participate in the war?*
- *Why did Mexico's past leave it so vulnerable?*
- *Why did people support or oppose the war?*
- *What was the role of "patriotism" in the war?*

A century and a half after it began, the Mexican War has become a footnote to American history. When not forgotten, it has been misinterpreted as America's first imperial venture or its first unpopular war. The truth about the conflict, and its effect on the nation, is far more interesting.

1 "Long after we are dead" wrote the popular mid-19th-century novelist George Lippard, "History will tell the children of ages yet to come, how the hosts gathered for the Crusade, in the year 1846."

2 It was that year the United States took up arms against Mexico, engaging in a war fought wholly on foreign soil for the first time in its history. It was a conflict fraught with significance for both nations. Yet for all its importance (and despite Lippard's confident prediction), the war with Mexico has become America's forgotten war. Few today can recite its causes. Few Americans even recall the battlefield triumphs. If remembered at all, it is thought of, wrongly, as an unpopular war, in large part because certain luminaries of the day, including Ralph Waldo Emerson and Henry David Thoreau, inveighed so eloquently against it.

3 To be sure, wars often create more problems than they settle, and the Mexican War was no exception.

A bitter and divisive sectional struggle over the issue of slavery's expansion into the territories gained from Mexico was an unintended consequence of the conflict. Many Americans were later convinced, as was Ulysses S. Grant (himself a participant in the war), that "the Southern rebellion was largely an outgrowth of the Mexican War." Writing 40 years after the fact, failing in health, the old general influenced much subsequent thinking about the war when he charged that it was "one of the most unjust ever waged by a stronger against a weaker nation." The Civil War, he declared, was "our punishment." The war with Mexico, when it was viewed at all, was considered within the context of the struggle over slavery and as a precursor to what Grant called "the most sanguinary and expensive war of modern times."

4   But the Mexican War had importance far beyond its contributions to the outbreak of the Civil War–and in its day was viewed far more favorably than subsequent opinion would have us think. The first major national crisis faced during a period of unprecedented economic and social change, it came at a crucial moment in the young life of the United States. Rapid commercial and industrial expansion, with new opportunities for material advancement, was changing people's lives. Social reformers, utopian visionaries, political theorists, and religious enthusiasts were offering a host of projects and schemes in their quest for individual improvement. Questions were being raised about the true nature and purpose of republican government, as older values of patriotism and civic virtue—the heart of classical republicanism—seemed to be giving way before the new "spirit of gain."

5   The United States at midcentury was a nation in search of itself, and the war with Mexico became an important step toward self-definition. For a time and for some people, the war offered reassurance, giving new meaning to patriotism, providing a new arena for heroism, and reinforcing popular convictions regarding the superiority of republican government. The war was seen as a test of democratic institutions, as legitimizing America's mission as the world's "model republic."

6   The outbreak of the Mexican War had a long and complex background in years of uneasy relations between the two countries. To many Americans, the frequency of revolutions in Mexico rendered that country's republican government more a sham than a reality. The United States had lodged claims against Mexico for losses incurred by American citizens during the revolutions, but even though the claims were arbitrated in 1842 at Mexico's request, they remained unpaid.

7   Yet for all the moments of irritation and tension, the cause of the Mexican War might be simply stated in a single word—Texas. The United States wanted Texas, and Mexico did not mean for the Americans to have it. From the moment Texas gained its independence from Mexico in 1836, Mexico blamed the United States for its loss and nurtured hopes for its recapture. The boundary with the United States, as far as Mexico was concerned, continued to be the Sabine River, which separated Louisiana and Texas. For the United States, it was the Rio Grande, the "traditional" line claimed in the 1803 treaty with France, which suggested that Texas was a part of the Louisiana Purchase, and confirmed by John Quincy Adams in his 1819 negotiations with Spain. The land between the two rivers—the Sabine and the Rio Grande—was the disputed territory.

8   Sentiment in support of the annexation of Texas to the United States gained strength as it was linked with questions of western settlement and territorial expansion. John L. O'Sullivan, outspoken New York journalist and editor of the *Democratic Review*, reflecting the romantic idealism of the time, placed the issue in broader perspective (and unwittingly coined a phrase that soon became a popular American idiom) when he asserted that America's claim to Texas was "by right of our manifest destiny to overspread and possess the whole of the continent which Providence has given us for the development of the great experiment of liberty and federated self government."

9   Any action by the United States aimed at acquiring Texas, Mexican authorities repeatedly warned, would be regarded as a declaration of war against Mexico. When Congress passed a joint resolution annexing Texas, on March 1, 1845, Mexico broke diplomatic relations with the United States. As he left Washington, the Mexican minister angrily denounced annexation as an act of aggression against Mexico, "the most unjust which can be found recorded in the annals of modern history."

10   The ensuing year was marked by the rapid breakdown of relations, by threats and ultimatums, by military movements and countermovements, by bellicose invective and futile peace feelers. Mexico's repeated threats of invasion, the mobilization of its armed forces, the massing of Mexican troops on the south bank of the Rio Grande, and the appeals from Austin for protection following the official acceptance of annexation prompted President James K. Polk to order General Zachary Taylor's army into Texas. Taylor's force crossed the Sabine River and by late August 1845 was camped near the village of Corpus Christi.

11   The outbreak of hostilities now appeared certain. In a last-ditch effort to avert war, Polk dispatched John Slidell to Mexico City with authority to negotiate the differences between the two countries, a futile gesture that only inflamed anti-American feeling. Slidell was rebuffed, and a short time later Mexico's government was toppled by a revolution

led by military hardliners who pledged to defend Mexican territory as far east as the Sabine River.

12   The admission of Texas to statehood in December 1845 raised the stakes. When news of Slidell's failure reached Washington shortly afterward, an impatient President Polk ordered General Taylor to move his army to the Rio Grande. By the end of March 1846, the troops were in position on the river opposite the Mexican town of Matamoros. Taylor had been instructed not to treat Mexico as an enemy unless its forces committed an "open act of hostility."

13   Within weeks of Taylor's movement, the new Mexican president, General Mariano Paredes, declared a "defensive war" against the United States, and the Mexican commander on the Rio Grande informed Taylor that hostilities had commenced. A Mexican force crossed the Rio Grande and ambushed a detachment of American dragoons on a reconnaissance mission, killing and wounding a number of them in the process. When Polk received the news on May 9, he summoned his cabinet into an emergency meeting. On May 11, he submitted his war message to Congress. Within two days, both houses had concurred, authorizing the president to raise 50,000 volunteers and appropriating $10 million to meet the expenses.

14   What neither Polk nor Congress could know was that the Mexican army had already crossed the Rio Grande in force and had engaged Taylor's army in the first major battles of the war, Palo Alto and Resaca de la Palma, in and near the present city of Brownsville. In both engagements, Taylor's outnumbered soldiers sent the invaders reeling in disorganized retreat back across the river.

15   The call for volunteers coincided with the news reports of the victories on the Rio Grande. The response was electric. Quotas, initially assigned to those states nearest the scene of operations, were quickly oversubscribed. Thousands of young men had to be turned back; Illinois provided enough men for 14 regiments when only four were called. The rush of volunteers, according to one writer, confirmed the superior nature of republican government: "We had to show the Mexicans that a people without being military, may be *warlike*."

16   The volunteers came from all walks of life. Individuals from the upper ranks of society–sons of Henry Clay and Daniel Webster, a descendant of John Marshall, and Edward Everett's nephew, as well as scions of families with proud Revolutionary War connections–mixed with farmers, merchants, lawyers, journalists, members of fire companies, students, recent immigrants, and even a sprinkling of American Indians. As one Illinois volunteer looked about him at a rendezvous where recruits had gathered, he noted "lead-miners from Galena; wharf rats and dock loafers from Chicago; farmers on unpurchased lands from the interior; small pattern politi-

cians, emulous of popularity; village statesmen, pregnant with undeveloped greatness, and anxious to enlarge the sphere of their influence by a military *accouchement*; briefless lawyers and patientless physicians; and a liberal allowance of honest, hard-fisted "Suckers." Whatever their background or occupation, the volunteers were united by a spirit of adventure, eagerly anticipating a "grand jubilee in the halls of the Montezumas." It was an army of democracy, and the citizen soldier became an honored symbol of the republic.

17   Many of the volunteers had military experience, in the War of 1812 or the Seminole wars in Florida, and a large number of them had spent time at West Point. One-third of the volunteer regiments were commanded by West Pointers, and well over a third of the field officers had had at least some West Point training.

18   Everywhere they went, the volunteers attracted crowds of well-wishers. Residents of the towns and farms along the Ohio and Mississippi rivers gathered on the riverbanks to shout their encouragement, waving flags and handkerchiefs, as the volunteers passed on their way down river to New Orleans. There, they camped on the Chalmette battlefield, where Andrew Jackson had humbled a proud British army only 31 years before. At what they called Camp Jackson, they awaited transportation by sea to the mouth of the Rio Grande.

19   The Civil War has customarily been regarded as America's first literate war, that is, the first war in which significant numbers of literate individuals served as soldiers. Although statistics are sketchy or nonexistent, a good case for possession of this distinction might be made for the Mexican War. Numbered among the volunteers were many men of education, including college graduates and products of the country's common-school systems. They were avid letter writers, corresponding with their families and friends and often serving as special correspondents for their hometown newspapers. Following the hard-fought battle for the northern Mexican city of Monterrey in September 1846, the volume of letters that passed through the New Orleans post office from the men in Taylor's army doubled in number to more than 14,000 pieces.

20   Reading materials–books and newspapers–were also in heavy demand and short supply. That many of the soldiers were exceptionally well-read was evident from the literary and historical allusions that filled their letters and diaries. European travelers to the United States had observed that the Americans were a "reading people," and the volunteers confirmed this judgment. Soldiers carried books in their knapsacks, received books in the mail from their families (often asking for specific titles), and sought out booksellers in the Mexican towns they occupied. Still, there were never enough books

Mexico's War of 1847

As the specter of war loomed over Mexico during the spring of 1846, its leaders pondered the prospect of an armed conflict with the United States. The outlook was not promising. Only 25 years before, after a destructive 11-year war to win its independence from Spain, the new nation had begun a long and largely unsuccessful struggle to achieve social, economic, and political stability. But apart from a widespread determination to preserve Mexico's honor and its territorial integrity, little unified the bankrupt and divided nation in the mid-1840s.

The lack of domestic solidarity was largely the result of Mexico's failure to establish a durable political arrangement. Since independence, the nation had experimented with an empire, a federal republic, and various forms of centralized rule, but none of these had lasted. By midcentury, most of the country's roughly seven million inhabitants were ill-assimilated Indians who performed manual labor, while anti-Spanish sentiment had long driven off many of Mexico's better-trained elites. To make matters worse, the nation had little industry, a poor transportation network, and almost no government revenue apart from import tariffs.

On the eve of the war, the Catholic church and the military (whose chief strong-man was General Antonio Lopez de Santa Anna) were firmly established as the country's most powerful institutions. Separate entities within the state, they had their own courts and privileges, and any effort by reformers to curb their power ignited political disputes, including one that pitted three powerful factions against one another during the 1840s.

Led by Valentin Gomez Farias, the radicals (or *puros*) wanted to eradicate all vestiges of traditionalism by limiting the Church's economic and political privileges and by establishing a volunteer civic militia to break the regular army's power. Enlisting the support of the lower classes, the radicals hoped to bring back the federal form of government (set forth in the 1824 constitution), believing that it would give Mexico the strength and unity to regain Texas.

Like the *puros*, the moderates, led by Manuel Gomez Pedraza, favored putting restraints on the regular army and the Church, though only gradually in the case of the latter. Wary of the lower classes, the *moderados* wanted only property owners to serve in the civic militias. While preferring a constitutional monarchy, in 1845 they supported efforts to reform the centralist constitution of 1843. In foreign affairs, they stood almost alone in hoping to reach an amicable accord with the United States on the Texas question.

available to satisfy the demand. Newspapers were even more scarce. Some of the eastern metropolitan dailies established papers in the larger Mexican cities, the so-called "Anglo-Saxon press," but this effort did not meet the needs of the troops.

21 The volunteer system was at the heart of America's vision of responsible republican government, the principal means of defense during times of national crisis. Although President Polk called for a modest increase in the size of the regular army and later authorized 10 additional regiments, he shared the popular bias against a large professional military force. A standing army, he declared, was "contrary to the genius of our free institutions, would impose heavy burdens on the people and be dangerous to public liberty." Reliance, he insisted, must be on "our citizen soldiers." From the beginning of the war, there was no love lost between the regulars and the volunteers. To the volunteers, the regular soldier was a "drilled automaton," while the regulars, resentful of all the attention given to the volunteers, viewed them as little better than an untrained and undisciplined rabble, useless as fighting men and ignorant of even the basic rules of survival in the field.

22 General Winfield Scott, who commanded large numbers of volunteers, complained that they knew nothing of camp discipline, cleanliness, sanitation, and proper diet. Scott and his fellow officers had reason for concern. More than 6,000 volunteers died from exposure and disease, principally dysentery and chronic diarrhea, about 10 times the number killed in action, though regulars hardly fared much better.

23 Although there were numerous examples of friendly relations between the soldiers and Mexican civilians, including instances of the U.S. Army's defense of Mexican towns against marauding Indians

For their part, conservatives such as Lucas Alaman sought to salvage those elements of the Spanish colonial state that had benefited them. They wanted a strong centralized government, preferably a monarchy, built upon an alliance between the church and the regular army, and only limited citizenship for the lower classes. Finding it impossible to resist the pro-war atmosphere, they reluctantly took up the jingoistic banner against the United States.

The episode that best illuminates Mexico's crippling political divisiveness is the February 1847 "rebellion of the *polkos*." On January 11 of that year, then-vice president Gomez Farias, the acting chief executive, issued a decree authorizing the government to raise 15 million pesos by mortgaging or selling ecclesiastical property. Designed to finance the war against the United States, the law set off a furor. *Moderado* politicians, senior army chiefs, and high-ranking clerical leaders plotted to overthrow Farias, relying on civic militia battalions (known as the *polkos* because the polka had become the most popular dance of elite society) organized during the fall of 1846 by Mexico City's well-to-do. The revolt, which erupted just a few days before General Winfield Scott's expeditionary army landed in Veracruz, prevented the Mexican government from coming to the defense of the port city.

Eventual defeat in what Mexicans called the War of 1847 did not bring unity to the nation. A new generation of *puro* and *moderado* thinkers concluded that Mexico's main problem had been the failure to extirpate the Spanish colonial legacy, while conservatives argued that monarchy was the best means of restoring national well-being. Debate grew increasingly rancorous and fumed to open conflict in 1854. Only in 1867, after overcoming yet another round of civil war and foreign intervention by Napoleon III, who in 1862 installed Maximilian of Hapsburg as emperor, did the *puros* manage to establish a new republic and greater national consensus.

–Pedro Santoni

- PEDRO SANTONI *is a professor of history at California State University, San Bernardino.*

and bandits, breaches of discipline among the soldiers were not uncommon, especially during long periods of inactivity. Individual acts of violence against the lives and property of civilians, often retaliatory in nature, generally went unpunished. Only rarely did large bodies of men engage in such acts. Following the destruction by Mexican irregulars of a three-mile-long supply trainbound for Taylor's army in which the teamsters were slaughtered, a passing group of volunteers, said to be Texas Rangers whose thirst for vengeance against Mexicans was widely feared, avenged the massacre by murdering up to 40 inhabitants of a nearby village.

24 More widely publicized and condemned was the murder by Arkansas cavalry, "wild and reckless fellows" known as Rackensackers, of 30 Mexican men, women, and children who had sought safety in a mountain cave following the murder of one of the Arkansas officers. Taylor was outraged, and the incident was reported in gory detail in the American press, arousing an immediate popular reaction. The massacre was denounced as behavior inconsistent with "one of the most enlightened and civilized nations of the globe." "Let us no longer complain of Mexican barbarity."

25 In spite of what regulars said about them, the volunteers proved their mettle as combat soldiers, fighting with courage and tenacity. Their role in each of the three areas of military operation was crucial to the ultimate success of American arms. Victory owed much to the superior organization and efficiency of the regulars and to the high quality of training offered by West Point, but in many respects the Mexican War was a volunteers' war.

26 Following his early victories at Palo Alto and Resaca de la Palma, Taylor moved his army into northern Mexico, his first target the "stronghold of northern Mexico," the fortified city of Monterrey. Anticipated by the volunteers with exhilaration, the battle for Monterrey in late September 1846 proved to be a costly struggle, marked by bloody, desperate street and house-to-house fighting before the city was secured. Taylor's campaign culminated the following February in the Battle of Buena Vista, fought in a narrow pass between mountain ranges south

of the city of Saltillo against a larger force commanded by General Santa Anna. Except for about 200 dragoons and three batteries of artillery, Taylor's men were volunteers, all but a few facing enemy fire for the first time. It was another hard-fought engagement, one the volunteers were not sure they could win. Exhaustion turned to rejoicing when Santa Anna withdrew his army under cover of darkness and began a long retreat southward, his force diminished by heavy casualties and mounting desertions.

27   A second army, commanded by General Stephen Watts Kearny, moved westward from Missouri along the Santa Fe Trail, occupying New Mexico without a shot, and, in conjunction with naval forces, going on to take possession of California.

28   A third front was opened in March 1847, after months of planning that required the careful coordination of military and naval operations and the collection of vast amounts of ordnance and quartermaster stores. General Scott, in the greatest amphibious operation to that time, landed 9,000 men on the beach south of Veracruz in five hours without suffering a single casualty. In addition to regular troops transferred from Taylor's command, Scott's army included volunteer regiments from Pennsylvania, New York, South Carolina, Tennessee, and Illinois. By the end of March, Veracruz had fallen to the Americans, and Scott began his march inland toward Mexico City, on the route followed by Cortes in the 16th century. Santa Anna's army blocked his path in Cerro Gordo, a wild, mountainous region, but by unexpectedly following a treacherous mountain path and scaling peaks under fire, Scott's force flanked an apparently impregnable Mexican position, sending the enemy's soldiers into headlong retreat. After several sharp engagements in the vicinity of Mexico City—at Contreras, Churubusco, Molino del Rey, and Chapultepec—Scott occupied the Mexican capital in September 1847. With the occupation of Mexico City the fighting came to an end, except for sporadic guerrilla raids along the lines of supply.

29   The logistical problems faced by Polk in directing the war were enormous and unprecedented. Large numbers of troops had to be raised in a short time, trained and equipped, and moved quickly over long distances to the scenes of the fighting. That the problems were met was a tribute to Polk's single-minded dedication to what he conceived to be the responsibilities of presidential leadership in time of war.

30   Polk was the first president to give full definition to the role of commander in chief. "Polk gave the country its first demonstration of the administrative capacities of the presidency as a war agency," historian Leonard D. White has written. "He proved that a president could run a war." He not only placed the nation on a wartime footing almost overnight, but

he also involved himself directly in all the countless details that sprang from prosecuting a war in a distant, and, to a large extent, unknown land. He took the initiative in securing war legislation and finance, made many of the tactical decisions that were conveyed to the armies by the War Department, appointed generals and drafted their instructions, and coordinated the work of the various bureaus and cabinet departments. Polk was, as one author has written, "the center on which all else depended." Later, dealing with his own crisis, Abraham Lincoln devoted careful study to Polk's management of the war.

31   Anticipating a short conflict, Polk undertook negotiations to end the war almost from the moment it began. The terms of the treaty that finally concluded the war were Polk's terms from the beginning. Signed in early February 1848 in a suburb of Mexico City, the Treaty of Guadalupe Hidalgo recognized the Rio Grande boundary and provided for the cession of New Mexico and California to the United States. The United States canceled its long-standing claims against Mexico and agreed to pay Mexico $15 million. The two countries further agreed to submit all future disputes to arbitration.

32   The Mexican War provided combat experience and valuable military lessons for many young officers who would later become leaders in the Civil War. But the war had consequences far beyond the battlefield. It touched the lives of Americans more intimately and with greater immediacy than any major event to that time. Coinciding with the "print explosion" of the mid-19th century, of which the penny press was one manifestation, the war was reported in more detail than any previous conflict. Fast, steam-powered presses, innovative techniques in news gathering, the employment of war correspondents for the first time, the use of the new magnetic telegraph, and the rapid proliferation of books and periodicals all combined to carry the war into the lives of Americans on an unprecedented scale.

33   The first news of the war was greeted by an outburst of enthusiasm from one end of the country to the other: public demonstrations, bonfires, and illuminations, war rallies from Massachusetts to Illinois. "A military ardor pervades all ranks;" wrote Herman Melville from his New York home. "Nothing is talked of but the 'Halls of the Montezuma.'"

34   How to explain the outburst of public support and the sudden rush of volunteers to the colors? How to account for what one newspaper called "this sublime spectacle of military preparations?" One explanation was found in America's commitment to a republican form of government. Where the people were the rulers, the security of the country in times of crisis was in the hands of its citizens.

35   There is no doubt that the war awakened a latent spirit of patriotism among Americans, but there

were other, less lofty reasons for the rush of volunteers. It was a time when Americans were "reaching out" beyond their borders; the expansion of commerce, the increase in travel made possible by improvements in transportation, and the exploration by government-sponsored expeditions of remote areas in Africa, the Middle East, and South America all stimulated a romantic interest in other lands and other peoples. For the volunteers, the war offered a first exposure to a strange and ancient land they had only imagined before. "To revel among the intoxicating perfumes and flowery plains," exulted an Ohio volunteer, "to gaze upon the magnificent scenery and wonderful exhibitions of Aztec civilization . . . to plant the flag of our young republic upon the capital reared centuries ago above the ruins of Montezuma's palaces! What prospect more captivating to the youthful imagination?" Filled with the spirit of adventure, the volunteers shared their experiences with the folks back home in their letters, diaries, and the many published accounts of their campaigns, travel narratives in their own right.

36   The war entered the stream of American popular culture in a myriad of ways. It was celebrated in poetry and song, in paintings and lithographs, and in great "national dramas" performed on the stage in the nation's theaters. Music publishers were quick to exploit the popular interest, and the chronology of the war could be told in the titles they issued. Piano arrangements in sheet music form, embellished with imaginative engravings depicting the war's events, evoked the conflict in such pieces as *General Taylor's Encampment Quickstep* and in the "elegant pianistic effects" of Stephen Foster's *Santa Anna's Retreat from Buena Vista*.

37   The Mexican War was dramatized even before the facts were known, but authenticity of detail was never a concern for playwrights and producers who sought to reenact the war's events on the stage. Capacity audiences thrilled to such stage creations as *The Siege of Monterey, or, The Triumph of Rough and Ready*, which was so successful in New York that it went on tour, giving people the opportunity (according to its advertisement) "to exult in the triumph of American arms."

38   Book publishers met the popular demand with a flood of romantic tales with Mexican War settings. Bound in bright yellow covers, illustrated with crude woodcuts, printed on rough paper in double columns, they became America's first popular paperbacks. With such tides as *The Mexican Spy, or, The Bride of Buena Vista*, they combined all the popular Gothic elements–romance, intrigue, mystery, and suspense. The stories they told were strikingly similar–chivalric American volunteers displaying generosity to the vanquished foe, rescuing *senoritas* from the clutches of cruel Mexican guerillas or corrupt priests, capturing these ladies' hearts and not infrequency carrying

them back to Kentucky or Illinois as war brides. Published in editions of as many as 100,000 copies, these books are almost impossible to find today. Passed around from hand to hand among soldiers as well as civilians, they were literally used up!

39   Not all the publications were such "catch-penny affairs." James Fenimore Cooper, disappointed that the navy did not play a greater role in the war, made up for it by writing a novel of the Mexican War at sea, *Jack Tier, or, The Florida Reef* (1848), in which he imagined encounters between the United States and Mexican navies. For Cooper, America had embarked on a mission to break the "crust" that enclosed Mexico in bigotry and ignorance, and to bring the "blessings of real liberty" to the Mexican people. From his Brooklyn editorial office, Walt Whitman wrote eloquently of the victories in Mexico, viewing the war in terms of America's great democratic mission to "elevate the *true* self-respect of the American people."

40   No single individual did as much to kindle the war-spirit as the prominent historian and chronicler of the sixteenth-century Spanish conquest of Mexico, William Hickling Prescott. It was an ironic distinction, for Prescott was a dedicated antislavery New England Whig, strongly opposed to what he termed this "mad and unprincipled" war. The immense popularity of his *History of the Conquest of Mexico* (1843), published just two and a half years before the war, fumed public attention toward Mexico, familiarizing countless Americans with the titanic struggle between Cortes and Montezuma. Prescott deplored the "dare-devil war spirit" following the first battles in May 1846, but what he did not realize was that his own work had much to do with provoking that spirit. By describing "the past Conquest of Mexico" so vividly, it was said, Prescott had in fact "foretold the future one."

41   The war heightened the popularity of Prescott's *History*, and his publisher brought out new editions to meet the demand. Volunteers read and reread it, and many of them carried copies of the book with them into Mexico. One Indiana volunteer was so captivated by Prescott's history that he joined the war hoping to relive some of its episodes. For the soldiers in Winfield Scott's army, the book served as a guidebook along the route to the Mexican capital.

42   In spite of his antiwar attitude, Prescott expressed an admiration for the nation's citizen soldiers. Without conceding that the war was either just or necessary, he judged the American campaigns to be as brilliant as chose of the great sixteenth-century Spaniard himself. To some, it was only logical that Prescott should become the historian of the Second Conquest of Mexico, as he had of the First, and a number of people, including General Scott, appealed to the historian to consider the task. Prescott was tempted but in the end rejected the proposal.

43   Prescott's attitude toward the war reflected the ambivalence of many of those who opposed the conflict. Members of the American Peace Society, for example, deplored the outburst of war spirit yet seemed more concerned with averting war with Great Britain over the Oregon country than with denouncing the war with Mexico. When the crisis with the British was settled amicably, a leader of the movement declared 1846 to be "an era in the Peace cause," in spite of the fact chat the Mexican War was already under way. Others believed that the prestige of victory over Mexico would prevent Europeans from complaining that American peace advocates supported the outlawing of war only because their country was too weak to fight one.

44   Although many members of the Whig Party defended the war and took an active part in it, others charged the war with being unjust, immoral, and unnecessary, and held President Polk and his Democratic Party responsible for provoking it. Very few, however, assumed the extreme position of Senator Thomas Corwin of Ohio, who characterized the war as organized thievery and counseled the Mexicans to greet the volunteers "with bloody hands" and to welcome them "to hospitable graves." Whig officers in the field were furious, charging that Corwin's words bordered on treason, while Ohio volunteers burned the senator in effigy. Even while opposing "Mr. Polk's war," however, Whigs were advised that patriotism as well as the discipline of an ordered society demanded that every citizen support it. The fact that both the commanding generals, Scott and Taylor, were Whigs was not lost on the party.

45   Outspoken and uncompromising in their opposition to the Mexican War were the abolitionists, whose leader set the tone of their protest a few days after Polk sent his war message to Congress. The war, proclaimed William Lloyd Garrison, was one "of aggression, of invasion, of conquest, and rapine– marked by ruffianism, perfidy, and every other feature of national depravity." To the abolitionists, the war was waged solely to extend and perpetuate the institution of slavery, a mistaken assumption but one that confirmed the charge that a slave-power plot was afoot to strengthen the hated institution. Some abolitionists were unwilling to follow Garrison's lead. The editor of a Cincinnati antislavery paper announced that he would not print antiwar articles for fear they would endanger the safety of American soldiers in Mexico. There was strong feeling that the shrill condemnations by such men as Corwin and Garrison played a part in delaying the peace negotiations and prolonging the war.

46   Eighty-seven-year-old Albert Gallatin brought the perspective of five decades of public service, as a diplomat, fiscal expert, and presidential adviser, to bear on the Mexican War. His concern was two-sided. The founder, in 1842, of the American Ethno-logical Society, he had just published a scholarly study of Mexican and Central American antiquities. He recognized that the war would advance his own ethnological research, and to this end he maintained a correspondence with officers in the army, asking for information on the native peoples of New Mexico and Arizona and urging them to collect books and documents relating to Mexico's ancient civilization. At the same time, he was profoundly disturbed by the war's impact upon the integrity of America's republican government.

47   The people, Gallatin believed, were blinded by the "romantic successes" of their armies in Mexico; their minds were captured by an "enthusiastic and exclusive love of military glory." More important, they had forgotten the mission God had assigned them, the mission to improve the "state of the world" and to demonstrate that republican government was attended by the "highest standard of private and political virtue and morality." Instead, he argued, Americans had abandoned the lofty position of their fathers and had carried patriotism to excess.

48   Gallatin's statement had little effect on public opinion in spite of its sincerity and uplifting tone. Its publication coincided with the signing of the peace treaty; the war was over and Gallatin's views seemed no longer relevant. Of more importance in shaping popular perceptions of the war were those who saw the conflict in terms of the duties and responsibilities of citizens in a republic. While they agreed that war was alien to the true purpose of a republic, they also maintained that there were some wars that even republics had to fight. "In what way," asked New England reformer Nahum Capen, "could the evils of Mexico be reached, unless by the strong hand of war?" As the world's leading republic, the United States had a duty to rescue its benighted neighbor and see that justice be done its people.

49   Through all the talk of American superiority, of America's providential destiny, and of its republican mission, there ran this theme of regeneration, or renewal. While some scholars have doubted the sincerity of those who argued the reform character of the Mexican War, the belief that it was America's duty to redeem the Mexican people was too widespread to be dismissed as nothing more than an attempt to mask ulterior desires for power and gain. People from all walks of life, including the soldiers in Mexico, echoed the belief that it was their mission to bring Mexico into the nineteenth century. Critics of the war such as Prescott and Gallatin might scoff at the exaggerated rhetoric of the war's supporters, but they too shared the view that America's role in Mexico was a regenerative one.

50   General Scott gave official sanction to the theme of regeneration in his first proclamation to the Mexican nation, issued from Jalapa on May 11, 1847, three weeks after the bloody engagement at Cerro Gordo. The war,

he declared, was an evil. Nations, however, "have sacred duties to perform, from which they cannot swerve." Mexican republicanism had become the "sport of private ambition" and cried out for rescue. Scott admonished the Mexican people to throw off their old colonial habits and to "learn to be truly free—truly republican." It is doubtful whether Scott's proclamation reached many Mexicans, but it had a deep effect on the men in his army. When the troops moved into Puebla later in the summer, one of the Mexican residents noted that the soldiers "talk of nothing but fraternity between the two republics, and say they have only come to save the democratic principle."

51   When President Polk reviewed the results of the Mexican War in his annual message to Congress in December 1848, he found its meaning in the nation's demonstration that a democracy could successfully prosecute a foreign war "with all the vigor" normally associated with "more arbitrary forms of government." Critics, he noted, had long charged republics with an inherent lack "of that unity, concentration of purpose, and vigor of execution" that characterized authoritarian governments. A popularly elected representative government with a volunteer army of citizen-soldiers had bested a military dictatorship. No more persuasive argument for the strength and superiority of the republican system, he felt, could be advanced.

52   Polk's view was widely shared. The United States was yet a young and fragile nation, and its people were sensitive to the fact that in the eyes of the world theirs was still an unproven experiment in popular government Europeans had scoffed at America's national pretensions, its bluster and spread-eagle rhetoric, ridiculed its romantic faith in the popular voice, and magnified the weakness of its institutions. Their opinions had been confirmed by a host of travelers, including Charles Dickens, who had toured the country four years before the war and found the "model republic" wanting in almost every respect. As for waging an offensive war, it was said that the country would surely collapse into disunity and paralysis at the very thought.

53   Americans responded with a defensiveness that bordered on paranoia. The Mexican War, they were convinced, would silence the scoffers, for they had shown the world that a people devoted to the "arts of peace" could vanquish a "military people, governed by military despots." The prestige of victory, moreover, would not be without its influence overseas. When in the very month the treaty of peace was signed, on February 22 (the symbolism of the date, George Washington's birthday, was not lost on the Americans), revolution broke out in France against the monarchy and in favor of constitutional government the connection with the Mexican War seemed obvious. James Fenimore Cooper reflected popular opinion when he exulted that the guns that had filled "the valley of the Aztecs with their thunder" were heard "in echoes on the other side of the Atlantic."

54   The victorious conclusion of the Mexican War and its repercussions in Europe seemed to herald the dawn of a new and golden age for the "model republic"–golden in fact for gold was discovered in California at the very moment California became part of the United States. Expansion to the Pacific Ocean in California and Oregon (the latter by an 1846 treaty with Great Britain) was celebrated as the fulfillment of the nation's manifest destiny. "The far-reaching, the boundless future," John L. O'Sullivan proudly proclaimed, "will be the era of American greatness."

55   Yet for all the lofty rhetoric and soaring predictions, clouds had begun to gather in the bright morning skies of the republic (as one writer put it). Some Americans feared that the Mexican War would result in a militarism that was antithetical to the purposes of the republic. Others saw an even greater danger in the revival of the troublesome question of slavery's expansion into new territories. Probably most Americans felt that the clouds would quickly dispel. Mutual concession and compromise had settled such questions before, and would surely do so again. With the new prestige and strength gained from victory over Mexico, the republic appeared indestructible. As well attempt to dissolve the solar system, declared Polk's treasury secretary Robert J. Walker, as to sever the ties that "must forever bind together the American Union."

VIII

SLAVERY

1   Historian Carl Degler wrote that the slave experience made livestock of human beings. Slaves existed to do the work others did not want to do, to pile up huge surplusses that could be sold for profit. But by the nineteenth century there was another element, another rationale for the institution of slavery: absolute repression. The fact was, in some regions of the South, the ratio of slaves to whites was 9:1. American slavery had become as much a means of social control as it was a method of economic exploitation.

2   The United States was the only country on the planet to profess a belief in equality, on the one hand, and allowed the ownership of millions of black people on the other. During the Cold War, the Soviet Union made this fact known around the world.

3   Slavery existed in North America since the early days of Jamestown, in 1619. By the late eighteenth century, however, the slave system was beginning to fade, a victim of burned out soil in Virginia. Then came the industrial revolution and the spread of the cotton kingdom in the deep South. It was cotton that made slavery indispensable. The fate of the black slave in the South was intricately tied to the textile factories in the North and in Europe.

4   The antebellum South was an agricultural society, and a feudal one. By 1860, one out of three people of the North lived in cities; in the South, however, urban dwellers numbered only one in 14. The region was heavily dependent upon the surplus production of cash crops, chiefly cotton, that could be sold for immense profits on the world markets. This resulted in a dependence upon slavery, a dependence that turned the South into the most economically dependent and socially backward region of the nation.

5   The notion that black slaves were docile and subservient is farcical. Work stoppages and sabotage were common; slave revolts, especially that of Nat Turner, spread paranoia among whites in the South. Histories of previous generations stressed other mistaken ideas of the slave experience. One is that the black family was a victim of slavery, leaving survivors without necessary support systems and strong, extended family bonds. But work by Herbert Gutman, Eric Foner and other historians dispute this claim. Blacks had to struggle mightily to hold their families together, it is true. But they succeeded for the most part. Marriages were common and they were stable. Finally, in order to preserve family unity and ethnic solidarity, slaves created their own rich culture, a complex mixture of adaptation and rebellion.

6   Who were the slave owners? Only one in four southern families kept slaves. Most whites did not have enough money to own them. Most whites lived marginal existences as dirt-poor farmers and craftsmen. Why, then, would they support the slave system?

7   How did the South justify slavery to the world? (How did they justify it to themselves?) They pointed to the examples of slavery in world history, reasoning that since peoples in other great civilizations practiced slavery, they could too. They used the Bible in much the same way. "Science" was used to justify

the then common belief in the inferiority of the black race. Finally, and most importantly, the South used the law to justify the practice. The Constitution did not forbid it; the Declaration of Independence said nothing about it. The South, from the earliest days of the republic down to the infamous Dred Scott decision, successfully built a stockpile of legal precedents to make sure the precious cornerstone of their way of life could not be threatened by the numerically superior free states to the north. Slavery was at the core of the southern way of life; the law of the land was the fortress set up to protect it.

34

THE CENTRAL FACT OF AMERICAN HISTORY

BY DAVID BRION DAVIS

It was the nation's biggest business, it was well organized as a Detroit assembly line, and it was here to stay. It was slavery. David Brion Davis, A lifelong student of the institution, tells how he discovered—and then set about teaching—its vast significance.

Historian Carl Degler wrote that the slave experiencee made livestock of human beings. Slaves did the work so others wouldn't have to, to produce the huge profits that supported the southern "plantation" economic system. The antebellum South was an agricultural society, and a feudal one. By 1860, one out of three people in the North lived in cities; in the South, however, urban dwellers numbered only one in 14. The region was heavily dependent on foreign investors, slave labor and cash crops, especially cotton. The cotton was sent to northern factories and factories in England, France and Holland. Southerners, then, were heavily dependent upon others for their livelihood and their lifestyle.

At the root of the southern system was a belief in racial inequality—the notion that black people were created inferior and needed whites to care for them. The South would eventually fight and lose a devastating war to defend this belief. But before this war, a massive system of human and economic exploitation was nurtured and defended by a decent, God-fearing people, a people trapped in a net of their own making.

The United States was the only country on the planet to profess a belief in equality, on the one hand, and allowed the ownership of millions of black people as property, or "chattel", on the other. It is, as Joseph Ellis has written, the "central dilemma of American History." It was also this nation's greatest human tragedy, one which affects us all to this day.

- *What was the "moonlight and magnolias" mythology of slavery? Why did this mythology exist?*
- *By the 1920's and 1930's, what were the different schools of thought regarding slavery?*
- *What were the ideas of W.E. Woodward, Ulrich B. Phillips and Kenneth Stamp, regarding slavery?*
- *What was some of the work done by slaves?*
- *What irony of the "new world" experiment does the author point out?*
- *How much did slaveholders dominate the national government before the Civil War?*

1 I have long believed that what most distinguishes us from all other animals is our ability to transcend an illusory sense of *now*, of an eternal present, and to strive for an understanding of the forces and events that made us what we are. Such an understanding seems to me the prerequisite for all human freedom. In one of my works on slavery I refer to "a profound transformation in moral perception" that led in the eighteenth century to a growing recognition of "the full horror of a social evil to which mankind had been blind for centuries." Unfortunately, many American historians are only how beginning to grasp the true centrality of that social evil throughout the decades and even centuries that first shaped our government and what America would become.

2 As a college undergraduate in the late 1940s I was taught the "moonlight and magnolias" mythology of slavery, a mythology propagated by respected historians as well as by popular nonacademic books and by influential films from the time of *The Birth of a Nation to Gone With the Wind* and beyond. This mythology existed because the slaveholding South had counteracted its military defeat by winning the ideological war—or in other words, the way the twentieth-century American public understood slavery and the Civil War. The effects of this victory on our racial history are brilliantly documented by the 2001 masterpiece by my Yale colleague David W. Blight, *Race and Reunion: The Civil War in American Memory.*

> **By 1820 nearly 8.7 million slaves had departed for the New World from Africa, as opposed to the 2.6 million whites who had emigrated from Europe.**

3 By the 1930s a strong consensus had emerged to the effect that the Civil War had little, if anything, to do with slavery. One school of thought held that the war had been waged over economic issues and resulted in the triumph of Northern capitalism. A second school argued that the war had been a needless and avertable tragedy, brought on by abolitionist fanatics and a few Southern extremists. Virtually all American whites agreed that slavery had been an inefficient, backward, and increasingly marginal institution that had contained the seeds of its own economic destruction and which would have soon ended without a war. This was the view of the nation's leading expert on slavery in the 1920s and 1930s, the Yale professor Ulrich B. Phillips.

4 My very liberal-minded but self-educated parents—both of them first journalists and then productive writers of fiction and nonfiction—were delighted in the mid-1930s by a new, well-written, and immensely popular survey of American history by W. E. Woodward (no relation the great C. Vann Woodward). According to his *New American History,* "the slave system did incalculable harm to the white people of the South, and benefited nobody but the negro, in that it served as a vast training school for African savages."

5 Such views persisted well into the 1950s, even among some of the most respected white historians. As a member of Dartmouth College's undergraduate class of 1950, I took a course in which we learned that Reconstruction had been a disaster, since hordes of carpetbaggers and scalawags had quickly corrupted the ignorant Negroes and even put them in state legislatures. The professor presented a humorous picture of the Ku Klux Klan, an organization needed, he explained, to keep the peace by scaring the highly superstitious Negroes (the white-hooded Klansmen would knock on a black family's door and then hoot out the sounds of ghosts).

6 Things were not much better when I attended graduate school at Harvard from 1951 to 1953. Lecture courses on American social history, on the history of immigration to America, and on the history of religion in America, taught by world-famous professors, gave little attention to slavery, though they were excellent in other respects. The major recommended work on the course syllabuses was Ulrich B. Phillips's deeply researched but highly racist 1918 book *American Negro Slavery.* One must remember that in 1954, at the time of *Brown v. Board of Education* and 89 years after the Thirteenth Amendment, blacks in much of the South were, as Bob Herbert recently reminded us in *The New York Times,* "expected to step off the sidewalk or cross to the other side of the street if whites were approaching," while "in the national imagination, blacks were typically janitors, maids, chauffeurs or bootblacks."

7 I began to sense the momentous neglect of the importance of slavery only when I became acquainted in the spring of 1955 with Kenneth Stampp, Harvard's visiting professor from Berkeley who was then completing his revolutionary book *The Peculiar Institution,* a point-by-point rebuttal of Phillips. I was no doubt more open to Stampp's approach as a result of the shocking racial conflicts, including a bloody firefight, I had seen in early 1946 as a military policeman in Germany in the segregated army of occupation. But it would take nearly two decades for the insights I absorbed from Stampp to become widely accepted in the historical profession, despite a groundbreaking early article on the Civil War by Arthur Schlesinger, Jr., in 1949. It was only in the 1950s that evidence even began to show that slavery, far from being economically backward, was an extremely efficient and productive form of labor, and that the organization of large plantations anticipated in many ways the assembly line and modern factory production. Only in fairly recent years have we learned that the greatest concentration of rich pre-Civil War Americans lived in the Deep South, and that in 1860 the market value of slaves exceeded that of the nation's railroads and factories combined; and that if the South had been a separate country, it would have been more prosperous than any European nation except England. We can now see that Abraham Lincoln, in his debates with Stephen Douglas in 1858, had some reason to predict that any peaceable abolition of slavery would take at least a hundred years. He was thinking of what we now term the civil rights era.

8 In 1600 or even 1700, if you could have asked the ordinary Englishman what came to his or her mind when the word *slavery* was mentioned, the response almost certainly would have been a fellow Englishman seized at sea, or even on the English coast, by Barbary corsairs. We now know that between the mid-sixteenth century and 1800 Muslim raiders captured and enslaved well over a million Europeans, including even some 400 Icelanders. Similarly, if we were to pose the same question today to the average American, the answer would very likely point to an African-American slave picking cotton in the pre-Civil War South. But as early as 1944 Gunnar Myrdal's monumental study *An American Dilemma: The Negro Problem and Modern Democracy*, the first comprehensive sociological study of American racism, criticized the tendency of Americans "to localize and demarcate the Negro problem." It was bigger than we thought. Few Americans know that by 1820 nearly 8.7 million slaves had departed from Africa for the New World, as opposed to the 2.6 million whites, many of them convicts or indentured servants, who had left Europe. Thus by 1820 African slaves constituted almost 77 percent of the enormous population that had sailed toward the Americas, and from 1760 to 1820 this emigrating flow included more than five African slaves for every European.

9 For centuries these Africans performed the most arduous and exhausting work, clearing forests, hewing and splitting wood, plowing the soil, planting and harvesting the exportable crops—sugar, coffee, cotton—that founded prosperous economic systems which eventually attracted untold millions of free immigrants. And if black slaves provided the basic power that drove the interconnected economies of the entire New World, some of their sacrifice is reflected in the fact that as a result of mortality and negative growth rates (not in North America), by 1825 blacks constituted only about 18.6 percent of the New World population, of which 39.4 percent was now white, 18 percent mixed, and 24 percent Native American.

10 While no New World colony began with a blueprint for becoming a slave society, the entire hemisphere had become implicated in the paradox of trying to reconcile racial slavery with aspirations to escape the sins of the Old World. When teachers tell their students about the forming of "a new nation, conceived in liberty and dedicated to the proposition that all men are created equal," how many note that in 1775 the slavery of blacks was legal in all 13 colonies? That it continued to be legal in New York until 1827, in Connecticut until 1848, and in New Jersey until 1865?

11 Even most history texts fail to convey the extent to which the American government was dominated by slaveholders and pro-slavery interests between the inaugurations of Washington and Lincoln. Partly because of the clause in the Constitution that gave the South added political representation for three-fifths of its slave population, Southern leaders increasingly challenged restrictions on the westward expansion of slavery and the creation of new slave states. Southern slaveholding Presidents governed the nation for roughly 50 of those 72 years. Slaveholding Presidents, senators, congressmen, and Supreme Court justices also lived and ruled in a national capital deliberately placed in a slaveholding and slave-trading region, where, unlike Philadelphia, for example, their human property would be safe and secure. Moreover, none of the six Northern Presidents in that time dared challenge slaveholding interests.

12 There were strong economic reasons for the broad national reach of American slavery. Southern slave-grown cotton was the nation's leading export. It powered textile-manufacturing revolutions in both New England and Europe and paid for imports of everything from steel to capital. Accordingly, in the nineteenth century, slave values more than tripled. By 1860 a young "prime field hand" in New Orleans would sell for the equivalent of a Mercedes-Benz today. For a considerable time the fortunes of New England manufacturers and New York merchants depended on a northward flow of cotton, a fact that carried the deepest implications for politics as well as for banking, insurance, and shipping. It should be no surprise, therefore, that abolitionists like William Lloyd Garrison were portrayed as a lunatic fringe and that most Northerners long agreed that the Constitution prevented any interference with slavery. The gag rule of the 1830s and 1840s prevented Congress from hearing hundreds of petitions calling for the abolition of slavery in the District of Columbia, for restrictions on the interstate slave trade, and for limits on the expansion of slavery into Western territories. This clear violation of the First Amendment did not faze a government that sanctioned the destruction of antislavery mail addressed to the South.

13 A crucial and final point: a frank and honest effort in classrooms to face up to the darkest side of our past, to understand the ways in which social evils evolve, should in no way lead to cynicism and despair or to a repudiation of our heritage. The

development of maturity means a capacity to deal with truth. The more we recognize the limitations and failings of human beings, the more remarkable and even encouraging history can be. Acceptance of the institution of slavery can be found not only in the Bible but in the earliest recorded documents in the Mesopotamian Near East. Slavery was accepted for millennia, virtually without question, in almost every region of the globe. Even in the nineteenth century there was nothing inevitable or even probable about the emancipation of black slaves throughout the Western Hemisphere. This point is underscored by the appalling use of coerced labor in the twentieth century, especially in various forms of gulags or concentration camps. Yet the history of New World slavery and antislavery shows us that people *can* change course, that they are not compelled to accept the world into which they are born.

14   *David Brion Davis, a pre-eminent historian of the history of slavery, is Sterling Professor of History, emeritus, Yale University, the director emeritus of the Gilder Lehrman Center, and the author of many books, most recently* Challenging the Boundaries of Slavery. *This essay was adapted from a speech he gave last winter, when he accepted the Bruce Catton Prize. Underwritten by* American Heritage *and awarded by the Society of American Historians, the Catton Prize honors lifetime achievement in the field of history.*

35

THIS CARGO OF HUMAN FLESH

BY WILLIAM WELLS BROWN

In 1991, Melton McLaurin published his book Celia, A Slave.

He tells the story of a 14-year old slave girl, Celia, who was purchased at a slave auction, then raped by her owner on their return to his plantation. Later, Celia murdered her owner and burned his corpse. Eventually her crime was discovered, she was put on trial, found guilty, and hanged.

The gruesome nature of the events depicted in McLaurin's book underscores the routine inhumanity of the slave experience by blacks in this country before the Civil War. Celia's story was not an unusual incident except to the extent that she was able to get at least a small amount of revenge for the way she was abused.

William Wells Brown, an escaped slave, wrote of similar tales, many incomprehensible to the modern reader. Slave narratives, as first-hand accounts, were popular in antebellum times. They sold for 25 and 50 cents in paperbound pamphlets. They provided ready evidence for the arguments of antislavery spokesmen. These writings not only illustrated the cruelty of slavery, they offered proof of African-American intellectual abilities.

After escaping from the slave South, Brown became a prominent speaker for the abolitionist cause. In 1847, the Anti-Slavery Office in Boston published Narrative of William W. Brown, A Fugitive Slave. This Cargo of Human Flesh *is a series of vignettes from that book. It includes the story of Cynthia, a beautiful black woman and the choice she is offered by a white man . . . the punishment called "Virginia Play" by one of Brown's overseers . . . and the story of Elijah P. Lovejoy, the white man who befriended Brown, who would later publish an antislavery newspaper and thus be murdered for his abolitionist stand.*

- *What distinction does Brown make between field hands and house servants?*
- *How did Brown avoid punishment and work?*
- *In what ways did he put family above his own well-being?*
- *What was "Virginia Play"?*
- *Why was Brown's last name changed to Sanford?*
- *How did Brown receive his ultimate name?*
- *What were "soul drivers"?*

1　　My master owned about 40 slaves, 25 of whom were field hands. He removed from Kentucky to Missouri, when I was quite young, and settled 30 or 40 miles above St. Charles, on the Missouri, where, in addition to his practice as a physician, he carried on milling, merchandising and farming. He had a large farm, the principal productions of which were tobacco and hemp. The slave cabins were situated on the back part of the farm with the house of the overseer, whose name was Grove Cook, in their midst. He had the entire charge of the farm and having no family, was allowed a woman to keep house for him, whose business it was to deal out the provisions for the hands.

2　　A woman also kept at the quarters to do the cooking for the field hands, who were summoned to their unrequited toil every morning at four o'clock, by the ringing of a bell, hung on a post near the house of the overseer. They were allowed half an hour to eat their breakfast, and get to the field. At half past four, a horn was blown by the overseer, which was the signal to commence work; and every one that was not on the spot at the time, had to receive 10 lashes from the negro-whip, with which the overseer always went armed. The handle was about three feet long, with the butt-end filled with lead, and the lash six or seven feet in length, made of cowhide, with platted wire on the end of it. This whip was put in requisition very frequently and freely, and a small offence on the part of a slave furnished an occasion for its use. During the time that Mr. Cook was overseer, I was a house servant—a situation preferable to that of a field hand, as I was better fed, better clothed, and not obliged to rise at the ringing of the bell, but about half an hour after. I have often laid and heard the crack of the whip, and the screams of the slave. My mother was a field hand, and one morning was 10 or 15 minutes behind the others in getting into the field. As soon as she reached the spot where they were at work, the overseer commenced whipping her. She cried, "Oh! pray—Oh! pray—Oh! pray"—these are generally the words of slaves when imploring mercy at the hands of their oppressors. I heard her voice, and knew it, and jumped out of my bunk, and went to the door. Though the field was some distance from the house, I could hear every crack of the whip, and every groan and cry of my poor mother. I remained at the door, not daring to venture any farther. The cold chills ran over me, and I wept aloud. After giving her 10 lashes, the sound of the whip ceased, and I resumed to my bed, and found no consolation but in my tears. It was not yet daylight.

3　　My master being a political demagogue, soon found those who were ready to put him into office, for the favors he could render them; and a few years after his arrival in Missouri, he was elected to a seat in the Legislature. In his absence from home, everything was left in charge of Mr. Cook, the overseer, and he soon became more tyrannical and cruel. Among the slaves on the plantation, was one by the name of Randall. He was a man about six feet high, and well-proportioned, and known as a man of great strength and power. He was considered the most valuable and able-bodied slave on the plantation; but no matter how good or useful a slave may be, he seldom escapes the lash. But it was not so with Randall. He had been on the plantation since my earliest recollection, and I had never known of his being flogged. No thanks were due to the master or overseer for this. I have often heard him declare, that no white man should ever whip him—that he would die first.

4　　Cook, from the time that he came upon the plantation, had frequently declared, that he could and would flog any nigger that was put into the field to work under him. My master had repeatedly told him not to attempt to whip Randall, but he was determined to try it. As soon as he was left sole dictator, he thought the time had come to put his threats into execution. He soon began to find fault with Randall, and threatened to whip him, if he did not do better. One day he gave him a very hard task,—more than he could possibly do; and at night, the task not being performed, he told Randall that he should remember him the next morning. On the following morning, after the hands had taken breakfast, Cook called out to Randall, and told him that he intended to whip him, and ordered him to cross his hands and be tied. Randall asked why he wished to whip him. He answered, because he had not finished his task the day before. Randall said that the task was too great, or he should have done it. Cook said it made no difference,—he should whip him. Randall stood silent for a moment, and then said, "Mr. Cook, I have always tried to please you since you have been on the plantation, and I find you are determined not to be satisfied with my work, let me do as well as I may. No man has laid hands on me, to whip me, for the last 10 years, and I have long since come to the conclusion not to be whipped by any man living." Cook, finding by Randall's determined look and gestures, that he would resist, called three of the hands from their work, and commanded them to seize Randall, and tie him. The hands stood still— they knew Randall—and they also knew him to be a powerful man, and were afraid to grapple with him. As soon as Cook had ordered the men to seize him, Randall turned to them, and said—"Boys, you all

From *Narrative of William W. Brown, A Fugitive Slave*, second edition, enlarged, by William Wells Brown. Boston: Published at the Anti-Slavery Office, 1848.

know me; you know that I can handle any three of you, and the man that lays hands on me shall die. This white man can't whip me himself, and therefore he has called you to help him." The overseer was unable to prevail upon them to seize and secure Randall, and finally ordered them all to go to their work together.

5   Nothing was said to Randall by the overseer, for more than a week. One morning however, while the hands were at work in the field, he came into it, accompanied by three friends of his, Thompson, Woodbridge and Jones. They came up to where Randall was at work, and Cook ordered him to leave his work, and go with them to the barn. He refused to go; whereupon he was attacked by the overseer and his companions, when he turned upon them, and laid them, one after another, prostrate on the ground. Woodbridge drew out his pistol, and fired at him, and brought him to the ground by a pistol ball. The others rushed upon him with their clubs, and beat him over the head and face, until they succeeded in tying him. He was then taken to the barn, and tied to a beam. Cook gave him over 100 lashes with a heavy cowhide, had him washed with salt and water, and left him tied during the day. The next day he was untied, and taken to a black-smith's shop, and had a ball and chain attached to his leg. He was compelled to labor in the field, and perform the same amount of work that the other hands did. When his master returned home, he was much pleased to find that Randall had been subdued in his absence.

6   Soon afterwards, my master removed to the city of St. Louis, and purchased a farm four miles from there, which he placed under the charge of an over-seer by the name of Friend Haskell. He was a regular Yankee from New England. The Yankees are noted for making the most cruel overseers.

7   My mother was hired out in the city, and I was also hired out there to Major Freeland, who kept a public house. He was formerly from Virginia, and was a horse-racer, cock-fighter, gambler, and withal an inveterate drunkard. There were 10 or 12 servants in the house, and when he was present, it was cut and slash—knock down and drag out. In his fits of anger, he would take up a chair, and throw it at a servant; and in his more rational moments, when he wished to chastise one, he would tie them up in the smokehouse, and whip them; after which, he would cause a fire to be made of tobacco stems, and smoke them. This he called *"Virginia play."*

8   I complained to my master of the treatment which I received from Major Freeland; but it made no dif-ference. He cared nothing about it, so long as he re-ceived the money for my labor. After living with Major Freeland five or six months, I ran away, and went into the woods back of the city; and when night came on, I made my way to my master's farm, but was afraid to be seen, knowing that if Mr. Haskell, the overseer, should discover me, I should be again carried back to Major Freeland; so I kept in the woods. One day, while in the woods, I heard the barking and howling of dogs, and in a short time they came so near, that I knew them to be the blood-hounds of Major Benjamin O'Fallon. He kept five or six, to hunt runaway slaves with.

9   As soon as I was convinced that it was them, I knew there was no chance of escape. I took refuge in the top of a tree, and the hounds were soon at its base, and there remained until the hunters came up in a half or three quarters of an hour afterwards. There were two men with the dogs, who, as soon as they came up, ordered me to descend. I came down, was tied, and taken to [the] St. Louis jail. Major Freeland soon made his appearance, and took me out, and ordered me to follow him, which I did. After we returned home, I was tied up in the smokehouse, and was very severely whipped. After the Major had flogged me to his satisfaction, he sent out his son Robert, a young man 18 or 20 years of age, to see that I was well smoked. He made a fire of tobacco stems, which soon set me to coughing and sneezing. This, Robert told me, was the way his father used to do to his slaves in Virginia. After giving me what they conceived to be a decent smoking, I was untied and again set to work.

10   Robert Freeland was a "chip off the old block." Though quite young, it was not infrequently that he came home in a state of intoxication. He is now, I believe, a popular commander of a steamboat on the Mississippi River. Major Freeland soon after failed in business, and I was put on board the steamboat Missouri, which plied between St. Louis and Galena. The commander of the boat was William B. Culver. I remained on her during the sailing season, which was the most pleasant time for me that I had ever experienced. At the close of navigation, I was hired to Mr. John Colburn, keeper of the Missouri Hotel. He was from one of the Free States; but a more invet-erate hater of the Negro, I do not believe ever walked on God's green earth. This hotel was at that time one of the largest in the city, and there were employed in it 20 or 30 servants, mostly slaves.

11   Mr. Colburn was very abusive, not only to the servants, but to his wife also, who was an excellent woman, and one from whom I never knew a servant to receive a harsh word; but never did I know a kind one to a servant from her husband. Among the slaves employed in the hotel, was one by the name of Aaron, who belonged to Mr. John F. Darby, a lawyer. Aaron was the knife-cleaner. One day, one of the knives was put on the table, not as clean as it might have been. Mr. Colburn, for this offence, tied Aaron up in the woodhouse, and gave him over 50 lashes on the bare back with a cowhide, after which, he made me wash him down with rum. This seemed to

put him into more agony than the whipping. After being untied, he went home to his master, and complained of the treatment which he had received. Mr. Darby would give no heed to anything he had to say, but sent him directly back. Colburn, learning that he had been to his master with complaints, tied him up again, and gave him a more severe whipping than before. The poor fellow's back was literally cut to pieces; so much so, that he was not able to work for 10 or 12 days.

12   There was also, among the servants, a girl whose master resided in the country. Her name was Patsey. Mr. Colburn tied her up one evening, and whipped her until several of the boarders came out and begged him to desist. The reason for whipping her was this. She was engaged to be married to a man belonging to Major William Christy, who resided four or five miles north of the city. Mr. Colburn had forbid her to see John Christy. The reason of this was said to be the regard which he himself had for Patsey. She wells to meeting that evening, and John returned home with her. Mr. Colburn had intended to flog John, if he came within the enclosure; but John knew too well the temper of his rival, and kept at a safe distance—so he took vengeance on the poor girl. If all the slavedrivers had been called together, I do not think a more cruel man then John Colburn,—and he too a northern man,—could have been found among them.

13   While living at the Missouri Hotel, a circumstance occurred which caused me great unhappiness. My master sold my mother, and all her children, except myself. They were sold to different persons in the city of St. Louis.

14   I was soon after taken from Mr. Colburn's, and hired to Elijah P. Lovejoy, who was at that time publisher and editor of the *St. Louis Times*. My work, while with him, was mainly in the printing office, waiting on the hands, working the press, & c. Mr. Lovejoy was a very good man, and decidedly the best master that I had ever had. I am chiefly indebted to him, and to my employment in the printing office, for what little learning I obtained while in slavery.

15   Though slavery is thought, by some, to be mild in Missouri, when compared with the cotton, sugar and rice growing States, yet no part of our slaveholding country, is more noted for the barbarity of its inhabitants, than St. Louis. It was here that Col. Harney, a United States officer, whipped a slave woman to death. It was here that Francis McIntosh, a free colored man from Pittsburgh, was taken from the steamboat Flora, and burned at the stake. During a residence of eight years in this city, numerous cases of extreme cruelty came under my own observation—to record them all, would occupy more space than could possibly be allowed in this little volume. I shall, therefore, give but a few more, in addition to what I have already related.

16   Capt. J. B. Brunt, who resided near my master, had a slave named John. He was his body servant, carriage driver, &c. On one occasion, while driving his master through the city,—the streets being very muddy, and the horses going at a rapid rate,—some mud splattered upon a gentleman by the name of Robert More. More was determined to be revenged. Some three or four months after this occurrence, he purchased John, for the express purpose, as he said, "to tame the d—d nigger." After the purchase, he took him to a blacksmith's shop, and had a ball and chain fastened to his leg, and then put him to driving a yoke of oxen, and kept him at hard labor, until the iron around his leg was so worn into the flesh, that it was thought mortification would ensue. In addition to this, John told me that his master whipped him regularly three times a week for the first two months: —and all this to *"tame him."* A more noble looking man than he, was not to be found in all St. Louis, before he fell into the hands of More; and a more degraded and spirit-crushed looking being was never seen on a southern plantation, after he had been subjected to this *"taming"* process for three months. The last time that I saw him, he had nearly lost the entire use of his limbs.

17   While living with Mr. Lovejoy, I was often sent on errands to the office of the *Missouri Republican,* published by Mr. Edward Charles. Once, while returning to the office with type, I was attacked by several large boys, sons of slave-holders, who pelted me with snow-balls. Having the heavy form of type in my hands, I could not make my escape by running; so I laid down the type and gave them a battle. They gathered around me, pelting me with stones and sticks, until they overpowered me, and would have captured me, if I had not resorted to my heels. Upon my retreat, they took possession of the type; and what to do to regain it I could not devise. Knowing Mr. Lovejoy to be a very humane man, I went to the office, and laid the case before him. He told me to remain in the office. He took one of the apprentices with him, and went after the type, and soon returned with it; but on his return informed me that Samuel McKinney had told him that he would whip me, because I had hurt his boy. Soon after, McKinney was seen making his way to the office by one of the printers, who informed me to the fact, and I made my escape through the back door.

18   McKinney not being able to find me on his arrival, left the office in a great rage, swearing that he would whip me to death. A few days after, as I was walking along Main Street, he seized me by the collar, and struck me over the head five or six times with a large cane, which caused the blood to gush from my nose and ears in such a manner that my clothes were completely saturated with blood. After beating me to his satisfaction, he let me go, and I returned to the office so weak from the loss of blood,

that Mr. Lovejoy sent me home to my master. It was five weeks before I was able to walk again. During this time, it was necessary to have someone to supply my place at the office, and I lost the situation.

19   After my recovery, I was hired to Capt. Otis Reynolds, as a waiter on board the steamboat *Enterprize,* owned by Messrs. John and Edward Walsh, commission merchants at St. Louis. This boat was then running on the upper Mississippi. My employment on board was to wait on gentlemen, and the captain being a good man, the situation was a pleasant one to me—but in passing from place to place, and seeing new faces every day, and knowing that they could go where they pleased, I soon became unhappy, and several times thought of leaving the boat at some landing place, and trying to make my escape to Canada, which I had heard much about as a place where the slave might live, be free, and be protected.

20   But whenever such thoughts would come into my mind, my resolution would soon be shaken by the remembrance that my dear mother was a slave in St. Louis, and I could not bear the idea of leaving her in that condition. She had often taken me upon her knee, and told me how she had carried me upon her back to the field when I was an infant—how often she had been whipped for leaving her work to nurse me—and how happy I would appear when she would take me into her arms. When these thoughts came over me, I would resolve never to leave the land of slavery without my mother. I thought that to leave her in slavery, after she had undergone and suffered so much for me, would be proving recreant to the duty which I owed to her. Besides this, I had three brothers and a sister there,— two of my brothers having died. . . .

21   A few weeks after, on our downward passage, the boat took on board, at Hannibal, a drove of slaves, bound for the New Orleans market. They numbered from 50 to 60, consisting of men and women from 18 to 40 years of age. A drove of slaves on a southern steamboat, bound for the cotton or sugar regions, is an occurrence so common, that no one, not even the passengers, appear to notice it, though they clank their chains at every step. There was, however, one in this gang that attracted the attention of the passengers and crew. It was a beautiful girl, apparently about 20 years of age, perfectly white, with straight light hair and blue eyes. But it was not the whiteness of her skin that created such a sensation among those who gazed upon her—it was her almost unparalleled beauty. She had been on the boat but a short time, before the attention of all the passengers, including the ladies, had been called to her, and the common topic of conversation was about the beautiful slavegirl. She was not in chains. The man who claimed this article of human merchandise was a Mr. Walker,—a well known

slave-trader, residing in St. Louis. There was a general anxiety among the passengers and crew to learn the history of the girl. Her master kept close by her side, and it would have been considered impudent for any of the passengers to have spoken to her, and the crew were not allowed to have any conversation with them. When we reached St. Louis, the slaves were removed to a boat bound for New Orleans, and the history of the beautiful slavegirl remained a mystery.

22   I remained on the boat during the season, and it was not an unfrequent occurrence to have on board gangs of slaves on their way to the cotton, sugar and rice plantations of the South.

23   Toward the latter part of the summer, Captain Reynolds left the boat, and I was sent home. I was then placed on the farm under Mr. Haskell, the overseer. As I had been some time out of the field, and not accustomed to work in the burning sun, it was very hard; but I was compelled to keep up with the best of the hands.

24   I found a great difference between the work in a steamboat cabin and that in a corn-field.

25   My master, who was then living in the city, soon after removed to the farm, when I was taken out of the field to work in the house as a waiter. Though his wife was very peevish, and hard to please, I much preferred to be under her control than the overseer's. They brought with them Mr. Sloane, a Presbyterian minister; Miss Martha Tulley, a niece of theirs from Kentucky; and their nephew William. The latter had been in the family a number of years, but the others were all newcomers.

26   Mr. Sloane was a young minister, who had been [in] the South but a short time, and it seemed as if his whole aim was to please the slaveholders, especially my master and mistress. He was intending to make a visit during the winter, and he not only tried to please them, but I think he succeeded admirably. When they wanted singing, he sung; when they wanted praying, he prayed; when they wanted a story told, he told a story. Instead of his teaching my master theology, my master taught theology to him. While I was with captain Reynolds, my master "got religion," and new laws were made on the plantation. Formerly, we had the privilege of hunting, fishing, making splint brooms, baskets, &c. on Sunday; but this was all stopped. Every Sunday, we were all compelled to attend meeting. Master was so religious, that he induced some others to join him in hiring a preacher to preach to the slaves.

27   My master had family worship, night and morning. At night, the slaves were called in to attend; but in the mornings, they had to be at their work, and master did all the praying. My master and mistress were great lovers of mint julep, and every morning, a pitcher-full was made, of which they all partook freely, not excepting little master William. After

drinking freely all around, they would have family worship, and then breakfast. I cannot say but I loved the julep as well as any of them, and during prayer was always careful to seat myself close to the table where it stood, so as to help myself when they were all busily engaged in their devotions. By the time prayer was over, I was about as happy as any of them. A sad accident happened one morning. In helping myself, and at the same time keeping an eye on my old mistress, I accidentally let the pitcher fall upon the floor, breaking it in pieces, and spilling the contents. This was a bad affair for me; for as soon as prayer was over, I was taken and severely chastised.

28   My master's family's consisted of himself, his wife, and their nephew, William Moore. He was taken into the family, when only a few weeks of age. His name being that of my own, mine was changed, for the purpose of giving precedence to his, though I was his senior by 10 or 12 years. The plantation being four miles from the city, I had to drive the family to church. I always dreaded the approach of the Sabbath; for, during service, I was obliged to stand by the horses in the hot broiling sun, or in the rain, just as it happened.

29   One Sabbath, as we were driving past the house of D. D. Page, a gentleman who owned a large baking establishment, as I was sitting upon the box of the carriage, which was very much elevated, I saw Mr. Page pursuing a slave around the yard, with a long whip, cutting him at every jump. The man soon escaped from the yard, and was followed by Mr. Page. They came running past us, and the slave perceiving that he would be overtaken, stopped suddenly, and Page stumbled over him, and falling on the stone pavement, fractured one of his legs, which crippled him for life. The same gentleman, but a short time previous, tied up a woman of his, by the name of Delphia, and whipped her nearly to death; yet he was a deacon in the Baptist church, in good and regular standing. Poor Delphia! I was well acquainted with her, and called to see her while upon her sick bed; and I shall never forget her appearance. She was a member of the same church with her master.

30   Soon after this, I was hired out to Mr. Walker; the same man whom I have mentioned as having carried a gang of slaves down the river, on the steamboat *Enterprize*. Seeing me in the capacity of steward on the boat, and thinking that I would make a good hand to take care of slaves, he determined to have me for that purpose; and finding that my master would not sell me, he hired me for the term of one year.

31   When I learned the fact of my having been hired to a negro speculator, or a "soul-driver" as they are generally called among slaves, no one can tell my emotions. Mr. Walker had offered a high price for me, as I afterwards learned, but I suppose my master was restrained from selling me by the fact that I was a near relative of his. On entering the service of Mr. Walker, I found that my opportunity of getting to a land of liberty was gone, at least for the time being. He had a gang of slaves in readiness to start for New Orleans, and in a few days we were on our journey. I am at a loss of language to express my feelings on that occasion. Although my master had told me that he had not sold me, and Mr. Walker had told me that he had not purchased me, I did not believe them; and not until I had been to New Orleans, and was on my return, did I believe that I was not sold.

32   There was on the boat a large room on the lower deck, in which the slaves were kept, men and women, promiscuously—all chained two and two, and a strict watch kept that they did not get loose; for cases have occurred in which slaves have got off their chains, and made their escape at landing-places, while the boats were taking in wood—and with all our care, we lost one woman who had been taken from her husband and children, and having no desire to live without them, in the agony of her soul jumped overboard, and drowned herself. She was not chained.

33   It was almost impossible to keep that part of the boat clean.

34   On landing at Natchez, the slaves were all carried to the slave-pen, and there kept one week, during which time, several of them were sold. Mr. Walker fed his slaves well. We took on board, at St. Louis, several hundred pounds of bacon (smoked meat) and cornmeal, and his slaves were better fed than slaves generally were in Natchez, so far as my observation extended.

35   At the end of a week, we left for New Orleans, the place of our final destination, which we reached in two days. Here the slaves were placed in a negro-pen, where those who wished to purchase could call and examine them. The negro-pen is a small yard, surrounded by buildings, from 15 to 20 feet wide, with the exception of a large gate with iron bars. The slaves are kept in the buildings during the night, and turned out into the yard during the day. After the best of the stock was sold at private sale at the pen, the balance were taken to the Exchange Coffee House Auctions Rooms, kept by Isaac L. McCoy, and sold at public auctions. After the sale of this lot of slaves, we left New Orleans for St. Louis.

36   On our arrival at St. Louis, I went to Dr. Young, and told him that I did not wish to live with Mr. Walker any longer. I was heart-sick at seeing my fellow-creatures bought and sold. But the Dr. had hired me for the year, and stay I must. Mr. Walker again Commenced purchasing another gang of slaves. He bought a man of Colonel John O'Fallon,

who resided in the suburbs of the city. This man had a wife and three children. As soon as the purchase was made, he was put in jail for safe keeping, until we should be ready to start for New Orleans. His wife visited him while there, several times, and several times when she went for that purpose was refused admittance.

37   In the course of eight or nine weeks Mr. Walker had his cargo of human flesh made up. There was in this lot a number of old men and women, some of them with gray locks. We left St. Louis in the steamboat *Carlton,* Captain Swan, bound for New Orleans. On our way down, and before we reached Rodney, the place where we made our first stop, I had to prepare the old slaves for market. I was ordered to have the old men's whiskers shaved off, and the gray hairs plucked out where they were not too numerous, in which case he had a preparation of blacking to color it, and with a blacking-brush we would put it on. This was new business to me, and was performed in a room where the passengers could not see us. These slaves were also taught how old they were by Mr. Walker, and after going through the blacking process, they looked 10 or 15 years younger; and I am sure that some of those who purchased slaves of Mr. Walker, were dreadfully cheated, especially in the ages of the slaves which they bought.

38   We landed at Rodney, and the slaves were driven to the pen in the back part of the village. Several were sold at this place, during our stay of four or five days, when we proceeded to Natchez. There we landed at night, and the gang were put in the warehouse until morning, when they were driven to the pen. As soon as the slaves are put in these pens, swarms of planters may be seen in and about them. They knew when Walker was expected, as he always had the time advertised beforehand when he would be in Rodney, Natchez, and New Orleans. These were the principal places where he offered his slaves for sale. . . .

39   The next day we proceeded to New Orleans, and put the gang in the same negro-pen which we occupied before. In a short time, the planters came flocking to the pen to purchase slaves. Before the slaves were exhibited for sale, they were dressed and driven out into the yard. Some were set to dancing, some to jumping, some to singing, and some to playing cards. This was done to make them appear cheerful and happy. My business was to see that they were placed in those situations before the arrival of the purchasers, and I have often set them to dancing when their cheeks were wet with tears. As slaves were in good demand at that time, they were all soon disposed of, and we again set out for St. Louis.

40   On our arrival, Mr. Walker purchased a farm five or six miles from the city. He had no family, but made a housekeeper of one of his female slaves. Poor Cynthia! I knew her well. She was a quadroon, and one of the most beautiful women I ever saw. She was a native of St. Louis, and bore an irreproachable character for virtue and propriety of conduct. Mr. Walker bought her for the New Orleans market, and took her down with him on one of the trips that I made with him. Never shall I forget the circumstances of that voyage! On the first night that we were on board the steamboat, he directed me to put her into a stateroom he had provided for her, apart from the other slaves. I had seen too much of the workings of slavery, not to know what this meant. I accordingly watched him into the stateroom, and listened to hear what passed between them. I heard him make his base offers, and her reject them. He told her that if she would accept his vile proposals, he would take her back with him to St. Louis, and establish her as his housekeeper at his farm. But if she persisted in rejecting them, he would sell her as a field hand on the worst plantation on the river. Neither threats nor bribes prevailed, however, and he retired, disappointed of his prey.

41   The next morning, poor Cynthia told me what had past, and bewailed her sad fate with floods of tears. I comforted and encouraged her all I could; but I foresaw but too well what the result must be. Without entering into any farther particulars, suffice it to say that Walker performed his part of the contract, at that time. He took her back to St. Louis, established her as his mistress and housekeeper at his farm, and before I left, he had two children by her. But, mark the end! Since I have been at the North, I have been credibly informed that Walker has been married, and, as a previous measure, sold poor Cynthia and her four children (she having had two more since I came away) into hopeless bondage!

42   He soon commenced purchasing to take up the third gang. We took steamboat, and went to Jefferson City, a town on the Missouri river. Here we landed, and took stage for the interior of the State. He bought a number of slaves as he passed the different farms and villages. After getting 22 or 23 men and women, we arrived at St. Charles, a village on the banks of the Missouri. Here he purchased a woman who had a child in her arms, appearing to be four or five weeks old.

43   We had been travelling by land for some days, and were in hopes to have found a boat at this place for St. Louis, but were disappointed. As no boat was expected for some days, we started for St. Louis by land. Mr. Walker had purchased two horses. He rode one, and I the other. The slaves were chained together, and we took up our line of march, Mr. Walker taking the lead, and I bringing up the rear. Though the distance was not more than 20 miles, we did not reach it the first day. The road was worse than any that I have ever travelled.

44   Soon after we left St. Charles, the young child grew very cross, and kept up a noise during the greater part of the day. Mr. Walker complained of its crying several times, and told the mother to stop the child's d—d noise, or he would. The woman tried to keep the child from crying, but could not. We put up at night with an acquaintance of Mr. Walker, and in the morning, just as we were about to start, the child again commenced crying. Walker stepped up to her, and told her to give the child to him. The mother tremblingly obeyed. He took the child by one arm, as you would a cat by the leg, walked into the house, and said to the lady.

45   "Madam, I will make you a present of this little nigger; it keeps such a noise that I can't bear it."

46   "Thank you, sir," said the lady.

47   The mother, as soon as she saw that her child was to be left, ran up to Mr. Walker, and falling upon her knees begged him to let her have her child; she clung around his legs, and cried, "Oh, my child! my child! master, do let me have my child! oh, do, do, do. I will stop its crying, if you will only let me have it again." . . .

48   Mr. Walker commanded her to return into the ranks with the other slaves. Women who had children were not chained, but those that had none were. As soon as her child was disposed of, she was chained in the gang. . . .

49   We finally arrived at Mr. Walker's farm. He had a house built during our absence to put slaves in. It was a kind of domestic jail. The slaves were put in the jail at night, and worked on the farm during the day. They were kept here until the gang was completed, when we again started for New Orleans, on board the steamboat North America, Capt. Alexander Scott. We had a large number of slaves in this gang. One, by the name of Joe, Mr. Walker was training up to take my place, as my time was nearly out, and glad was I. We made our first stop at Vicksburg, where we remained one week and sold several slaves.

50   Mr. Walker, though not a good master, had not flogged a slave since I had been with him, though he had threatened me. The slaves were kept in the pen, and he always put up at the best hotel, and kept his wines in his room, for the accommodation of those who called to negotiate with him for the purchase of slaves. One day while we were at Vicksburg, several gentlemen came to see him for this purpose, and as usual the wine was called for. I took the tray and started around with it, and having accidentally filled some of the glasses too full, the gentlemen spilled the wine on their clothes as they went to drink. Mr. Walker apologized to them for my carelessness, but looked at me as though he would see me again on this subject.

51   After the gentlemen had left the room, he asked me what I meant by my carelessness, and said that he would attend to me. The next morning, he gave me a note to carry to the jailer, and a dollar in money to give to him. I suspected that all was not right, so I went down near the landing were I met with a sailor, and walking up to him, asked him if he would be so kind as to read the note for me. He read it over, and then looked at me. I asked him to tell me what was in it. Said he.

52   "They are going to give you hell."

53   "Why?" said I.

54   He said, "This is a note to have you whipped, and says that you have a dollar to pay for it."

55   He handed me back the note, and off I started. I knew not what to do, but was determined not to be whipped. I went up to the jail—took a look at it, and walked off again. As Mr. Walker was acquainted with the jailer, I feared that I should be found out if I did not go, and be treated in consequence of it still worse.

56   While I was meditating on the subject, I saw a colored man about my size walk up, and the thought struck me in a moment to send him with my note. I walked up to him, and asked him who he belonged to. He said he was a free man, and had been in the city but a short time. I told him I had a note to go into the jail, and get a trunk to carry to one of the steamboats; but was so busily engaged that I could not do it, although I had a dollar to pay for it. He asked me if I would not give him the job. I handed him the note and the dollar, and off he started for the jail.

57   I watched to see that he went in, and as soon as I saw the door close behind him, I walked around the corner, and took my station, intending to see how my friend looked when he came out. I had been there but a short time, when a colored man came around the corner, and said to another colored man with whom he was acquainted—

58   "They are giving a nigger scissors in the jail."

59   "What for?" said the other. The man continued,

60   "A nigger came into the jail, and asked for the jailer. The jailer came out, and he handed him a note, and said he wanted to get a trunk. The jailer told him to go with him, and he would give him the trunk. So he took him into the room, and told the nigger to give up the dollar. He said a man had given him the dollar to pay for getting the trunk. But that lie would not answer. So they made him strip himself, and then they tied him down, and are now whipping him."

61   I stood by all the while listening to their talk, and soon found out that the person alluded to was my customer. I went into the street opposite the jail, and concealed myself in such a manner that I could not be seen by any one coming out. I had been there but a short time, when the young man made his appearance, and looked around for me. I, unobserved, came forth from my hiding-place, behind a pile of back, and he pretty soon saw me and came up to me

complaining bitterly, saying that I had played a trick upon him. I denied any knowledge of what the note contained and asked him what they had done to him. He told me in substance what I heard the man tell who had come out of the jail.

62   "Yes," said he, "they whipped me and took my dollar, and gave me this note."

63   He showed me the note which the jailer had given him, telling him to give it to his master. I told him I would give him 50 cents for it,—that being all the money I had. He gave it to me, and took his money. He had received 20 lashes on his bare back, with the negro-whip.

64   I took the note and started for the hotel where I had left Mr. Walker. Upon reaching the hotel, I handed it to a stranger whom I had not seen before, and requested him to read it to me. As near as I can recollect, it was as follows:—

Dear Sir:—By your direction, I have given your boy twenty lashes. He is a very saucy boy, and tried to make me believe that he did not belong to you, and I put it on to him well for lying to me. I remain.

Your obedient servant.

65   It is true that in most of the slave-holding cities, when a gentleman wishes his servants whipped, he can send him to the jail and have it done. Before I went in where Mr. Walker was, I wet my cheeks a little, as though I had been crying. He looked at me, and inquired what was the matter. I told him that I have never had such a whipping in my life, and handed him the note. He looked at it and laughed—"and so you told him that you did not belong to me." "Yes, sir," said I. "I did not know that there was any harm in that." He told me I must behave myself, if I did not want to be whipped again.

66   This incident shows how it is that slavery makes its victims lying and mean; for which vices it afterwards reproaches them, and uses them as arguments to prove that they deserve no better fate. I have often, since my escape, deeply regretted the deception I practiced upon this poor fellow; and I heartily desire that it may be, at some time or other, in my power to make him amends for his vicarious sufferings in my behalf.

67   In a few days we reached New Orleans, and arriving there in the night, remained on board until morning. While at New Orleans this time, I saw a slave killed; an account of which had been published by Theodore D. Weld, in his book entitled, *Slavery as it is*. The circumstances were as follows. In the evening, between seven and eight o'clock, a slave came running down the levee, followed by several men and boys. The whites were crying out, "Stop that nigger, stop that nigger"; while the poor panting slave, in almost breathless accents, was repeating, "I did not steal the meat—I did not steal the meat." The poor man at last took refuge in the river. The whites who were in pursuit of him, ran on board of one of the boats to see if they could discover him. They finally espied him under the bow of the steamboat *Trenton*. They got a pike-pole, and tried to drive him from his hiding place. When they would strike at him, he would dive under the water. The water was so cold, that it soon became evident that he must come out or be drowned.

68   While they were trying to drive him from under the bow of the boat or drown him, he would in broken and imploring accents say, "I did not steal the meat; I did not steal the meat. My master lives up the river. I want to see my master. I did not steal the meat. Do let me go home to master." After punching him, and striking him over the head for some time, he at last sank in the water, to rise no more alive.

69   On the end of the pike-pole with which they were striking him was a hook which caught in his clothing, and they hauled him on the bow of the boat. Some said he was dead, others said he was *"playing possum,"* while others kicked him to make him get up, but it was no use—he was dead.

70   As soon as they became satisfied of this, they commenced leaving, one after another. One of the hands on the boat informed the captain that they had killed the man, and that the dead body was lying on the deck. The captain came on deck, and said to those who were remaining, "You have killed this nigger; now take him off my boat." The captain's name was Hart. The dead body was dragged on shore and left there. I went on board of the boat where our gang of slaves were, and during the whole night my mind was occupied with what I had seen. Early in the morning, I went on shore to see if the dead body remained there. I found it in the same position that it was left the night before. I watched to see what they would do with it. It was left there until between eight and nine o'clock, when a cart, which takes up the trash out of the streets, came along, and the body was thrown in, and in a few minutes more was covered over with dirt which they were removing from the streets. During the whole time, I did not see more than six or seven persons around it, who, from their manner, evidently regarded it as no uncommon occurrence.

71   During our stay in the city, I met with a young white man with whom I was well acquainted in St. Louis. He had been sold into slavery, under the following circumstances. His father was a drunkard, and very poor, with a family of five or six children. The father died, and left the mother to take care of and provide for the children as best she might. The eldest was a boy, named Burrill, about 13 years of age, who did chores in a store kept by Mr. Riley, to assist his mother in procuring a living for the family.

After working with him two years, Mr. Riley took him to New Orleans to wait on him while in that city on a visit, and when he resumed to St. Louis, he told the mother of the boy that he had died with the yellow fever. Nothing more was heard from him, no one supposing him to be alive. I was much astonished when Burrill told me his story. Though I sympathized

with him, I could not assist him. We were both slaves. He was poor, uneducated, and without friends; and if living, is, I presume, still held as a slave.

72   After selling out this cargo of human flesh, we returned to St. Louis, and my time was up with Mr. Walker. I had served him one year, and it was the longest year I ever lived.

36

CHILDREN OF DARKNESS

BY STEPHEN B. OATES

In 1793, Eli Whitney invented the cotton ginny, or gin. This contraption separated the cotton fibers from the seeds. Its mechanical principles were simple; its effects upon the southern economy and perhaps the rest of American history were enormous. The cotton gin made the cultivation of short-staple cotton more profitable. The result was a renewed demand for legions of slaves to clear the land, plant, cultivate and harvest the South's biggest cash crop.

August, 1831, Southampton, Virginia. Thomas Jefferson has been dead for five years; Andrew Jackson is the country's president. Abolitionist literature, urging slaves to rebel, is circulating in many areas of the South.

Nat Turner was a small, mysterious and intelligent black man who would become what every white southerner feared most. Jefferson once remarked that owning slaves was like "holding a wolf by the ears." Nat Turner became that wolf. And one night in the summer of 1831, the wolf got away . . . and the South would not forget.

- *How did Turner use his prodigious knowledge of the Bible?*
- *What did Turner do before beginning his rebellion?*
- *Why did Turner deliberately avoid an extensive plot involving a number of slaves?*
- *After Turner was captured and put on trial, how did he respond when asked do you find yourself mistaken now?*
- *After Turner's Rebellion in 1831, how did southerners view northern abolitionism and slave rebellion?*
- *How did Turner change the antebellum South?*

---

1   Until August, 1831, most Americans had never heard of Virginia's Southampton County, an isolated, impoverished neighborhood located along the border in the southeastern part of the state. It was mostly a small farming area, with cotton fields and apple orchards dotting the flat, wooded landscape. The farmers were singularly fond of their apple crops: from them they made a potent apple brandy, one of the major sources of pleasure in this hardscrabble region. The county seat, or "county town," was Jerusalem, a lethargic little community where pigs rooted in the streets and old-timers spat tobacco juice in the shade of the courthouse. Jerusalem lay on the bank of the Nottoway River some 70 miles south of Richmond. There had never been any large plantations in Southampton County, for the soil had always been too poor for extensive tobacco or cotton cultivation. Although one gentleman did own 80 slaves in 1830, the average was around three or four per family. A number of whites had moved on to new cotton lands in Georgia and Alabama, so that Southampton now had a population that was nearly 60 percent black. While most of the blacks were still enslaved, an unusual number—some 1,700, in fact—were "free persons of color."

2   By southern white standards, enlightened benevolence did exist in Southampton County—and it existed in the rest of the state, too. Virginia whites

allowed a few slave schools to operate—then a crime by state law—and almost without complaint permitted slaves to hold illegal religious meetings. Indeed, Virginians liked to boast that slavery was not so harsh in their "enlightened" state as it was in the brutal cotton plantations in the Deep South. Still, this was a dark time for southern whites—a time of sporadic insurrection panics, especially in South Carolina, and of rising abolitionist militancy in the North—and Virginians were taking no chances. Even though their slaves, they contended, were too happy and too submissive to strike back, Virginia was nevertheless almost a military garrison, with a militia force of some 100,000 men to guard against insurrection.

3   Southampton whites, of course, were caught in the same paradox: most of the white males over 21 voluntarily belonged to the militia and turned out for the annual drills, yet none of them thought a slave revolt would happen here. *Their* blacks, they told themselves, had never been more content, more docile. True, they did get a bit carried away in their religious meetings these days, with much too much singing and clapping. And true, there were white preachers who punctuated their sermons with what a local observer called "ranting cant about equality" and who might inspire black exhorters to retail that doctrine to their congregations. But generally things were quiet and unchanged in this remote tidewater county, where time seemed to stand as still as a windless summer day.

4   It happened with shattering suddenness, an explosion of black rage that rocked Southampton County to its foundations. On August 22, 1831, a band of insurgent slaves, led by a black mystic called Nat Turner, rose up with axes and plunged southeastern Virginia—and much of the rest of the South—into convulsions of fear and racial violence. It turned out to be the bloodiest slave insurrection in southern history, one that was to have a profound and irrevocable impact on the destinies of southern whites and blacks alike.

5   Afterward, white authorities described him as a small man with "distinct African features." Though his shoulders were broad from work in the fields, he was short, slender, and a little knock-kneed, with thin hair, a complexion like black pearl, and large, deep-set eyes. He wore a mustache and cultivated a tuft of whiskers under his lower lip. Before that fateful August day, whites who knew Nat Turner thought him harmless, even though he was intelligent and did gabble on about strange religious powers. Among the slaves, though, he enjoyed a powerful influence as an exhorter and self-proclaimed prophet.

6   He was born in 1800, the property of Benjamin Turner of Southampton County and the son of two strong-minded parents. Tradition has it that his African-born mother threatened to kill him rather than see him grow up in bondage. His father eventually escaped to the North, but not before he had helped inculcate an enormous sense of self-importance in his son. Both parents praised Nat for his brilliance and extraordinary imagination; his mother even claimed that he could recall episodes that happened before his birth—a power that others insisted only the Almighty could have given him. His mother and father both told him that he was intended for some great purpose, that he would surely become a prophet. Nat was also influenced by his grandmother, who along with his white masters taught him to pray and to take pride in his superior intelligence. He learned to read and write with great ease, prompting those who knew him to remark that he had too much sense to be raised in bondage—he "would never be of any service to any one as a slave," one of them said.

7   In 1810 Benjamin Turner died, and Nat became the property of Turner's oldest son Samuel. Under Samuel Turner's permissive supervision Nat exploited every opportunity to improve his knowledge: he studied white children's school books and experimented in making paper and gunpowder. But it was religion that interested him the most. He attended black religious meetings, where the slaves cried out in ecstasy and sang hymns that expressed their longing for a better life. He listened transfixed as black exhorters preached from the Bible with stabbing gestures, singing out in a rhythmic language that was charged with emotion and vivid imagery. He studied the Bible, too, practically memorizing the books of the Old Testament, and grew to manhood with the words of the prophets roaring in his ears.

8   Evidently Nat came of age a bit confused if not resentful. Both whites and blacks had said he was too intelligent to be raised a slave; yet here he was, fully grown and still in bondage. Obviously he felt betrayed by false hopes. Obviously he thought he should be liberated like the large number of free blacks who lived in Southampton County and who were not nearly so gifted as he. Still enslaved as a man, he zealously cultivated his image as a prophet, aloof, austere, and mystical. As he said later in an oral autobiographical sketch, "Having soon discovered to be great, I must appear so, and therefore studiously avoided mixing in society, and wrapped myself in mystery, devoting myself to fasting and prayer."

9   Remote, introspective, Turner had religious fantasies in which the Holy Spirit seemed to speak to him as it had to the prophets of old. "Seek ye the kingdom of Heaven," the Spirit told him, "and all things shall be added unto you." Convinced that he "was ordained for some great purpose in the hands of the Almighty," Turner told his fellow slaves about his communion with the Spirit. "And they believed,"

Turner recalled, "and said my wisdom came from God." Pleased with their response, he began to prepare them for some unnamed mission. He also started preaching at black religious gatherings and soon rose to prominence as a leading exhorter in the slave church. Although never ordained and never officially a member of any church, he was accepted as a Baptist preacher in the slave community, and once he even baptized a white man in a swampy pond. There can be little doubt that the slave church nourished Turner's self-esteem and his desire for independence, for it was not only a center for underground slave plottings against the master class, but a focal point for an entire alternate culture—a subterranean culture that the slaves sought to construct beyond the white man's control. Moreover, Turner's status as a slave preacher gave him considerable freedom of movement, so that he came to know most of Southampton County intimately.

10   Sometime around 1821 Turner disappeared. His master had put him under an overseer, who may have whipped him, and he fled for his freedom as his father had done. But 30 days later he voluntarily returned. The other slaves were astonished. No fugitive ever came back on his own. "And the negroes found fault, and murmured against me," Turner recounted later, "saying that if they had my sense they would not serve any master in the world." But in his mind Turner did not serve any earthly master. His master was Jehovah—the angry and vengeful God of ancient Israel—and it was Jehovah, he insisted, who had chastened him and brought him back to bondage.

11   At about this time Turner married. Evidently his wife was a young slave named Cherry who lived on Samuel Turner's place. But in 1822 Samuel Turner died, and they were sold to different masters—Cherry to Giles Reese and Nat to Thomas Moore. Although they were not far apart and still saw each other from time to time, their separation was nevertheless a painful example of the wretched privations that slavery placed on black people, even here in mellowed Southampton County.

12   As a perceptive man with a prodigious knowledge of the Bible, Turner was more than aware of the hypocrisies and contradictions loose in this Christian area, where whites gloried in the teachings of Jesus and yet discriminated against the "free coloreds" and kept the other blacks in chains. Here slave owners bragged about their benevolence (in Virginia they took care of their "niggers") and yet broke up families, sold blacks off to whip-happy slave traders when money was scarce, and denied intelligent and skilled blacks something even the most debauched and useless poor whites enjoyed: freedom. Increasingly embittered about his condition and that of his people, his imagination fired to incandescence by prolonged fasting and Old Testament prayers,

Turner began to have apocalyptic visions and bloody fantasies in the fields and woods southwest of Jerusalem. "I saw white spirits and black spirits engaged in battle," he declared later, "and the sun was darkened—the thunder rolled in the heavens, and blood flowed in streams—and I heard a voice saying, 'Such is your luck, such you are called to see, and let it come rough or smooth, you must surely bear it.'" He was awestruck, he recalled, but what did the voice mean? What must he bear? He withdrew from his fellow slaves and prayed for a revelation; and one day when he was plowing in the field, he thought the Spirit called out, "Behold me as I stand in the Heavens," and Turner looked up and saw forms of men there in a variety of attitudes, "and there were lights in the sky to which the children of darkness gave other names than what they really were—for they were the lights of the Saviour's hands, stretched forth from east to west, even as they extended on the cross on Calvary for the redemption of sinners."

13   Certain that Judgment Day was fast approaching, Turner strove to attain "true holiness" and "the true knowledge of faith." And once he had them, once he was "made perfect," then the Spirit showed him other miracles. While working in the field, he said, he discovered drops of blood on the corn. In the woods he found leaves with hieroglyphic characters and numbers etched on them; other leaves contained forms of men—some drawn in blood—like the figures in the sky. He told his fellow slaves about these signs—they were simply astounded—and claimed that the Spirit had endowed him with a special knowledge of the seasons, the rotation of the planets, and the operation of the tides. He acquired an even greater reputation among the county's slaves, many of whom thought he could control the weather and heal disease. He told his followers that clearly, something large was about to happen, that he was soon to fulfill "the great promise that had been made to me."

14   But he still did not know what his mission was. Then on May 12, 1828, "I heard a loud noise in the heavens," Turner remembered, "and the Spirit instantly appeared to me and said the Serpent was loosened, and Christ had laid down the yoke he had borne for the sins of men, and that I should take it on and fight against the Serpent." Now at last it was clear. By signs in the heavens Jehovah would show him when to commence the great work, whereupon "I should arise and prepare myself, and slay my enemies with their own weapons." Until then he should keep his lips sealed.

15   But his work was too momentous for him to remain entirely silent. He announced to Thomas Moore that the slaves ought to be free and would be "one day or other." Moore, of course, regarded this as dangerous talk from a slave and gave Turner a thrashing.

16   In 1829 a convention met in Virginia to draft a new state constitution, and there was talk among the slaves—who communicated along a slave grapevine—that they might be liberated. Their hopes were crushed, though, when the convention **emphatically** rejected emancipation and restricted **suffrage** to whites only. There was also a strong backlash against antislavery publications thought to be infiltrating from the North, one of which—David Walker's *Appeal*—actually called on the slaves to revolt. In reaction the Virginia legislature enacted a law against teaching slaves to read and write. True, it was not yet rigorously enforced, but from the blacks' viewpoint slavery seemed more entrenched in "enlightened" Virginia than ever.

17   There is no evidence that Turner ever read antislavery publications, but he was certainly sensitive to the despair of his people. Still, Jehovah gave him no further signs, and he was carried along in the ebb and flow of ordinary life. Moore had died in 1828, and Turner had become the legal property of Moore's nine-year-old son—something that must have humiliated him. In 1829 a local wheelwright, Joseph Travis, married Moore's widow and soon moved into her house near the Cross Keys, a village located southwest of Jerusalem. Still known as Nat Turner even though he had changed owners several times, Nat considered Travis "a kind master" and later said that Travis "placed the greatest confidence in me."

18   In February, 1831, there was an eclipse of the sun. The sign Turner had been waiting for—could there be any doubt? Removing the seal from his lips, he gathered around him four slaves in whom he had complete trust—Hark, Henry, Nelson, and Sam—and confided what he was called to do. They would commence "the work of death" on July 4, whose connotation Turner clearly understood. But they formed and rejected so many plans that his mind was affected. He was seized with dread. He fell sick, and Independence Day came and passed.

19   On August 13 there was another sign. Because of some atmospheric disturbance the sun grew so dim that it could be looked at directly. Then it seemed to change colors—now pale green, now blue, now white—and there was much excitement and consternation in many parts of the eastern United States. By afternoon the sun was like an immense ball of polished silver, and the air was moist and hazy. Then a black spot could be seen, apparently on the sun's surface—a phenomenon that greatly aroused the slaves in southeastern Virginia. For Turner, the black spot was unmistakable proof that God wanted him to move. With awakened resolution he told his men that "as the black spot passed over the sun, so shall the blacks pass over the earth."

20   It was Sunday, August 21, deep in the woods near the Travis house at a place called Cabin Pond. Around a crackling fire Turner's confederates feasted on roast pig and apple brandy. With them were two new recruits—Jack, one of Hark's cronies, and Will, a powerful man who intended to gain his freedom or die in the attempt. Around mid-afternoon Turner himself made a dramatic appearance, and in the glare of pine-knot torches they finally made their plans. They would rise that night and "kill all the white people." It was a propitious time to begin, because many whites of the militia were away at a camp meeting. The revolt would be so swift and so terrible that the whites would be too panic-stricken to fight back. Until they had sufficient recruits and equipment, the insurgents would annihilate everybody in their path—women and children included. When one of the slaves complained about their small number (there were only seven of them, after all), Turner was quick to reassure him. He had deliberately avoided an extensive plot involving a lot of slaves. He knew that blacks had "frequently attempted similar things," but their plans had "leaked out." Turner intended for his revolt to happen completely without warning. The "march of destruction," he explained, "should be the first news of the insurrection," whereupon slaves and free blacks alike would rise up and join him. He did not say what their ultimate objective was, but possibly he wanted to fight his way into the Great Dismal Swamp some 20 miles to the east. This immense, snake-filled quagmire had long been a haven for fugitives, and Turner may have planned to establish a slave stronghold there from which to launch punitive raids against Virginia and North Carolina. On the other hand, he may well have had nothing in mind beyond the extermination of every white on the 10-mile route to Jerusalem. There are indications that he thought God would guide him after the revolt began, just as He had directed Gideon against the Midianites. Certainly Turner's command of unremitting carnage was that of the Almighty, who had said through his prophet Ezekiel: "Slay utterly old and young, both maids and little children, and women. . . . "

21   The slaves talked and schemed through the evening. Night came on. Around two in the morning of August 22 they left the woods, by-passed Giles Reese's farm, where Cherry lived, and headed for the Travis homestead, the first target in their crusade.

22   All was still at the Travis house. In the darkness the insurgents gathered about the cider press, and all drank except Turner, who never touched liquor. Then they moved across the yard with their axes. Hark placed a ladder against the house, and Turner, armed with a hatchet, climbed up and disappeared

---

emancipation: freedom from bondage, oppression, or restraint; liberation.
suffrage: the right or privilege of voting.

through a second-story window. In a moment he unbarred the door, and the slaves spread through the house without a sound. The others wanted Turner the prophet, Turner the black messiah, to strike the first blow and kill Joseph Travis. With Will close behind, Turner entered Travis' bedroom and made his way to the white man's bed. Turner swung his hatchet—a wild blow that glanced off Travis' head and brought him out of bed yelling for his wife. But with a sure killer's instinct Will moved in and hacked Travis to death with his axe. In minutes Will and the others had slaughtered the four whites they found in the house, including Mrs. Travis and young Putnam Moore, Turner's legal owner. With Putnam's death Turner felt that at last, after 30 years in bondage, he was free.

23   The rebels gathered up a handful of old muskets and followed "General Nat" out to the barn. There Turner paraded his men about, leading them through every military maneuver he knew. Not all of them, however, were proud of their work. Jack sank to his knees with his head in his hands and said he was sick. But Hark made him get up and forced him along as they set out across the field to the next farm. Along the way somebody remembered the Travis baby. Will and Henry returned and killed it in its cradle.

24   And so it went throughout that malignant night, as the rebels took farm after farm by surprise. They used no firearms, in order not to arouse the countryside, instead stabbing and decapitating their victims. Although they confiscated horses, weapons, and brandy, they took only what was necessary to continue the struggle, and they committed no rapes. They even spared a few homesteads, one because Turner believed the poor white inhabitants "thought no better of themselves than they did of negroes." By dawn on Monday there were 15 insurgents—nine on horses—and they were armed with a motley assortment of guns, clubs, swords, and axes. Turner himself now carried a light dress sword, but for some mysterious reason (a fatal irresolution? the dread again?) he had killed nobody yet.

25   At Elizabeth Turner's place, which the slaves stormed at sunrise, the prophet tried once again to kill. They broke into the house, and there, in the middle of the room, too frightened to move or cry out, stood Mrs. Turner and a neighbor named Mrs. Newsome. Nat knew Elizabeth Turner very well, for she was the widow of his second master, Samuel Turner. While Will attacked her with his axe the prophet took Mrs. Newsome's hand and hit her over the head with his sword. But evidently he could not bring himself to kill her. Finally Will moved him aside and chopped her to death as methodically as though he were cutting wood.

26   With the sun low in the east, Turner sent a group on foot to another farm while he and Will led the horsemen at a gallop to Caty Whitehead's place. They surrounded the house in a rush, but not before several people fled into the garden. Turner chased after somebody, but it turned out to be a slave girl, as terrified as the whites, and he let her go. All around him, all over the Whitehead farm, there were scenes of unspeakable violence. He saw Will drag Mrs. Whitehead kicking and screaming out of the house and almost sever her head from her body. Running around the house, Turner came upon young Margaret Whitehead hiding under a cellar cap between two chimneys. She ran crying for her life, and Turner set out after her—a wild chase against the hot August sun. He overtook the girl in a field and hit her again and again with his sword, but she would not die. In desperation he picked up a fence rail and beat her to death. Finally he had killed someone. He was to kill no one else.

27   After the Whitehead massacre the insurgents united briefly and then divided again, those on foot moving in one direction and Turner and the mounted slaves in another. The riders moved across the fields, kicking their horses and mules faster and faster, until at last they raced down the lane to Richard Porter's house, scattering dogs and chickens as they went. But the Porters had fled—forewarned by their own slaves that a revolt was under way. Turner knew that the alarm was spreading now, knew that the militia would soon be mobilizing, so he set out alone to retrieve the other column. While he was gone Will took the cavalry and raided Nathaniel Francis' homestead. Young Francis was Will's owner, but he could not have been a harsh master: several free blacks voluntarily lived on his farm. Francis was not home, and his pregnant young wife survived Will's onslaught only because a slave concealed her in the attic. After killing the overseer and Francis' two nephews Will and his men raced on to another farm, and another, and then overran John Barrow's place on the Barrow Road. Old man Barrow fought back manfully while his wife escaped in the woods, but the insurgents overwhelmed him and slit his throat. As a tribute to his courage they wrapped his body in a quilt and left a plug of tobacco on his chest.

28   Meanwhile Turner rode chaotically around the countryside, chasing after one column and then the other, almost always reaching the farms after his scattered troops had done the killing and gone. Eventually he found both columns waiting for him at another pillaged homestead, took charge again, and sent them down the Barrow Road, which intersected the main highway to Jerusalem. They were 40 strong now and all mounted. Many of the new recruits had joined up eager "to kill all the white people." But others had been forced to come along as though they were hostages. A black later testified that several slaves—among them three teen-age boys "were constantly guarded by negroes with guns

who were ordered to shoot them if they attempted to escape."

29   On the Barrow Road, Turner's strategy was to put his 20 most dependable men in front and send them galloping down on the homesteads before anybody could escape. But the cry of insurrection had preceded them, and many families had already escaped to nearby Jerusalem, throwing the village into pandemonium. By midmorning church bells were tolling the terrible news—*insurrection, insurrection*—and shouting men were riding through the countryside in a desperate effort to get the militia together before the slaves overran Jerusalem itself.

30   As Turner's column moved relentlessly toward Jerusalem one Levi Waller, having heard that the blacks had risen, summoned his children from a nearby schoolhouse (some of the other children came running too) and tried to load his guns. But before he could do so, Turner's advance horsemen swept into his yard, a whirlwind of axes and swords, and chased Waller into some tall weeds. Waller managed to escape, but not before he saw the blacks cut down his wife and children. One small girl also escaped by crawling up a dirt chimney, scarcely daring to breathe as the insurgents decapitated the other children—10 in all—and threw their bodies in a pile.

31   Turner had stationed himself at the rear of his little army and did not participate in these or any other killings along the Barrow Road. He never explained why. He had been fasting for several days and may well have been too weak to try any more killing himself. Or maybe as God's prophet he preferred to let Will and the eight or nine other lieutenants do the slaughtering. All he said about it afterward was that he "sometimes got in sight in time to see the work of death completed" and that he paused to view the bodies "in silent satisfaction" before riding on.

32   Around noon on Monday the insurgents reached the Jerusalem highway, and Turner soon joined them. Behind them lay a zigzag path of unredeemable destruction: some 15 homesteads sacked and approximately 60 whites slain. By now the rebels amounted to 50 or 60—including three or four free blacks. But even at its zenith Turner's army showed signs of disintegration. A few reluctant slaves had already escaped or deserted. And many others were roaring drunk, so drunk they could scarcely ride their horses, let alone do any fighting. To make matters worse, many of the confiscated muskets were broken or too rusty to fire.

33   Turner resolved to march on Jerusalem at once and seize all the guns and powder he could find there. But a half mile up the road he stopped at the Parker farm, because some of his men had relatives and friends there. When the insurgents did not return, Turner went after them—and found his men not in the slave quarters but down in Parker's brandy cellar. He ordered them back to the highway at once.

34   On the way back they met a party of armed men—whites. There were about 18 of them, as far as Turner could make out. They had already routed his small guard at the gate and were now advancing toward the Parker house. With renewed zeal Turner rallied his remaining troops and ordered an attack. Yelling at the top of their lungs, wielding axes, clubs, and gun butts, the blacks drove the whites back into Parker's cornfield. But their advantage was short-lived. White reinforcements arrived, and more were on the way from nearby Jerusalem. Regrouping in the cornfield, the whites counterattacked, throwing the rebels back in confusion. In the fighting some of Turner's best men fell wounded, though none of them died. Several insurgents, too drunk to fight any more, fled pellmell into the woods.

35   If Turner had often seemed irresolute earlier in the revolt, he was now undaunted. Even though his force was considerably reduced, he still wanted to storm Jerusalem. He led his men away from the main highway, which was blocked with militia, and took them along a back road, planning to cross the Cypress Bridge and strike the village from the rear. But the bridge was crawling with armed whites. In desperation the blacks set out to find reinforcements: they fell back to the south and then veered north again, picking up new recruits as they moved. They raided a few more farms, too, only to find them deserted, and finally encamped for the night near the slave quarters on Ridley's plantation.

36   All Monday night news of the revolt spread beyond Southampton County as express riders carried the alarm up to Petersburg and from there to the capitol in Richmond. Governor John Floyd, fearing a statewide uprising, alerted the militia and sent cavalry, infantry, and artillery units to the stricken county. Federal troops from Fortress Monroe were on the way, too, and other volunteers and militia outfits were marching from contiguous counties in Virginia and North Carolina. Soon over 3,000 armed whites were in Southampton County, and hundreds more were mobilizing.

37   With whites swarming the countryside, Turner and his lieutenants did not know what to do. During the night an alarm had stampeded their new recruits, so that by Tuesday morning they had only 20 men left. Frantically they set out for Dr. Simon Blunt's farm to get volunteers—and rode straight into an ambush. Whites barricaded in the house opened fire on them at pointblank range, killing one or more insurgents and capturing several others—among them Hark Travis. Blunt's own slaves, armed with farm tools, helped in the defense and captured a few rebels themselves.

38   Repulsed at Blunt's farm, Turner led a handful of the faithful back toward the Cross Keys, still hoping to gather reinforcements. But the signs were truly ominous, for armed whites were everywhere. At last the militia overtook Turner's little band and in a final, desperate skirmish killed Will and scattered the rest. Turner himself, alone and in deep anguish, escaped to the vicinity of the Travis farm and hid in a hole under some fence rails.

39   By Tuesday evening a full-scale manhunt was under way in southeastern Virginia and North Carolina as armed whites prowled the woods and swamps in search of fugitive rebels and alleged collaborators. They chased the blacks down with howling dogs, killing those who resisted—and many of them resisted zealously—and dragging others back to Jerusalem to stand trial in the county court. One free black insurgent committed suicide rather than be taken by white men. Within a week nearly all the bona fide rebels except Turner had either been executed or imprisoned, but not before white vigilantes—and some militiamen—had perpetrated barbarities on more than a score of innocent blacks. Outraged by the atrocities committed on whites, vigilantes rounded up blacks in the Cross Keys and decapitated them. Another vigilante gang in North Carolina not only beheaded several blacks but placed their skulls on poles, where they remained for days. In all directions whites took blacks from their shacks and tortured, shot, and burned them to death and then mutilated their corpses in ways that witnesses refused to describe. No one knows how many innocent blacks died in this reign of terror—at least 120, probably more. Finally the militia commander of Southampton County issued a proclamation that any further outrages would be dealt with according to the articles of war. Many whites publicly regretted these atrocities but argued that they were the inevitable results of slave insurrection. Another revolt, they said, would end with the extermination of every black in the region.

40   Although Turner's uprising ended on Tuesday, August 24, reports of additional insurrections swept over the South long afterward, and dozens of communities from Virginia to Alabama were seized with hysteria. In North Carolina rumors flew that slave armies had been seen on the highways, that one—maybe led by Turner himself—had burned Wilmington, butchered all the inhabitants, and was now marching on the state capital. The hysteria was even worse in Virginia, where reports of concerted slave rebellions and demands for men and guns swamped the governor's office. For a time it seemed that thousands of slaves had risen, that Virginia and perhaps the entire South would soon be ablaze. But

Governor Floyd kept his head, examined the reports carefully, and concluded that no such widespread insurrection had taken place. Actually no additional uprisings had happened anywhere. Out of blind panic whites in many parts of the South had mobilized the militia, chased after imaginary insurgents, and jailed or executed still more innocent blacks. Working in cooperation with other political and military authorities in Virginia and North Carolina, Floyd did all he could to quell the excitement, to reassure the public that the slaves were quiet now. Still, the governor did not think the Turner revolt was the work of a solitary fanatic. Behind it, he believed, was a conspiracy of Yankee agitators and black preachers—especially black preachers. "The whole of that massacre in Southampton is the work of these Preachers," he declared, and demanded that they be suppressed.

41   Meanwhile the "great bandit chieftain," as the newspapers called him, was still at large. For more than two months Turner managed to elude white patrols, hiding out most of the time near Cabin Pond where the revolt had begun. Hunted by a host of aroused whites (there were various rewards totalling $1,100 on his head), Turner considered giving himself up and once got within two miles of Jerusalem before turning back. Finally on Sunday, October 30, a white named Benjamin Phelps accidentally discovered him in another hideout near Cabin Pond. Since the man had a loaded shotgun, Turner had no choice but to throw down his sword.

42   The next day, with lynch mobs crying for his head, a white guard hurried Turner up to Jerusalem to stand trial. By now he was resigned to his fate as the will of Almighty God and was entirely fearless and **unrepentant**. When a couple of court justices examined him that day, he stated emphatically that *he* had conceived and directed the slaughter of all those white people (even though he had killed only Margaret Whitehead) and announced that God had endowed him with extraordinary powers. The justices ordered this "fanatic" locked up in the same small wooden jail where the other captured rebels had been incarcerated.

43   On November 1 one Thomas Gray, an elderly Jerusalem lawyer and slaveholder, came to interrogate Turner as he lay in his cell "clothed with rags and covered with chains." In Gray's opinion the public was anxious to learn the facts about the insurrection—for whites in Southampton could not fathom why their slaves would revolt. What Gray wanted was to take down and publish a confession from Turner that would tell the public the truth about why the rebellion had happened. It appears that Gray had already gathered a wealth of

---

unrepentant: having or exhibiting no remorse.

information about the outbreak from other prisoners, some of whom he had defended as a court-appointed counsel. Evidently he had also written unsigned newspaper accounts of the affair, reporting in one that whites had located Turner's wife and lashed her until she surrendered his papers (remarkable papers, papers with hieroglyphics on them and sketches of the Crucifixion and the sun). According to Gray and to other sources as well, Turner over a period of three days gave him a voluntary and authentic confession about the genesis and execution of the revolt, recounting his religious visions in graphic detail and contending again that he was a prophet of Almighty God. "Do you not find yourself mistaken now?" Gray asked. Turner replied testily, "Was not Christ crucified?" Turner insisted that the uprising was local in origin but warned that other slaves might see signs and act as he had done. By the end of the confession Turner was in high spirits, perfectly "willing to suffer the fate that awaits me." Although Gray considered him "a gloomy fanatic," he thought Turner was one of the most articulate men he had ever met. And Turner could be frightening. When, in a burst of enthusiasm, he spoke of the killings and raised his manacled hands toward heaven, "I looked on him," Gray said, "and my blood curdled in my veins."

44   On November 5, with William C. Parker acting as his counsel, Turner came to trial in Jerusalem. The court, of course, found him guilty of committing insurrection and sentenced him to hang. Turner, though, insisted that he was not guilty because he did not feel so. On November 11 he went to his death in resolute silence. In addition to Turner, the county court tried some 48 other blacks on various charges of conspiracy, insurrection, and treason. In all, 18 blacks—including one woman—were convicted and hanged. Ten others were convicted and "transported"—presumably out of the United States.

45   But the consequences of the Turner revolt did not end with public hangings in Jerusalem. For southern whites the uprising seemed a monstrous climax to a whole decade of ominous events, a decade of abominable tariffs and economic panics, of **obstreperous** antislavery activities, and of growing slave unrest and insurrection plots, beginning with the Denmark Vesey conspiracy in Charleston in 1822 and culminating now in the worst insurrection Southerners had ever known. Desperately needing to blame somebody besides themselves for Nat Turner, Southerners linked the revolt to some sinis-

ter Yankee-abolitionist plot to destroy their cherished way of life. Southern zealots declared that the antislavery movement, gathering momentum in the North throughout the 1820s, had now burst into a full-blown crusade against the South. In January, 1831, William Lloyd Garrison had started publishing *The Liberator* in Boston, demanding in bold, strident language that the slaves be immediately and unconditionally emancipated. If Garrison's rhetoric shocked Southerners, even more disturbing was the fact that about eight months after the appearance of *The Liberator* Nat Turner embarked on his bloody crusade—something southern politicians and newspapers refused to accept as mere coincidence. They charged that Garrison was behind the insurrection, that it was his "bloodthirsty" invective that had incited Turner to violence. Never mind that there was no evidence that Turner had ever heard of *The Liberator;* never mind that Garrison categorically denied any connection with the revolt, saying that he and his abolitionist followers were Christian pacifists who wanted to free the slaves through moral **suasion.** From 1831 on, northern abolitionism and slave rebellion were inextricably associated in the southern mind.

46   But if Virginians blamed the insurrection on northern abolitionism, many of them defended emancipation itself as the only way to prevent further violence. In fact, for several months in late 1831 and early 1832 Virginians engaged in a momentous public debate over the feasibility of **manumission.** Out of the western part of the state, where antislavery and anti-black sentiment had long been smoldering, came petitions demanding that Virginia eradicate the "accursed," "evil" slave system and colonize all blacks at state expense. Only by removing the entire black population, the petitions argued, could future revolts be avoided. Newspapers also discussed the idea of emancipation and colonization, prompting one to announce that "Nat Turner and the blood of his innocent victims have conquered the silence of 50 years." The debate moved into the Virginia legislature, too, and early in 1832 proslavery and antislavery orators harangued one another in an unprecedented legislative struggle over emancipation. In the end most delegates concluded that colonization was too costly and too complicated to carry out. And since they were not about to **manumit** the blacks and leave them as free men in a white man's country, they rejected emancipation. Indeed, they went on to revise and implement the slave codes in order to restrict blacks so stringently

---

obstreperous: noisily and stubbornly defiant.
suasion: persuasion.
manumission: emancipation, freeing from slavery or bondage.
manumit: to free from slavery or bondage; to emancipate.

that they could never mount another revolt. The modified codes not only strengthened the patrol and militia systems, but sharply curtailed the rights of free blacks and all but eliminated slave schools, slave religious meetings, and slave preachers. For Turner had taught white Virginians a hard lesson about what might happen if they gave slaves enough education and religion to think for themselves.

47   In the wake of the Turner revolt, the rise of the abolitionists, and the Virginia debates over slavery, the other southern states also expanded their patrol and militia systems and increased the severity of their slave codes. What followed was the Great Reaction of the 1830s and 1840s, during which the South, threatened it seemed by internal and external enemies, became a closed, martial society determined to preserve its slave-based civilization at whatever cost. If Southerners had once apologized for slavery as a necessary evil, they now trumpeted that institution as a positive good—"the greatest of all the great blessings," as James H. Hammond phrased it, "which a kind providence has bestowed." Southern postmasters set about confiscating abolitionist literature, lest these "incendiary" tracts invite

the slaves to violence. Some states actually passed sedition laws and other restrictive measures that prohibited blacks and whites alike from criticizing slavery. And slave owners all across the South tightened up slave discipline, refusing to let blacks visit other plantations and threatening to hang any slave who even looked rebellious. By the 1840s the Old South had devised such an oppressive slave system that organized insurrection was all but impossible.

48   Even so, southern whites in the **antebellum** period never escaped the haunting fear that somewhere, maybe even in their own slave quarters, another Nat Turner was plotting to rise up and slit their throats. They never forgot him. His name became for them a symbol of terror and violent retribution.

49   But for antebellum blacks—and for their descendants—the name of Nat Turner took on a profoundly different connotation. He became a legendary black hero who broke his chains and murdered white people because slavery had murdered blacks. Turner, said an elderly black man in Southampton County only a few years ago, was "God's man. He was a man for war, and for legal rights, and for freedom."

---

antebellum: belonging to the period before a war, especially the American Civil War.

37

THE LIBERATOR

BY WILLIAM LLOYD GARRISON

Concern over the evils of slavery developed slowly in the United States. Humanitarians focused their attention on the slave trade, which was ended legally in 1808, and on a plan for the gradual return of blacks to Africa. In 1817 a group of prominent Americans, including Henry Clay and John Marshall, formed the American Colonization Society. Carefully observing the legality of slavery, the new society sought to colonize free Negroes and emancipated slaves either in Haiti or in what eventually became the new republic of Liberia. Despite great fanfare, the colonizers' achievements were slight; by 1830 less than 1,500 blacks had emigrated, and nearly all of those were freemen.

William Lloyd Garrison first entered the antislavery movement as an advocate of colonization. As an orphaned boy in New England, he had learned the printing trade and in 1829 he joined with Benjamin Lundy, a Quaker reformer, in publishing the Genius of Universal Emancipation in Baltimore. Garrison quickly became impatient with Lundy's moderate approach. A stubborn, dogmatic man, he saw slavery as an absolute evil that required an all-out frontal attack if it were to be abolished. After serving a seven-week jail sentence for libel in 1830, Garrison broke with Lundy and returned to New England determined to found his own newspaper. The powerful oratory of a speech he gave in Boston converted two Unitarian ministers, Samuel Sewall and Samuel May, who later commented, "That night my soul was baptized in his spirit, and ever since I have been a disciple and fellow laborer of William Lloyd Garrison."

On January 1, 1831, the 25-year-old Garrison and his partner Isaac Knapp began publishing The Liberator in Boston. Living ascetically on water and stale bread from a neighboring bakery, and using borrowed type, week after week Garrison issued a strident call for the immediate end of slavery and transformed a slumbering antislavery movement into the abolitionist crusade.

- *Why did William Lloyd Garrison edit the newspaper The Liberator?*
- *How did Garrison's abolitionist views reflect the influence and zeal of early 19th century Christian revivals?*
- *Why was there no compromise in Garrison's stance?*
- *How do you suppose white southerners viewed Garrison's paper?*

---

1   To the Public.

     In the month of August, I issued proposals for publishing *The Liberator* in Washington City; but the enterprise, though hailed in different sections of the country, was **palsied** by public indifference. Since that time, the removal of the *Genius of Universal Emancipation* to the Seat of Government has rendered less **imperious** the establishment of a similar periodical in that quarter.

2   During my recent tour for the purpose of exciting the minds of the people by a series of discourses on the subject of slavery, every place that I visited gave fresh evidence of the fact, that a greater revolution in public sentiment was to be effected in the free states—*and particularly in New England*—than at the south. I found contempt more bitter, opposition more active, detraction more relentless, prejudice more stubborn, and apathy more frozen, than among slave owners themselves. Of course, there were individual exceptions to the contrary. This state of things afflicted, but did not dishearten me. I determined, at every hazard, to lift up the standard of emancipation in the eyes of the nation, *within sight of Bunker Hill and in the birth place of liberty*. That standard is now unfurled; and long may it float, unhurt by the **spoliations** of time or the missiles of a desperate foe—yea, till every chain be broken, and every bondman set free! Let Southern oppressors tremble—let their secret abettors tremble—let their Northern **apologists** tremble—let all the enemies of the persecuted blacks tremble.

3   I deem the publication of my original Prospectus unnecessary, as it has obtained a wide circulation. The principles therein inculcated will be steadily pursued in this paper, excepting that I shall not array myself as the political partisan of any man. In defending the great cause of human rights, I wish to derive the assistance of all religions and of all parties.

4   Assenting to the "self evident truth" maintained in the American Declaration of Independence, "that all men are created equal, and endowed by their Creator with certain inalienable rights—among which are life, liberty and the pursuit of happiness," I shall strenuously contend for the immediate enfranchisement of our slave population. In Park-Street Church, on the Fourth of July, 1829, in an address on slavery, I unreflectingly assented to the popular but **pernicious** doctrine of *gradual* abolition. I seize this opportunity to make a full and unequivocal **recantation**, and thus publicly to ask pardon of my God, of my country, and of my brethren the poor slaves, having uttered a sentiment so full of timidity, injustice and absurdity. A similar recantation, from my pen, was published in the *Genius of Universal Emancipation* at Baltimore, in September, 1829. My conscience is now satisfied.

5   I am aware, that many object to the severity of my language; but is there not cause for severity? I *will be* as harsh as truth, and as uncompromising as justice. On this subject, I do not wish to think, or speak, or write, with moderation. No! No! Tell a man whose house is on fire, to give a moderate alarm; tell him to moderately rescue his wife from the hands of the ravisher; tell the mother to gradually extricate her babe from the fire into which it has fallen; —but urge me not to use moderation in a cause like the present. I am in earnest—I will not equivocate—I will not excuse—I will not retreat a single inch—*AND I WILL BE HEARD*. The apathy of the people is enough to make every statue leap from its pedestal, and to hasten the resurrection of the dead.

6   It is pretended, that I am retarding the cause of emancipation by the coarseness of my invective, and the **precipitancy** of my measures. *The charge is not true*. On this question my influence,—humble as it is,—is felt at this moment to a considerable extent, and shall be felt in coming years—not perniciously, but beneficially—not as a curse, but as a blessing; and posterity will bear testimony that I was right. I desire to thank God, that he enables me to disregard "the fear of man which bringeth a snare," and to speak his truth in its simplicity and power. . . .

---

palsied: paralyzed.
imperious: urgent, pressing.
spoliation: the act of plundering.
apologist: a person who argues in defense or justification of slavery.
pernicious: destructive; causing great harm.
recantation: formal retraction or disavowal of a previously held statement or belief.
precipitancy: excessive haste.

38

No Day of Triumph

BY FREDERICK DOUGLASS

The Fourth of July evoked no enthusiasm among many abolitionists; they held that it was inconsistent to celebrate independence and freedom in a land in which slavery existed. Black abolitionist and ex-slave Frederick Douglass shared this view, preferring to let the day pass in silence. However, when he was invited by the Rochester Ladies' Anti-Slavery Society to deliver the Fourth of July oration in 1852, he made the most of the occasion. His speech was not devoted to patriotic themes but addressed itself to the question, "What, to the American slave, is your Fourth of July?"

---

1 The papers and placards say that I am to deliver a Fourth of July Oration. This certainly sounds large, and out of the common way, for me. It is true that I have often had the privilege to speak in this beautiful Hall, and to address many who now honor me with their presence. But neither their familiar faces, nor the perfect gage I think I have of Corinthian Hall seems to free me from embarrassment. The fact is, ladies and gentlemen, the distance between this platform and the slave plantation, from which I escaped, is considerable—and the difficulties to be overcome in getting from the latter to the former are by no means slight. That I am here to-day is, to me, a matter of astonishment as well as of gratitude. You will not, therefore, be surprised, if in what I have to say I evince no elaborate preparation, nor grace my speech with any high sounding exordium. With little experience and with less learning, I have been able to throw my thoughts hastily and imperfectly together; and trusting to your patient and generous indulgence, I will proceed to lay them before you.

2 This, for the purpose of this celebration, is the Fourth of July. It is the birthday of your National Independence, and of your political freedom. This, to you, is what the Passover was to the emancipated people of God. It carries your minds back to the day, and to the act of your great deliverance; and to the signs, and to the wonders, associated with that act, and that day. This celebration also marks the beginning of another year of your national life; and reminds you that the Republic of America is now 76 years old. I am glad, fellow-citizens, that your nation is so young. Seventy-six years, though a good old age for a man, is but a mere speck in the life of a nation. Three score years and ten is the allotted time for individual men; but nations number their years by thousands. According to this fact, you are, even now, only in the beginning of your national career, still lingering in the period of childhood. I repeat, I am glad this is so. There is hope in the thought, and hope is much needed, under the dark clouds which lower above the horizon. The eye of the reformer is met with angry flashes, portending disastrous times; but his heart may well beat lighter at the thought that America is young, and that she is still in the impressible stage of her existence. May he not hope that high lessons of wisdom, of justice and of truth, will yet give direction to her destiny? Were the nation older, the patriot's

---

From *Oration, Delivered in Corinthian Hall, Rochester, by Frederick Douglass, July 5, 1852* (Rochester: Lee, Mann and Company, 1852), pp. 3–5, 14–15, 20, 32–35, 37–39.

heart might be sadder, and the reformer's brow heavier. Its future might be shrouded in gloom, and the hope of its prophets go out in sorrow. There is consolation in the thought that America is young—Great streams are not easily turned from channels, worn deep in the course of ages. They may sometimes rise in quiet and stately majesty, and inundate the land, refreshing and fertilizing the earth with their mysterious properties. They may also rise in wrath and fury, and bear away, on their angry waves, the accumulated wealth of years of toil and hardship. They, however, gradually flow back to the same old channel, and flow on as serenely as ever. But, while the river may not be turned aside, it may dry up, and leave nothing behind but the withered branch, and the unsightly rock, to howl in the abyss-sweeping wind, the sad tale of departed glory. As with rivers so with nations . . .

3   Fellow-citizens, pardon me, allow me to ask, why am I called upon to speak here to-day? What have I, or those I represent, to do with your national independence? Are the great principles of political freedom and of natural justice, embodied in that Declaration of Independence, extended to us? and am I, therefore, called upon to bring our humble offering to the national altar, and to confess the benefits and express devout gratitude for the blessings resulting from your independence to us?

4   Would to God, both for your sakes and ours, that an affirmative answer could be truthfully returned to these questions! Then would my task be light, and my burden easy and delightful. For *who* is there so cold, that a nation's sympathy could not warm him? Who so obdurate and dead to the claims of gratitude, that would not thankfully acknowledge such priceless benefits? Who so stolid and selfish, that would not give his voice to swell the hallelujahs of a nation's jubilee, when the chains of servitude had been torn from his limbs? I am not that man. In a case like that, the dumb might eloquently speak, and the "lame man leap as an hart."

5   But such is not the state of the case. I say it with a sad sense of the disparity between us. I am not included within the pale of this glorious anniversary! Your high independence only reveals the immeasurable distance between us. The blessings in which you, this day, rejoice, are not enjoyed in common—The rich inheritance of justice, liberty, prosperity and independence, bequeathed by your fathers, is shared by you, not by me. The sunlight that brought light and healing to you, has brought stripes and death to me. This Fourth of July is *yours*, not *mine*. *You* may rejoice, *I* must mourn. To drag a man in fetters into the grand illuminated temple of liberty, and call upon him to join you in joyous anthems, were inhuman mockery and sacrilegious irony. Do you mean, citizens, to mock me, by asking me to speak today? If so, there is a parallel to your

conduct. And let me warn you that it is dangerous to copy the example of a nation whose crimes, towering up to heaven, were thrown down by the breath of the Almighty, burying that nation in irrevocable ruin! I can to-day take up the plaintive lament of a peeled and woe-smitten people! . . .

6   What, to the American slave, is your 4th of July? I answer; a day that reveals to him, more than all other days in the year, the gross injustice and cruelty to which he is the constant victim. To him, your celebration is a sham; your boasted liberty, an unholy license; your national greatness, swelling vanity; your sounds of rejoicing are empty and heartless; your denunciation of tyrants, brass fronted impudence; your shouts of liberty and equality, hollow mockery; your prayers and hymns, your sermons and thanksgivings, with all your religious parade and solemnity, are, to him, mere bombast, fraud, deception, impiety, and hypocrisy—a thin veil to cover up crimes which would disgrace a nation of savages. There is not a nation on the earth guilty of practices more shocking and bloody than are the people of the United States, at this very hour.

7   Go where you may, search where you will, roam through all the monarchies and despotisms of the Old World, travel through South America, search out every abuse, and when you have found the last, lay your facts by the side of the everyday practices of this nation, and you will say with me, that, for revolting barbarity and shameless hypocrisy, America reigns without a rival . . .

8   Americans! your republican politics, not less than your republican religion, are flagrantly inconsistent. You boast of your love of liberty, your superior civilization, and your pure Christianity, while the whole political power of the nation (as embodied in the two great political parties) is solemnly pledged to support and perpetuate the enslavement of three millions of your countrymen. You hurl your anathemas at the crowned headed tyrants of Russia and Austria and pride yourselves on your Democratic institutions, while you yourselves consent to be the mere *tools* and *body-guards* of the tyrants of Virginia and Carolina. You invite to your shores fugitives of oppression from abroad, honor them with banquets, greet them with ovations, cheer them, toast them, salute them, protect them, and pour out your money to them like water; but the fugitives from your own land you advertise, hunt, arrest, shoot, and kill. You glory in your refinement and your universal education; yet you maintain a system as barbarous and dreadful as ever stained the character of a nation—a system begun in avarice, supported in pride, and perpetuated in cruelty. You shed tears over fallen Hungary, and make the sad story of her wrongs the theme of your poets, statesmen, and orators, till your gallant sons are ready to fly to arms to vindicate her cause against the oppressor; but, in regard to the ten thousand wrongs

of the American slave, you would enforce the strictest silence, and would hail him as an enemy of the nation who dares to make those wrongs the subject of public discourse! You are all on fire at the mention of liberty for France or for Ireland; but are as cold as an iceberg at the thought of liberty for the enslaved of America. You discourse eloquently on the dignity of labor; yet, you sustain a system which, in its very essence, casts a stigma upon labor. You can bare your bosom to the storm of British artillery to throw off a three-penny tax on tea; and yet wring the last hard earned farthing from the grasp of the black laborers of your country. You profess to believe "that, of one blood, God made all nations of men to dwell on the face of all the earth," and hath commanded all men, everywhere, to love one another; yet you notoriously hate (and glory in your hatred) all men whose skins are not colored like your own. You declare before the world, and are understood by the world to declare that you *"hold these truths to be self-evident, that all men are created equal; and are endowed by their Creator with certain inalienable rights; and that among these are, life, liberty, and the pursuit of happiness"*; and yet, you hold securely, in a bondage which, according to your own Thomas Jefferson, *"is worse than ages of that which your fathers rose in rebellion to oppose,"* a seventh part of the inhabitants of your country.

9 Fellow-citizens, I will not enlarge further on your national inconsistencies. The existence of slavery in this country brands your republicanism as a sham, your humanity as a base pretense, and your Christianity as a lie. It destroys your moral power abroad; it corrupts your politicians at home. It saps the foundation of religion; it makes your name a hissing and a bye-word to a mocking earth. It is the antagonistic force in your government, the only thing that seriously disturbs and endangers your *Union*. It fetters your progress; it is the enemy of improvement; the deadly foe of education; it fosters pride; it breeds insolence; it promotes vice; it shelters crime; it is a curse to the earth that supports it; and yet you cling to it as if it were the sheet anchor of all your hopes. Oh! be warned! be warned! a horrible reptile is coiled up in your nation's bosom; the venomous creature is nursing at the tender breast of your youthful republic; *for the love of God, tear away*, and fling from you the hideous monster, and *let the weight of twenty millions crush and destroy it forever!* . . .

10 Allow me to say, in conclusion, notwithstanding the dark picture I have this day presented, of the state of the nation, I do not despair of this country. There are forces in operation which must inevitably work the downfall of slavery. "The arm of the Lord is not shortened," and the doom of slavery is certain. I, therefore, leave off where I began, with hope. While drawing encouragement from "the Declaration of Independence," the great principles it contains, and the genius of American Institutions, my spirit is also cheered by the obvious tendencies of the age. Nations do not now stand in the same relation to each other that they did ages ago. No nation can now shut itself up from the surrounding world and trot round in the same old path of its fathers without interference. The time was when such could be done. Long established customs of hurtful character could formerly fence themselves in, and do their evil work with social impunity. Knowledge was then confined and enjoyed by the privileged few, and the multitude walked on in mental darkness. But a change has now come over the affairs of mankind. Walled cities and empires have become unfashionable. The arm of commerce has borne away the gates of the strong city. Intelligence is penetrating the darkest corners of the globe. It makes its pathway over and under the sea, as well as on the earth. Wind, steam, and lightning are its chartered agents. Oceans no longer divide, but link nations together. From Boston to London is now a holiday excursion. Space is comparatively annihilated. Thoughts expressed on one side of the Atlantic are distinctly heard on the other.

11 The far off and almost fabulous Pacific rolls in grandeur at our feet. The Celestial Empire, the mystery of ages, is being solved. The fiat of the Almighty, "Let there be Light," has not yet spent its force. No abuse, no outrage whether in taste, sport or avarice, can now hide itself from the all-pervading light. The iron shoe, and crippled foot of China must be seen in contrast with nature. Africa must rise and put on her yet unwoven garment. "Ethiopia shall stretch out her hand unto God." In the fervent aspirations of William Lloyd Garrison, I say, and let every heart join in saying it:

God speed the year of jubilee
The wide world o'er!

39

THE LAW THAT RIPPED AMERICA
IN TWO

BY ROSS DRAKE

Slavery helped start our country. It then divided our country, and then tore our country apart. Never facing the "peculiar institution" head on, politicians from the North and South tried to finesse it. In Thomas Jefferson's Declaration of Independence, the black slave is denied equality; in the Constitution, blacks are denied their humanity; during Andrew Jackson's presidency, the issue of slavery couldn't even be talked about because of the infamous "gag rule". In short, when it came to the issue of slavery, early America was in denial. We simply couldn't face up to it.

The 1850's finally brought the issue to a head. Harriet Beecher Stowe's book, Uncle Tom's Cabin was a best-seller, both in the United States and in Europe. Readers were appalled, many for the first time, by the human tragedy depicted in Stowe's book. As a result of the treaty of Guadalupe-Hidalgo, the nation had grown by one-third, moving west. What to do with these new lands was a central issue facing Congress. Instead of deciding, once and for all, the legality of spreading slavery into these western lands, Congress let people living in these lands decide the issue for themselves. It sounded "democratic", but in reality the Kansas-Nebraska Act was yet another dodge, a finessing of the issue by Congress. The results were "bleeding Kansas", and, ultimately, the emergence of one Abraham Lincoln onto the national political scene.

- *Who was John Brown, and what were his actions?*
- *Who was Stephen A. Douglass? What were his motives?*
- *What was the Kansas Nebraska Act, and why did it fail?*

---

1   Abolitionist John Brown, failed businessman, sometime farmer and full-time agent, he believed, of a god more disposed to retribution than mercy, rode into the Pottawatomie Valley in the new territory of Kansas on May 24, 1856, intent on imposing "a restraining fear" on his proslavery neighbors. With him were seven men, including four of his sons. An hour before midnight, Brown came to the cabin of a Tennessee emigrant named James Doyle, took him prisoner despite the pleadings of the man's desperate wife, and shot him dead. After butchering Doyle and two of his sons with broadswords, the party moved on to kill two other men, leaving one with his skull crushed, a hand severed, and his body in Pottawatomie Creek.

2   In a sense, the five proslavery settlers were casualties not merely of Brown's bloody-mindedness but also of a law described by the historians William and Bruce Catton as possibly "the most fateful single piece of legislation in American history." Ironically, the Kansas-Nebraska Act, passed by Congress in May 1854, was meant to quiet the furious national argument over slavery by allowing settlers in the new Western territories to accept the institution or

not, without the intrusion of the federal government. Yet in repealing the Missouri Compromise of 1820, which had outlawed slavery everywhere in the Louisiana Purchase north of the latitude of Missouri's southern border (except for Missouri itself), the new law's impact was precisely the opposite, inflaming the emotions it was intended to calm and wrenching the country apart at its fault lines.

3   By the time the act's consequences were totaled, sectional resentments had turned to bloody hostilities, the Democratic party lay shattered, the Republican party had formed to oppose it, and an obscure Illinois lawyer named Abraham Lincoln had been set on the road to the presidency. Had civil war been made unavoidable? "I'd put it this way," says historian George B. Forgie of the University of Texas. "Whatever the chances of avoiding disunion before Kansas-Nebraska, they fell dramatically as a result of it."

4   The author of the bill—officially called "An Act to Organize the Territories of Nebraska and Kansas"—was Senator Stephen A. Douglas of Illinois, eclipsed in history by his rival Lincoln, but for most of his lifetime a figure of far greater national consequence. Short-legged and barrel-chested, with a head disproportionately large for his body, the 5'4" Democrat, known to admirers as the Little Giant, was a gifted, dynamic, rough-mannered man who seemed destined one day to be president. Ferocious in debate (the author Harriet Beecher Stowe likened his forensic style to "a bomb… [that] bursts and sends red-hot nails in every direction"), he first ran for Congress at 25 against Lincoln's law partner John T. Stuart, losing by just 36 votes. Douglas biographer Robert W. Johannsen reports that Stuart once became incensed at Douglas's language, "took him under his arm, and carried him around the Springfield marketplace. Douglas, in return, gave Stuart's thumb such a bite that Stuart carried the scar for many years afterward."

5   Douglas was equally combative in Congress. An avid backer of the Mexican war of 1846-48, he looked forward, if not to an American empire, at least to a republic spanning the continent. But his ambitions could hardly be realized by a nation at war with itself. The problem, as always, was slavery. As the boundaries of the nation moved westward, threatening the tenuous North-South balance of power, Congress had struck the bargains needed to keep the Union intact, without confronting the issue head-on. One accommodation had followed another, but time was not on the side of evasion. Observes historian Paul Finkelman of the University of Tulsa: "As Lincoln said in his second inaugural address, 'all knew that this interest'—slavery—'was somehow the cause of the war.' That 'interest' was not likely to go away peacefully. Sooner or later the American people had to come to terms with it."

6   Mildly opposed to slavery in principle—though as absentee manager of his first wife's Mississippi plantation, he was barely one step removed from being a slaveholder—Douglas regarded the issue as more a dangerous distraction than a fundamental obstacle to the republic's survival. White America's destiny, in his view, was to extend its domain from the Atlantic to the Pacific, not to agonize over the dubious rights of those he considered its racial inferiors. With that in mind, he had helped arrange the historic Compromise of 1850, which admitted California to the union as a free state while placing no restrictions on slavery in the new territories of Utah and New Mexico. Voters there would decide for themselves whether or not to permit it, and the principle would be known as popular sovereignty.

7   Four years later, Douglas had another agenda. Early in 1854, hoping to open the way for a railroad linking California with Illinois and the East, he wanted Congress to approve the establishment of a territorial government in the intervening wilderness known as Nebraska. Douglas had asked for such approval before, but lacked the southern votes needed to get it. Further bargaining would now be required, and the stakes this time would include the Missouri Compromise, for more than 30 years the foundation of federal policy restricting the expansion of slavery. If Nebraska were organized with the Compromise still in place, slave-state Missouri would be bordered on three sides by free states and territories. The state's rabidly proslavery senator David Atchison had a problem with that; he wanted Nebraska opened to slavery, and vowed to see it "sink in hell" if it weren't.

8   Thus began a delicate negotiation in which Douglas, who had once described the Missouri Compromise as "a sacred thing which no ruthless hand would be reckless enough to disturb," searched for a politic way of disturbing it—something short of outright repeal. But his would-be southern allies, fearing any ambiguity about the Compromise's survival might discourage slaveholders from moving into Nebraska, wanted language striking it down unequivocally. Douglas was reluctant, but finally agreed. "By God, sir," he is said to have exclaimed to Kentucky senator Archibald Dixon, "you are right, and I will incorporate it into my bill, though I know it will raise a hell of a storm."

9   He was right about that. Even as he saw his bill through the Senate (it now called for the division of Nebraska into two territories, one of them Kansas), and an uneasy House of Representatives, vilification rained from the pulpit, the press, and a congressional vanguard of outraged Free-Soilers, as those who opposed slavery's extension were known. At one point the Senate received a petition 250 feet long and signed by more than 3,000 New England clergymen urging the defeat of Kansas-Nebraska "in the name

of Almighty God." Douglas detested abolitionists and sought to cast the protests as the work of extremists. But if much of the abuse he received was surely excessive—Douglas was hardly the "Illinois man-stealer . . . who trades in little children" that one newspaper made him out to be—the anger was deep and not confined to the radicals.

10   There was, in fact, a growing antipathy in the North toward slavery. Moreover, observes Professor Forgie, "The upending of a permanent deal naturally antagonizes people disadvantaged by it, and [Kansas-Nebraska] fed existing worries that the slaveholding class was bent on extending its power nationally, with the goal of ultimately destroying republican institutions. Also, the law seemed to promise the movement of blacks into areas northern whites had assumed were to be reserved for them."

11   Though Douglas later observed that he could have made his way from Boston to Chicago "by the light of my own effigy," he could not be intimidated. He was, after all, a practical man, and he saw Kansas-Nebraska as a practical bill. By transferring authority over slavery from Congress to the territories themselves, he believed he was removing a threat to the union. Nor did he think it likely that slavery would spread from the 15 states where it existed to the areas being opened for settlement. But when it came to judging the intensity of public feeling on the issue, the senator was, unhappily, tone-deaf.

12   "He was a northern man who was southern in his views on race," explains Professor Finkelman. "He said he didn't care whether slavery was voted up or down, but most northerners *did* care. He may have been the only person in America who didn't. Many northerners, and Lincoln is a great example, thought the Missouri Compromise was just a notch below the Constitution as a fundamental part of the American political framework. They saw it as putting slavery on the road to extinction, and that was for them a sacred goal. Kansas-Nebraska betrayed this." And so, the battle lines were drawn.

13   Douglas seemed unfazed at first, confident he could undo the damage. He soon discovered otherwise. Speaking in Chicago to kick off the 1854 off-year election campaign in Illinois—though he wasn't on the ballot himself—Douglas was interrupted by "an uproar of shouts, groans and hisses," reports Johannsen. "Missiles" were thrown, and "to the delight of the crowd, Douglas lost his temper, denouncing the assemblage as a mob and replying to their taunts by shaking his fist, which only intensified the din. . . ." Douglas put up with the heckling for more than two hours, then angrily strode from the platform. "It is now Sunday morning," he was said to have shouted back at his tormentors (though some historians doubt that he did). "I'll go to church and you may go to hell!"

14   The election that followed confirmed the devastating impact of Douglas's bill on his party. Opponents of Kansas-Nebraska carried both houses of the Illinois legislature, which would soon elect a United States senator, and Democrats in the free states lost 66 of their 91 seats in the House of Representatives. Suddenly, the Democrats found themselves primarily a southern party, capable after 1856 of electing only one president in what remained of the century.

15   Meanwhile, Abraham Lincoln, a former one-term congressman nearly five years out of office, had joined the fray. Stumping for Richard Yates, a candidate for Congress in the 1854 election, Lincoln tore into Kansas-Nebraska, finding in its passage "covert zeal for the spread of slavery." In so doing, he was directly challenging Douglas, setting the stage for the crucial debates between them four years later that would make Lincoln a national figure. "I was losing interest in politics" he wrote in a letter in 1859, "when the repeal of the Missouri Compromise aroused me again."

16   Motivated as he surely was by his sense that Douglas had made himself vulnerable, Lincoln spoke also from a sense of moral commitment and was capable of raising the slavery debate to a level at which Douglas seems profoundly disadvantaged now (as he wasn't then) by his obvious disdain for blacks, slave or free. "I care more for the great principle of self-government," Douglas would one day declare, ". . . than I do for all the negroes in Christendom. I would not blot out the great inalienable rights of all white men for all the negroes that ever existed." (According to his biographer William Lee Miller, Lincoln quoted Douglas as saying, more colorfully, that in all contests between the Negro and the crocodile, he was for the Negro, but that in all questions between the Negro and the white man, he was for the white man.)

17   While Douglas viewed popular sovereignty as a bedrock democratic value, Lincoln saw in its application to slavery a callous statement of moral indifference. Revoking the Missouri Compromise he equated with a repudiation of the Declaration of Independence itself. "Near 80 years ago," he observed, "we began by declaring that all men are created equal; but now . . . we have run down to the other declaration, that for some men to enslave others is a 'sacred right of self-government.'"

18   Though Lincoln's feelings about what he called "the monstrous injustice of slavery" were sincere, he was no abolitionist and felt bound to accept it where it existed. He was, like Douglas, a practical man, with whom the union always came first. He endorsed the spirit of compromise on which it depended, and which he believed Kansas-Nebraska subverted. "And what shall we have in lieu of [this spirit]?" he asked. "The South flushed with triumph and tempted to excesses; the North, betrayed, as

they believe, brooding on wrong and burning for revenge. One side will provoke; the other resent. The one will taunt, the other defy; one aggresses, the other retaliates."

19   That is precisely what happened. "Any plausible explanation of the failure to find another sectional compromise in 1860–61 would have to include the fact that [trust in such agreements] took a deadly hit with Kansas-Nebraska," says Forgie. "Why would anyone sign on to a compromise again?" And once awakened, the South's hope that Kansas might become the sixteenth slave state took on a tenacious life of its own. When the North proved equally determined to keep Kansas free, the territory turned into a battlefield.

20   Events quickly took an ominous turn. When New England abolitionists formed the Emigrant Aid Company to seed Kansas with antislavery settlers, proslavery Missourians sensed an invasion. "We are threatened," an acquaintance complained to Senator Atchison, "with being made the unwilling receptacle of the filth, scum and offscourings of the East . . . to preach abolition and dig underground Railroads."

21   In fact, most emigrants didn't come to preach anything, much less to dig. As likely to be anti-black as they were antislavery, they came to Kansas for land, not a cause. Likewise, most proslavery settlers had neither slaves nor the prospect of having any. Yet these distinctions didn't much matter. Kansas quickly became part of the larger American drama, and the few thousand settlers who made their home in the territory found themselves surrogates, reluctant or not, of the inexorable issues that threatened the union. "Kansas," says Forgie, "much like Korea or Berlin in the Cold War, readily took form as the arena in which a battle was being waged for much larger stakes. Which section's institutions would shape the future of the continent?"

22   What happened in Kansas has been called a bushwhackers' war, and it began with a bushwhacked election. Defending themselves against what they saw as Yankee fanatics and slave stealers, thousands of Missourians, led by Senator Atchison, crossed the border in March 1855 to elect, illegally, a pro-slavery territorial legislature. "There are 1,100 coming over from Platte County to vote," Atchison shouted at one point, "and if that ain't enough we can send 5,000—enough to kill every God-damned abolitionist in the territory!" When the new legislature promptly expelled its few antislavery members, disenfranchised Free-Soilers set up their own shadow government.

23   The territory was soon awash with secret societies and informal militias, formed ostensibly for self-defense, but capable of deadly mischief on both sides. Kansas was a powderkeg awaiting a match, and it found one in the shooting of Douglas County sheriff Samuel Jones, an unrestrained proslavery man, as he sat in his tent outside the Free-Soil stronghold of Lawrence. Soon afterward, the Douglas County grand jury, instructed by a judge angered by what he regarded as Free-Soilers' treasonous resistance to the territorial government, returned indictments against the Free-Soil "governor," Charles Robinson, two Lawrence newspapers charged with sedition, and the town's Free State Hotel, supposedly being used as a fortress. Soon a posse descended on Lawrence, led by a federal marshal who made several arrests before dismissing the troops. It was then that Sheriff Jones, recovered from his wound (but not, in the view of historian Allan Nevins, from being "a vindictive, blundering fool"), took over the posse, which looted the town, wrecked the newspapers' presses, set fire to Robinson's house, and burned the hotel after failing to destroy it with cannon fire.

24   It was a bad day for Lawrence, but a better one for the nation's antislavery press, which made the sack of Lawrence, as it was called, sound like the reduction of Carthage. "Lawrence in Ruins," announced Horace Greeley's New York *Tribune*. "Several Persons Slaughtered—Freedom Bloodily Subdued." (In fact, the only fatality in Lawrence was a slave-stater struck by falling masonry.)

25   As exaggerated as the "sack" may have been, in the climate of the day it was bound to have consequences. John Brown quickly set them in motion. On his way to Lawrence with a group called the Pottawatomie Rifles, he learned they were too late to defend the town and turned his attention to the unfortunate Doyles and their neighbors. (Three years later, on October 16, 1859, Brown and his followers would stage a bloody attack on a federal armory in Harpers Ferry, Virginia. Cornered by U.S. Marines under the command of Col. Robert E. Lee, a wounded Brown would be taken prisoner, convicted and hanged.)

26   Reaction in Kansas to Brown's Pottawatomie killing spree was swift. Proslavery settlers were furious, fearful and primed for revenge, and many Free-Soilers were horrified—as well they might have been, since the incident was followed by an outbreak of shootings, burnings and general mayhem. Yet the larger Eastern audience hardly knew what had happened. Like the sack of Lawrence, the Pottawatomie murders were transformed in the telling. Either they hadn't happened at all, or had been committed by Indians, or had occurred in the heat of battle. In the great propaganda war being waged and won in the northern press, slave-state Kansans were invariably cast as the villains, and it was a role they were not to escape.

27   Sometimes they didn't seem to be trying, as when the tainted proslavery legislature made it a felony

even to question the right to hold slaves in Kansas, and a capital offense to aid a fugitive slave. Neither law was enforced, but probably that wasn't the point. Unable to match the flood of free-soil emigrants pouring in from the Ohio Valley and elsewhere, slave-staters seemed more determined than ever to make the territory inhospitable to those who opposed them.

28 And they had allies. "The admission of Kansas to the Union as a slave state is now a point of honor with the South," wrote South Carolina congressman Preston Brooks in March 1856. "It is my deliberate conviction that the fate of the South is to be decided with the Kansas issue." Thus freighted with national consequence, resolution of the Kansas question would hardly be left to Kansans alone. Under the circumstances, it seems unsurprising that presidents Franklin Pierce and James Buchanan, northern men of pronounced southern sympathies, endorsed the legitimacy of the illegitimate legislature over the objections of a succession of territorial governors.

29 Among the latter was Robert J. Walker, a former Treasury Secretary and an ally of Douglas. Meeting with President Buchanan before leaving Washington in the spring of 1857, he spelled out his understanding, with which Buchanan agreed, that Kansas would be admitted to statehood only after residents were able to vote freely and fairly on a state constitution.

30 It sounded simple enough, but in execution, of course, it would not be. That was made clear when, at a welcoming banquet, the diminutive Walker was upbraided by one of his proslavery hosts: "And do you come here to rule us? You, a miserable pygmy like you? Walker, we have unmade governors before, and by God, I tell you, sir, we can unmake them again!" Certainly they were ready to try. After Free-Soilers refused to participate in what they believed, with reason, would be a rigged election for constitutional convention delegates, the proslavery convention, meeting in the town of Lecompton, made a crucial decision.

31 Rather than being allowed to vote up or down on a proposed constitution, Kansans would be given a choice between a constitution with slavery and a constitution without it. But the constitution without it contained a clause allowing slaveholders already in the territory to retain not only their slaves but the slaves' offspring. Free-Soilers, naturally, saw their choice as being not between slavery and its absence, but between a little bit of slavery and a lot of it—or, as one Kansan put it, between taking arsenic with bread and butter and taking it straight. When the options were put to a vote, Free-Soilers once again declined to take part.

32 By this time, the battle had been joined back in Washington. Over the strenuous objections of Walker, Buchanan had decided to accept the verdict of the Lecompton convention and the inevitable approval of its slave-state constitution. This led him to an angry confrontation with Douglas, who saw the president's decision as a betrayal of popular sovereignty, on which the senator had staked his career.

33 Now, as always, Douglas saw himself as the defender of the sane middle ground, where the union might be saved from extremists. But his rejection of Lecompton meant trouble. When the House of Representatives, at Douglas's urging, refused to accept the slave-state constitution submitted by Kansas, Southerners who had supported Douglas's notion of popular sovereignty when it suited their purposes, now abandoned both it and Douglas. And Buchanan, who had boldly proclaimed Kansas "as much a slave state as Georgia or South Carolina," became Douglas's implacable enemy. The South had elected him; he was desperately afraid of secession; he couldn't bring himself to back down on Lecompton.

34 Yet neither could Douglas. Whatever compromising on Lecompton might have gained him in the South would have been lost in the North and the West, where the Democrats were already in deep disarray. And though Douglas had made his reputation as a canny career politician, he was also, at bottom, a patriot. He believed a national Democratic party was needed to hold the Union together, and he believed he was needed to lead it. Douglas had never been a man of cautious habits, and his health in recent years had been suspect. But when, in 1860, he was at long last nominated for the presidency, and found the party irretrievably broken—southern Democrats promptly chose a candidate of their own, John C. Breckinridge, to oppose both him and the Republican nominee, Lincoln—he turned all that was left of his energy into a campaign that was as much for the Union as it was for himself.

35 In October, accepting the inevitability of Lincoln's election, and knowing secession was no idle threat, Douglas courageously decided on a final tour of the South, hoping to rally sentiment to keep the nation whole. But though his reception was generally civil, the time for persuasion had passed. Symbolically, the deck of an Alabama riverboat on which he and his wife were traveling collapsed, injuring them both and forcing Douglas to continue with the aid of a crutch—for which someone later sent him a bill. He received news of his defeat in Mobile, realized it augured a country divided and likely a war, and retired to his hotel "more hopeless," reported his secretary, "than I had ever before seen him." The following June, exhausted in body and spirit, Douglas died at age 48, just seven weeks after the fall of Fort Sumter and the start of the Civil War he had dedicated himself to prevent.

40

TOMBEE

Portrait of a Cotton Planter

BY THOMAS BENJAMIN CHAPLIN

In 1971, antebellum historian Kenneth Stampp remarked that "I know of not a single slave diary." Since slaves were prevented from learning to read or write by their owners, we are left with few slave primary source documents. As a result of this lack of materials, students of history must rely upon other documentation—such as slavemasters' written records of wills, deeds, mortgages, and journals.

Diary keeper Thomas Benjamin Chaplin owned the Tombee Plantation on St. Helena Island in Beaufort District, South Carolina. Born in 1822, Chaplin was heir to a considerable fortune consisting of rice lands, cotton fields, and numerous slaves. Chaplin received an aristocratic formal education, which never raised questions about the South's peculiar institution—slavery.

Chaplin saw himself as a benevolent slaveowner, who cared for his chattel better than they would have cared for themselves . . . or so he would have us—the readers of his journal—believe. If students are shocked by Chaplin's recollections as they probably will be, remember two things: (1) Chaplin had little intention of having the public read his journal; and (2) slaves were not viewed as human beings by those who owned them.

*As you read Chaplin's 1845 journal entries, from historian Theodore Rosengarten's edited book—*Tombee: Portrait of a Cotton Planter, *consider these questions:*

- *What are Chaplin's main worries?*
- *How did weather conditions affect Chaplin's ownership of slaves?*
- *Do you believe Chaplin's assessment that his slaves were disconsolate (unhappy) "but this will soon blow over"?*

---

1   *April 27th, 1845.* Sunday, went to church. Was taken with a violent toothache, & returned home without hearing the service. There is to be a great baptizing at the Baptist meeting house today.[1]

2   Robert was taken very sick last night with an attack very like cholera. Man Tony was taken in the same way today. They were taken very suddenly with spasmatic pains in the stomach, with frequent operations[2] & excessive vomiting of green stuff like beet grass, and extreme debility in every part. Opium brings relief.

3   This is the day of my birthday, the 23rd year of my age—

4   *April 30th.* Went hunting, killed nothing. Saw the ship[3] ashore. It was quite a curiosity to some of the men. She was sold to a Mr. King[4] in Savannah for 52½ dollars so I did not expect to get anything more out of her. The men are now cutting her to pieces. Returned home about 8 o'clock. My tooth pained me very much. Sent for Mr. Jenkins. Had it extracted, it came out very easy.

5   *May 2nd*. Stayed at home all day—had toothache. Find that the tooth is broken off in the gum.

6   *May 3rd*. Went to Beaufort, parade day.[5] Got off from parade on account of my tooth. Returned after dark. Had a heavy shower of rain after I left the ferry. Was very much disappointed when I got as far as Wm. Chaplin's[6] to find there had not been a drop there. I do not think it rained farther this way than the marsh, if so far. This is the second rain they have had at the other end of the Island when we have had none for several weeks. Everything is suffering for want of rain. The little cotton that is up is dying. Potatoes and sugarcane also dying. The corn looks green in spots, but not growing. Water is getting scarce. My pump is almost dry—it sucks every evening. Nearly every pump & well in Beaufort has gone dry. Trouble gathers thicker & thicker around me. I will be compelled to send about 10 prime Negroes to town[7] next Monday, to be sold. I do this rather than have them seized and sold in Beaufort by the sheriff—or rather sacrificed.

7   I never thought that I would be driven to this very unpleasant extremity. Nothing can be more mortifying and grieving to a man than to select out some of his Negroes to be sold. You know not to whom, or how they will be treated by their new owners. And Negroes that you find no fault with— to separate families, mothers & daughters, brothers & sisters—all to pay for your own extravagances. People will laugh at your distress, and say it serves you right, you lived beyond your means, though some of the same never refused to partake of that hospitality and generosity which caused me to live beyond my means. Those beings I shall find out and will then know how to treat them.

8   *May 4th*. Sunday—did not go to church— toothache all day. The Negroes pulled up the floor to one of the outhouses & killed 56 rats—fine Sunday's work. A few clouds flying about. Wind very fresh but no rain. Things look worse & worse. Rode over to J. L. Chaplin's to get him to take the Negroes up to Beaufort for me tomorrow.

9   Just as had finished writing the foregoing sentence, I perceived Chaplin, James Clark[8] coming down the road. After they had eaten dinner, they went to the Negro houses & took 10 Negroes, viz.— Prince, Sib, Moses, Louisa, Tom, Hannah, Paul, Titus, Marcus & Joe. Carried them over to the Riverside where Clark's boat was. Got them on board, but it was so rough the boat nearly swamped, so they had to come on shore & stop until the next day. I cannot express my feelings on seeing so many faithful Negroes going away from me forever, not for any fault of their own but for my extravagance. It is a dearly bought lesson, and I hope I will benefit by it. The Negroes did not appear at all inclined to get off,[9] but apparently quite willing and in good spirits, particularly Prince & Paul. I hope they will bring a good price in Charleston where I have sent them under the charge of Wm. B. Fickling, to be sold, and not have to sell any more. Mickler the deputy levied on them they got in Beaufort, but Fickling jockied him and got them on steamboat quite safe.[10]

10   *May 5th*. Went to Beaufort. Could not go down to the boat to see the Negroes off, but am glad it is all over for it is the most unpleasant thing I have ever had to do, and truly hope it may never occur again. The Negroes at home are quite disconsolate, but this will soon blow over. They may see their children again in time. Returned home after dusk. DaCosta rode from the ferry with me.

11   *NOTE TO 4th & 5th MAY. It was a trying thing then. But could I or anyone foreseen how things would be 19 years after, when every Negro was set free by "force of war" I & everyone else would have gladly put them all in their pockets.[11] Besides, I would not have felt bad about it, for in truth, the Negroes did not care as much about us as we did for them.* [Editor's Note: This aside was written in 1876 by Thomas Chaplin, 11 years after all slaves were emancipated.]

Endnotes

1. A baptizing of Negroes. At this time on St. Helena, only the Baptist Church baptized and catechized slaves.

2. Bowel movements.

3. The shipwreck *Clio*.

4. Probably William King (1804–1884), cotton factor (one who sells cotton) and insurance agent.

5. Day when the Beaufort Volunteer Artillery assembled for the display, inspection, and procession.

6. William S. Chaplin's plantation, on the road to the Ladies Island Ferry.

7. Charleston, South Carolina.

8. James S. Clark (b. 1811). The census of 1850 lists his occupation as "none."

9. Off the boat.

10. Some of the court judgments that forced this sale involve creditors in Beaufort. The deputy attempted to seize the property before it left the District. In Fickling, Chaplin has chosen an experienced and influential man to see the slaves safely to Charleston, where they will bring more though a broker's sale than at a sheriff's auction in Beaufort.

11. Would have sold them then and there.

41

SLAVES IN THE FAMILY: ONE GENERATION'S SHAME IS ANOTHER'S REVELATION

BY BRENT STAPLES

In the summer of 2001, New York Times editorial writer Brent Staples noted that:

"Northerners tend to believe that slavery was confined to the South and that the North was composed of "free" states. The truth is that slavery was practiced all over the early United States, including the Dutch colonial settlement of New Amsterdam, which later became New York. The Dutch established New Amsterdam in the early 1600's and immediately imported Africans to work on farms and public works like the fortress wall from which Wall Street gets its name. By the 18th century, New York had more enslaved Africans than any other city in the country, with the exception of Charleston, South Carolina."

In 1991, a construction crew uncovered a colonial-era African burial ground while digging the foundation of an office tower in lower Manhattan. It was the first time for many New Yorkers to discover that the North wasn't as free as they had been taught in school. Many were shocked. After all, wasn't slavery confined solely to the South? Weren't white northerners free of such insidiousness?

New York abolished slavery in 1827. However, that did not stop many northern-ers from slave profiteering. Contemporary historians are discovering numerous primary source documents that establish the direct link between northern businesses—many of which are still exist—that provided insurance to southern slave owners and to those who trafficked in slaves. Antebellum northerners might have felt good about not owning slaves, while they still turned a profit from "that peculiar institution." As Brent Staples explains, such revelations remind us once again why history is ever-changing.

- *How did Brent Staples uncover his past?*
- *According to Staples, how did black families deal with slavery after moving north?*
- *How did schools teach slavery to children?*
- *What role did insurance companies play with slavery?*
- *Research one of the insurance companies within the article and find out its reaction to this revelation.*
- *How can families keep you from better knowing the past?*
- *What steps could you take to uncover a part of that past?*

1   Those of us who write about our families inevitably dig up secrets having to do with petty crime, infidelity or children born out of wedlock. I encountered similar domestic dramas while writing the history of my family a decade ago. The most dramatic discovery was that my great-grandfather was conceived in the fading days of the Confederacy, had several ex-slaves among his siblings and narrowly missed being born a slave himself. He died just 11 years before I was born.

2   I had always known at least in the abstract that slavery was somewhere in the past. But it startled me to realize that it was so recent and that my life had overlapped with the lives of people who had been bought and sold. I learned this not from my uncles who talked ceaselessly about the family but from a mimeographed family bulletin I came across when I was nearly 40.

3   A genealogical chart showed that some of the given names in my generation had come from slave-era relatives, including the white slave owner who sired my great-grandfather. A prime source for this information was my favorite uncle, Paul, who died this spring at the age of 81. He told me hundreds of stories over the years but somehow skipped this one.

4   Black families have commonly dealt with slavery by leaving it behind when they moved north in the **Great Migration**, sometimes bringing relatives who had once stood upon the auction block. The memory of enslavement was too fresh to be anything but stigmatizing and shameful. Families elected to bury this harrowing past and sometimes forbade their elders to speak of it.

5   Concealment of slavery at home was matched by dishonesty about it at school, where slavery was addressed superficially and incorrectly if it was addressed at all. Most Americans, both black and white, grew up believing that the North was always made up of "free" states dominated by fire-breathing abolitionists and that the evils of slavery were confined to the downy white cotton fields of the South.

6   Many present-day New Yorkers, for example, were made aware of their state's slave history only in the years since 1991, when a construction crew uncovered a colonial-era African burial ground while digging the foundation of a federal office tower in Lower Manhattan. The surprise was palpable in New York and beyond, even though Gotham in the eighteenth century was a capital of human bondage, with more enslaved people than any other American city, with the possible exception of Charleston, South Carolina.

7   The rediscovery of slave history in the North is racing along. A prime example is last fall's special issue of *The Hartford Courant's Sunday Magazine*, which presented an extensive, and shattering, review of slavery in Connecticut and which is now being made the basis of a book.

8   Historians working on business records are showing that the good, rich citizens of the Northeast were vigorously seeking business with Southern slavers and trafficking in slaves even after abolitionists had seized the day and Northeastern states had outlawed the slave trade. The mother lode of data can be found on the State Insurance Department Web site of California, which passed a law requiring insurance companies doing business in the state to scan their archives for documents related to the coverage of slave ships as well as slave injuries and deaths.

9   While eight companies reported slave business, only three: Aetna of Hartford, and the New York Life Insurance Company and the United States Life Insurance Company, both of New York could locate ledgers that named slaves and their owners. Insurance records figure prominently in federal lawsuits filed against companies in several states. The attempt to penalize present-day corporations for the conduct of their eighteenth and nineteenth century predecessors is controversial and unlikely to succeed. But the airing of records that have long lain hidden in corporate archives will give sharper focus to the portrait of Northern involvement in slavery.

10   What is striking in the records is that some companies operated with the clear intent of taking in slave-related business, even after abolition in the North. Manhattan Life quoted an old speech by a former president discussing what he believed to be one of the first group policies, if not the first group policy, ever issued by an American life insurance company. The 1854 policy insured 700 Chinese indentured workers (described as "coolies"), some of whom drowned themselves during the trip from China to Panama aboard the clipper ship *Sea Witch*.

11   The most striking records, deposited at the Schomburg Center for Research in Black Culture in Harlem, include voluminous ledgers and copies of two slave policies issued by the Nautilus Insurance Company of New York, the predecessor company of New York Life. Slavery had been abolished in New York for nearly 20 years when Nautilus set up shop in 1845. Yet the company's official history notes without shame that "among the first 1,000 policies issued, 339 were upon the lives of negro slaves in Maryland and Virginia." The company stopped

---

Great Migration: the period from World War One through teh 1940's when large numbers of southern blacks migrated to the North for a better life and employment opportunities.

issuing slave policies in 1848, probably because of pressure from abolitionist like Henry Ward Beecher.

12   One company, Royal and Sun Alliance, gives a harrowing account of an African slave insurrection on board a ship it insured, which resulted in some of the crew members being killed and the ship being run aground.

13   The records dredged up by California are just beginning to tell their stories. By the time that tale is done, the myth of the "free" North will have been put to rest for good, and Americans will know that the ligaments and tendons of slavery reached into the highest levels of the Northern elite and stretched the length and breadth of this country.

42

BITTER HARVEST

BY KIMBERLY FRENCH

Slavery isn't history—and we're reaping its fruit
How do we benefit from slavery today? In many, many ways. Here are just a few examples of how ALL of us benefits from slavery RIGHT NOW: chocolate, cotton, coffee, tea, tobacco, sugar, tomatoes, oranges, clothing, sneakers, gold, diamonds, cell phones, carpet and rugs.

Slavery is illegal everywhere in the world. But surprisingly, slavery is MORE common now than it was before the Civil War. Yes. An Estimated 27 million people are enslaved around the world today, including most states here in America. This is twice the number of Africans enslaved during the four centuries of the transatlantic slave trade. It is estimated that 50,000 people are forced to work as slaves in the United States today.

What is a slave? A slave is:

- *forced to work—through mental or physical threat;*
- *owned or controlled by an 'employer', usually through mental or physical abuse or threatened abuse;*
- *de-humanized, treated as a commodity or bought and sold as 'property';*
- *physically constrained or has restrictions placed on his/her freedom of movement*

In her article, **Bittter Harvest,** *Kimberly French writes that "we are all complicit." How? What does the average American do to encourage the modern slave trade?*

- *How is today's slavery different from that of "chattel slavery"?*
- *Why are there so many slaves now?*
- *How does debt bondage work?*
- *How are people lured into slavery?*
- *What will it take to solve this problem, in the author's opinion?*
- *Share this article with others. How did they react to this?*

---

1   You, in all likelihood, own items that were produced by slaves:

Chocolate. Hand-woven carpets. Cotton. Coffee. Tea. Tobacco. Sugar. Tomatoes. Cucumbers. Oranges. Grains. Clothing. Sneakers. Soccer balls. Gold. Diamonds. Jewelry. Fireworks. Steel. Glassware. Charcoal. Timber. Stone. Tantalum (a mineral used in laptops, pagers, personal digital assistants, and cell phones). Products in all of these industries have been found made with slave labor, then sold in the global market.

2   More items that you consume every day are tainted by slavery in less direct ways. "Your computer terminal may be made in Japan, but that company may reward executives with sex tours of enslaved prostitutes in Southeast Asia," says Barney

Freiberg-Dale, founder of Unitarian Universalists Against Slavery, one of several Unitarian Universalist groups working to fight modern slavery.

3   All of us who are lucky enough to be housed, clothed, and fed every day benefit from prices kept low by slave labor. Global companies we invest in, or whose stocks are part of our mutual or pension funds, provide higher returns because they buy from suppliers that pay workers very little—or not at all.

4   As participants in the world's largest consumer economy, with its drive for lower and lower prices, we contribute to the global economic pressure for slave labor. We are all complicit.

But didn't slavery end in the nineteenth century?

5   Many of today's new abolitionists admit to having held that same assumption, until a news story or pamphlet or lecture shocked them out of it.

6   Or you may have thought the reports of human trafficking that periodically make the news—such as sex slavery rings or forced migrant farm work—were isolated cases, somewhere far from you. I did.

7   The truth is that slavery exists in virtually every country of the world and in almost every U.S. state, according to human rights organizations, scholars, government agencies, and journalists. A growing antislavery movement has been hard at work documenting and exposing this troubling fact. Surveying their reports and interviewing antislavery spokespeople is eye-opening, answering not only my question about the nineteenth-century "end" of slavery but raising other questions as well.

8   In fact, legal slavery did end. Slavery is illegal in every country of the world. Nonetheless there are more slaves today than ever before: 27 million, twice as many as the number of Africans enslaved during the four centuries of the transatlantic slave trade, according to a calculation that slavery expert Kevin Bales calls conservative. Bales, a sociologist at Roehampton University in London who spoke at the UUA's 2003 General Assembly, estimates that 50,000 people are forced to work as slaves in the United States today.

How can this be? If slavery is illegal everywhere, how can there be slaves, and in such numbers?

9   In the United States our image of slavery is defined by our own horrific history. The antebellum slavery that was practiced here is called chattel slavery, meaning one person is owned completely by another and can be inherited as property.

10   Today's slavery is different. Simply put, slavery is one person forcing another to work without pay, using the threat of violence or psychological manipulation. Ownership no longer defines slavery.

11   When slaves could be legally owned, when buying slaves required a substantial financial investment, there was an incentive for owners to take care of their "property," to provide for their slaves' housing, food, health, children's care, and other needs. In contrast, when today's slaves are no longer economically useful, they are cast aside, worked or starved into permanent illness or death, sometimes even killed.

So why are there so many slaves now?

12   First, the world's population has nearly tripled in 50 years, most dramatically in developing countries, creating a huge pool of people who are desperately poor, vulnerable, and easily preyed on.

13   At the same time, globalization has transformed national and local economies. Corporations turn to unregulated suppliers in developing countries, and keep pressing for lower costs. In some cases, suppliers use forced, unpaid labor.

14   In many countries, widespread corruption allows slavery to thrive and grow.

15   The most common form of slavery today is debt bondage, a tradition throughout southern Asia that keeps a society's lowest castes or tribes perpetually in debt to their masters. The number of bonded laborers in India, Pakistan, and Nepal is estimated in the millions. They must work however much the master says and ask for permission for their every move. Bonded laborers have told human rights workers they are paying off loans as small as $10 to $50 . But the interest is always more than they can pay, and the debts are passed on through the generations.

16   Forced labor exists in many countries, including the United States. Wartime slavery is a problem in countries like Sudan, where government-backed militias and raiders have been kidnapping and enslaving village children and women since at least the mid-1980's, according to United Nations reports. Even chattel slavery persists: The military dictatorship of Mauritania has repeatedly declared slavery abolished, yet the U.S. State Department reports that 90,000 people are held there as chattel slaves.

---

17   The pitfall of focusing mainly on the most concentrated and brutal slavery hotspots is that we can compartmentalize slavery as something that is happening somewhere else, to someone far removed us, with little we can do. In fact, we need look no farther than our own country to find the fastest-growing form of slavery, called contract slavery, in which the poor, weak, young, and vulnerable are tricked with promises of legitimate work.

18   The Department of Justice estimates that 14,500 to 17,500 people are trafficked into the United States

annually. Slavery cases are being investigated in 46 states. In this country, most slavery victims are foreign-born and are found working as farm workers, live-in domestics, or prostitutes. Slavery has also been found in small businesses that typically rely on low-wage temporary labor, such as restaurants, nursing homes, and small manufacturers.

19   A 2002 case that resulted in federal sentences of 10 to 15 years for three family members who contracted farm labor from Florida to North Carolina shows how contract slavery works:

20   In early 2001 three Mixe Indians from Mexico each paid $250 to be smuggled into the United States. Penniless and stranded in an abandoned trailer with 30 others in Arizona, the three men agreed to go with a recruiter promising them jobs picking oranges in Florida. For three days they were packed in vehicles with no food and no stops to relieve themselves.

21   They were met in Florida by the Ramos brothers, who wrote a check to the recruiter and said each man owed $1,000 for transportation. Anyone who tried to leave without paying would be beaten. The workers were housed in a filthy converted bar, six to a room, on bare mattresses. They worked 12 hours a day, six to seven days a week, under 24-hour surveillance by guards with weapons. Each week the Ramoses deducted exorbitant fees for rent, food, work equipment, and daily transportation from the workers' "wages," then claimed to credit whatever remained to their "debt." The Ramoses were found to have "employed" thousands of undocumented workers in a similar pattern over a decade, according to Florida State University's Center for the Advancement of Human Rights.

22   Variations of this scenario are replayed every day in industries and countries throughout the world:

- Cacao plantations in Cote d'Ivoire, which produce half of the world's cocoa, have lured teenage boys from Mali, Burkina Faso, and Liberia with promises of jobs, then paid them nothing and beaten them into submission. Thus, a small but significant portion of the chocolate imported to the United States and Europe is slave-produced.
- Tens of thousands of children as young as six have been kidnapped or tricked to work in India's Carpet Belt in Uttar Pradesh, where they may be kept round-the-clock in the rooms where they are forced to weave.
- Wealthy people in New York, London, Paris, and other Western cities have promised young women jobs as nannies or household help and a chance to go to school, then forced them to work without pay. Joy Zarembka, director of the Break the Chain Campaign in Washington, D.C., told me she was shocked to discover an enslaved domestic worker on her very own street.

- Girls in Eastern Europe and Southeast Asia have been promised factory or restaurant jobs, then forced to work in brothels in their region or in Europe and the United States.

23   This list could go on and on. The story often turns out the same way: Once the victims arrive to work—with no money, no idea where they are, no understanding of their rights, and unable to speak the local language—they are told they must work to pay a debt for transportation or perhaps an advance paid to their families. They may be beaten, humiliated, or threatened with harm to themselves or their families. They are often kept in deplorable conditions, forced to work long hours with little sleep, forbidden to talk to outsiders. Their debt is never paid.

---

24   Slavery has been with us since the birth of civilization. About 11,000 years ago, humans began to form agrarian communities and organize themselves into hierarchical societies. Those at the top of the hierarchies enslaved others for domestic, agricultural, and construction work.

25   As long ago as Aristotle, people have argued that slavery may in fact be a condition of civilization. William Harper, a nineteenth-century proslavery judge and senator from South Carolina, argued: "Without it, there can be no accumulation of property, no providence for the future, no taste for comfort or elegancies, which are the characteristics and essentials of civilization."

26   Contemporary slavery is more complex and victimizes more people than ever before. And yet the new abolitionists see reasons to hope.

27   "We don't face the problems we faced in the past," Kevin Bales says. "We don't have to win the legal fight. We don't have to win the moral argument. In many ways it's simply a resource question and an awareness question."

28   Free the Slaves, the U.S. branch of the London-based Antislavery International, estimates that it costs $32 to free a slave family in northern India—not to buy their freedom, but to support local organizations that help slaves escape or walk away, then provide education and long-term rehabilitation so they don't fall back into slavery. At that rate, the cost to help every enslaved person on earth step to freedom can be roughly estimated at $10 billion—about the same cost as Boston's Big Dig.

29   In recent years, the new abolitionists have seen heartening successes. Pressure on Congress led to the 2000 passage of the U.S. Trafficking Victims Protection Act, specifying new slavery-related crimes and expanding protection for victims. Slavery investigations and prosecutions in this country have increased threefold.

30   The United Nations Convention on Transnational Organized Crime, ratified in 2003 , includes a large section on human trafficking. For the first time slavery cases are being prepared for trial before the International Criminal Court.

31   Underlying these successes is one essential factor: better public awareness. In order for antislavery strategies to work, governments and corporations must know that people are watching and that they demand an end to slavery.

32   Journalistic exposés and political action have curtailed slavery in Brazilian forests and mines and Dominican sugar fields. Grassroots organizations have helped free tens of thousands of slaves in India and other countries.

33   "Whether we like it or not, we are now a global people," Bales writes in *Disposable People: New Slavery in the Global Economy*. "We must ask ourselves: Are we willing to live in a world with slaves? If not, we are obligated to take responsibility for things that are connected to us, even when far away. . . . What good is our economic and political power, if we can't use it to free slaves? If we can't choose to stop slavery, how can we say that we are free?"

43

THE DEATH OF JOHN BROWN

BY R. EDWARD LEE

"I, John Brown, am now quite certain that the crimes of this guilty land will never be purged away but with blood."

No individual in America polarized Americans and their respective beliefs on slavery more so than John Brown. When Brown and his small band of followers attempted to incite slaves to revolt against their southern owners in 1858 at Harper's Ferry, Virginia, the nation moved one giant step closer to war. As abolitionist newspaper editor William Lloyd Garrison wrote—"In firing his gun, John Brown has merely told what time of day it is. It is high noon, thank God."

Although Brown's armed rebellion failed, the abolitionist cause solidified those who argued by any means of necessary. With the trial and hanging of Brown, he became a martyr to abolitionists. Henry David Thoreau likened Brown's death to Christ's crucifixion "as two ends of a chain which is not without its links. He is not old Brown any longer; he is an angel of light." Abolitionists sang John Brown's body lies a smoldering in the grave. His death would not be in vain.

Others entrenched themselves to maintain slavery no matter what the costs. Slaveholders and those sympathetic toward "the peculiar institution" were determined to make the execution of Brown an example to those who felt a kindred spirit to the enslaved. The Richmond Whig editorialized that the miserable old traitor and murderer belongs to the gallows. Woe to those who follow in Brown's footsteps! There was little middle ground. Compromises on slavery ceased.

- *What was John Brown's background? Why did he feel compelled to overthrow slavery?*
- *Why didn't freed blacks and slaves follow Brown's rebellion?*
- *Herman Melville called Brown the meteor of the Civil War. Do you agree with his assessment?*
- *How might the media portray a modern-day type Brown and similar actions today?*

---

1   The misguided aims of John Brown in 1859 at Harpers Ferry will long be remembered. The raid he carried out was in preparation a long time with the assistance of many who hated slavery. Many people of wealth and intellect believed in his aims. According to C. Vann Woodward in *The Burden of Southern History*, Brown's chief conspirators were "the Secret Six": Gerrit Smith, a philanthropist; Dr. Samuel G. Howe, husband of Julia Ward Howe; George L. Steams, a prosperous Boston manufacturer; Thomas Wentworth Higginson, son of a Boston merchant, and who later became a Unitarian minister in Worcester, Massachusetts; and Franklin B. Sanborn, a disciple of Ralph Waldo Emerson. While not a member of the Secret Six, Frederick Douglass provided advice, and helped raise funds even though he expected failure. He told John Brown that he was stepping into "a perfect steel trap."

2   Many New England intellectuals sympathized with his plan, such as Ralph Waldo Emerson, Henry David Thoreau, William Ellery Channing, Louisa May Alcott, and James Russell Lowell, among others.

3   Brown was certain—though not all others sympathizers were, that with a small army and hundreds of slaves and Free Blacks in the immediate area who would join him, they would hide out in the dense Appalachian forests and gather strength from thousands of other runaways, hold off great numbers of their attackers, and move slowly down the mountain chain collecting more slaves and black freedmen as they progressed Southward.

4   Brown had set up a plan for an abolitionist republic. It was presented to his supporters in the spring of 1858.

5   At the same time much less is known about the Secret Order of Twelve—completely black, and organized by one Rev. John Dickson, who decided to lie back with some 138,000 recruits and wait. They would permit Brown to strike first.

6   By the spring of 1858, about $23,000 in "cash, credit, and supplies" had been raised to support Brown's guerrilla activities.

7   His supplies included some 200 hundred rifles, 200 hundred revolvers, ammunition, and nearly 1,000 specially manufactured pikes for the slaves he fully expected to join him.

8   Brown's "army" finally consisted of 21 men, including two of his sons and five black men: Dangerfield Newby, Shields Green, John A. Copeland, Sherrard Lewis Leafy, and Osborn P. Anderson. Shields Green, a runaway slave, had been recruited by Douglass, and joined Brown during a visit to the Maryland farmhouse in the company of Douglass. Douglass departed after remaining overnight discussing the matter with Brown.

9   Shields Green was sent on special recruiting missions after he arrived. Free Blacks and slaves did not join Brown in his efforts. There were several reasons why. The major reason was that they saw the action as one stamped with failure.

10   A second reason was that free Blacks in the vicinity were reasonably content. There were no large plantations. Thirdly, the slaves in the area were few. Those that were about were of the first opinion. Their duties and responsibilities were easier than for those who toiled in plantation life.

11   On the evening of October 16, Brown left three men standing guard at the farmhouse, and took 17 others with him to the federal arsenal. Taking the arsenal would be an easy task since there were no guards stationed there.

12   He took enough ammunition to field an army much larger than the one he had.

13   President Buchanan, notified, by wire, promptly sent then Colonel Robert E. Lee with a detachment of marines to quell the disturbance. One marine was killed along with four residents of Harpers Ferry. Counted among the dead were the mayor and a black freeman, the local baggage handler. He was the first person killed, as he ran to inform other townspeople of what was taking place.

14   When Brown was captured, 10 of his small army were killed, including his own two sons, five were captured including Brown himself, and seven escaped. Two were captured later.

15   Except for the first day of the trial at Charles Town, which started eight days after his capture, Brown lay on a stretcher on the floor as arguments swirled about him. Few men could look the old warrior in the eye, according to Thomas J. Fleming writing in "American Heritage."

16   On that first day in court, Brown walked into the room erect with a steady gait. He stared at the prosecutor, Charles Harding, an alcoholic, "his coat stained and dirty, his hair uncombed, [with] a stubble of whiskers and a weak chin." When he asked Brown if he had proper legal counsel, or would the court have to assign him counsel, Brown addressed the court. Among other things, he said:

17   "Virginians, I did not ask for any quarter at the time I was taken. I did not ask to have my life spared . . . I am ready for my fate. I do not ask a trial. I beg for no mockery of a trial—no insult—nothing but that which conscience gives, or cowardice would drive you to practice . . . I have now little further to ask, other than that I may not be foolishly insulted only as cowardly barbarians insult those who fall into their power."

18   Brown was described as a monomaniac with a fixation on the Bible. Henry David Thoreau had already declared that Brown's sure execution would be like "the crucifixion of Christ."

19   Members of Brown's family pointed out the family members who had been classified as insane. Some "nineteen affidavits were signed by relatives and friends attesting to the record of insanity in the Brown family."

20   His maternal grandmother and his mother died insane. Three of his aunts and two of his uncles (on his mother's side) were classified as crazy. One of his sons died insane, and another had intermittent episodes of insanity. Most of Brown's six first cousins had been mentally deranged from time to time. But Brown steadfastly refused to plead insanity.

21   The Boston Post observed wryly, "John Brown may be a lunatic (but if so) then one-fourth of the people of Massachusetts are madmen."

22   Governor Henry A. Wise of Virginia thought Brown mad, and once ordered him to be examined by the superintendent of the state insane asylum, but on reflection countermanded his order. Brown himself said that Governor Wise was crazy.

23 Speaking at Henry Ward Beecher's church, Wendell Phillips said it was "Hard to tell who was mad. The world says one man's mad. John Brown said the same of the Governor."

24 Abolitionist firebrand the Rev. Theodore Parker said that Brown would not only become a martyr, "but also a saint." He boldly predicted slave insurrection—"the Fire of Vengeance—and only the white man's blood will be able to put it out." Parker continued, "Do we shrink from the violence?" He said that such a fire could "not be put out with rose water."

25 After a parade of witnesses, the display of papers taken from the Maryland farmhouse, and a full review of what had occurred, the court was ready for sentencing.

26 From his stretcher on the floor, Brown listened and delayed the proceedings. But on October 26, he was brought into the courtroom on a cot, claiming he was too weak to walk. He accused his captives of taking his money ($250 in gold) after he was "sacked and stabbed." Part of the time, Brown lay on his cot and listened with his eyes closed.

27 When called upon to speak, Brown responded:

28 "Now, if it is deemed necessary that I would give up my life for the furtherance of ends of justice, and mingle my blood rather with blood of my children and with blood of millions in this slave country lose rights are disrespected by wicked, cruel, and unjust enactments, I submit: let it be done!"

29 On October 31—two weeks after the Harpers Ferry Raid, the jury brought in a verdict of guilty. On November 2, the judge sentenced Brown to death by hanging. The act would be carried out one month later.

30 Governor Wise received many letters asking that Brown be given a life sentence instead of hanging. Some of his friends thought of storming the jail. Governor Wise even considered putting Brown on a ship at sea, and holding him there until the day of the hanging.

31 There are at least two famous paintings and one lithograph showing Brown in the presence of a black mother and child.

32 The story had been spread by *The New York Tribune* on the day of his hanging, that Brown had leaned down to kiss a black child. The artists were T.S. Noble (*John Brown's Blessing*), and *The Last Moments of John Brown*, by Thomas Hovenden. The lithograph is by Currier and Ives. Indeed, one of the pictures shows the Captain kissing the black child.

33 Not only that, Brown was of such heroic proportions that Victor Hugo in France got into the act by painting a picture of Brown on the gallows. John Greenleaf Whittier said Brown "had stooped between the jeering ranks and kissed the negro's child." The rumor was untrue, and the figment of a reporter's imagination. Brown did kiss a child on that day, December 2, 1859, but it was the child of his jailer, John Avis.

34 Brown went to his hanging wearing a frock coat and pants, "a black slouch hat, and red slippers." When he saw some 1,500 armed men in the street, Brown commented laconically, "I had no idea that Governor Wise considered my execution so important."

35 As he left the jail, he gave to one of the guards a note which read:

36 "I, John Brown. am now quite certain that the crimes of this guilty land will never be purged away; but with Blood. I had as I now think, vainly flattered myself that without very much bloodshed it might be done."

37 He rode to the scaffold seated on his coffin, and commented on the beauty of the scenery on a clear warm day: "This is a beautiful country. I never truly had the pleasure of seeing it before."

38 When they put the white bag over his head, the old man never wavered. When the sheriff cut the rope to the trap door, Brown fell about five inches; his arm, bent at the elbows, went upward, and in a few moments he was dead.

39 The hanging of John Brown was a cause célèbre. The North and South hardened in their separate resolves, perhaps knowing that the nation was moving closer and closer to civil war. There are those who say that the Civil War had nothing to do with slavery, but I think they're wrong. It depends on how one looks at things. Less than a year and a half after the execution of John Brown, Confederate troops fired on Fort Sumter, signaling the beginning of the war. In many ways, John Brown had brought the slavery issue to a head: no, a boil, in the conscience of the nation.

THE CIVIL WAR AND IT'S AFTERMATH

1 The Civil War was the most violent episode in our nation's history. It was also the most revolutionary. The war killed more people than all of our other wars combined. It destroyed cities and ravaged the countryside of many states, North and South. The war changed us. We were a different country in 1865. In essence, the United States went into the Civil War an agricultural society, loosely held together by a national government that was constantly beset by threats from bitter factions, North, South, East, and West. We emerged from the war an industrial juggernaut, with the southern plantation system crushed, slavery abolished, and a new, truly national government that grew in power and influence over the next century.

2 The conflict was an outgrowth of the vast differences between the two regions: differences in geography, economy, class structure, and temperament. For over 30 years before the war, the South felt itself increasingly threatened by explosive growth in the North. Southerners believed that as population growth in the North outstripped their own, southern control of the federal government could slip away. This, it was believed, would threaten the legal structure that protected the South's "peculiar institution", slavery. Prior to the Civil War, leadership of the federal government lied firmly in southern hands. Two-thirds of the presidents were southern;

two-thirds of the pro-tems of the Senate and Speakers of the House were southern; 20 of 34 Supreme Court justices were southern. By 1860, there were nine million people living in the South, with over 22 million living in the North.

3 A bewildering series of events in the 1850s set the stage for the conflict. In 1852, Harriet Beecher Stowe published *Uncle Tom's Cabin*. The book brought the human tragedy of slavery out into the open for the first time. Northerners and Europeans alike were outraged by the treatment of people that Stowe's novel so vividly portrayed. It was a monumental best-seller, and, like Thomas Paine's *Common Sense* before, it recast American public opinion at a crucial time.

4 In 1857, the Supreme Court handed down its decision in the Dred Scott case. Scott, a black man, had sued for his freedom based upon the fact that his "owner" had taken him into a free state, Illinois, and a free territory, Wisconsin. The courts decision nullified the Missouri Compromise of 1820, which prevented slaveowners from taking slaves (their legal property) into territories north of the 36° 30' latitudinal line. Further, Chief Justice Roger Taney, a southerner, wrote in the majority opinion that black persons, whether free or slave, "had no rights which the white man was bound to respect," and that the *Declaration of Independence* and the Constitution did

not apply to black people. The Court's decision deepened the sectional split.

5   The sparks that set the conflict off were twofold: In 1859, John Brown, a radical abolitionist bent on freedom at all costs for the slaves, led an ill-fated raid on the federal arsenal at Harper's Ferry, Virginia. His goal was to get weapons to slaves so they could rise up and slay their owners. That his raid failed miserably does not really matter. Because of Brown, the South was further convinced that northerners were bent on the destruction of their way of life. "Fire-eaters," radicals in the South who wanted a total break with the North, were gaining ground.

6   When he was elected president in 1860, Abraham Lincoln was faced with a divided country. Lincoln was a northerner, and he was opposed to the extension of slavery in the territories, though he conceded that he could do nothing about its practice where it already existed. He received only 39 percent of the popular vote. This put him at a serious disadvantage from election day onward. By the time he took office in March, 1861, six southern states, led by South Carolina, had already seceded from the union.

7   According to Civil War historian James McPherson, the War started out as one kind of conflict and ended up as something quite different. Lincoln's goal at the beginning was very basic: to keep the union together. To him, if secession were allowed to succeed, the United States "would fragment into a dozen pitiful, squabbling countries, the laughing stock of the world." And if the confederacy were allowed to succeed, the idea of inequality would live, perhaps even spread. He prosecuted the war, then, to preserve the union, not to save or destroy slavery. Not in the beginning, anyway . . .

8   The South saw the conflict in entirely different terms, naturally. They left the nation in the name of their own liberties—of property rights and state sovereignty—in the name of their right proclaimed by the *Declaration of Independence* to "alter or abolish" the form of government, if it became destructive of the purpose of protecting their property. One Texan who enlisted in the Confederate Army said that, like their forefathers of 1776, he and his brothers "are now enlisted in the 'Holy Cause of Liberty and Independence.'" Both sides, in their own way, were fighting for their liberties.

9   It was a harder war by 1863, harder for both sides. Lincoln upped the ante in 1863: With his Emancipation Proclamation, he made the freeing of the slaves an additional goal for fighting the war. What had begun as a war to preserve the Union had now become a war to tear down the entire southern social structure. Emancipation, and the decision to recruit black troops, became the heaviest blow dealt to the southern rebellion. By 1863, then, there was no room left for compromise: the South either won the war and formed a new country, or it lost not only the conflict but also its entire way of life . . .

10   The South did lose the war, and it lost just about everything else, too. To James McPherson, the war for independence from Great Britain was not nearly as revolutionary as the Civil War. How could this be so? First, the Civil War resulted in the abolition of slavery. The American Revolution had left slavery intact. The Civil War also destroyed the social structure of the old South and radically altered the power balance between North and South. Mark Twain wrote that the war "uprooted institutions that were centuries old . . . transformed the social life of half the country, and wrought so profoundly upon the entire national character." Charles Beard called it a "social cataclysm . . . making vast changes in the arrangement of classes, in the distribution of wealth, in the course of industrial development."

11   Lincoln himself was shaken by the presidency. As President, the burden of responsibility was terrifying for him. His personal victory, winning the office he so long had coveted, meant death for 630,000 men and women. He shouldered this burden and was aware of his own role in causing the disaster. Stephan B. Oates wrote: "His utter lack of personal malice toward the South, his humanity and his tragic sense of life have no parallel in American history."

12   The war changed us. In 1858, Lincoln laid out our national political agenda with his "House Divided" speech. He then carried it out, crushing forever the outdated notion of human inequality and scaling back the then modern southern notion of state sovereignty. In 1863, Lincoln picked up where Jefferson left off in 1776. In his Gettysburg Address, Lincoln re-defined what is meant by the words freedom and democracy, the consequences of which Americans are still grappling with today.

44

CLARKSDALE

BY NICHOLAS LEMANN

It's hard to find people to do the work you don't want to do. The first Euro-Americans started off by using indentured servants to do the work. Seven years of room and board and you got your freedom. But lots of people died off, so servants stopped coming to America. So they started buying and selling black slaves. Slaves produced huge agricultural surpluses, resulting in profits, investment, and more profits. It worked for the white people. But then they figured slavery wasn't fair, so they replaced it with sharecropping. Lots of the same folks, same abusive labor practices, but at least they were "free". Up North, where cash crops were not the foundation of the economy, they used children and immigrants in their factories to generate profits. Coal mines, steel mills, and textile factories chewed up labor by the millions. With depressions and wars we learned a lesson: labor should be valued. So now we have minimum wage. A benchmark, a subsistence wage, complete with no benefits, retirement or job security. The cheap labor source continues.

Each group of abused workers discovered ways to beat the system that took their labor: slaves fought for their freedom; immigrants assimilated and moved up the ladder; students finish their degrees and said goodbye to minimum wage. But what about sharecroppers? Many had been abused by the system of chattel slavery. Many were illiterate, with little or no understanding of the law. And with time came Jim Crow and lynchings to keep black people "in their place." The southern economic and political culture was a caste system—set up to keep people separate—economically, legally, socially, and culturally. It succeeded. If success can be marked by gross inequalities.

Nicholas Lemann's book The Promised Land *detailed black folks' attempts to break out of the southern system and gain new opportunities and identities in northern cities. This first chapter of* The Promised Land *illustrates how sharecropping worked. Clarksdale, Mississippi is in the Delta, ground zero for sharecropping in that former slave state. To understand how sharecropping worked in Mississippi is to grasp the reasoning behind black folks' decision to leave it.*

- *What does Lemann mean when he said the Mississippi Delta was a quintessential sharecropping area? Provide examples.*
- *Why did many black people refer to Chicago as "The Promised Land"?*
- *What were the realities of sharecroppers' lives in the Delta?*
- *Define the following: "furnish", "seed money", "chopped", "take up", "the settle", and "soak".*
- *How did planters cheat sharecroppers?*
- *How did planters explain the poverty experienced by sharecroppers?*

1   Segregation's heyday and sharecropping's heyday substantially coincided. Together the two institutions comprised a system of race relations that was, in its way, just as much a thing apart from the mainstream of American life as slavery had been, and that lasted just about as long as slavery did under the auspices of the government of the United States. The Mississippi Delta, which was only a footnote in the history of slavery because it was settled so late, was central to the history of the sharecropper system, especially the part of the system that involved blacks working on large plantations. The Delta had the largest-scale farming of the quintessential sharecropping crop, cotton. It was in the state that had the quintessential version of Jim Crow. The intellectual defense of sharecropping emerged from the Delta more than from any other place. The study of sharecropping by outsiders took place more in the Delta than in any other place. The black culture associated with sharecropping—including that culture's great art form, the blues—found its purest expression in the Delta. The Delta was the locus of our own century's peculiar instruction.

2   The greatest days of the Delta were during World War I. The veneer of civilization had by then been pretty well laid down. There were clubs, schools, libraries, businesses, and solid homes in the towns. Agricultural prices were high nationally all through the 'teens, and World War I created an especially great demand for cotton. In 1919 the price of Delta cotton went to $1 a pound, its all-time high relative to inflation. Land prices were as high as $1,000 an acre, which meant that all the big plantations were worth millions. In 1920 disaster struck: the price of cotton fell to 10 cents a pound. The Delta began struggling on and off with economic depression a decade earlier than the rest of the country.

3   Before the cotton crash, through, the Delta's main problem was that black people had begun to migrate to the North to work in factories. The main transportation routes out of the Delta led straight north. The Illinois Central Railroad, which was by far the most powerful economic actor in Mississippi, had bought the Delta's main rail system in 1892; its passengers and freight hooked up in Memphis with the main Illinois Central line, which ran from New Orleans to Chicago, paralleling the route of U.S. Highway 51. U.S. Highway 61, paralleling the Mississippi River, passed through Clarksdale; U.S. 49, running diagonally northwest through the Delta from Jackson, Mississippi, met 61 on the outskirts of Clarksdale. These were famous routes. The Illinois Central trains were household names: the Panama Limited, the City of New Orleans, the Louisiane. One of the canonical blues songs is called *Highway Forty-Nine*. The closest cities to Clarksdale were Jackson, Memphis, New Orleans, and St. Louis, but none of them

was fully removed from the social orbit of Southern segregation, or in a state of flat-out industrial expansion. The main place where all the routes out of Clarksdale really led was Chicago—job-rich Chicago.

4   Chicago was home to the *Chicago Defender*, the country's leading black newspaper, with a wide readership in the rural South, Robert S. Abbott, the *Defender's* publisher, a small, round, well-dressed man who artfully combined the roles of race crusader and businessman, launched what he called "The Great Northern Drive" on May 15, 1917. The object of the drive was to exhort Southern blacks to come to Chicago, in order to make money and live under the legal benefits of citizenship. Abbott invented slogans ("The Flight Out of Egypt") and promoted songs (*Bound for the Promised Land*, *Going Into Canaan*) that pounded home a comparison to the events described in the Book of Exodus for his audience of extremely religious children of slaves. He persuaded the railroads to offer "club rates" to groups of blacks migrating to Chicago. At the same time strong-back businesses like the stockyards and packing houses, desperately short of labor because of the war, hired white labor agents and black preachers to tour the South recruiting. Black porters on the Illinois Central, who at the time were a prosperous, respected elite in black America, spread the word (and passed out the *Defender*) on their stops in Mississippi towns. E. Franklin Frazier, the black sociologist, reported that, "In some cases, after the train crossed the Ohio River, the migrants signalized the event by kissing the ground and holding prayer services." The black population of Chicago grew from 44,000 in 1910 to 109,000 in 1920, and then to 234,0000 in 1930. A local commission on race relations reported that 50,000 black people had moved to Chicago from the South in 18 months during the war.

5   The South naturally wanted to stop the migrations. Some towns levied heavy "licensing fees" on labor agents to prevent them from coming around. Some threatened to put the agents in jail. In some places the police would arrest black people for vagrancy if they were found in the vicinity of the train station, or even pull them off of trains and put them in jail. There was a great deal of local propagandizing against migration by planters, politicians, black preachers in the hire of whites, and the press. A headline of the time from the *Memphis Commercial Appeal*, the big-city paper most read in the Delta said:

6   *SOUTH IS BETTER FOR NEGRO, SAY MISSISSIPPIANS*

7   *COLORED PEOPLE FOUND PROSPEROUS AND HAPPY*

8   None of these tactics seem to have worked, but it didn't matter. When the soldiers came home in 1918,

the demand for labor in Chicago slackened immediately. Later, the Depression hit Chicago especially hard, and the effect in the South of the high unemployment rate in Chicago was to discourage migration; the black population of Chicago grew by just 44,000 in the 1930's.

9   Anyway, the planters of the Delta had, during and after World War I, created a significant, though unpublicized, black migration of their own, from the hills of northern and central Mississippi to the Delta. The most common family history among black families in the Delta is exactly like Ruby Daniel's: the family scratching out an existence in the mediocre soil of the hills; the Delta plantation manager painting his enticing picture of the bountiful cotton crop in the Delta and the economic promise of the sharecropper system; and then the move.

10   This inside-Mississippi migration almost always ended with the family feeling that it had been badly gulled, because it turned out to be nearly impossible to make any money sharecropping. The sharecropper's family would move, early in the year, to a rough two- or three-room cabin on a plantation. The plumbing consisted of, at most, a washbasin, and usually not even that. The only heat came from a woodburning stove. There was no electricity and no insulation. During the winter, cold air came rushing in through cracks in the walls and the floor. Usually the roof leaked. The families often slept two and three to a bed.

11   Every big plantation was a fiefdom; the small hamlets that dot the map of the Delta were mostly plantation headquarters rather than conventional towns. Sharecroppers traded at a plantation-owned commissary, often in scrip rather than money. (Martin Luther King, Jr., on a visit to an Alabama plantation in 1965, was amazed to meet sharecroppers who had never seen United States currency in their lives.) They prayed at plantation-owned Baptist churches. Their children walked, sometimes miles, to plantation-owned schools, usually one- or two-room buildings without heating or plumbing. Education ended with the eighth grade and was extremely casual until then. All the grades were taught together, and most of the students were far behind the normal grade level for their age. The textbooks were tattered hand-me-downs from the white schools. The planter could and did shut down the schools whenever there was work to be done in the fields, so the school year for the children of sharecroppers usually amounted to only four or five months, frequently interrupted. Many former sharecroppers remember going to school only when it rained. In 1938 the average American teacher's salary was $1,374, and the average value of a school district's buildings and equipment per student was $274. For blacks in Mississippi, the figures were $144 and $11.

12   Each family had a plot of land to cultivate, varying in size from 15 to 40 acres depending on how many children there were to work and how generous the planter was. In March, the planter would begin to provide the family with a "furnish," a monthly stipend of anywhere from $15–$50 that was supposed to cover their living-expenses until the crop came in in the fall. The planter also provided "seed money" for cotton seed, and roots for cultivation. He split the cost of fertilizer with the sharecropper. Thus equipped, the sharecropper would plow his land behind a mule, plant the cotton, and cultivate a "garden spot" for vegetables. Between planting and harvest, the cotton had to be regularly "chopped"—that is, weeded with a hoe—to ensure that it would grow to full height. The standard of living provided by the furnish was extremely low – cheap homemade clothes and shoes, beans, bread, and tough, fatty cuts of pork—but nonetheless the money often ran out before the end of the month, in which case the family would have to "take up" (borrow) at the commissary.

13   The cotton was picked in October and November and then was taken to the plantation's gin, where it was separated from its seeds and then weighed. The planter packed it into bales and sold it. A couple of weeks would pass during which the planter would do his accounting for the year. Then, just before Christmas, each sharecropper would be summoned to the plantation office for what was called "the settle." The manager would hand him a piece of paper showing how much money he had cleared from his crop, and pay him his share.

14   For most sharecroppers, the settle was a moment of bitterly dashed hope, because usually the sharecropper would learn that he had cleared only a few dollars, or nothing at all, or that he owed the planter money. The planters explained this by saying that ever since the cotton crash of 1920 they hadn't made much money either; what every sharecropper believed was that they were cheating. There was one set of accounting practices in particular that the sharecroppers considered cheating and the planters didn't: a series of fees the planters levied on the sharecroppers over the course of the year. The goods sold at the commissary were usually marked up. Many planters charged exorbitant interest on credit at the commissary, and sometimes on the furnish as well—20 percent was a typical rate. When tractors came in during the 1930's, the planters would charge the sharecroppers for the use of them to plow the fields. None of these charges were spelled out clearly as they were made, and usually they appeared on the sharecropper's annual statement as a single unitemized line, "Plantation Expense."

15   Then there was indisputable cheating. There was no brake on dishonest behavior by a planter toward a sharecropper. For a sharecropper to sue a planter was

unthinkable. Even to ask for a more detailed accounting was known to be an action with the potential to endanger your life. The most established plantations were literally above the law where black people were concerned. The sheriff would call the planter when a matter of criminal justice concerning one of his sharecroppers arose, and if the planter said he preferred to handle it on his own (meaning, often, that he would administer a beating himself), the sheriff would stay off the place. Some planters were allowed to sign their sharecroppers out of the county jail if it was time to plant or chop or pick, and pay the bond later on credit. (If a sharecropper committed a crime serious enough for him to be sent to the state penitentiary, in Parchman, he would pick cotton there too—it was a working plantation in the Delta.) If a planter chose to falsify a sharecropper's gin receipt, lowering the weight of cotton in his crop, there was nothing the sharecropper could do about it; in fact a sharecropper was not allowed to receive and sign for a gin receipt on his own. If a planter wanted to "soak" a sharecropper, by adding a lot of imaginary equipment repairs to the expense side of his statement, the sharecropper had no way of knowing about it. As one Clarksdale planter puts it, quoting a proverb his father used to quote to him, "When self the wavering balance holds, 'tis seldom well adjusted."

16   Everybody agrees that some planters cheated and some didn't. Numbers are understandably difficult to come by. Hortense Powdermaker, an anthropologist from Yale who spent a year in the 1930s studying the town of Indianola, Mississippi, 60 miles down the road from Clarksdale, estimated that only a quarter of the planters were honest in their accounting.

17   The end of every year presented a sharecropper who had come up short with not many good options. He could stay put, piling up debt at the commissary until the furnish started again in March, and hope that the next year he would make a good enough crop to clear his debt. He could move to town, live in an unheated shack there, and try working for wages as a filed hand or a domestic. He could, finally, try sharecropping on another place, and this was the choice that most sharecroppers made sooner or later. Some of them would pack up and move, and some of them would "slip off" in the night, to escape a too-onerous debt or some other kind of bad trouble with white people. The great annual reshuffling of black families between plantations in the Delta during the time after the settle and before the furnish is in retrospect one of the most difficult aspects of the sharecroppers system to understand. The relatively few plantations where the sharecroppers regularly cleared money rarely had openings, so the families that moved usually wound up at another dishonest place where they would end the year in debt. The constant churning of the labor force couldn't have been good business for the planters, either.

18   Many of the sharecroppers and planters obviously weren't thinking all that far ahead. The more marginal the planter, the more likely he was to cheat, so that he could see some money himself at the end of the year. The more he cheated, the more likely he was to lose his labor after the settle. The sharecropper's rationale for moving was, in part, some mix of optimism and disgust. John Dollard, the Yale psychologist who helped develop the theory that frustration leads to aggression, also spent time during the thirties in Indianola, Mississippi, and wrote the book *Caste and Class in a Southern Town* about it. Dollard explained sharecroppers' moving by saying, "It seems that one of the few aggressive responses that the Negroes may make . . . is to leave a particular plantation . . . it is exactly what they could not do in prewar days, and it probably represents a confused general distrust, resentment, and hope for betterment . . . ."

19   The false-promise aspect of sharecropping, the constant assertion by planters that your poverty was your own fault—you and he were simply business partners, your loss was right there in cold type on the statement—made it especially painful. As a sharecropper, your found your life was organized in a way that bore some theoretical relation to that of a free American—and yet the reality was completely different. There were only two ways to explain it, and neither one led to contentment: either there was a conspiracy dedicated to keeping you down, or—the whites' explanation—you were inferior, incapable. Poverty and oppression are never anything but hard to bear, but when you add to them the imputation of failure, it multiplies the difficulty.

About the Editors

Peter J. Myers is an Associate Professor of History at Palo Alto College in San Antonio, Texas, where he has taught since 1988. He earned his B.A. in history from Muhlenberg College in Allentown, Pennsylvania and his M.A. in history from New York University. Born in New York City, he was raised on Long Island and taught high school in Papua New Guinea before re-locating to south Texas. Students in his classes learn to do artifact research and oral history. Their oral history projects can be viewed at: http://www.accd.edu/pac/faculty/InteractiveHistory/

Robert R. Hines is an Assistant Professor of History at Palo Alto College since 1989. He earned his B.S. and M.S. degrees from Illinois State University. His graduate work allowed him the opportunity to study in China. Later, he journeyed to Papua New Guinea, where he taught English and history for two years as a Peace Corps Volunteer. Students in his classes learn to research the history of small towns in south Texas. These histories can be viewed at: http://www.accd.edu/pac/faculty/InteractiveHistory/

Rex Lewis Field is an Associate Professor of History at Palo Alto, where he has taught since 1989. He was raised in Ft. Worth, "where the west begins," earning a B.A. in history at the University of Texas at Arlington. He earned an M.A. in history, concentrating on foreign affairs, at the University of Houston. He has devoted considerable time and interest toward travel and study in Mexico, Europe, and Asia. His article on Mission Espada in *Flyover History—Volume I* is the product of an ongoing love of the early period of Texas.

CREDITS

This page constitutes an extension of the copyright page. We have made every effort to trace the ownership of all copyrighted material and to secure permission from copyright holders. In the event of any question arising as to the use of any material, we will be pleased to make the necessary corrections in future printings. Thanks are due to the following authors, publishers, and agents for permission to use the material indicated.

Chapter 1. 3: Evan Hadingham, "America's First Immigrants," in Smithsonianmagazine.com, November 2004, http://www.smithsonian magazine.com/issues/2004/november/immigrants.php. Copyright (c) 2004 by Smithsonianmagazine.com. All rights reserved. Reproduced by permission. **9:** From Alan Linn, "Corn, the New World's Secret Weapon and the Builder of Its Civilizations", originally appeared in SMITHSONIAN MAGAZINE, August 1, 1973, pp. 59-63. **13:** David Roberts, "Secrets of the Maya: Deciphering Tikal," in Smithsonianmagazine.com, July 2004, http://www.smithsonianmagazine.com/issues/2004/july/tikal.php. Copyright (c) 2004 by Smithsonianmagazine.com. All rights reserved. Reproduced by permission. **17:** From Lewis Lord and Sarah Burke, "America Before Columbus," U.S. NEWS & WORLD REPORT, July 8, 1991, pp. 30-37. Copyright (c) 1991 U.S. News & World Report, L.O. Reprinted with permission.

Chapter 2. 25: "The Sailors of Palos" by Peter F. Copeland. This article is reproduced from the March/April 1993 issue of AMERICAN HISTORY ILLUSTRATED with the permission of PRIMEDIA Enthusiast Publications (History Group), copyright (c) American History Illustrated. **33:** "The Great Disease Migration" by Geoffrey Cowley from NEWSWEEK, Fall/Winter, 1991 pp. 54-56. (c) 1991 Newsweek Inc. All rights reserved. Reprinted by permission. **37:** Mission San Francisco de la Espada of San Antonio" by Rex Lewis Field. Used by permission of the author. **41:** Jeffery L. Sheler, "Rethinking Jamestown," in Smithsonianmagazine.com, January, 2005, http://www.smithsonian magazine.com/issues/2005/january/index.php. Copyright (c) 2004 by Smithsonianmagazine.com. All rights reserved. Reproduced by permission. **47:** "Africa and the Slave Trade" by Olaudah Equiano and Omar Ibn Seid from AFRO-AMERICAN HISTORY, 2nd, ed., edited by Thomas Frazier, Wadsworth Publishing, 1988, pp. 2-4. **55:** Saxton, Martha. "Bearing the Burden? Puritan Wives," HISTORY TODAY, October 1994, pp. 28-33.

Chapter 3. 73: From William C. Kashatus, "Revolution with Pen and Ink." This article is reproduced from the February 2000 issue of AMERICAN HISTORY ILLUSTRATED with the permission of PRIMEDIA Enthusiast Publications (History Group), copyright (c) American History Illustrated. **63:** Fred Anderson, "The Real First World War and the making of America," in America Heritage Magazine, Vol. 56, Issue 6, 2005, http://www.americanheritage.com/articles/magazine/ah/2005/6/2005_6_75.shtml. Copyright (c) 2005 by American Heritage. All rights reserved. Reproduced by permission of AMERICAN HERITAGE, Inc. **67:** From Robert Cecil, "The Famous Tax Included, Tea Was Still Cheaper Here," AMERICAN HERTIAGE, April 1961. **79:** John Ferling, "The Rocky Road to Revolution," in Smithsonianmagazine.com, July 2004, http://www.smithsonian magazine.com/issues/2004/july/revolution.php. Copyright (c) 2004 by Smithsonianmagazine.com. All rights reserved. Reproduced by permission. **85:** Reprinted by permission of the publisher from THE ADAMS FAMILY CORRESPONDENCE, VOLUME I: December 1761 - May 1776, edited by L.H. Butterfield, pp. 29-31, Cambridge, Mass: The Belknap Press of Harvard University Press, Copyright (c) 1963 by the Massachusetts Historical Society. **89:** From Joseph T. Ellis, "Jefferson's Cop-Out," CIVILIZATION, December 1966/January 1967, pp. 46-53. Copyright (c) 1966/1967 Joseph T. Ellis. Reprinted by permission of Joseph T. Ellis.

Chapter 4. 99: Eric Niderost, "Capital in Crisis" 1793," in American History, August, 2004. Copyright (c) 2004 by American History. All rights reserved. REproduced by permission. **105:** From Robert S. Kyff, "The Whiskey Rebellion." This article is reproduced from the August 1994 issue of AMERICAN HISTORY ILLUSTRATED with the permission of PRIMEDIA Enthusiast Publications (History Group), copyright (c) American History Illustrated. **111:** Andro Linklater, "The Measurement That Built America," in America Heritage Magazine, Vol. 53, Issue 6, 2002, http://www.americanheritage.com/articles/magazine/ah/2002/6/2002_6_44.shtml. Copyright (c) 2002 by American Heritage. All rights reserved. Reproduced by permission of AMERICAN HERITAGE, Inc.

Chapter 5. 119: From Dennis Maurizi, "Erie Canal: Viable East-West Trade Started in New York," NEW YORK STTE CONSERVATIONIST, Vol. 57, I. 4 (February) 2003, p. 2 (6). Used by permission of the author. **123:** From John Steele Gordon, "When Our Ancestors Became Us," AMERICAN HERITAGE, 1989, Vol. 40, No. 8, pp. 106-121. Copyright (c) 1989 American Heritage. Reprinted by permission of Forbes, Inc. **133:** From Maury Klein, "From Utopia to Mill Town." This article is reproduced from the October/November 1981 issue of AMERICAN HISTORY ILLUSTRATED with the permission of PRIMEDIA Enthusiast Publications (History Group), copyright (c) American History Illustrated.

Chapter 6. 141: From Diana Ross McCain, "The Temperance Movement," EARLY AMERICAN LIFE, February 1993. Used by permission of Diana Ross McCain. **145:** From Constance Rynder, "All Men and Women are Created Equal." This article is reproduced from the August 1998 issue of AMERICAN HISTORY ILLUSTRATED with the permission of PRIMEDIA Enthusiast Publications (History Group), copyright (c) American History Illustrated. **151:** From James S. Olson, "Wounded and Presumed Dead: Dying of Breast Cancer in Early America," AMERICAN EXPERIENCES: READINGS IN AMERICAN HISTORY, 3rd ed., Randy Roberts and James S. Olson, eds., 1994 HarperCollins Publishers. Copyright (c) 1994 James S. Olson. Reprinted by permission of James S. Olson. **157:** From Charles E. Rosenberg, "The Epidemic: 1849," THE CHOLERA YEARS, 1962, pp. 101-120. Copyright (c) 1962 The University of Chicago Press. Reprinted by permission of The University of Chicago Press. **165:** "Burned Over: Joseph Smith and The Book of Mormon" by Todd Velasco. Used by permission. **175:** Jon Grinspan, "America's Worst Immigration War," in American Heritage, November 2006, http://www.americanheritage.com/events/articles/web/20061104-know-nothing-nativism-american-party-immigration-catholicism.shtml. copyright (c) 2006 by American Heritage. All rights reserved. Reproduced by permission.

Chapter 7. 181: "The Agony of Removal" from THE CHEROKEES AND THEIR CHIEFS: IN THE WAKE OF EMPIRE by Stanley W. Hoig, pp. 163-176. Reprinted by permission of the University of Arkansas Press. Copyright (c) 1998 by Stanley W. Hoig. **189:** Bruce Watson, "George Catlin's Obsession," Smithsonianmagazine.com, December 2002, www.smithsonianmagazine.com/issues/2002/december/catlin.php. Copyright (c) 2002 by Smithsonian. All rights reserved. Reproduced by permission. **193:** "The Great Migration" by Gregory M. Franzwa. This article is reproduced from teh May/June 1993 issue of AMERICAN HISTORY ILLUSTRATED with the permission of PRIMEDIA Enthusiast Publications (History Group), copyright (c) American History Illustrated. **203:** "Santa Fe Trail" by Eric Niderost. This article is reproduced from the August 1996 issue of WILD WEST MAGAZINE with the permission of PRIMEDIA Enthusiast Publications (History Group), copyright (c) Wild West Magazine. **209:** "America's Forgotten War" by Robert W. Johannesen from the WILSON QUARTERLY, Vol. 20, No. 2 (Spring), 1996. Copyright (c) 1996 The Woodrow Wilson International Center for Scholars.